Television Game
Show Hosts

Television Game Show Hosts

Biographies of 32 Stars

David Baber

McFarland & Company, Inc., Publishers
Jefferson, North Carolina, and London

LIBRARY OF CONGRESS CATALOGUING-IN-PUBLICATION DATA

Baber, David, 1975–
Television game show hosts : biographies of 32 stars /
David Baber.
p.   cm.
Includes bibliographical references and index.

ISBN-13: 978-0-7864-2926-4
illustrated case binding : 50# alkaline paper ∞

1. Game shows—United States.   2. Television personalities—
United States—Biography.   I. Title.
PN1992.8.Q5B33   2008   791.4502'8092273—dc22   2007022695

British Library cataloguing data are available

Cover photograph: Host Bob Barker of *The Price Is Right*
30th Anniversary Special January 31, 2002 (CBS/Photofest)

Manufactured in the United States of America

*McFarland & Company, Inc., Publishers
Box 611, Jefferson, North Carolina 28640
www.mcfarlandpub.com*

To the memory of my grandmother,
Doris Gleason Baber (1918–1990),
who spent countless hours watching game shows with me
and nurtured my interest in the subject

Acknowledgments

This book has been 13 years in the making and would not be possible without the help of the following people:

Teresa Keller (my advisor at Emory & Henry College) and Lou Ferrarini (my next door neighbor the first year at E&H), who first suggested that I take my interest in game shows and write a book.

To Carol Andrews, Bob Burton, Dick Clark, Ann Cullen, Burt Dubrow, Geoff Edwards, Donna Ellerbusch, Bob Eubanks, Howard Felsher, Monty Hall, Art James, Leo James, Gaby Johnston, Tom Kennedy, Richard Kline, Jim Lange, Peter Marshall, Wink Martindale, Jack Narz, Robert Noah, Jim Peck, Joanie Perciballi, Jim Perry, Sandy Pietron, Richard Reid, Rocky Schmidt, Ira Skutch, Bob Stewart, Amy Striebel, Peter Tomarken, Alex Trebek, and Betty White, who very graciously granted telephone interviews or supplied written information.

Fred Wostbrock of Kazarian Spencer and Associates, Inc., who supplied the majority of the pictures featured in this book.

Amanda Dugan and David Schwartz of Game Show Network and Michelle Mastrobattista and Sean Perry of Endeavor Talent Agency, who helped me find many of the people interviewed for this project.

Jane Caldwell, Claudine Daniel, Patty Greany, and Juanita Ratliff of Kelly Library at Emory & Henry College, who provided research help by locating out-of-print books and long-forgotten magazine articles. They are the greatest at finding obscure resources.

Ken Brown, Gabe Dempsey and Bart DiPietro of the IT Department at Emory & Henry College, who provided technical help with scanning the book's pictures.

My great friends Alison Baker, Diane Baker, John Davis, Andrea Gaylor, Jack Gaylor, David Lyons, Robin Reid, and Linda Springer, who provided valuable editorial suggestions.

And most importantly to Almighty God our Heavenly Father. This book was a real test of faith. Thank you for your guidance and for giving me the patience to endure.

Contents

Introduction

"Come on Down!" "Big bucks! No Whammies!" "Sign in please." "From Hollywood, here come the Newlyweds." "You failed to tell the truth. Now you must pay the consequences." "Be sure to phrase your response in the form of a question." "Will the real ___ please stand up?" "I'd like to buy a vowel." "Joker, joker, joker!" "Survey said..." Throughout television history, these phrases became widely known to millions of viewers. Game shows have been a part of American popular culture since the days of radio. There have been thousands of game shows, but not nearly as many hosts. When one stops to count the number of game show hosts, the figure is astonishingly low.

Yes, there have been many hosts who came and went, but there is a small fraternity that came and stayed. These people have become legends in the entertainment world, although they usually never attract the same prestige awarded to major movie or primetime television stars. Game show hosts were never even awarded Emmys on a regular basis until 1974.

This book will take you into the lives of 32 game show hosts who graced the airwaves in radio and television over the past 60-plus years. The selection process for these hosts was at times difficult because there are so many more than just 32. The hosts included here are those who made a career out of game shows. Some hosts in this book enjoyed tremendous success and some did not, but all their stories made for fascinating reading.

Each chapter begins with biographical facts about the host, including a comprehensive list of radio and television shows on which the host appeared on a regular basis and the dates for the programs. Credits include not just shows on which the person served as host, but also those in which the person appeared as a celebrity panelist, and programs produced, directed, or created by the individual.

Personal information for each host includes date and place of birth, name(s) of spouse(s), number of children, and a list of other careers outside of the entertainment industry. This is followed by a complete biography highlighting the most important parts of the person's life.

So without further ado, here are your hosts, the stars of television's game shows!

BOB BARKER

Birth Name: Robert William Barker
Born: December 12, 1923, in Darrington, Washington
Marriage: Dorothy Jo Gideon (January 12, 1945–October 19, 1981) (Deceased)
Military Service: United States Navy (1942–1945)
Radio Career: Announcer (KTTS-AM, Springfield, MO) 1946–1949; Announcer (WWPG-AM, Palm Beach, FL) 1949–1950; *The Bob Barker Show* (KWIK-FM, Burbank, CA) 1950–1958; *Ken and Bob Saturday Special* (KABC-AM, Los Angeles, CA) 1982–1983
TV Career: HOST—*Your Big Moment* (KNBH-TV, Los Angeles, CA) Sept. 26, 1951–Dec. 23, 1951; *Talent in High* (KHJ-TV, Los Angeles, CA) October 31, 1954–January 18, 1955; *Truth or Consequences* (NBC Daytime) December 31, 1956–September 24, 1965; *The End of the Rainbow* (NBC Primetime) February 1, 1958–February 15, 1958; *Truth or Consequences* (Syndicated) September 19, 1966–September 1975; *Miss Universe Pageant* (Annually) 1966–1987; *Miss U.S.A. Pageant* (Annually) 1966–1987; *The Family Game* (ABC Daytime) June 19, 1967–December 15, 1967; *Indianapolis 500 Parade* (Annually) 1969–1980; *Pillsbury Bakeoff* (Annually) 1969–1985; *Tournament of Roses Parade* (New Year's Day) 1969–1988; *Simon Says* (Unsold Game Show Pilot) 1971; *The Price Is Right* (CBS Daytime) September 4, 1972–September 2007, (Syndicated) September 1977–September 1980, (CBS Primetime) August 14, 1986–September 18, 1986, (CBS Primetime) May 17, 2002–July 12, 2002; *That's My Line* (CBS Primetime) August 9, 1980–August 23, 1980, (CBS Primetime) February 3, 1981–April 11, 1981; *The Price Is Right Million Dollar Spectacular Specials* (CBS Primetime) February 5, 2003–May 16, 2007. EXECUTIVE PRODUCER—*Lucky Pair* (KNXT-TV, Los Angeles, CA) September 3, 1968–September 4, 1970; *The Price Is Right* (CBS) 1987–2007
Theatrical Movie: *Happy Gilmore* (1996)

"Come on down! You're the next contestant on *The Price Is Right*." For 35 years these words have been a part of the American jargon. Thousands of people have been fortunate to hear those words and run down the aisle to play *The Price Is Right*. On the stage presiding over the festivities stands a deeply tanned 6'1" tall man named Bob Barker. As host of *The Price Is Right* since the age of 48, Barker is one of the most recognized entertainers to both the young and old alike.

Early Life

In the early 1920s, a young couple named Byron and Matilda Barker lived in Mission, South Dakota.

Bob Barker (Fred Wostbrock)

Byron worked as a power-line foreman and traveled to different parts of the country for his job. He was working on a job near Darrington, Washington, when Matilda gave birth to their only child, Robert William, on December 12, 1923.

When Byron died from complications after falling off a pole in 1930, Bob and his mother remained in Mission where she taught school at the Rosebud Indian Reservation. Barker told *People Magazine* in 1999 that he was surrounded by Cowboys and Indians and that it was like growing up in the west. Barker, who is one-eighth Sioux Indian, felt right at home in this setting.

Look for the Dogs

From an early age, he showed a love for animals and could usually be found running around with a pack of dogs. Barker and his mother lived in a hotel, the only two-story building in the small town of Mission. Matilda, also known as "Tillie," never had to worry about locating Bob whenever he was outside playing. According to a 1999 story he told to *The Pet Press*, whenever Barker's mother needed him, she climbed to the top of the hotel and simply looked across the area for the large pack of dogs.

Barker was very active in sports playing baseball, football, basketball, and running track during his growing years. He spent the winter months ice skating with his friends in the community.

Going Midwest

When Barker was 12 years old, his mother married a tire salesman named Louis Valandra and the family moved to Springfield, Missouri. Barker's half brother Kent was born in 1938. After graduating from Springfield High School in 1941, Barker attended Drury College in Springfield where he received a basketball scholarship. Interrupting his college career in 1942, Barker enlisted in the United States Navy during World War II, training as a fighter pilot.

Marrying, Graduating, and Announcing

On January 12, 1945, Barker and his high school sweetheart, Dorothy Jo Gideon, eloped in St. Louis, Missouri while he was on rest leave from the service. Barker and Dorothy Jo had dated since he was 15 years old when he asked her out to an Ella Fitzgerald concert. After Barker received his discharge in 1945, he and Dorothy Jo moved back to Springfield, Missouri where he resumed his studies at Drury College.

Meanwhile, Barker worked at radio station KTTS-AM in Springfield to earn money for college tuition. He graduated summa cum laude with a B.A. in economics in 1947, but his interest in radio had taken root. He remained with KTTS working as a news and sports announcer and disc jockey. One particular day, the host of an audience participation show that aired on KTTS was unable to report to work. The station manager pressed Barker into service as the last minute host. Before Barker had a chance to get nervous, he found himself on the air live before a studio audience.

In a 2000 interview with Fred Wostbrock for the American Academy of TV Arts and Sciences, Barker recalled that Dorothy Jo heard the show and told him that he did audience participation better than anything else he had done in radio. From then on, Barker actively pursued hosting jobs. Barker told Wostbrock in the interview that Dorothy Jo was the major reason for his successful career. She not only convinced him to become a host, but also worked along side of him for many years.

In 1949 the Barkers moved to Palm Beach, Florida where he worked as a news editor and announcer at WWPG-AM while Dorothy Jo taught school. The highlight of his one year in Florida came that Christmas when Barker played Santa Claus at a local department store.

3,000 Announcers Walking the Streets

In August 1950 with no promise of a job waiting for him, Barker and Dorothy Jo took a leap of faith and moved to Hollywood. In a 1976 *TV Guide* interview, Barker said that there were 3,000 announcers walking the streets looking for work. Barker and Dorothy Jo put together the idea for an audience participation show where the members played a series of mini-games for small prizes.

With Barker hosting and Dorothy Jo producing, *The Bob Barker Show* was picked up by KWIK-FM in Burbank and became a local hit. Before long, Southern California Edison, the local power company, picked up sponsorship and the show traveled around southern California originating live from different auditoriums each weekday for the next eight years.

Your Big Moment

In the autumn of 1951, Westinghouse hired Barker to host *Your Big Moment*, a local talent show, for KNBH-TV in Los Angeles. That show only lasted 13 weeks, but it inspired Barker and Dorothy Jo to create *Talent in High*, a talent competition for the area high school students. KHJ-TV picked up the weekly series in 1954, but it too lasted a mere 13 weeks. Although his radio series was going strong, Barker was intrigued with television.

Barker's real break came two years later when Ralph Edwards was looking for someone to host a daytime version of *Truth or Consequences* for NBC. Edwards hosted the show on radio and television from 1940 to 1951 while Jack Bailey hosted a nighttime revival from 1954 to 1956. Bailey was not interested in returning for the weekday version so Edwards began searching feverishly for a new host.

Give Me a Break NBC!

One day in December 1956, Edwards was driving to pick up his daughters from an ice skating rink in Los Angeles and happened to tune in to Barker's radio show in the car. Edwards liked what he heard so he located Barker and had him record an audition film for NBC. Because Barker was still an unknown, the network was not impressed.

Using his clout, Edwards insisted that the network give Barker a chance and NBC relented. At 12:05 p.m. (Pacific Time) on December 21, 1956, Edwards called Barker to tell him that he was now the host of *Truth or Consequences*. For many years, Barker and Edwards met for lunch to drink a toast celebrating the event every December 21 at 12:05 p.m. until Edwards' death in 2005.

Since NBC was not sold on Barker as a host, the network only gave him four weeks to make his mark. For Barker it was a make it or break it situation when *Truth or Consequences* debuted on December 31, 1956. The show originated live each day from the El Capitan Theater in Hollywood. Within four weeks, NBC had a hit show and Barker had a long-term contract.

Tell the Truth or Pay the Consequences

Truth or Consequences used the same format that had carried it from its radio days. Contestants were chosen from the audience and brought onstage where Barker asked trick questions. Players were required to answer quickly before "Beulah the Buzzer," sounded. If the players answered incorrectly, or more likely failed to answer fast enough since the buzzer sounded almost immediately after the question, they were told that since they failed to tell the truth, they would have to pay the consequences.

Players who answered the question were simply asked more trick questions until they were stumped. In other words, the contestants were going to pay the consequences regardless. The consequences were usually outlandish and embarrassing stunts such as riding unicycles around the stage or dressing up in crazy costumes. One stunt involved a man rowing from Los Angeles to New York in a boat mounted on top of a car. On many occasions, the stunts reunited long-separated friends and relatives.

More Consequences, More Exposure

Truth or Consequences left NBC on September 24, 1965, but proved too popular to sit idle. Ralph Edwards quickly syndicated a new version, and the show returned in September 1966. Only five stations in the country initially carried the game, but by the end of the 1966–1967 season, *Truth or Consequences* was seen in almost every part of the U.S. It settled in for another nine years.

Nineteen sixty-six also saw Barker hosting the annual Miss U.S.A. and Miss Universe pageants for the first time. Both pageants aired on all three of the major networks through the years. For six months in 1967, Barker squeezed in *The Family Game* for ABC. Chuck Barris produced this show in which two teams of families answered questions about themselves to see how much they really knew each other.

On January 1, 1969, Barker began a 20 year stint hosting the annual Tournament of Roses Parade. Later that year he took over the Pillsbury Bakeoff, a popular contest where people baked various food dishes for cash prizes. Barker also hosted the annual Indianapolis 500 Parade.

The Making of a Winner

It seemed that nearly every show Barker hosted lasted for 20 years or more. He joked in a 2000 interview with Fred Wostbrock that unless a show was going to run for 20 years, there was no point in taking the job. Barker's star continued to shine brightly in the early 1970s, but he was only getting started.

In 1972 Goodson-Todman Productions launched a new version of *The Price Is Right*, a game show hosted by Bill Cullen from 1956 to 1965. Four contestants competed each day guessing the retail prices of merchandise. The player who was closest to the actual retail price without going over won the prize. This guessing game was played through several rounds with the player accruing the most cash and prizes becoming the day's winner.

Mark Goodson intended to syndicate *The New Price Is Right* for primetime viewing when CBS expressed interest in a daytime series. After doing a run-through of the game, Goodson realized that the old format was way too slow for the fast paced 1970s. He told CBS that unless he could totally restructure the show, there was no way *The Price Is Right* could survive. CBS told Goodson to do whatever was necessary to make the show work.

The Goodson-Todman staff redesigned the show to employ several mini-games, all of which adhered to the main premise of guessing the actual retail prices of prizes. *The New Price Is Right* selected contestants from the studio audience to play a preliminary round of guessing the price of a prize for the right to come up on stage and play a game. The pricing games rotated each day giving the show variety. Some of the first games developed for the show in 1972 included "Any Number," "The Clock Game," "The Bonus Game," "Double Prices," "5 Price Tags," and "The Grocery Game."

The Price Is Definitely Right

With the format in place, CBS picked up *The New Price Is Right* as a daily series with Barker as host while a weekly nighttime version was syndicated to local stations. Veteran game show host Dennis James emceed the nighttime show. The big doors on the set of *The New Price Is Right* opened for the first time on September 4, 1972. The show attracted a whopping 40 percent of the daytime audience in its time slot. Announcer Johnny Olson developed the show's legendary "come on down" phrase that has been echoed by succeeding announcers Rod Roddy and Rich Fields.

During its first three years, *The Price Is Right* was only 30 minutes long and featured three pricing games per show. The two players with the highest cash and prize total competed in the Showcase round where they viewed two prize packages. Each contestant guessed the price of one of the showcases and the player guessing the closest to the retail price without going over won their prize package.

One Hour

In December 1975 *The Price Is Right* expanded to one hour and the format changed. The show was divided into two segments with a total of six pricing games. After the first three pricing games, the three participants spun a giant wheel containing money amounts from $.05 to $1.00. Each player was given two spins on the wheel to score as close to $1.00 without going over. The winner earned the right to compete in the Showcase round.

As an added bonus, players who spun $1.00 exactly in one spin or a combination of two spins received $1,000 and a bonus spin. In the bonus spin, if the wheel stopped on the $1.00, the contestant won $10,000. Later in the run, two "green" sections were added to the $.05 and $.15 spaces on the wheel. Landing on either of the green sections in the bonus spin netted the player $5,000. After playing three more pricing games, the second batch of contestants spun the wheel and the winner advanced to the Showcase round.

Between 1972 and 1975, Barker hosted *Truth or Consequences* along with *The Price Is Right*. He was one of the few television stars to have two daily half hour shows running concurrently. In May 1976 Barker received his star on the Hollywood Walk of Fame. After Dennis James left the weekly nighttime version of *The Price Is Right* in 1977, Barker took over for the show's final three seasons.

She Came On Down and They Came On Out

Through the years, *The Price Is Right* has produced a number of memorable moments. One of the most famous was the "tube top" lady from June 1977. She was wearing one of the flimsy

Bob Barker stands in front of the big doors on *The Price Is Right* (Fred Wostbrock).

tube tops popular in the 1970s and was the second of the first four players called to contestant's row at the start of the show. The lady jumped up from her seat and sailed down the aisle jumping up and down in excitement. As she turned to enter contestant's row, her tube top slipped downward and her breasts came out. When this episode aired, the woman's upper torso was blacked out by electronic effects.

At another taping, a woman in the audience went into labor during a commercial break. Barker asked the pages to help her out of the studio, but the woman insisted on staying. The taping stopped until the woman was safely escorted out and driven to the hospital. There have been at least two occasions where contestants fainted on stage and two episodes where male contestants proposed to their girlfriends on camera. For the record, both girlfriends said, "yes."

That's My Line

In August 1980, Barker stepped outside of *The Price Is Right* arena to host *That's My Line*. The premise was to showcase real people with unusual occupations or talents such as the world's fastest typist, a man who designed skirts for men, and a 76 year old newspaper carrier who delivered the papers from an airplane. After a three week nighttime trial on CBS in the summer of 1980, *That's My Line* returned for a two month run in February 1981. The new version focused more on bizarre and unusual happenings than on occupations.

The Love of His Life

In the spring of 1981, Barker's wife, Dorothy Jo, was diagnosed with lung cancer. After fighting the illness for six months, she passed away on October 19, 1981, at the age of 57. Barker went into a deep depression and spent the next two years dealing with the loss. Refusing to sink into total despair, Barker immersed himself into his work.

Another comfort for Barker was taking an active interest in animal rights, something that Dorothy Jo had long enjoyed. He had become a vegetarian in 1979 following Dorothy Jo's lead. Now he set out to work on behalf of protecting animals from abuse and to encourage people to adopt pets from animal shelters. In 1995 he set up the DJ&T Foundation (named for his wife "Dorothy Jo" and his mother "Tillie") to provide financial support for animal protection.

Barker began using *The Price Is Right* as a platform to get his message across. He closed each episode of the show with the advice, "Help control the pet population. Have your pets spayed or neutered." Those words remained Barker's signature sign-off until his retirement in 2007. He also insisted that *The Price Is Right* stop awarding fur coats as prizes.

Working for Animal Rights

In 1983 Barker met Nancy Burnet, the founder of the United Activists for Animal Rights in Riverside, California. The two became close friends and full time activists for animal rights. In 1989 Barker and Burnet were sued by the American Humane Association after they charged that the organization failed to protect animals used in movie productions. In the late 1990s, they took on the CBS series *Dr. Quinn, Medicine Woman* stating that the show mistreated horses.

Barker found another media outlet for his views on the *Ken and Bob Saturday Special* radio show broadcast over KABC-AM in Los Angeles. After more than a year on the show, KABC executives asked Barker to tone down his animal rights viewpoints. Complaints from listeners claimed that the show was too one sided on the issue. When Barker refused to tone down his cause, the station fired him from the show in November 1983. Barker's dismissal prompted about 75 to 100 people to march in the rain outside of KABC in protest of the action.

In 1987 Barker protested the use of fur coats worn by the contestants in the Miss U.S.A. pageant, which he had been hosting for 21 years. Barker threatened to resign as host unless the furs were not used. The pageant producers found synthetic furs and the show went on as scheduled. However in 1988, the pageant producers decided to resume using real fur coats. Barker promptly quit hosting the Miss U.S.A. and Miss Universe pageants. His departure resulted in the Miss U.S.A. pageant losing 29 percent of its audience the following year. Barker was also not afraid to turn down lucrative offers to do commercials for fast food chains and cosmetic companies because of the use of animals in their products.

Black to Gray

Although animal rights were very important to Barker, he also remained committed to *The Price Is Right*. On March 27, 1987, *The Price Is Right* became the longest-running daytime game show after breaking the record previously held by *Concentration*. Another highlight of 1987 was when Barker stopped dying his hair to hide the gray. He made the decision after repeated colorings had turned his hair pink.

When he returned to work after a vacation, his hair had suddenly gone from black to gray. On the air, the transition from black to gray literally seemed to happen overnight to the viewers. Barker told *People Magazine* in 1999 that he received a postcard from a viewer who said he looked like he had "one hell of a night."

When *The Price Is Right* executive producer Frank Wayne died in 1987, Barker took over Wayne's duties. With Barker now calling many of the shots, the popularity of *The Price Is Right* continued into the 1990s as the show broke all records in longevity. In April 1990, the show finally became the longest running game show of all time after breaking the 18-year record held by the primetime winner *What's My Line?*

The Price Is Wrong

Barker and the show's popularity were put to the test in May 1994 when former model Dian Parkinson sued Barker for sexual harassment. Parkinson, who worked on the show from 1975 to 1993, claimed that Barker had forced her to have sex with him for an extended period in the late 1980s and early 1990s or lose her job on the show.

According to a 1994 *People Weekly* report, Barker responded with a press conference in which he admitted to having a sexual relationship with Parkinson from December 1989 to September 1991, but that it had been consensual and that Parkinson initiated the whole thing. Parkinson dropped the lawsuit in April 1995 because of the effect it was having on her health and the heavy legal expenses.

See You in Court

No sooner had the Parkinson case ended when Barker found himself in more hot water. In July 1995 Holly Hallstrom, a model on *The Price Is Right* since 1977, departed the show under a cloud of controversy. Hallstrom recounted in a 2005 *Park Record* interview that trouble began when she held a press conference. Hallstrom told reporters that she had been fired from the show for refusing to defend Barker publicly during the Parkinson lawsuit. When she refused, Hallstrom said that Barker used her recent weight gain due to prescribed medication as a reason to let her go.

In an interview with Larry King in December 2002, Barker stated that the reason Hallstrom was off the show was because of budget cuts. Mark Goodson Productions, the owner of the show, decided to reduce the number of models from four to three. He said that Hallstrom was offered a retirement package.

In December 1995, Barker sued Hallstrom for slander and defamation of character. She in turn filed a wrongful termination suit against Barker and *The Price Is Right*. The case dragged on for the next five years until Barker dropped his defamation suit against Hallstrom in 2000.

She continued with her suit until the case was finally settled out of court in 2005 in which she was awarded an undisclosed sum.

Milestones

Barker emerged from the scandals with his popularity intact. In the spring of 1996, he surprised many viewers with an appearance in the theatrical movie *Happy Gilmore*, starring Adam Sandler. Barker played himself competing in a celebrity golf tournament as Sandler's partner. After losing the tournament, Barker and Sandler get into a fistfight with Barker using karate kicks and punches to win the brawl. The success of *Happy Gilmore* opened the door for Barker to act in guest roles on the NBC sitcom *Something So Right* during the 1996-1997 season.

On August 23, 1996, CBS broadcast a special primetime edition of *The Price Is Right* to mark the beginning of the show's 25th season on television. Then in March 1998, the show taped its 5,000th episode. To commemorate the occasion, CBS renamed the famous Studio 33 at Television City in Hollywood, where the show taped, The Bob Barker Studio.

Up to that point, Barker could also claim another milestone. Of the 5,000 episodes of *The Price Is Right* he had missed only three episodes in early 1975 while recovering from broken ribs. Dennis James substituted for him on those shows. Barker had actually set a world's record for hosting the most consecutive broadcasts of a show with no absences. Between December 1956 and January 1973, he hosted 3,524 consecutive episodes of *Truth or Consequences*. He finally broke the chain on January 8, 1973, when he was forced to cancel a taping of the show. He suffered an allergic reaction that caused his face to swell and he could not open his eyes. When Barker broke a toe in 1976, he hosted *The Price Is Right* on crutches until his recovery.

A Scare

As he graced through his eighth decade of life, Barker enjoyed good health and remained physically active. A onetime student of karate expert and actor Chuck Norris, Barker had earned a black belt in karate a number of years earlier. He seemed to be in perfect health as he began each morning with exercises and a few kicks to stay in shape.

Nothing, however, prepared Barker for a scare he received on September 16, 1999. He went to Washington, D.C. to speak to a group of congressmen about the Captive Elephant Act, which prohibited the use of elephants in circuses. Just before leaving his hotel room for a breakfast meeting, Barker felt a tingling sensation in his right arm.

After undergoing tests at George Washington University Hospital, doctors found that Barker had suffered a mini-stroke and was on the verge of having a massive one. The cause was a partially obstructed carotid artery, which was impeding the flow of blood to his brain. Barker underwent surgery to clear the blocked artery and returned home to California to recuperate. Meanwhile, all tapings for *The Price Is Right* were canceled until Barker returned to work in October 1999.

Is the Price Still Right?

On October 19, 2000, another earthquake rocked *The Price Is Right*. Pearson Television, who bought out Mark Goodson Productions and were now the show's owners, dismissed models Janice Pennington and Kathleen Bradley. Other people dismissed that day included longtime director Paul Alter and executive assistant Sherrell Paris, editorial consultant Sharon Friem, and production assistant Linda Riegert.

According to a December 2000 *Los Angeles Times* story, Pennington and Bradley had given depositions for the earlier Holly Hallstrom case that contradicted Barker's side of the story. Bradley believed that Barker had them fired as a result.

In the same article, Barker told *The Los Angeles Times* that he had nothing to do with their abrupt dismissals. He stated that the decision came from Pearson Television, who recently bought the show, and that Pennington's and Bradley's dismissals were part of massive budget cuts. *The Price Is Right* began using a series of rotating models from week to week so there were no longer any permanent "Barker's Beauties" as the models were called.

Price Turns 30, Barker Turns 80

These scandals did nothing to hurt Barker's or the show's popularity. In January 2002, *The Price Is Right* aired a primetime special marking the show's 30th anniversary. Impressed by the high ratings, CBS aired a series of six primetime specials in the spring of 2002 honoring members of all branches of the United States Armed Forces along with the New York and Los Angeles Fire Departments. In 2003 CBS launched another round of specials titled *The Price Is Right Million Dollar Spectacular*. It was on the December 13, 2003, special that Barker celebrated his 80th birthday. *The Price Is Right* hit yet another milestone in March 2004 when it aired its 6,000th episode.

Now in his ninth decade of life and fifth decade of performing, Bob Barker continued to entertain the viewers each day. Year after year, *The Price Is Right* remained largely unchanged from its original 1972 format as Barker kept the laughter, fun, and games rolling nonstop.

Hanging It Up

Bob Barker and *The Price Is Right* were so synonymous that it was hard to imagine one without the other. In a day that had to come sooner or later, Barker announced on October 31, 2006, that he would retire from *The Price Is Right* at the end of the show's 35th season in June 2007. Barker had contemplated retirement since 1996, but he enjoyed hosting the show so much that he found it difficult to quit. After reaching his 80s, Barker noted that taping the show was becoming more and more demanding physically and mentally.

The year 2007 marked two milestones in Barker's career: his 50th year in show business and the 35th season on *The Price Is Right*. These two coinciding events convinced Barker that it was a good time to retire. He noted that he could probably do a 36th season, but that it was better to quit too soon than too late. Barker taped his final episode on June 6, 2007.

Barker resides in Los Angeles in the 15 room Spanish-style home he purchased many years ago. He spends most of his time working for animal rights through his DJ&T Foundation and sunbathing when weather permits. A lifelong fan of the sun, Barker has undergone occasional minor surgeries to remove small skin cancers, but otherwise has no problem with lying in the sun. He is also a Civil War buff and enjoys books on the subject.

What's His Secret?

In his long career, Barker weathered scandal and occasional health problems to become the oldest man to host a daily television show. He survived long after most emcees have hung up their microphones. So what is his secret? In Maxine Fabe's 1979 book *TV Game Shows*, Barker explained that his job was to make contestants funny rather than to be funny himself. By creating a relaxed atmosphere, Barker helps contestants feel comfortable enough to be themselves.

His biggest compliment came from an elderly lady who appeared on *The Price Is Right* in the 1970s. After her appearance, she sent Barker a letter telling him that she had never been as funny as she was on that show. Drawing from his years of hosting audience-participation shows dating back to the radio days, Barker's secret is to draw average folks from an audience, get to know them, and then play a little game all without cue cards. And that method has served Barker well since the day he first substituted as host of that audience-participation show back in Springfield, Missouri, in the late 1940s.

JACK BARRY

Birth Name: Jack Barasch
Born: March 20, 1918 in Lindenhurst, Long Island
Died: May 2, 1984 in New York, New York
Marriages and Family: Marcia Van Dyke (1948–1959) (Divorced) 2 sons; Patty Preble (February 14, 1960-May 2, 1984) 1 daughter, 1 son
Radio Career: Announcer (WTTM-AM, Trenton, NJ) 1943–1945; *The Uncle Don Carney Show* (WOR-AM, New York) 1945–1946; *Juvenile Jury* (WOR-AM, New York City) May 11, 1946–June 8, 1946, (MBS) June 15, 1946–April 1, 1951, (NBC) September 28, 1952–February 15, 1953; *Life Begins at 80* (MBS) July 4, 1948–September 24, 1949; *The Joe Dimaggio Show* (CBS) September 17, 1949–March 11, 1950, (NBC) April 15, 1950–August 19, 1950; *It's the Barrys* (Syndicated) 1953
TV Career: HOST—*Juvenile Jury* (NBC Primetime) April 3, 1947–September 28, 1953, (CBS Primetime) October 11, 1953–September 14, 1954, (NBC Daytime) January 2, 1955–March 27, 1955; *Life Begins at 80* (NBC Primetime) January 13, 1950–August 25, 1950, (ABC Primetime) October 3, 1950–March 10, 1952, (DuMont Primetime) March 21, 1952–July 24, 1955, (ABC Primetime) July 31, 1955–February 25, 1956; *Oh Baby!* (Syndicated) 1952; *Wisdom of the Ages* (DuMont Primetime) December 16, 1952–June 30, 1953; *Winky Dink and You* (CBS Daytime) October 10, 1953–April 27, 1957; *The Big Surprise* (NBC Primetime) October 8, 1955–March 3, 1956; *Tic Tac Dough* (NBC Daytime) July 30, 1956–October 6, 1958; *Twenty-One* (NBC Primetime) September 12, 1956–October 16, 1958; *High Low* (NBC Primetime) July 4, 1957–September 12, 1957; *Concentration* (NBC Primetime) October 30, 1958–November 20, 1958; *Kidding Around* (WNTA-TV, New York City) May 6, 1961–June 24, 1961; (KTLA-TV, Los Angeles, CA) November 5, 1962–January 25, 1963; *You Don't Say* (KTLA-TV, Los Angeles, CA) December 9, 1962–January 20, 1963; *The Jack Barry Show* (KTLA-TV, Los Angeles, CA) January 28, 1963–August 22, 1964; *By the Numbers* (KTLA-TV, Los Angeles, CA) March 3, 1963–September 28, 1963; *L.A. Today* (KTLA-TV, Los Angeles, CA) May 17, 1963–September 1, 1963; *Addograms* (KTLA-TV, Los Angeles, CA) September 2, 1963–April 3, 1964; *Pick 'N' Choose* (KTLA-TV, Los Angeles, CA) May 29, 1964–August 30, 1964; *It's a Match* (Toronto, Canada) 1966–1967; *Photo Finish* (Toronto, Canada) 1967–1968; *Generation Gap* (ABC Primetime) April 18, 1969–May 23, 1969; *Juvenile Jury* (Syndicated) September 1970–September 1971; *The Reel Game* (ABC Primetime) January 18, 1971–May 3, 1971; *The Joker's Wild* (CBS Daytime) September 4, 1972–June 13, 1975; *We've Got Your Number* (Unsold Game Show Pilot) May 1975; *People Are Funny* (Unsold Game Show Pilot) November 1975; *Break the Bank* (Syndicated) September 18, 1976–September 11, 1977; **The Joker's Wild* (Syndicated) September 5, 1977–September 1984 *(Episodes of Joker's Wild with Barry as host continued after his death until Bill Cullen took over as host in the fall of 1984); *Joker, Joker, Joker* (Syndicated) September 8, 1979-September 1981.   PRODUCER & CREATOR—*Back That Fact* (Producer)(ABC Primetime) October 22, 1953–November 26, 1953; *You're on Your Own* (Producer)(CBS Primetime) December 22, 1956–March 16, 1957; *Everybody's Talking* (Creator)(ABC Daytime) February 6, 1967–December 29, 1967; *The Honeymoon Game* (Producer)(Unsold Game Show Pilot) October 3, 1970; *Make the Scene* (Producer)(Unsold ABC Game Show Pilot) 1971; *The Joker's Wild* (Creator & Executive Producer) 1972–1975, 1977–1984; *Hollywood's Talking* (Executive Producer) (CBS Daytime) March 26, 1973–June 22, 1973; *Blank Check* (Executive Producer) (NBC Daytime) January 6, 1975–July 4, 1975; *Break the Bank* (Co-Producer)(ABC Daytime) April 12, 1976–July 23, 1976; *Way Out Games* (Co-Producer)(CBS Day-

time) September 11, 1976–September 4, 1977. PACKAGER WITH DAN ENRIGHT—*Dough Re Mi* (NBC Daytime) February 24, 1958–November 1958; *Concentration* (NBC Daytime) August 25, 1958–November 1958; *The Hollywood Connection* (Syndicated) September 5, 1977–April 1978; *Tic Tac Dough* (NBC Daytime and Primetime) 1956–1958; (CBS Daytime) July 3, 1978–September 1, 1978; (Syndicated) 1978–1984; *Play the Percentages* (Syndicated) January 7, 1980–September 12, 1980; *The Bert Convy Show* (Unsold Talk Show Pilot) 1980; *Four In Love* (Unsold CBS Sitcom Pilot) 1980; *Jake's Way* (Unsold CBS Drama Pilot) 1980; *Bullseye* (Syndicated) September 29, 1980–September 24, 1982; *Soap World* (Syndicated) September 1982–September 1983; *Hot Potato* (NBC Daytime) January 23, 1984–June 29, 1984; *Mama Malone* (CBS Primetime) March 7, 1984–July 21, 1984

Theatrical Movies: *Everything You Have Always Wanted to Know About Sex* But Were Afraid to Ask* (1972) (Actor); *Search and Destroy* (1980) (Producer); *Private Lessons* (1981) (Producer); *Private School* (1983) (Producer)

Jack Barry (Fred Wostbrock)

Business Interests: Partner, Jack Barry-Dan Enright Productions (1946–1959) & (1975–1984); Co-owner, WGMA-AM Radio Station, Hollywood, Florida (1957–1966); Co-owner, Melody Music Inc.; Executive Vice-President, Fragrance Process Co., Manhattan, N.Y. (1959–1961); Owner, KKOP-FM Radio Station, Redondo, Beach, California (1968–1978); Co-owner, Jack Barry Cable Company, Los Angeles, CA (1978–1984); Co-owner, Barry-Enright Films Inc. (1979–1984)

Other Career: Handkerchief Salesman (1939–1943)

Every host had career ups and downs, but probably no other host had such a colorful and checkered career as Jack Barry. Though he had huge success with *The Joker's Wild* for more than a decade, Barry's early television career gives his story a bit of an edge over the rest of the game show fraternity. Jack Barry was born as Jack Barasch in Lindenhurst, Long Island on March 20, 1918. He led a jazz band in high school called "The Melody Five," but abandoned his musical aspirations in college for the world of business. He graduated from the Wharton School of Finance and Commerce at the University of Pennsylvania in 1939, and went into the handkerchief business with his father.

Nothing to Sneeze At

The handkerchief business soon grew tedious, but Barry was not sure what other options to pursue. The answer came at a house party one night when someone brought in a tape recorder and asked Barry to say a few words into the microphone. When the tape was played, his voice impressed all the guests, and they urged him to become a radio announcer.

Barry worked for his father's handkerchief business until 1943 when he became a radio announcer while taking courses in radio at Northwestern University. He then moved up to a staff announcer at WTTM in Trenton, New Jersey at a salary of $12 a week. Within a year, he had worked his way up to $400 a week but resigned when the station refused to make him an executive. In New York he became the announcer for *The Uncle Don Carney Show* on WOR. It was here that Barry met Dan Enright, a production manager. The two became fast friends and formed Barry-Enright Productions.

Here Come the Juveniles

Barry was the warm up man for the kids before Uncle Don made his entrance. As part of his warm up, Barry began asking the kids tricky questions. The often-comical answers he received gave him an idea for a children's show. The result was *Juvenile Jury*, and it premiered over WOR on May 11, 1946. A panel of five children ranging in age from three to twelve was read a series of common everyday problems submitted by listeners. Barry polled the children to come up with solutions. The children's off-the-cuff remarks made the show a hit.

Five weeks later, *Juvenile Jury* began airing nationally. In 1947 it began an eight year run on NBC television. A September 1953 *TV Guide* article told the amusing story of Barry promoting the sponsor's health tonic on one *Juvenile Jury* episode. In the commercial, Barry was required to take a couple of swigs of the tonic to show its benefits. When he resumed his interviews with the children, one child sniffed the air and said, "Have you been drinking?" Barry thoroughly enjoyed working with the children and made the task look easy. As a father of two sons, Jonathan and Jeffrey, he had plenty of experience.

More Creations

In July 1948 Barry started the radio series *Life Begins at 80*, a show where a panel of octogenarians dispensed advice to questions submitted by listeners. *Life Begins at 80* jumped to television in 1950 hop-scotching on NBC, ABC, and the DuMont networks for six years.

Barry also enjoyed a four year run hosting the children's show, *Winky Dink and You*. Winky Dink was a little boy who starred in a cartoon featured each week.

Surprise! You're Out of a Job

In 1955 Barry moved into game shows hosting *The Big Surprise* for NBC. This was his first show not produced or packaged by Barry-Enright Productions. However, Barry was considered too dull as a quiz show host and was fired from *The Big Surprise* in March 1956.

Two of Barry's former employees thought otherwise of Barry's talents.

> **Robert Noah (Twenty-One** *executive producer, June 2006 telephone interview):*
> "Jack was an absolute first rate emcee. He was very bright and very able and was also a very good businessman."

Game show producer Howard Felsher, who later worked with Barry on *Tic Tac Dough*, echoed Noah's sentiments:

> **Howard Felsher (Tic Tac Dough** *producer, June 2006 telephone interview):*
> "As a person, my favorite [of the hosts] was probably Jack Barry. He was a very easy man to get along with. He had no temperament at all. As a talent, he was one of the better ones and certainly one of the more agreeable ones."

Twenty-One

By now, almost all quiz shows were giving away thousands of dollars in cash and prizes. Barry and Enright followed the trend by developing two big money game shows. The result was *Tic Tac Dough* and *Twenty-One* with Barry hosting both shows. *Twenty-One* has the more interesting history and so this show will be examined in further detail.

Two contestants competed on *Twenty-One* wearing headphones. The players stood in separate isolation booths on stage. At the start of each round, Barry announced a category and the sound was eliminated in one player's booth. The other player selected a question worth 1 to 11 points. The difficulty of the question increased with its point value. A correct answer added points to the player's score. Then the second player selected a point value for his or her question while the sound was cut in the first player's booth.

The purpose of eliminating the sound in the booths was to keep each player from knowing their opponent's score. The object was to amass 21 points in two or more rounds. Players could stop the game at any time, a risky decision, since they automatically lost if their opponent had a higher score. The winner received $500 for each point. If both players tied, they started a new game with the point values doubling to $1,000. If another tie resulted, the point value increased to $1,500 and so on for any succeeding rounds.

Twenty-One premiered on September 12, 1956. In the first game the questions were so hard that the contestants tied 0–0 after missing 17 questions in a row. Unless the contestants were walking encyclopedias, they stood no chance of winning. The producers decided that the only way to make the show work was to rig the game thereby creating dramatic and suspenseful competitions.

Fixing the Game

In a 1979 *TV Guide* interview by Dick Russell, Barry told the story of how the practice of rigging *Twenty-One* began. He remembered receiving a phone call from the network, the sponsor, or the advertising agency. The voice on the other end of the line warned Barry and Enright to never have another fiasco like *Twenty-One*'s premiere ever again. According to Barry, he had heard of the practice of rigging quiz shows from his radio days. He and Enright decided to coach the contestants by giving answers to the questions in advance. To heighten suspense, contestants were taught to stutter and hesitate when answering. The idea was to make it seem as if they would miss the question and then suddenly blurt out the correct answer. In the isolation booths on stage, the heat was turned up to make the contestants sweat.

In October 1956, Herbert Stempel became one of the first contestants to be coached for the show. Stempel, a 29-year-old Army veteran who was attending the City College of New York, had an incredible photographic memory for facts and details and was no educational slouch. Stempel became the first big winner on *Twenty-One*, and over the next several weeks he knocked down one opponent after another. The show's ratings climbed and Stempel became a national celebrity.

Enter Charles, Exit Herb

In November 1956, Charles Van Doren, an English professor at Columbia University, was brought on the show to face Stempel. Van Doren was also coached and given answers to the questions. In their first match on November 28, 1956, the game ended in a 21–21 tie. For the program of December 5, 1956, Stempel was instructed to miss a question on which he already knew the answer.

The question was, "Which 1955 movie won the Oscar for Best Picture?" Stempel knew the answer was *Marty*, because it was his favorite movie, but he was instructed to say *On the Waterfront*. Stempel took the dive and left the program with $49,500 in winnings. Charles Van Doren became the new champion and proceeded to win $129,000 by the time he was defeated in March 1957. *Twenty-One*'s ratings went through the roof and began to make a significant dent in the audience of CBS's *I Love Lucy*, which ran against it on Monday nights.

What Do You Know?

Just how much Jack Barry himself knew about the rigging of his game show has long been debated. Depending on the story you read, some sources say Barry knew everything that happened. Others say he was totally in the dark and only discovered the truth when the scandals hit the newspapers.

In his 1979 *TV Guide* interview with Dick Russell, Barry noted that as host of *Twenty-One*, he allowed the coaching to take place but kept himself uninformed on details. He feared that knowing who was going to win would affect his role as the host. He wanted to show genuine surprise when a contestant won the game. Former *Tic Tac Dough* producer Howard Felsher confirmed that Barry knew about the rigging, but did not know all the details.

> *Howard Felsher:*
> "Dan Enright was the mastermind of it all. But Jack certainly knew what was going on."

Raking in the Green

In May 1957, Barry and Enright sold their rights to *Tic Tac Dough* and *Twenty-One* to NBC for $2 million. They continued their association with the shows by working as producers for the network. Barry and Enright purchased radio station WGMA in Hollywood, Florida, and a music publishing company, Melody Music Inc. In August 1958, the duo packaged the highly successful game *Concentration* with Hugh Downs, best known as co-anchor of ABC's *20–20* in recent years, as the host.

Blackmail

Barry and Enright were riding high, but a storm cloud was brewing on the horizon preparing to bring down the whole empire. Herbert Stempel, who was less than pleased at being cut from *Twenty-One* during his prime, began telling the newspapers about the rigging process. At first, no one would believe him, and to keep the cat from getting out of the bag, Dan Enright took measures to keep him quiet. When Stempel met with Enright at the producer's office on March 7, 1957, Stempel again threatened to expose the deception. What Stempel did not realize was that Enright secretly taped their meeting. The tape was then used against Stempel at a press conference and he was accused of blackmailing Enright.

There was no stopping Stempel, however. With the added testimony from other *Twenty-One* contestants James Snodgrass, Hank Bloomgarden, and Vivienne Nearing, the show came under fire from the New York District Attorney's office. NBC launched an investigation on their shows. The network allowed Barry to defend *Twenty-One* on the program of September 8, 1958, in which he denied to the viewers that anything was wrong.

Bailing Out

With *Twenty-One* going down in defeat in the ratings, Barry and Enright sold their rights to *Concentration*, an unrigged show, to NBC. This was the only way of saving the show from cancellation since the Barry-Enright name was now tarnished. The newspapers finally carried stories of the riggings based on interviews from contestants. NBC fired Barry and Enright as producers. Barry hosted his last *Tic Tac Dough* episode on October 6, 1958, while *Twenty-One* left the air on October 16.

Two weeks later, Barry hosted a primetime version of *Concentration* hastily scheduled by NBC to replace *Twenty-One*. Hugh Downs continued to hold down the fort on the daytime version while the nighttime series crashed in the ratings and was gone in four weeks. After November 1958 Barry disappeared from national television for the next seven years. When the subsequent Congressional investigations finally ended, no one was charged with a crime except perjury to the Grand Jury during testimonies.

As it turned out, there were no laws saying that quiz shows could not be rigged. Congress passed tougher legislation in 1960 making it a felony to rig a game show. The three networks soon created Standards and Practices departments as a means of keeping an eye on the happenings of future television game shows. During the shows, members of the network Standards and Practices Department were present in the studio to ensure that everything was honest.

Despite the lack of criminal charges, Jack Barry and Dan Enright were blackballed from television because, in the minds of the public, a great deception had taken place. The big money quiz fad had fizzled out, and after that, no game show ever asked such challenging questions as did *Twenty-One* or *Tic Tac Dough*. Since Barry and Enright were no longer welcome at NBC, or anywhere else for that matter, they dissolved their partnership and went their separate ways.

Sweet Smell of Success

Dan Enright went to Canada producing game, talk, and dramatic shows for Screen Gems. Barry left television to become executive vice-president of The Fragrance Process Company, a Manhattan-based chemical firm of which he had been part owner since the mid 1950s. The company produced scented pellets used in the packaging of plastic bags for clothing, bedding, and hosiery products.

Barry's business knowledge was paying him dividends in a new career, but his marriage to Marcia Van Dyke ended in divorce in 1959. On Valentine's Day 1960, he married Patte Preble, an associate producer on *Concentration*. They had two children, Barbara and Douglas.

Kidding Around

In 1961 while on a trip in Japan, Barry and his wife ran into some American tourists who recognized him. They were fans of his old *Juvenile Jury* show and asked if he would ever return to television in something like it. Barry developed an idea for a children's show similar to *Jury*, but with some changes. The new show, *Kidding Around*, seated the children around a table instead of in a panel, and featured skits. Going back to New York, Barry talked station WTNA-TV into airing the show. *Kidding Around* debuted in the New York area on May 6, 1961.

Barry had plans to syndicate the show nationally and to produce a new quiz show with a public service angle. Unfortunately, *Kidding Around* failed to attract a local audience and vanished after six weeks, taking Barry's hopes and dreams with it. He moved his family to Hollywood, Florida where he and Enright still owned radio station WGMA. However, the Federal Communications Commission (FCC) eventually forced Barry and Enright to sell the station in 1966 due to their checkered past.

L.A. Today

After spending a year out of work, Barry moved to Los Angeles in 1962. He secured a job as a program packager and host on station KTLA-TV. Between 1962 and 1964, Barry produced and hosted the game shows *You Don't Say*, *By the Numbers*, *Addograms*, and *Pick 'n' Choose*. NBC picked up *You Don't Say*, but the hosting job went to Tom Kennedy, who had also hosted the local version for a few weeks.

Barry hosted an updated version of *Kidding Around* and *L.A. Today*, a two hour magazine show. He also hosted his own variety series, *The Jack Barry Show*. With all of his local successes it seemed that Barry's career was on the rise. The bubble burst in 1964 when new owners took over KTLA and immediately fired Barry.

Bitter Years

After losing his KTLA job, Barry grew extremely bitter. Nobody in the television industry wanted anything to do with him. He told *TV Guide's* Mary Murphy in 1984 that television executives who saw him on the street crossed to the other side to avoid him. Barry became a heavy drinker and nearly lost his life in the process. Despite the hardships, his family stayed together during those lean years. Barry stayed afloat working as a consultant for some game shows during the mid 1960s, but never received credit for his participation.

Canadian Television

In 1966 Barry received an offer from Dan Enright, who was still working in Canada, to emcee several game and children's shows he was producing. Rather than move to Canada, Barry chose to commute from Los Angeles, taping shows for ten days at a time and then coming home until the next tape day. It was a bone-crushing schedule, but Barry wanted to keep his ties to the United States in case another television job came his way.

He created the game show *Everybody's Talking*, which debuted on ABC in February 1967 with Los Angeles disc jockey Lloyd Thaxton as host. Barry turned production of the show over to producer Jerome Schnur and kept his own name out of the credits. The network was still afraid to have Barry's name associated with the show. Instead, he received a royalty for developing the concept.

Getting Approval

Still unable to get a television job in the United States, Barry continued his Canadian commute until 1968 when his wife threatened to walk out on him with their children. By now, the family's financial problems were so severe that Barry moved them to Spain where they found an inexpensive place to stay until he could figure out what to do. Barry decided that the only way to end his broadcasting exile was to get approval to work in the industry from the FCC.

Returning to the U.S., he persuaded his father-in-law to loan him $40,000. Barry made a down payment on radio station KKOP-FM in Redondo Beach, California. He applied for an operator's license and spent the summer of 1968 waiting for the FCC's verdict. The tide finally turned on September 17, 1968, when Barry's Washington, D.C. lawyer, Marcus Cohn, called and informed him that he now owned KKOP-FM. At long last, he had the FCC's approval, and the 50-year-old Barry began his second climb to fame with a new lease on life.

Life Begins at 50

Shortly afterward, a CBS programming executive named Fred Silverman contacted Barry about coming up with new game show ideas. He produced a pilot for CBS called *The Joker's Wild*, but the network wanted a different host. That job was given to former *Password* host Allen Ludden and the pilot was taped in 1969. While CBS rejected *The Joker's Wild* pilot, ABC asked Barry to take over as host of a failing primetime game show called *Generation Gap*. On April 18, 1969, Barry finally returned to national television. Although ABC canned *Generation Gap* five weeks later, Barry had finally overcome the television blacklist.

During the 1970-1971 season, he hosted a one season revival of *Juvenile Jury* and an ABC primetime show, *The Reel Game*. In 1971 Barry produced, and this time hosted, a second pilot for *The Joker's Wild*. Again CBS passed, but Los Angeles station KTLA-TV picked up the show for a short run to test audience reaction.

The Joker Is Wild

Several months later, CBS decided to give Barry and *The Joker's Wild* a chance. With Barry as host, the show premiered on September 4, 1972, leading off an hour and a half of new game shows including *The Price Is Right* with Bob Barker and *Gambit* with Wink Martindale. On *The Joker's Wild*, players pulled a lever that activated a large slot machine on the stage. The machine contained three wheels displaying a combination of categories. Contestants selected a category and the question was worth $50. If a category appeared twice on the board the question value doubled to $100, and if it appeared three times the question was worth $200.

Many times, Jokers appeared on one or more of the wheels and could be used to double or triple the value. The first contestant to reach $500 won the game and played a bonus round in which the contestant played the slot machine for money. The player tried to accumulate $1,000 or more and could quit after each spin and keep their winnings. If the "devil" appeared on any of the wheels, the contestant lost their bonus round winnings.

Jack Barry (right) invites us to check out the huge slot machine on *The Joker's Wild* (Fred Wostbrock).

Staying in the Game

The Joker's Wild continually beat its competition on NBC. It ran *The Dinah Shore Show* off the air in 1974 and knocked out its replacement game show *Name That Tune* in early 1975. However, when NBC moved its popular show *Celebrity Sweepstakes* to 10:00 a.m., *The Joker's Wild* went into a slump. After three years on CBS, *The Joker's Wild* was canceled on June 13, 1975.

Later in 1975 Barry and Dan Enright renewed their partnership. Their first pilot, *We've Got Your Number*, failed to sell, but in early 1976 the team sold *Break the Bank* to ABC and a second version for syndication. Tom Kennedy hosted the ABC version until it was canceled after three months. When Kennedy was unavailable to host the syndicated version in September 1976, Barry took over as host, but that version faded after one season.

The Joker Is Wilder

Barry and Enright sold repeats of *The Joker's Wild* to select television stations testing the waters for a possible revival. The reruns drew a large enough audience to convince Colbert TV Sales in Los Angeles to market a new syndicated version of the show. *The Joker's Wild* returned to the airwaves in September 1977 with Barry as host and Enright as executive producer.

Barry and Enright quickly cranked out new game shows for syndication. In 1978 they launched a revival of *Tic Tac Dough* with host Wink Martindale. A children's version of *The Joker's Wild* called *Joker, Joker, Joker* aired from 1979 to 1981 with Barry doing double duty as host. Barry-Enright Productions grew into a larger operation than it was in the 1950s.

Oh, brother! Jack Barry knows this is going to be one of those days on *The Joker's Wild* **(Jack Barry Productions; Kline and Friends, Inc.).**

Barry finally sold the radio station that had relaunched his career, KKOP-FM. Using the money from the sale, he formed The Jack Barry Cable Company, which brought cable television to subscribers in Los Angeles. Barry and Enright also branched out into the movies producing *Search and Destroy* in 1980 and *Private Lessons* in 1981. However, *The Joker's Wild* and *Tic Tac Dough* remained the company's primary source of revenue. Adding the game shows *Play the Percentages* and *Bullseye* to their roster, Barry and Enright were the most successful syndicated game show producers of the early 1980s.

Ironically, as creative as Barry was at developing game shows, he told *The Saturday Evening Post* in 1975 that he was a "duffer" at playing games in real life.

The Sunset

Barry and Enright had made a very successful comeback and were now widely respected by their colleagues in the business. The bitterness from the quiz show scandals was finally a thing of the past. The long years of strain had clearly affected Barry's health. Suffering from high blood pressure, by the late 1970s, Barry began having heart problems. His doctors placed him on a diet and a strict exercise regiment which included jogging and swimming fifty laps a day in his home pool.

By 1979 Barry had lost 40 pounds and was much stronger. Nearing 65 years of age, he cut

Jack Barry with contestant on *The Joker's Wild*: Will she continue to play or stop and take the money? (Fred Wostbrock).

back his work load in 1983, so Jim Peck was hired to occasionally substitute as host of *The Joker's Wild*. Peck said in a 2002 interview that Barry was gradually phasing himself out as host of *The Joker's Wild* and looking to retire. He planned to work behind the scenes with the company however.

After finishing the 1983-1984 season on *The Joker's Wild*, Barry and his wife visited their daughter in Europe. Upon returning to the United States, the Barrys stopped in New York City before heading home to Los Angeles. Late in the morning on May 2, 1984, Barry suffered a massive heart attack while jogging in New York City's Central Park. He was rushed to Lenox Hill Hospital but was pronounced dead on arrival at the age of 66.

He was survived by his wife Patte and four children. After Barry's death, veteran host Bill Cullen took over *The Joker's Wild*. Dan Enright continued operating their company, keeping *The Joker's Wild* and *Tic Tac Dough* on the air until 1986. He later worked on made-for-TV movies until his death in 1992 at the age of 75.

The popularity of big money game shows caused by the success of ABC's *Who Wants to Be a Millionaire?* in the summer and fall of 1999 prompted NBC to bring out a revival of *Twenty-One*. The program debuted on January 9, 2000, with talk show personality Maury Povich as host. NBC canceled it after a few months, but it later moved to the cable network PAX-TV.

Containing only a few new twists, the basic game remained the same with two contestants competing in separate isolation booths answering questions to score 21 points. The major difference between the new version and the Jack Barry edition was that the questions were multiple choice making them much easier to answer. This was one result from the quiz show scandals of the 1950s. Never again would the questions be so difficult that the game would have to be rigged in order for the contestants to win.

Dick Clark

Birth Name: Richard Wagstaff Clark

Born: November 30, 1929, in Mount Vernon, New York

Marriages and Families: Barbara Mallery (1952–1961) (Divorced) 1 son; Loretta Martin (1962–1971) (Divorced) 1 son, 1 daughter; Kari Wigton (1977–Present)

Radio Career: Announcer (WRUN-AM/FM, Utica, NY) 1946; Announcer/Disc Jockey (WAER-FM, Syracuse, NY) 1946–1950; Announcer (WOLF-AM, Syracuse, NY) 1950–1951; Announcer (WRUN-AM, Syracuse, NY) 1951; Announcer (WFIL-AM, Philadelphia, PA) 1952–1956; *The Dick Clark National Music Survey* (MBS) 1982–1985; *Dick Clark's Rock, Roll, and Remember* (Syndicated) 1982–Present; *Countdown America* (Syndicated) 1985–1994; *Dick Clark's U.S. Music Survey* (Syndicated) 1994–2005; *Dick Clark's Music Calendar* (Syndicated) 2001–Present

TV Career: HOST—*Cactus Dick and the Santa Fe Riders* (WKTV-TV, Utica, NY) 1951–1952; *What's the Next Line?* (WFIL-TV, Philadelphia, PA) 1954–1955; *Bandstand* (WFIL-TV, Philadelphia, PA) July 9, 1956–August 2, 1957; *American Bandstand* (ABC Daytime) August 5, 1957–August 30, 1963, (ABC Primetime) October 7, 1957–December 30, 1957, (ABC Saturdays) September 7, 1963–September 5, 1987, (Syndicated) September 19, 1987–April 8, 1989; *Talent Trend* (WFIL-TV, Philadelphia, PA) 1957–1958; *The Dick Clark Show* (ABC Primetime) February 16, 1958–September 10, 1960; *Dick Clark's World of Talent* (ABC Primetime) September 27, 1959–December 20, 1959; *The Object Is* (ABC Daytime) December 30, 1963–March 27, 1964; *Missing Links* (ABC Daytime) March 30, 1964–December 25, 1964; *Where the Action Is* (ABC Daytime) June 27, 1965–March 31, 1967; *Dick Clark's New Year's Rockin' Eve* (ABC Annually) December 31, 1972–Present; *The $10,000 Pyramid* (CBS Daytime) March 26, 1973–March 29, 1974; *The Rock & Roll Years* (ABC Primetime) November 28, 1973–January 9, 1974; *The $10,000 Pyramid* (ABC Daytime) May 6, 1974–January 16, 1976; *The $20,000 Pyramid* (ABC Daytime) January 19, 1976–June 27, 1980; *Dick Clark's Live Wednesday* (NBC Primetime) September 20, 1978–December 27, 1978; *Strictly Confidential* (Unsold Game Show Pilot) November 1980; *The Dick Clark Show* (Unsold Talk Show Pilot) 1981; *The $50,000 Pyramid* (Syndicated) January 26, 1981–September 11, 1981; *Krypton Factor* (ABC Primetime) August 7, 1981–September 4, 1981; *Inside America* (ABC Primetime) April 4, 1982–April 25, 1982; *The $25,000 Pyramid* (CBS Daytime) September 20, 1982–December 31, 1987, (CBS Daytime) April 4, 1988–July 1, 1988; *TV's Bloopers & Practical Jokes* (NBC Primetime) January 9, 1984–February 24, 1986; *Dick Clark's Nitetime* (Syndicated) September 1985–September 1986; *The $100,000 Pyramid* (Syndicated) September 9, 1985–September 2, 1988; *Super Bloopers & New Practical Jokes* (NBC Primetime) May 20, 1988–September 2, 1988; *Live! Dick Clark Presents* (CBS Primetime) September 14, 1988–October 22, 1988; *The Challengers*

Dick Clark (Fred Wostbrock)

(Syndicated) September 3, 1990–August 31, 1991; *Scattergories* (NBC Daytime) January 18, 1993–June 11, 1993; *It Takes Two* (FAM) March 10, 1997–May 30, 1997; *TV's Censored Bloopers '98* (NBC Primetime) January 31, 1998–August 2, 1998; *Winning Lines* (CBS Primetime) January 8, 2000–February 19, 2000; *The Other Half* (Syndicated) September 10, 2001–September 5, 2003   PRODUCER—*Dick Clark's New Year's Rockin' Eve* (ABC) December 1972–Present; *In Concert* (ABC Late Night) January 1973–May 1975; *American Music Awards* (ABC) February 1974–Present; *The John Davidson Show* (NBC Primetime) May 24, 1976–June 14, 1976; *Easy Does It* (CBS Primetime) August 25, 1976–September 15, 1976; *Academy of Country Music Awards* (NBC/CBS) May 1979–Present; *Golden Globe Awards* (Syndicated) January 1983–January 1988, (TBS) January 1989–January 1995, (NBC) January 1996–Present; *Rock 'N' Roll Summer Action* (ABC Primetime) July 17, 1985–August 28, 1985; *Puttin' on the Hits* (Syndicated) September 1985–September 1986 ; *Keep on Cruisin'* (CBS Late Night) January 9, 1987–June 5, 1987; *In Person From The Palace* (CBS Late Night) June 12, 1987–August 21, 1987; *Trial By Jury* (Syndicated) September 1989–September 1990; *Let's Make a Deal* (NBC Daytime) July 9, 1990–January 11, 1991; *Greed* (FOX Primetime) November 4, 1999–July 14, 2000; *American Dreams* (NBC Primetime) September 29, 2002–March 30, 2005

Theatrical Movies: *Because They're Young* (1960); *The Young Doctors* (1961); *Psych-Out* (1968); *The Savage Seven* (1968); *Wild in the Streets* (1968); *Killers Three* (1969)

Made-for-TV Movies: *Telethon* (ABC) November 6, 1977; *Deadman's Curve* (CBS) February 3, 1978; *Elvis* (ABC) February 11, 1979; *Birth of the Beatles* (ABC) November 23, 1979; *The Man In the Santa Claus Suit* (NBC) December 13, 1979; *Valentine Magic on Love Island* (NBC) February 15, 1980; *Murder In Texas* (NBC) May 3–4, 1981; *The Demon Murder Case* (NBC) March 6, 1983; *Copacabana* (CBS) December 3, 1985; *Demon Murder Case* (1985); *Liberace* (1988); *Town Bully* (1988); *Promised a Miracle* (1988)

Business Interests: Chairman/CEO: Dick Clark Productions (1956–2005); Chairman/CEO: Dick Clark Company (2006–Present)

Books: *Your Happiest Years* (1959); *To Goof or Not to Goof* (1963); *Rock, Roll, and Remember* (1976); *Dick Clark's Program For Success in Your Business and Personal Life* (1980); *Looking Great, Staying Young* (1980); *The History of American Bandstand* (1985); *Dick Clark's Easygoing Guide to Good Grooming* (1986); *Murder on Tour: A Rock 'n' Roll Mystery* (1989); *Dick Clark's American Bandstand* (1997)

In the spring of 1995, Dick Clark was sent a list of the television shows on which he served as host and/or producer. When asked if the information was accurate, he replied that his association with television shows produced by his company took up 41 single spaced typewritten pages! To say the least, it would be difficult to put all of that information into one book. The list of Dick Clark's shows on the previous pages only scratches the surface of his prosperous run.

Richard Wagstaff Clark was born on November 30, 1929, in Mount Vernon, New York. As a child, Clark's keen business mind was evident when he peddled a neighborhood gossip sheet for five cents a copy. His older brother, Bradley, was killed when his plane was shot down during World War II. In his spare time, Clark listened to the radio and became interested in a broadcasting career. He then joined his high school's drama club where he refined his speaking skills.

Breaking into Broadcasting

In 1946 Clark's family moved to Utica, New York where his father worked for radio station WRUN. After high school, Clark worked in the mail room at WRUN during the summer of 1946. He was soon filling in for the station's announcer doing weather forecasts, station breaks and newscasts. Clark enrolled at Syracuse University in the fall of 1946 as an advertising major with a minor in radio. He racked up more broadcasting experience as a disc jockey on the campus station WAER-FM and working weekends at WOLF, the commercial station in Syracuse.

Upon graduating in June 1951, Clark worked for his father at WRUN in Utica for the summer before striking out on his own. At television station WKTV in Utica, Clark hosted a country music show called *Cactus Dick and the Santa Fe Riders*. In 1952 he moved to Philadelphia as a weekday disc jockey for WFIL. Clark also commuted to New York to do television beer commercials but his boyish looks got him into trouble. The brewery owner pulled Clark off the air saying that he looked too young to be drinking beer.

It's Got a Good Beat

Clark's first big television break came in the fall of 1955 when he filled in as host on the WFIL television show, *Bandstand*, while the regular host was on vacation. *Bandstand* had begun on WFIL in October 1952 with Bob Horn and Lee Stewart as co-hosts. In the summer of 1956, *Bandstand* host Bob Horn was arrested for drunk driving and summarily fired from his job. Clark was pressed into service to host *Bandstand*, and over the next year, the show climbed to the top of the ratings in Philadelphia. *Bandstand*'s success caught the attention of ABC, and Clark persuaded the network to give the show a brief run in August 1957. By that fall the show was popular enough to warrant a regular slot on ABC's daytime schedule. With the new name *American Bandstand*, the show took the country by storm.

Each day on *American Bandstand*, Clark introduced one or two popular rock and roll performers and interviewed them about their careers. The artists lip-synched their biggest hit records while the studio audience of teenagers danced to the music. Clark also played records of other recording stars for the remainder of the show. During the 1950s, *American Bandstand* featured just about every big name artist, most of whom were just starting their careers, such as Bill Haley and the Comets, Jerry Lee Lewis, the Supremes, and the Everly Brothers.

Breaking Records with Records

By 1958 Clark was fronting two ABC television shows including his own Saturday night music series, *The Dick Clark Show*. He became so identified with the music scene that everywhere Clark went he was besieged with requests to listen to people's ideas for songs. Everyone wanted a piece of the action at *American Bandstand*. Teenagers bought rock and roll records by the millions.

Any rock and roll artist knew that exposure on *American Bandstand* usually meant huge record sales of their material. Since he was responsible for so many record successes, Clark invested some of his earnings into the recording business. He worked with record companies helping with talent management, record pressing, and music publishing. By 1959 he had bought interest in a number of record labels and owned music publishing firms.

Payola Scandal

Clark was now a millionaire at the young age of 30, but his world nearly crashed down around him. Many music producers stopped at nothing to get their records played on radio and television. One of the underhanded methods was "payola," where disc jockeys received an under-the-table payment in exchange for playing certain records on their shows. Congress soon learned of the practice and took swift action to stop it. A number of disc jockeys and record producers lost their jobs after a massive investigation by the Representative Oren Harris House Special Subcommittee.

Clark became a target for the committee's investigation since he owned interests in the music business. When he was called to testify in April 1960, Clark successfully proved that he had never taken part in "payola" nor had received any payoffs to play music on *American Bandstand* or *The Dick Clark Show*. To prevent any future problems, however, ABC insisted that Clark relinquish all of his business interests in music.

The Object Is...

With his career and reputation intact, Clark returned to the *American Bandstand* set where he received a 10 minute ovation from the studio audience. He hosted *American Bandstand* each weekday afternoon until its popularity tapered with the changes in the public's musical tastes. In September 1963 ABC reduced the show to once a week and moved it to Saturday afternoons where it attracted a solid audience for the next 24 years. Clark also moved the show from Philadelphia to Los Angeles. With less time to spend on his musical activities, Clark looked for new projects. In December 1963 ABC assigned him to host his first game show, *The Object Is*.

In this game, three celebrities and three contestants identified famous people. The six participants sat together behind a long desk and each contestant played with two of the stars. One of the celebrities gave the clues while the second star guessed the subjects. The game began with one celebrity giving a clue. If the other celebrity guessed the subject, the player seated between them scored 10 points. A maximum of four clues were played with the point values decreasing to seven, five, and three points. Game play went down the line with each contestant getting a chance to score. The first player to collect 15 points won the game and played a bonus round. *The Object Is* was canceled on March 27, 1964.

A Missing Link

The following Monday, March 30, 1964, ABC picked up a discarded NBC game show called *Missing Links* with Clark replacing Ed McMahon as the host. Contestants read funny and humiliating real life stories to a panel of celebrities. The job of the celebrities was to guess key words deleted from the stories. When the player reading the story reached the key word, he/she paused to see if the panel could guess the all important word. If the panel guessed the "missing link," the player collected $50. Four "missing links" were played per story and three stories comprised a show. *Missing Links* left the air on Christmas Day 1964.

Clark's reputation as a workaholic was already becoming legendary in the business.

> *Ira Skutch (*Missing Links *producer, February 2006 telephone interview):*
> "Dick is the one of the hardest working people I know. He was living in California and we did *Missing Links* in New York. He would fly in, come to the theater and do the rehearsal. Dick would set himself up in the dressing room and immediately start making telephone calls, making notes, writing memos. He would come out and do the show. He would work through the lunch break [conducting business]. That's why he was so successful as a producer and entrepreneur."

After *Missing Links* left the air, Clark gave up on game shows. In addition to his weekly chores on *American Bandstand*, he acted in some theatrical movies and turned up periodically in episodes of the detective shows *Burke's Law* and *Honey West*. In a change of character, Clark played the murderer in the final episode of the law drama *Perry Mason*.

In the summer of 1965, Clark returned to ABC daytime hosting the half hour music series *Where the Action Is*. Dick Clark Productions also turned out a number of music specials for television and the theatrical movies *Psych-Out*, *The Savage Seven*, and *Killers Three*.

Rockin' New Year's Eve

The early 1970s found Clark producing more musically oriented television shows. On December 31, 1972, he took over as host and producer of ABC's annual New Year's Eve music show. The special had been hosted for many years by big band musician Guy Lombardo. Under Clark, the show took on a more youthful look by featuring current rock and roll musicians performing in Times Square in New York City.

Longtime fans of Guy Lombardo were shocked at the changes, but the viewers tuned in by the millions. The big moment for the show always came just before midnight when the famous ball started slowly down the pole counting down the last seconds before a new year began. *Dick Clark's New Year's Rockin' Eve* became an annual tradition that continues to this day on ABC.

Climbing the Pyramid

Looking for a new challenge, Clark again turned to game shows. He auditioned for CBS's *Gambit* in 1972, but the job went to Wink Martindale. Finally in March 1973, Clark landed his signature show: *The $10,000 Pyramid*. Two celebrity-contestant teams guessed a series of words using clues provided by their teammates. The team in control selected one of six categories and had 30 seconds to guess seven words related to their chosen category. Unlike *Password* where teams used one word clues, players could use whole sentence clues on *The $10,000 Pyramid*. Two categories were played per round and the team with the most points after three rounds moved to the "Winner's Circle." In the bonus game, the process was reversed and the player guessed six categories arranged on a pyramid-shaped board in 60 seconds from a list of short clues supplied by their celebrity partner. Going up the pyramid netted the winner $10,000.

The $10,000 Pyramid performed moderately well during its first season on CBS. As *Pyramid's* host, Clark was easy-going and low key, which initially brought him some criticism for not being more outgoing. Ignoring his critics in a 1986 *People Weekly* interview, Clark insisted that the game was exciting enough and that he did not need to be a high energy host.

In early 1974, the ratings took a dive and CBS dropped the show. ABC quickly grabbed the game for its daytime schedule and returned it to the air on May 6, 1974, where it fared much better than on CBS.

The Pyramid Grows

On January 19, 1976, the series was rechristened *The $20,000 Pyramid*. The show breezed through the next four years as one of the top-rated daytime shows. In 1981 Clark told *The Washington Post* that *The $20,000 Pyramid* was the best game ever created. Admitting that he was not a huge game show fan and that he had a short attention span, he never lost interest in the *Pyramid*.

A number of celebrities repeatedly turned up on *The $20,000 Pyramid* because they were such good players of the game. These included Tony Randall, Soupy Sales, William Shatner, Billy Crystal, and Patty Duke Astin. Shatner was a very devoted Pyramid player who took the game very seriously. On one episode, when he accidentally blew a clue that cost the player the big money during the bonus round, Shatner was so angry with himself that he tossed his chair out of the winner's circle.

Dedicated and Determined

Although Clark's business operations and home were in California, he commuted to New York each week to tape *The $20,000 Pyramid*.

> **Bob Stewart (The $20,000 Pyramid *executive producer, January 2006 telephone interview*):**
> "One stormy winter day his airplane was unable to land at Kennedy Airport in New York. He ended up in Washington, D.C. He hired a limousine to take him in the snow from Washington to New York and he got there in time, maybe 15 minutes before the taping was going to start. He never told us that happened to him and we learned about it many, many months later. He is probably the single most dependable man I ever met in my life with regard to his work ethic. He was there all the time and never complained. He took everything in stride."

In 1977 Clark produced *Dick Clark's Good Ol' Days*, a nostalgic music special for NBC. Its success prompted NBC to put the show on the air weekly. Clark agreed under the condition that the show be done live. Henceforth, *Dick Clark's Live Wednesday* was born in the fall of 1978. Each week past and present rock and roll artists performed on the show with clips from old *American Bandstand* episodes highlighting the evening. There was also a dangerous stunt performed each week by professional stuntmen.

Through the years, Clark has continually endured the criticism that his shows are a waste of time and energy. But it was frequently Dick Clark that the major networks called when a show faltered and they needed a quick replacement. His reputation for solid producing and beating impossible deadlines was widely known throughout the industry. Rick Ludwin, NBC's Vice President for Specials and Variety Programs, told *Newsweek* in 1986 that Clark could always "do it on time and within budget."

Raise the Pyramid

In June 1980 ABC pulled the plug on *The $20,000 Pyramid* after a seven year run. The idea was too good to sit idle, and in January 1981, the show was back in syndication. With Clark returning for the ride, the ante raised again to *The $50,000 Pyramid*. Game play remained the same except that winners returned to compete in a tournament of champions for the $50,000 grand prize at the end of the season. This version never caught on as well as the original and was gone in eight months.

Just Getting Warmed Up

By the early 1980s, Clark could point to a number of successes in his now two decade career. He was wealthy beyond his expectations from various enterprises, but he was only getting warmed

"**Relax and concentrate.**" Dick Clark gives final instructions to contestants as they prepare to go for $25,000 on *The $25,000 Pyramid* (Fred Wostbrock).

up. In 1981 he produced and hosted the NBC special *TV's Censored Bloopers*, which featured out-takes from television shows. The one-shot telecast was such a smash that it returned for eight additional specials on NBC over the next three years.

In the fall of 1982, Clark returned to a familiar perch hosting CBS's *The $25,000 Pyramid* for six seasons. This time the game originated from Los Angeles, but the format remained the same. By 1984 NBC had commissioned Clark to produce and host a weekly version of his bloopers specials called *TV's Bloopers and Practical Jokes*. With Ed McMahon as his co-host, a new feature was introduced where elaborate practical jokes were pulled on unsuspecting television stars.

Clark now had shows running on all three networks: *American Bandstand* for ABC, *The $25,000 Pyramid* on CBS, and *TV's Bloopers and Practical Jokes* for NBC. He also had two syndicated radio shows going strong: *Countdown America* and *Dick Clark's Rock, Roll, and Remember*. Away from broadcasting, Clark packaged and produced a live stage production called *Good Ol' Rock and Roll* in Las Vegas and Atlantic City.

Hurrying from Place to Place

In the fall of 1985, Clark's unbelievable schedule found him hurrying from place to place to carry out his work. Mondays were spent taping *TV's Bloopers and Practical Jokes*. Tuesdays found Clark taping episodes of his new weekly music series *Dick Clark's Nitetime*. Wednesdays put Clark in a radio studio to tape *Countdown America* and *Rock Roll and Remember*. On Thursdays he hustled to CBS Television City to tape five episodes of *The $25,000 Pyramid*. On Fridays he taped another five episodes of that show and five of the syndicated evening version, *The $100,000 Pyramid*. A few Saturdays each month, he taped episodes of *American Bandstand* for ABC.

Viewers who knew of Clark's easy-going personality on the air might have been in for a surprise to know that he was a demanding employer with a temper to go with it. Clark himself admitted to *People Weekly* in 1986 that he blew up and let out the steam adding that it was a great ulcer preventative.

Clark's wife, Kari Wigton, whom he married in 1977, served as Clark's personal secretary and helped people understand Clark's ways of working with people. Indeed his employees at Dick Clark Productions are fiercely loyal to him and respect him so much that they continually go the extra mile in their work.

Giving Up Projects, Taking on New Ones

By the late 1980s, Clark was seen less on television, but remained every bit as active behind the scenes. In a year's time *The $25,000 Pyramid*, *The $100,000 Pyramid*, and *American Bandstand* were all canceled but Clark immediately put *American Bandstand* in syndication. He finally stepped down as host on April 8, 1989, when *American Bandstand* moved to the USA cable network. Clark turned the hosting over to 26-year-old David Hirsch, but the show was axed after 26 weeks.

In a departure from his traditional shows, Clark produced the daily courtroom drama series, *Trial by Jury*, during the 1989-1990 season. He then co-produced a new version of *Let's Make a Deal* for NBC in the summer of 1990. Clark went before the camera to host the syndicated game *The Challengers* for one season. Players on this show had to be up to date on events in the news. Each day three contestants answered questions culled from a board of six categories. Each category had three questions worth various dollar amounts and players secretly selected a category and dollar amount. At the end of the game, all three players wagered all or part of their winnings on one final question to determine the winner.

In January 1993 Clark returned to NBC daytime hosting a 21 week run of *Scattergories*. Based on the popular board game, two teams of four players were given a subject and a letter of the alphabet. The team was given 15 seconds to name items related to the subject beginning with the given letter of the alphabet. Teams could pick up additional points by choosing four of the five celebrities who appeared via pre-recorded sequences. The celebrities gave their answers to the same subject played by the team and any new answers not already given by the team scored points.

Doling Out the Big Money

Although Clark remained out of the spotlight during much of the 1990s, he continued producing regular music specials and awards shows for the major networks. In November 1999 Clark jumped on the big money bandwagon after the success of ABC's *Who Wants to Be a Millionaire?* He produced *Greed*, a primetime game show for FOX, which offered a jackpot of $2 million. Chuck Woolery hosted the series, and *Greed* drew respectable ratings during the 1999-2000 season. Clark himself went before the cameras in January 2000 to host *Winning Lines*, a seven week entry into the big money sweepstakes.

Clark has not hosted another game show since *Winning Lines*, but he returned to television in the fall of 2001 with *The Other Half*. Clark produced and co-hosted with actor Danny Bonaduce, best known for his role on *The Partridge Family* in the 1970s. In September 2002 Clark launched *American Dreams*, an NBC drama series set in the 1960s. The show used a liberal amount of clips from *American Bandstand* to capture the flavor of the era. Clark himself did not appear in the show except in archival footage, but his unmistakable producer's touch was evident in the music and storylines.

What Happens Next?

Throughout his career, Clark remained the epitome of energy with his multiple activities. He never seemed to slow down, although he was more selective of his projects after being diagnosed with diabetes in 1994. With diet and exercise, Clark was able to keep his diabetes under control, and he became a spokesman on behalf of the disease. However, on December 6, 2004, Clark suffered a debilitating stroke that left him unable to speak or walk. For the first time in more than 30 years, Clark was forced to miss his annual *New Year's Rockin' Eve* show. Regis Philbin substituted for him on that broadcast while Clark began a slow recovery.

After seven weeks in the hospital, Clark underwent intense physical and speech therapy and regained part of his strength. He gave no interviews or appeared on television in the interim leading many people to speculate that he would not return to the New Year's show. But Clark had every intention of coming back and his prediction came true on December 31, 2005, when he returned to take the reins of the *New Year's Rockin' Eve* show. Joining Clark as co-host for the special was Ryan Seacrest, the host of FOX's popular series *American Idol*. Seacrest has signed to eventually take over the *New Year's Rockin' Eve* specials when Clark decides to step down as host.

Although his speech was still not perfect, Clark clearly held his own.

> *Bob Stewart:*
> "I thought it was very brave of him to come on and do that. What he did was magnificent because it gave so much hope to so many people recovering from strokes and they realized how far back he had come."

Although less involved in the day to day activities, he continues to keep a hand in the projects of Dick Clark Company. Today Clark lives with his wife Kari in Malibu, California. He has two sons and a daughter from two previous marriages in the 1950s and 1960s. One of Clark's best known traits through the years was his ability to never appear to age. He once revealed his secret in retaining one's youthful looks to *People Weekly*'s Christopher Andersen in 1986. According to Clark, the secret is to "pick your parents very carefully."

BUD COLLYER

Birth Name: Clayton Johnson Heermance, Jr.
Born: June 18, 1908, in New York, New York
Died: September 8, 1969, in Greenwich, Connecticut
Marriages and Family: Heloise Law Green (1936–1951) (Divorced) 2 daughters, 1 son; Marian Shockley (1952–1969)
Radio Career: *Just Plain Bill* (CBS & NBC) various supporting roles; *Pretty Kitty Kelly* (CBS) March 8, 1937–September 27, 1940; *Terry and the Pirates* (NBC) November 1, 1937–March 22, 1939; *The Guiding Light* (NBC & CBS); *Young Widder Brown* (NBC) 1938–1940; *The Adventures of Superman* (Syndicated) February 12, 1940–August 1942, (Mutual) August 31, 1942–June 17, 1949; *Cavalcade of America* (NBC) 1940–1943; *Kate Hopkins, Angel of Mercy* (CBS) October 7, 1940–April 3, 1942; *Man I Married* (CBS) July 21, 1941–April 3, 1942; *House in the Country* (NBC) 1941–1942; *Kitty Foyle* (CBS) October 5, 1942–June 9, 1944; *Abie's Irish Rose* (NBC) 1943–1944; *Mary Small* (ABC) February 27, 1944–March 24, 1946; *Break the Bank* (Mutual) October 20, 1945–April 13, 1946, (ABC) July 5, 1946–September 23, 1949, (NBC) October 5, 1949–September 21, 1951, (ABC) September 24, 1951–March 27, 1953; *By Popular Demand* (Mutual) June 27, 1946–November 14, 1946; *Time's a Wastin'* (CBS) October 6, 1948–December 29, 1948; *Winner Take All* (CBS) 1948–1950; *High Places; Listening Post; Big Sister; Chick Carter, Boy Detective; The Phillip Morris Playhouse; The Raleigh Room; Schaefer Revue; Stage Door Canteen; The Story of Mary Marlin; Road of Life*

Bud Collyer (courtesy Fred Wostbrock)

TV Career: Host—*Winner Take All* (CBS Primetime) July 1, 1948–October 3, 1950; *Break the Bank* (ABC Primetime) October 22, 1948–September 23, 1949, (NBC Primetime) October 5, 1949–January 9, 1952, (CBS Primetime) January 13, 1952–February 1, 1953, (NBC Daytime) March 30, 1953–September 1, 1953; *This Is the Missus* (CBS Daytime) November 17, 1948–December 1948; *Talent Jackpot* (DuMont Primetime) July 19, 1949–August 23, 1949; *Beat the Clock* (CBS Primetime) March 23, 1950–February 23, 1958, (CBS Daytime) September 16, 1957–September 12, 1958, (ABC Daytime) October 13, 1958–January 27, 1961; *Say It With Acting* (NBC Primetime) January 6, 1951–May 12, 1951; *Masquerade Party* (NBC Primetime) July 14, 1952–August 25, 1952; *Talent Patrol* (ABC Primetime) April 1953–June 1953; *Quick As a Flash* (ABC Primetime) May 1953–February 25, 1954; *On Your Way* (DuMont Primetime) September 9, 1953–January 20, 1954; *Feather Your Nest* (NBC Daytime) October 4, 1954–July 27, 1956; *To Tell the Truth* (CBS Prime-

time) December 18, 1956–May 22, 1967, (CBS Daytime) June 18, 1962–September 6, 1968; *Number Please* (ABC Daytime) January 31, 1961–December 29, 1961; *The Batman Superman Hour* (CBS Saturdays) September 14, 1968–September 1969
Broadway Career: *Fields Beyond* (1934); *Life Begins* (1936); *Angel Island* (1937)
Other Career: Law Clerk (1932–1934)
Books: *Thou Shalt Not Fear* (1962); *With the Whole Heart* (1966)

"Will the real _____ please stand up?" These words became a familiar phrase to many television viewers from the 1950s through the 1970s. Bud Collyer quoted this phrase on his long running game show *To Tell the Truth* for almost 12 years. Bud Collyer greeted viewers for more than 20 years with a warm, winning smile and a polite manner. When the show was over and it was time to part with the viewers for the day, he frequently said, "Goodbye and God bless you." He was never afraid to speak of his religious faith and he credited God with all of his successes.

Bud Collyer was born as Clayton Johnson Heermance, Jr. in New York City on June 18, 1908. Collyer came from a family with a theatrical background as his grandfather, Dan Collyer, acted on the stage for 50 years. His mother acted with the name Carrie Collyer, and his sister, June Collyer, starred in several silent films. Clayton "Bud" Collyer, as he eventually named himself, enrolled at Williams College around 1926 where he led a dance band. One evening at a school dance at the St. Regis Hotel in New York City, a fashion commentator heard Collyer singing. He helped Collyer land a part-time job with CBS Radio at a salary of $85 a week.

Lawyer vs. Actor

However, his call to show business did not come right away. Collyer instead followed in his father's footsteps to become a lawyer, so he attended Fordham Law School and worked as a law clerk for two years. He soon found law work boring. Once he saw that his mother, sister, and brother were making a good living as entertainers, he decided to ditch law and pursue an acting career. He began in 1934 with a bit part in the Broadway show *Fields Beyond*. Drawing on his experience with CBS radio during his college days, Collyer sought radio acting roles. During the mid to late 1930s, he found additional radio work serving as announcer or playing bit parts in such shows as *The Guiding Light, Just Plain Bill, Life Can Be Beautiful, Terry and the Pirates,* and *Pretty Kitty Kelly*.

Collyer married his first wife Heloise Law Green in 1936 and they had three children: daughters Patricia and Cynthia and son Michael. After their divorce, Collyer later married radio actress Marian Shockley in 1952. They had no children.

A Real Superman

In February 1940 Collyer began his most prominent role in radio as the lead in *The Adventures of Superman*. He portrayed the character for nine years, although Collyer kept his name anonymous until 1942 when *Time* published an article on the series. The article noted that Collyer stood six feet tall and weighed 165 pounds, which was not quite the size of Superman. At the time, Collyer was the superintendent of a 1,250 student interdenominational Sunday school in Manhasset, New York. The children in the classes viewed Collyer as the real Superman until he made sure they realized that he only played the character.

The Call of the Quiz Shows

Collyer broke into quiz shows in 1945 when he teamed with Bert Parks to co-host *Break the Bank*, which ran for eight years on radio and spawned a television version in 1948. Parks and Collyer co-hosted the television version as well. In July 1948, Collyer joined Mark Goodson–Bill Todman Productions to host one of their first television creations *Winner Take All*. This marked the beginning of a 20-year association with the company. Collyer also appeared on other television shows such as *Talent Jackpot* and *This Is the Missus*.

In 1950 Collyer began hosting the primetime game *Beat the Clock* for CBS. Contestants were required to perform tricky and comical stunts against a large ticking clock. Some stunts were more difficult than others, but almost all of them were messy and chaotic. Many contestants ended up with pies in the face, whipped cream and water sprayed on them, dishes breaking around them, and balloons exploding all over the place.

A Little Game in Itself

All of the stunts were devised by Bob Howard and Frank Wayne of the Goodson–Todman staff.

> *Ira Skutch (***Beat the Clock** *director, February 2006 telephone interview):*
> "*Beat the Clock* was a hard show for an emcee because you had to learn all those stunts. Every stunt was a little game in itself, and they all had different rules so Bud had to learn all that. We had to rehearse all the stunts, so Bud would physically learn how to do them, how to explain them and how to oversee them. We would go through the show piece by piece like that, then do a dress rehearsal, and then go on the air. That's not a lot of time to learn all that material and Bud would pick it up very, very quickly."

Each *Beat the Clock* game ended with a bonus stunt that was very difficult to perform. Sometimes the bonus stunt would be played for weeks before someone accomplished it. Early in the show's run, the stunt was usually worth only a few hundred dollars. By the mid 1950s when the big money quiz shows became the fad, the bonus stunt increased in value for each time it was not accomplished until it was worth several thousand dollars. The largest amount ever won on *Beat the Clock* was $64,000 by one couple in September 1956.

Jealous

Although Collyer was popular as the star of the show, there were rumors that he was jealous of the attention given to his beautiful young blonde assistant named Roxanne, who assisted contestants with the stunt props.

> *Ira Skutch:*
> "Bud was like most of us: somewhat complicated or contradictory. Personally, he was very pleasant and we got along very well. Of course he was like almost all performers. He had a performer's ego so you had to be considerate of that."

More Fun and Games

In September 1957 CBS added a daytime version of *Beat the Clock* to its schedule in addition to the primetime series. The nighttime version left the air in February 1958 and the daytime version switched to the ABC network in October 1958 continuing until January 27, 1961.

Collyer usually emceed at least one other game show during his *Beat the Clock* years. At one point in the spring of 1953, he hosted four shows simultaneously. Along with *Beat the Clock*, he hosted NBC's *Break the Bank*, an ABC military talent show used by the army for recruiting soldiers called *Talent Patrol*, and the ABC game show *Quick as a Flash*, where two contestant-celebrity teams viewed a film sequence and tried to be the first to guess its outcome. The players could stop the film anytime to give their answers. On the side, Collyer appeared in television commercials.

Despite his busy schedule with four television shows, Collyer brushed off any thoughts that he was overloaded with work in a 1953 *TV Guide* interview. Compared to doing 32 different radio shows a week at one point in his career during the 1940s, a mere four television shows a week were nothing.

Collyer left *Talent Patrol* in June 1953 while the daytime version of *Break the Bank* was canceled in September 1953. He then took the reigns of the DuMont quiz show *On Your Way*. This show gave contestants a chance to win a vacation to a destination of their choice by answering a series of questions. By the spring of 1954, Collyer was down to only *Beat the Clock*.

That fall he began hosting NBC's *Feather Your Nest*. Three couples competed in a three level quiz for the chance to win furniture. The three rounds of the game were represented by different colored feathers, red for round one, yellow in round two, and green for the third round. The feathers were worth from 1,000 to 3,000 points and the couples won feathers by correctly answering questions. The first team to amass 6,000 points earned the right to play for a jackpot prize. Couples also participated in a special drawing at the end of each show for the chance to win a house and a car. *Feather Your Nest* lasted just two seasons.

To Tell the Truth, You're a Star

In December 1956 Collyer struck gold again with *To Tell the Truth*, another popular game show from Goodson–Todman. The program featured three contestants, all of whom claimed to be a certain person. Only one of the players was telling the truth while two of them were imposters. Collyer then read a story containing unusual facts about the person. A panel of four celebrities took turns questioning the players to determine who the real person was and which two were bluffing. After all four celebrities cast their votes for who they thought was telling the truth, Collyer then asked the famous question "Will the real ____ please stand up?" The contestants divided $250 for each panelist they fooled for a possible $1,000.

Collyer was not the first choice to host *To Tell the Truth*. The pilot episode, which was titled *Nothing but the Truth*, was hosted by Mike Wallace, but he was replaced by Collyer before the show premiered. *To Tell the Truth* burned up the ratings on CBS' primetime schedule and later spawned a weekday afternoon version beginning in June 1962. The nighttime version continued until May 1967 while the daytime version lasted until September 6, 1968. When it was canceled, *To Tell the Truth* was the last game show left on CBS. The network did not air another game until 1972.

After *To Tell the Truth* left the air, Collyer brought his career full circle by portraying another comic book action hero. In the fall of 1968 he became the voice of Batman on the CBS Saturday morning cartoon series *The Batman/Superman Hour*. The show lasted only one season in original episodes before going into reruns in the fall of 1969.

Send Those Kids to Camp

Away from television, Collyer was very active in his hometown of Greenwich, Connecticut. In 1958 he and four other people created the nonprofit organization Sciences and Art Camps, Inc. The organization was designed for gifted school children primarily in grades four through six. The children were given the opportunity to attend a special summer camp to study art, music, science, mathematics, philosophy, creative writing, speech, and even the Russian language. The six week long summer camp was held in June 1960 in nearby Darien, Connecticut.

Sunday School Teacher

A deeply religious man, Collyer also taught Sunday school at his church in Greenwich every weekend. In 1950 he assumed the position of Sunday school superintendent at the First Presbyterian Church in Greenwich, Connecticut. Over time, his teaching style increased the Sunday school attendance from around 90 students to more than 700. Collyer used a folksy approach to teaching religion. His Sunday school sessions were loaded with debates on moral and theological questions, but he also had a penchant for pulling pranks to get a point across. During one session about walking the straight and narrow, Collyer demonstrated the point by tight-rope walking across a sofa.

Bud Collyer welcomes America to join in the fun on *To Tell the Truth* (Fred Wostbrock).

Many of Collyer's students were teenagers, and through the years he became a teenage counselor. Collyer wrote several articles on adolescent problems for major magazines and published two books of his Sunday school lessons called *Thou Shalt Not Fear* and *With the Whole Heart*. He also spoke out against religious and racial intolerance and raised money for various charities and the Boy Scouts. Collyer's religious views drew criticism from some circles, but he never let the critics stop him from stating his religious beliefs. He remained committed to religious work to the end of his life.

Complete Coincidence

In 1969 Collyer's popular game show, *Beat the Clock*, was revived for syndication with Jack Narz as the new host. That summer while on a flight, Collyer met Narz as he was flying to New York to begin taping for *Beat the Clock*.

Jack Narz (TV host, October 2004 telephone interview):
"When I got to my seat on the airplane, lo and behold, my seat-mate was Bud Collyer. [It was a] complete coincidence! He had been visiting his sister who was in the hospital at that time. We introduced ourselves and had a very pleasant flight, chatting all the way to New York. He was a real gentleman. He wished me luck and sent his regards to the staff and crew."

Goodnight and God Bless You

Collyer never lived to see the revival of *Beat the Clock*. Not long after his meeting with Narz, Collyer entered the Greenwich Hospital in Connecticut with a circulatory ailment. He died of heart failure at 61 years of age on the night of September 8, 1969. He was survived by his second wife Marian and three children. Ironically on the same day Collyer died, a syndicated revival of *To Tell the Truth* premiered with Garry Moore as host. Bud Collyer continued to entertain viewers more than 30 years after his death when Game Show Network aired reruns of his two most popular shows.

In his relatively short life, Collyer used his celebrity status to the fullest for a ministry to many people. He told *TV Guide* in 1962 that he once considered a career as a minister, but felt that he would be more effective as a layman. His strong religious faith was evident to those who knew him, but he never thought of himself as better than anyone. The best ending for any story about Bud Collyer would be to use his favorite closing, "God Bless You."

RAY COMBS

Birth Name: Raymond Neil Combs, Jr.
Born: April 3, 1956, in Hamilton, Ohio
Died: June 2, 1996, in Glendale, California
Marriage and Family: Debra Jo Mink (1977–1996) 2 sons, 4 daughters
TV Career: HOST—*Family Feud* (CBS Daytime) July 4, 1988–June 26, 1992; *Family Feud Challenge* (CBS Daytime) June 29, 1992–September 10, 1993, (Syndicated) September 19, 1988–September 9, 1994; *The Love Psychic* (Syndicated) 1994; *The Ray Combs Show* (Unsold Talk Show Pilot) 1995; **Family Challenge* (Family Channel) October 2, 1995–September 27, 1996 (*Reruns of *Family Challenge* continued for three months after Combs' death.)
Theatrical Movies: *Overboard* (1987); *Vampire in Brooklyn* (1995)
Business Interests: Co-Owner: Caddy Combs Comedy Club, Cincinnati, Ohio (1989–1990); Owner: Ray Combs Cincinnati Comedy Connection (1991–1995)
Other Careers: Foundry Worker (1974–1975); Mormon Missionary (1975–1977); Furniture Salesman (1977–1984); Audience warm-up man for TV sitcoms (1984–1988)

If you happen to catch a rerun or two of the sitcoms *Diff'rent Strokes*, *Amen*, *The Facts of Life*, or just about any NBC sitcom that ran during the mid 1980s, Ray Combs was there, although you rarely saw him on camera. Remember how loud the audience laughed at the zany stories and characters on those shows? An audience that laughs this hard and this long has to be feeling good. It takes a special person to warm up an audience, all of them tired and impatient from standing outside the studio for hours. The job of the warm up person is to put the audience in a good mood to enjoy the show.

Ray Combs was the man who brought down the house, warming up the audience. He could put people in a happy mood and help the audiences contribute to the success of the show. Combs spent many years developing his social skills in a series of increasingly challenging jobs from a foundry worker to a Mormon missionary to a furniture salesman to an audi-

Ray Combs (Fred Wostbrock)

ence warm up man and finally to a daytime television personality. His game show career spanned only eight years, but during that time he became a household name by hosting *Family Feud* and *Family Challenge.*

Raymond Neil Combs Jr. was born in Hamilton, Ohio, on April 3, 1956, one of six children born to Raymond Neil and Anita Jean Combs. When Combs was four years old, Mormon missionaries came by his house and told his parents about a weekly church program for children. His parents consented, and Combs slowly was indoctrinated into the Mormon belief. At the age of five, he delivered his first sermon, an experience that Combs credited with helping him speak comfortably before an audience. As he grew up, he showed a flair for being a comedian. His interest in show business was evident in high school where he was voted most humorous.

A Missionary and a Salesman

During his teenage years, Combs joined the Boys Club of America, an organization that engaged children in community service projects to keep them from joining street gangs. Combs won the title of Boy of the Year by the Hamilton, Ohio chapter of the club in 1974.

After high school, Combs attended Miami University in Ohio as a business major. He dropped out in 1975 for a two-year stint as a Mormon missionary in Arizona. Upon completing his missionary work in 1977, he married his childhood sweetheart, Debra Jo Mink, whom he had known since first grade. Ray and Debra moved to Indianapolis where he became successful as a furniture salesman earning as much as $70,000 a year by the time he was 22 years old. However, Combs never gave up on his dream of being a comedian.

California on My Mind

While working days as a furniture salesman, Combs worked nights at various Elks clubs and Moose lodges in the Indianapolis area doing a nightclub act. Finally Combs wrote a letter to comedian David Letterman, a native from Indianapolis, who was beginning to attract national attention. In the letter, Combs described his dreams and ambitions of being a comedian. Letterman wrote him back and urged him to come to California. Combs carried the letter for two years before mustering the courage to follow his dream. By now, he and Debra had two children and moving meant giving up a secure, high-paying career with no promise of another job.

In October 1981 Combs moved to California while Debra and the children remained in Indiana. He got in touch with Letterman, who took Combs to several comedy clubs to give him experience. His first performance at the Ice House in Pasadena took place before an audience of eight people. Combs began haunting nightclubs around the L.A. area, but found that he had to work for free just to gain the experience.

With a family to support, Combs took a job as a salesman for Levitz Furniture in Los Angeles. He made far less money than he did in the same job in Indianapolis. As a result, he could only afford a small apartment and had to sleep on the floor. He made trips back and forth between Indiana and California to be with his family.

There was another dark side, however, because his marriage began to falter. Debra Combs was frustrated with the long separations from Ray. The family's financial situation also suffered since Ray only made a fraction of what he once had in Indianapolis.

Great New Talent

Meanwhile, Combs got his first big break in 1984 when he finished fourth out of several hundred contestants in the Los Angeles Stand Up Comedy Competition. Combs gave up his furniture sales job and devoted full time to being a nightclub comedian. Debra and the family finally joined Ray in California where they purchased a home in Glendale.

According to a 1988 *Advertising Age* story, Combs began calling producers pretending to be an agent. He told them about a great new talent named Ray Combs. To fool the producers, he always called in the morning when his voice was deeper. Soon Combs was hired to do audience warm up work for several TV sitcoms such as *Diff'rent Strokes*, *The Facts of Life*, and *Golden Girls*. He became so good at warm-ups that producers of other shows changed their tape days just to get him. Being a successful audience warm-up man paid dividends as Combs earned $200,000 a year.

A Standing Ovation

One day in 1986, Combs was warming up an audience for the NBC sitcom *Amen*, which was produced by Johnny Carson Productions. Carson happened to be outside the studio during the warm up session and heard the laughter through what was supposed to be a soundproof wall. When Carson discovered it was Combs getting all the laughs, he immediately booked him for an appearance on *The Tonight Show*.

On October 23, 1986, Combs received a standing ovation after performing a six minute monologue on the show. During the applause, Combs was about to exit the stage when he saw Carson do something wonderful. Carson was so impressed that he invited Combs to join him during the interview segment.

One of the members in the studio audience that night was Combs' wife Debra. After witnessing the payoff for all of his hard work, Debra began supporting Ray's new career as a comedian 100 percent.

Getting the Work

The next day, NBC Entertainment President Brandon Tartikoff began looking for a way to keep Combs with the network. At Tartikoff's urging, producers offered Combs guest starring roles on NBC sitcoms. He appeared in episodes of *Golden Girls*, *You Again?* and *Nothing in Common*. In 1987 he auditioned to host NBC's *Classic Concentration*, but the job went to Alex Trebek. Combs also had a small role in the 1987 theatrical release *Overboard* starring Goldie Hawn and Kurt Russell.

The Feud Begins

Combs still had his sights set on a being a comedian when he was asked to audition as host for *Family Feud*. The popular game show aired on ABC from 1976 to 1985 with comedian Richard Dawson as host. In 1987 CBS bought the show for a weekday run while a nighttime version was sold in syndication. Dawson was not considered for the hosting job when CBS reactivated the show since he had clashed with *Family Feud's* creator, Mark Goodson. In the search for a new host, Combs' audience warm-ups attracted the attention of *Family Feud's* producers.

> *Gaby Johnston (***Family Feud*** producer, June 2006 telephone interview):*
> "I remember he came in and tried out for the show. He came in with his brother and said to me, 'If I ever get a big head, remind of this moment because I'm so happy.' I never did remind him of it. Ray was always a total pro."

After signing a seven year contract for $800,000 a year, Combs hosted his first *Family Feud* for CBS on July 4, 1988. Sporting a large colorful set that looked almost exactly like the original set from the ABC series, the new *Family Feud* also played like the original version. Two families competed to guess the most popular answers given to questions posed in a survey of 100 people.

Being His Own Man

Though the new version never quite matched the high ratings of the original series, it consistently outranked its NBC competition. At first, the viewers had mixed reactions to Combs,

Can you guess the number one answer to our survey? Ray Combs thinks this contestant family can do it on *Family Feud* (Fred Wostbrock).

frequently comparing him to *Family Feud's* first host, Richard Dawson. He immediately developed his own style and made sure that he was not just another Richard Dawson. Combs also enjoyed making the show a family occasion.

> *Gaby Johnston:*
> "He used to bring his kids. At Christmas they would all be dressed in their reds and greens. He had so many kids and a beautiful wife. It was a real joy to work with him. He never had a personality clash, wasn't mean spirited or self absorbed."

Off the Set

Away from the *Family Feud* set, Combs was a devoted family man. He enjoyed fishing, playing racquetball, and going to the mall with his six children: Ray III, Kelly, Whitney, Chelsy, Kirby, and Cody.

Combs' love for children prompted him to join the Boys and Girls Club of America where he became the National Alumni Association Chairman. Robbie Callaway, the senior vice-president of the Boys and Girls Club of America told the *Los Angeles Times* in June 1996 that Combs "helped to reach a million new youth." For his hard work, Combs won the organization's "Outstanding American" award. This award had previously been won by retired General, and later Secretary of State, Colin Powell.

Night Clubbing

Combs continued working as a stand-up comedian at Los Angeles comedy clubs. Seeking an outlet for his comedy act, he launched his own club in Cincinnati, Ohio called "Caddy Combs" with his business partner Charles Schneider in September 1989. The venture soon turned into a legal battle when differences on how to operate the club broke out between Schneider and Combs. Schneider, who owned the building housing "Caddy Combs," protested that Combs failed to keep his promise of bringing famous performers to the club while Combs charged that Schneider failed to keep accurate financial records and operate the club effectively.

On April 6, 1990, Schneider had Combs arrested after he performed at the club charging him with trespassing. Combs was quickly released at police headquarters and he returned to the stage at "Caddy Combs" a week later. Seeing that the club was more trouble than it was worth, Combs closed it soon after this incident.

However, the episode did not discourage Combs from trying again. In the fall of 1991, he opened "The Ray Combs Cincinnati Comedy Connection," in Cincinnati's tallest building, the Carew Tower Complex. Along with performing at the club himself, Combs booked several unknown and established comedians. He maintained a home in Cincinnati and traveled there once a month to check on his club operations.

The Final Feud

In June 1992, CBS expanded *Family Feud* to a full hour and renamed it *Family Feud Challenge*. In the new format, two complete games were played. The winning family on the first half hour faced another family in the second half of the show.

A new Bullseye Round was played at the beginning of each half hour allowing families to build bankrolls of money. In the Bullseye Round, the two families guessed only the number one answers to five survey questions. Guessing the number one answer, or "hitting the bullseye," earned money for the family's bankroll. Families could score a maximum of $10,000 in the first segment and $20,000 in the second half of the show. The team winning the main game played for their bankroll in the bonus round. The Bullseye Round was added to the syndicated version, but it remained a half hour in length.

However, the Bullseye Round took so much time to play that the rest of the show had to run at a breakneck speed to finish on time. As a result, much of the humor that was a vital part of the show was missed. A full hour of *Family Feud* also may have been too much for many viewers.

Many CBS affiliates dropped *Family Feud* in favor of syndicated programming. CBS finally canceled the daytime version on September 10, 1993. The syndicated series, also suffering in the ratings, remained on the air for the 1993-1994 season. In early 1994, with ratings still sliding, the producers decided to replace Combs with Richard Dawson to see if he could recapture the magic of the original version.

Losing *Family Feud* was a huge blow to Combs. On his last episode of the show, Combs walked off the set during the final moments of the taping leaving the winning family on stage alone.

> *Howard Felsher (***Family Feud*** executive producer, June 2006 telephone interview):*
> "There were about 30 or 45 seconds to go in the show when he left. He tried to make it not noticeable, but it was very noticeable because the show went off without the emcee. He knew it was going to be his last time as host of the show. He didn't want to say goodbye. That's very embarrassing for most people and he didn't want to have to go through it. He left the building. That is certainly understandable. It's not very professional, but it's certainly understandable."

Fighting to Survive

On July 11, 1994, Combs experienced another personal setback when an automobile accident on the Los Angeles Ventura Freeway left him temporarily paralyzed from the neck down. According to a *Los Angeles Times* story by Chip Johnson, Combs was driving west on the freeway near the Burbank-Glendale border when a speeding vehicle swerved from the passing lane and sideswiped Combs' 1991 Jaguar. He was then rear-ended by another vehicle.

The accident left Combs' head wedged between the dashboard and the steering wheel. Los Angeles Policeman Bill Mayfield, who was off-duty at the time and saw the accident scene, stopped and found Combs unconscious. He administered mouth-to-mouth resuscitation and brought Combs around. Doctors at the St. Joseph Medical Center in Burbank found that a swollen spinal disk was causing the paralysis. With intense physical therapy he eventually walked again, but he remained in almost constant pain for the rest of his life.

Combs returned to the home he and Debra maintained in Cincinnati, Ohio to continue his recuperation and to operate his comedy club. Investing a hefty sum of money into the venture, Combs lost out and closed the business in January 1995. Over the years he had charged almost $150,000 to his credit cards. He also owed nearly $100,000 in back taxes. His financial situation worsened when he faced the possibility of losing his five bedroom home in Glendale.

Also a man of compulsive generosity, Combs freely gave money to his family and friends back in Ohio, never asking to be reimbursed. The resulting total debt of nearly $500,000 put considerable strain on the family. These new anxieties further deteriorated his marriage. He and Debra separated in 1995 but later reconciled.

The Calm Before the Storm

In the spring of 1995, Combs hosted a pilot called *The Ray Combs Show*, which combined a talk format with home-shopping segments for viewers. The show was unique, but it never sold. His career picked up a bit with a second movie appearance in *Vampire in New York*. In October 1995 Combs began hosting the Family Channel cable game show *Family Challenge*. The game pitted two families in a series of messy and hilarious stunts for cash and prizes.

Despite the new career moves, Combs was increasingly unhappy. He wanted more than anything to fulfill his dream of being a comedian, but that seemed out of reach. In early 1996, he and Debra filed for divorce. Ray moved to an apartment in North Hollywood while Debra and the children remained in their Glendale home.

The combination of all these setbacks—the loss of *Family Feud*, the failure of his comedy clubs, the huge debt he had accumulated, the physical and emotional pain from the automobile accident, the possibility of losing his job as host of *Family Challenge*, and now the breakup of his 19-year marriage—pushed Combs over the edge. He attempted suicide twice in May 1996 by hitting his head on walls.

Tragedy

Events came to a boil on Saturday, June 1, 1996. According to *The Los Angeles Times*, Combs phoned Debra in the early morning hours from his apartment and threatened to take an overdose of the Valium pills prescribed by his doctors to help him sleep. An alarmed Debra called 911, and Combs was rushed to Providence St. Joseph Medical Center in Burbank. He was treated and released later that morning. While Debra drove him to their home, he demanded that she take him to his apartment. Combs suddenly jumped out of the car and ran toward the Ventura Freeway where he was picked up by a passing motorist.

Combs went to a friend's house in a fit of anger and repeatedly hit his head on a wall. With his head bleeding, Combs set out for the family's Glendale home to wreck the place. His friend contacted the police and told them about the threat. When Combs reached the house, he found that Debra and the children were gone. He was overturning furniture when police arrived and found him bleeding from his head injury. Combs told the police that the injury resulted from slipping in a hot tub. He was taken into custody, and later Debra told the police about his previous suicide attempts.

Combs was taken to the Glendale Adventist Medical Center and placed in a mental ward for 72 hours of observation. His room contained nothing a patient could use to harm himself. Although nurses checked on Combs every 15 minutes, he was not under constant supervision. Sometime around 4 a.m. on Sunday, June 2, 1996, Combs took some bed sheets and knotted them into a noose which he attached to a closet bar in his room. The bar was designed to break away under pressure. In this case, it failed to work properly, and Combs hanged himself bringing his life to an untimely end at the age of 40.

Since the bank foreclosed on their home, Debra moved with their six children to a smaller house she rented in another part of Glendale. When Johnny Carson learned of Combs' death and the family's financial struggles, he sent Debra a check for $25,000. Ray Combs' life may have ended tragically, but he lived a life filled with service to millions of children through his work in the Boys and Girls Club of America and he also gave the entertainment world many laughs as a comedian and host. Today, Combs remains popular with viewers through reruns of *Family Feud* on GSN: The Network for Games.

Ray Says...

Although his own life and career spiraled out of control, Combs once gave some sound advice to anyone wanting to break into show business. He told *The San Francisco Chronicle* in 1988 that he asked newcomers if they wanted to be actors or comedians because of a love for performing, or because they wanted to be stars. Combs' advice: If you want to be a star, you might be in for a hard time. If you enjoy the work and money is not an issue, relax and enjoy the trip.

BERT CONVY

Birth Name: Bernard Whalen Convy
Born: July 23, 1933, in St. Louis, Missouri
Died: July 15, 1991, in Los Angeles, California
Marriages and Family: Anne Anderson (1959–1991) (Divorced) 1 Daughter, 2 Sons; Katherine Hills (February 14, 1991–July 15, 1991)
TV Career: ACTOR—*Dear Mom, Dear Dad* (Unsold NBC Sitcom Pilot) May 18, 1959; *Love of Life* (CBS Daytime) 1963; *The Cliff Dwellers* (Unsold ABC Adventure Series Pilot) August 28, 1966; *Keep the Faith* (Unsold CBS Sitcom Pilot) April 14, 1972; *Lady Luck* (Unsold NBC Sitcom Pilot) February 12, 1973; *The Snoop Sisters* (NBC Primetime) December 19, 1973–August 20, 1974; *It's Not Easy* (ABC Primetime) September 29, 1983–October 27, 1983 HOST—*Tattletales* (CBS Daytime) February 18, 1974–March 31, 1978, (Syndicated) September 12, 1977–September 1978; *The Late Summer, Early Fall Bert Convy Show* (CBS Primetime) August 25, 1976–September 15, 1976; *The Bert Convy Show* (Unsold Talk Show Pilot) 1980; *Tattletales* (CBS Daytime) January 18, 1982–June 1, 1984; *People Do the Craziest Things* (NBC Primetime) Sept. 20, 1984–Sept. 27,

Bert Convy (Fred Wostbrock)

1984, (NBC Primetime) May 31, 1985–August 2, 1985; *Super Password* (NBC Daytime) September 24, 1984–March 24, 1989; *Win, Lose, or Draw* (Syndicated) September 7, 1987–September 1989; *3rd Degree* (Syndicated) September 11, 1989–September 7, 1990; *Match Game* (ABC Game Show Pilot) November 1989

Theatrical Movies: *Gunman's Walk* (1958); *A Bucket of Blood* (1959); *Susan Slade* (1961); *Act One* (1964); *Give Her the Moon* (1970); *Semi Tough* (1977); *Jennifer* (1978); *Racquet* (1979); *Hero at Large* (1980); *The Cannonball Run* (1981)

Made-for-TV Movies: *Death Takes a Holiday* (ABC) October 23, 1971; *The Girl on the Late Show* (NBC) April 1, 1974; *The Love Boat II.* (ABC) January 21, 1977; *Death Flight* (ABC) February 25, 1977; *Thou Shalt Not Commit Adultery* (NBC) November 1, 1978; *The Dallas Cowboys Cheerleaders* (ABC) January 14, 1979; *Hanging By a Thread* (NBC) May 8–9, 1979; *Ebony, Ivory, and Jade* (CBS) August 3, 1979; *The Man in the Santa Claus Suit* (NBC) December 13, 1979; *Jacqueline Susann's "Valley of the Dolls 1981"* (CBS) October 19–20, 1981; *Help Wanted: Male* (CBS) January 16, 1982; *Love Thy Neighbor* (ABC) May 23, 1984; *Weekend Warriors* (1986)

Broadway Career: *A Tree Grows in Manhattan*

(1958); *The Billy Barnes Revue* (August 4, 1959–Fall 1959); *Vintage '60* (September 12, 1960–September 18, 1960); *Nowhere to Go But Up* (November 10, 1962–November 16, 1962); *The Fantasticks* (1963); *The Beast in Me* (May 16, 1963–May 19, 1963); *Morning Sun* (1963); *Love and Kisses* (1963); *Fiddler on the Roof* (September 22, 1964–July 2, 1972); *The Impossible Years* (1965); *Cabaret* (1966–1969); *The Front Page* (1969); *Do It Again* (Director) (1971); *Nine* (1982)

Business Interests: Partner with Burt Reynolds, Burt & Bert Productions (1986–1991)

Other Careers: Baseball player, The Philadelphia Phillies (1951–1952); Member of the Rock 'n' Roll Music Group The Cheers (1954–1957); Member of the Matchmaker Players Ring Acting Troupe (1957–1958)

The list of Bert Convy's job titles was an unusual combination: minor league baseball player, actor, game show host, singer, producer, and director. From the time Convy began making a living in 1951 until his death in 1991 he took a stab at all seven careers and enjoyed great success in a few of them, limited success at a few others, and almost no success at one. Like many entertainers, it took several years of struggle before Convy found his niche, but once it arrived, he enjoyed a long career as an entertainer on the stage, and on the small and silver screens.

Batter Up

Bernard Whalen Convy was born in St. Louis, Missouri on July 23, 1933, as the only child of a businessman and a housewife. When his parents divorced in 1940, Bert, then only seven years old, moved with his mother to the San Fernando Valley in southern California. Convy attended North Hollywood High School where he was the class clown. His other main interest at the time was baseball, and he became a very good first baseman on his high school team. The day after graduating from high school in 1951, Convy signed to play baseball with the Philadelphia Phillies farm teams and was sent to Klamath Falls, Oregon.

After one season in Oregon, he switched to the Miami Eagles in the spring of 1952. The Eagles, who were based in Miami, Oklahoma, were part of the Kansas-Oklahoma-Missouri (KOM) League. In his book *Majoring In the Minors: A Glimpse of Baseball In a Small Town*, author John Hall states that Convy's batting average was .239 while he fielded at .875 in 24 games during the 1952 season. Unfortunately he lost his spot to Don Ervin from Kansas City, Missouri, who went on to set the all-time KOM League record of 24 home runs that year. In June 1952 Convy transferred to the Salina Bluejays in Kansas. Unable to bat .200 in 14 games, he decided that there was no future for him in baseball.

The Call of the Theatre

Moving back to Los Angeles, Convy enrolled at U.C.L.A. where he became interested in acting after playing the butler in Moliere's *The Imaginary Invalid*. In a 1983 *People Magazine* interview, Convy remembered that there were around 500 students in the drama department. The dean of the college told the students that only one of them would likely make a living as an actor.

Feeling confident in his future, Convy knew that the dean was referring to him. While at U.C.L.A., Convy joined a rock 'n' roll band called The Cheers. The group produced several singles including the hits *I Need Your Loving* and *Black Denim Trousers* (the latter sold more than a million copies).

Finding a Wife and a Career

After college, Convy worked as an actor with a Los Angeles troupe called The Matchmaker Players Ring. He later performed in several Broadway musicals such as *A Tree Grows in Manhattan* and *The Billy Barnes Revue*. It was during *The Billy Barnes Revue* that Convy met his future wife, Anne Anderson, an aspiring writer-actress. She attended *The Billy Barnes Revue* seven times and finally met Convy after the last show. They were married in 1959 and later had one daughter and two sons.

During the late 1950s and early 1960s, Anne Convy expanded her acting career with television appearances on *Alfred Hitchcock Presents, Cheyenne, Father Knows Best,* and *Sea Hunt.* Bert made his first television appearance on *77 Sunset Strip* in 1958 and appeared in guest shots on *One Step Beyond, Perry Mason,* and *Hawaiian Eye.* In 1959 a pilot for a proposed NBC sitcom *Dear Mom, Dear Dad* became the first of several television pilots in which he appeared. For a brief spell Convy played a regular role on the CBS daytime soap *Love of Life* in 1963. He also ventured into theatrical movies with minor roles in *Gunman's Walk* (1958), *A Bucket of Blood* (1959), and *Susan Slade* (1961).

Nowhere to Go But Up

In 1962 the Convys moved from Los Angeles to New York with their now two-year-old daughter Jennifer. Convy broke into Broadway with the short-lived musical *Nowhere to Go But Up,* which lasted only a week, causing him to nickname the musical "Nowhere to Throw But Up."

More short-lived musicals followed in 1963 with *The Beast in Me* and *The Fantasticks.* Finally, in 1964 Convy landed a role in *Fiddler on the Roof,* which lasted for eight years and 3,242 performances. Not one to put all his eggs in one basket, he also appeared in the Broadway shows *The Impossible Years, Cabaret,* and *The Front Page* during the late 1960s.

Meanwhile, Convy's television work remained sporadic. A 1966 ABC drama pilot called *The Cliff Dwellers* failed to become a series. A guest appearance on NBC's *Snap Judgment* launched Convy's game show career in 1967. Many guest appearances as a panelist on the syndicated edition of *What's My Line* followed in the early 1970s. After *Fiddler on the Roof* closed in July 1972, Convy moved his family back to Los Angeles. This time, he concentrated on television and landed roles on *The Mary Tyler Moore Show* and *Love, American Style.* He also starred in two more failed sitcom pilots, *Keep the Faith* and *Lady Luck.*

In late 1973 Convy joined the cast of *The Snoop Sisters* as police Lt. Steve Ostrowski, the nephew of two mystery writer sisters named Ernesta and Gwen Snoop. This show bit the dust in August 1974. With all of his film, television, and Broadway credits, Convy was still not considered a major star.

It Pays to Be a Tattletale

While looking for something new to boost his career, Convy auditioned to host *Tattletales,* a new CBS game show. At first he was unsure about this career move.

> *Ira Skutch (*Tattletales *executive producer, February 2006 telephone interview):*
> "Before the run-through, we went downstairs to get something to eat. He (Convy) said to me, 'Can I ask you something? You know I'm an actor and I'm interested in my acting career. Do you think if I were to do *Tattletales* that it would ruin my career as an actor and that people would no longer think of me as an actor but as only an emcee?' I said, 'No, I don't think it will do that. I think it will enhance you. It gives people a chance to see you in a different role.' And he said, 'Thank you,' and he took the part."

Skutch's prediction came true. *Tattletales* was a hit from its opening day on February 18, 1974. Finally the American public knew who Bert Convy was. Aided by his exposure on the show, Convy landed many lucrative acting gigs on made-for-television movies.

Tattletales aired immediately after the number one-rated daytime game show *Match Game '74.* Three celebrity couples answered often provocative questions about their personal lives. Every time the celebrity teams matched answers, they won money for members of the studio audience. The audience was divided into three sections identified by the colors red, yellow, and blue. Each of the celebrity couples played for one of the three sections. The game started with either the husbands or the wives sitting on stage while their mates were backstage out of earshot.

With host Bert Convy (left), celebrity wives Elaine Joyce, Anne Meara, and Barbara Stewart are ready to tattle on their mates during the first day of taping on *Tattletales* in 1974 (Fred Wostbrock).

Convy asked a question such as, "Which of the following is more likely to put you in the mood for romance: a look, a word, or a touch?" After the on stage celebrities in turn gave an answer, their mates were brought on via a television monitor to answer the question. If their answers matched, they won money for their rooting section of the audience. After two rounds, the husbands and wives changed places. The team with the most money after four rounds won the game. The audience members in the winning section split the money along with a $1,000 bonus.

Famous celebrities revealing their intimate secrets on national television made *Tattletales* a success. Convy found himself swamped with offers for television movies and the chance to guest host on NBC's *Tonight Show*. He even starred in his own primetime variety series for four weeks during the summer of 1976 called *The Late Summer, Early Fall Bert Convy Show*. At the Daytime Emmy Awards ceremony on May 12, 1977, Convy won an Emmy for his hosting duties on *Tattletales*. That fall, a syndicated version of the show aired along with the daytime series. The CBS version lasted until March 31, 1978, while the syndicated affair faded six months later.

It's Not Easy

Convy continued acting in a string of made-for-TV movies such as *Thou Shalt Not Commit Adultery*, *The Dallas Cowboys Cheerleaders*, and *The Man in the Santa Claus Suit*. He also turned up in the theatrical releases *Hero at Large* and *The Cannonball Run*. The latter movie starred Burt Reynolds, who became close friends with Convy.

In January 1982 Convy returned to host *Tattletales* for two additional seasons. The following year, Convy and his wife Anne finally got the chance to work together on a television project. Anne was hired as one of the four writers for the ABC sitcom *It's Not Easy*. In the show, a divorced couple, Jack and Sharon Long, lived across the street from each other in order to share custody of their two children. Sharon married Neil Townsend (portrayed by Bert) who also has a son. The plots of the show highlighted the confusion of everyone trying to adjust to this rather awkward situation. Scheduled against the popular CBS action show *Simon and Simon* on Thursday nights, *It's Not Easy* vanished after five weeks.

A Flop and a Winner

In the fall of 1984, Convy popped up on two shows. The first was host of ABC's *People Do the Craziest Things*, a takeoff of Allen Funt's long-running *Candid Camera* series. A hidden camera captured unsuspecting people on the streets in embarrassing situations. ABC pulled *People Do the Craziest Things* from its primetime schedule after two weeks. The show continued as a series of specials for the rest of the 1984-1985 season, but ended up as the lowest-rated primetime series that year ranking 97th among all programs.

Convy's biggest success that year, however, was *Super Password*. Two celebrity/contestant teams tried to guess a series of passwords from one word clues. The passwords were then posted on a board one at a time and served as clues to a puzzle. Teams won money for guessing the puzzles and the first team to score $500 won the game and advanced to the bonus round.

In the "Super Password" round, contestants tried to guess ten passwords from one-word clues provided by their celebrity partner. Guessing all ten words in sixty seconds won the player $5,000. If the player failed to win the bonus round, the value of the game increased by $1,000 each time until it was won. There was also a special "Cashword" feature during the main part of the game. One player was given three chances to guess a password from one-word clues provided by their celebrity partner. Guessing the "Cashword" earned the player an extra $1,000. The "Cashword" increased by $1,000 for each day it was not won.

A touch of controversy erupted in January 1988 when a contestant on *Super Password*, Kerry Ketchum, was spotted by viewers in Anchorage, Alaska as a fugitive in a credit card fraud case. Ketchum had appeared on the show using the alias Patrick Quinn. He was arrested at the producer's office in Burbank while picking up the check for $58,600 he had won in four appearances on the show.

Burt and Bert

In 1986 Convy formed Burt and Bert Productions with his friend Burt Reynolds. The team then packaged a new game show called *Win, Lose, or Draw*. Reynolds had invented the game many years before with several of his friends during a party at his home. Based on the parlor game Charades, two teams of three members each consisting of two celebrities and one contestant used a large easel sketch pad to draw clues for phrases their teammates tried to guess. NBC picked up the show for a daytime run while an evening version was launched in syndication. Both versions of the show debuted in September 1987. Actress Vicki Lawrence, best known for her roles on *The Carol Burnett Show* and *Mama's Family*, hosted the NBC version while Convy emceed the syndicated edition.

For a time, the show was extremely popular, and a home version of the game was sold in stores. Since the show was based on a parlor game, it was decided to give the program a homey feel. This was accomplished by modeling the show's set after Burt Reynolds' living room at his house. Reynolds frequently appeared as a celebrity player on both editions of the show. Other celebrities who frequently appeared included Dom DeLuise, Charles Nelson Reilly, Tony Danza, and Betty White.

In the spring of 1989, a third version of the game, *Teen Win, Lose, or Draw*, debuted on the Disney Cable Channel hosted by Marc Price. Show producer Richard Kline noted that *Win, Lose, or Draw* was the only game show to have three separate versions on the air at the same time.

NBC canceled the daytime version in September 1989, but Convy's syndicated edition was renewed for the 1989-1990 season. While he kept that job, Convy lost his other one when *Super Password* was also canceled by NBC in 1989.

Getting the 3rd Degree

Meanwhile Burt and Bert Productions, along with Kline and Friends Productions, developed a new game show called *3rd Degree*. The game featured two teams of two celebrities who tried to guess the relationship of two or more contestants by asking "yes" or "no" questions.

One episode featured 19 contestants who constituted an entire town. If both celebrity teams failed to make the connection, the players won $250 and if both teams of celebrities were stumped after two rounds, the players won $2,000. Veteran game show host Peter Marshall signed to emcee *3rd Degree*.

However, when Convy was unexpectedly dropped as host of *Win, Lose, or Draw* and replaced by Rob Weller for the 1989-1990 season, he stepped in to replace Marshall as host of *3rd Degree* before production commenced. On July 19, 1989, Marshall filed a $1 million plus lawsuit in Los Angeles County Superior Court against Burt and Bert Productions alleging fraud and breach of contract.

> *Richard Kline (***3rd Degree*** producer & director, May 2006 telephone interview):*
> "I was not aware of [the lawsuit]. We never defended a lawsuit. Our going ahead with Bert [to host *3rd Degree*] had nothing to do with Peter and his considerable talents. It was based on Bert's availability off of *Win, Lose, or Draw*. Peter is a gentleman and is very talented. I have always admired him as a host. He was wonderful at it and we would have loved to have had him. But again, the decision was based on Bert's availability."

In the end, Convy hosted *3rd Degree*, and Marshall later dropped the lawsuit. *3rd Degree* disappeared after one season.

Sudden Illness

Convy was scheduled to host the new ABC revival of *Match Game* in the summer of 1990. However on April 22, 1990, while visiting his mother, who was in the Cedars-Sinai Medical Center in Los Angeles recovering from a stroke, Convy passed out and fell to the floor hitting his head. After extensive testing for internal injuries revealed a brain tumor, Convy underwent chemotherapy and radiation treatments lasting for several months. He also endured two operations, both of which failed to remove all of the cancer.

Unable to return to work, Convy bowed out of *The Match Game* revival before production began. He was replaced by Ross Shafer and the game ran for one season on ABC beginning in July 1990.

After a lengthy separation from his wife Anne, their marriage ended in divorce in early 1991. Convy married 25-year-old Katherine Hills on Valentine's Day 1991. Because of his rapidly deteriorating condition, his second marriage only lasted five months. Convy's illness had him in and out of the hospital, but his last three months were spent at his Brentwood, California home. He finally succumbed to the brain tumor on July 15, 1991, at the age of 57. He was survived by his second wife Katherine, ex-wife Anne, and their three children Jennifer, Joshua, and Jonah.

Although Convy's career and life ended on rather somber notes, he left behind a wealth of light-hearted hosting that can be seen today in reruns on GSN: The Network For Games. If Convy's original plans for his acting career had progressed, he probably would not have pursued game shows. Had it not been for producer Ira Skutch's encouragement to Convy back in 1974 to take the gig on *Tattletales*, Convy may never have achieved the stardom that resulted from that show.

> *Ira Skutch:*
> "I always felt I had some small influence on him. I thought it was interesting that he would ask someone for that advice and that he had enough insight into himself, and to the business, to be curious about it."

BILL CULLEN

Birth Name: William Lawrence Cullen
Born: February 18, 1920, in Pittsburgh, Pennsylvania
Died: July 7, 1990, in Los Angeles, California
Marriages: Carol Ames (1949–1955) (Divorced); Ann Roemheld (December 24, 1955–July 7, 1990)
Military Service: Patrol Pilot and Instructor: Civilian Air Defense (1942–1944)
Radio Career: Announcer (WWSW-AM, Pittsburgh, PA) 1939–1941; Announcer (KDKA-AM, Pittsburgh, PA) 1941–1944; Staff Announcer (CBS Radio Network) 1944–1946; *Winner Take All* (CBS) June 14, 1946–February 1, 1952; *Hollywood Jackpot* (CBS) September 30, 1946–March 28, 1947; *This is Nora Drake* (NBC & CBS) October 27, 1947–1951; *Catch Me If You Can* (CBS) May 9, 1948–June 13, 1949; *Beat the Clock* (CBS) January 5, 1949–May 4, 1949; *Hit the Jackpot* (CBS) June 20, 1949–December 27, 1949; *Quick as a Flash* (ABC) December 12, 1949–June 29, 1951; *Hit*

Bill Cullen (Bob Stewart)

the Jackpot (CBS) May 28, 1950–September 3, 1950; *It Happens Every Day* (CBS) 1952–1953, (Mutual) 1953–1955; *Road Show* (NBC) 1954–1955; *Walk a Mile* (NBC) 1954–1955; *Stop the Music* (CBS) August 17, 1954–November 1954; *Pulse/The Bill Cullen Show* (WNBC-AM, New York, New York) 1955–1961; *Monitor* (NBC) 1971–1972

TV Career: HOST—*Act It Out* (WNBT-TV, New York City) February 20, 1949–August 7, 1949; *Meet Your Match* (WOR-TV, New York City) October 13, 1949–October 20, 1949; *Winner Take All* (CBS Daytime) February 25, 1952–October 5, 1952; *Give and Take* (CBS Daytime) March 20, 1952–June 12, 1952; *Why?* (ABC Primetime) December 29, 1952–April 20, 1953; *The Bill Cullen Show* (CBS Daytime) February 12, 1953–May 14, 1953; *Place the Face* (CBS Primetime) January 28, 1954–August 26, 1954, (NBC Primetime) September 18, 1954–December 25, 1954, (NBC Primetime) June 28, 1955–September 13, 1955; *Bank on the Stars* (NBC Primetime) May 15, 1954–July 10, 1954; *Professor Yes 'n' No* (Syndicated) 1954–1955; *Name That Tune* (CBS Primetime) September 2, 1954–March 24, 1955; *Inside NBC* (NBC Daytime) December 12, 1955–June 1, 1956; *Down You Go* (NBC Primetime)

June 16, 1956–September 8, 1956; *The Price Is Right* (NBC Daytime) November 26, 1956–September 6, 1963, (NBC Primetime) September 23, 1957–September 6, 1963, (ABC Daytime) September 9, 1963–September 3, 1965, (ABC Primetime) September 18, 1963–September 11, 1964; *Eye Guess* (NBC Daytime) January 3, 1966–September 26, 1969; *The Choice is Yours* (Unsold Game Show Pilot) 1970; *Three on a Match* (NBC Daytime) August 2, 1971–June 28, 1974; *Winning Streak* (NBC Daytime) July 1, 1974–January 3, 1975; *$25,000 Pyramid* (Syndicated) September 9, 1974–September 1979; *Blankety Blanks* (ABC Daytime) April 21, 1975–June 27, 1975; *I've Got a Secret* (CBS Primetime) June 15, 1976–July 6, 1976; *Pass the Buck* (CBS Daytime) April 3, 1978–June 30, 1978; *The Love Experts* (Syndicated) September 18, 1978–September 1979; *Punchliners* (Unsold Game Show Pilot) 1979; *Decisions, Decisions* (Unsold Game Show Pilot) 1979; *Chain Reaction* (NBC Daytime) January 14, 1980–June 20, 1980; *Password Plus* (NBC Daytime) April 14, 1980–May 12, 1980, *(Substituted for Allen Ludden); *Blockbusters* (NBC Daytime) October 27, 1980–April 23, 1982; *Child's Play* (CBS Daytime) September 20, 1982–September 16, 1983; *Hot Potato* (NBC Daytime) January 23, 1984–June 29, 1984; *The Joker's Wild* (Syndicated) September 1984–September 1986   PANELIST—*I've Got a Secret* (CBS Primetime) July 3, 1952–April 3, 1967; *Who's There* (CBS Primetime) July 14, 1952–August 1952; *Where Was I?* (Dumont Primetime) 1953; *You're Putting Me On* (NBC Daytime) June 30, 1969–December 26, 1969; *To Tell the Truth* (Syndicated) September 8, 1969–September 1978
Other Careers: Auto Mechanic and Tow Truck Driver (1938–1939); Owner & Operator, Appointment Airlines (1949–1953)

It would be hard to imagine anyone appearing on 25,000 individual radio and television episodes, but one man accomplished this feat. In a 49-year broadcasting career spanning from 1939 to 1988, Bill Cullen hosted, announced, or guest starred on game, variety and drama shows. He holds the all-time record for the number of television game shows hosted with an astonishing 23 different game shows. He made hosting look extremely easy while he never took himself seriously as a performer. Cullen's fun and engaging personality earned him the title as "The Dean of Game Show Hosts" by many of his colleagues and fans.

William Lawrence Cullen arrived on February 18, 1920, in Pittsburgh, Pennsylvania. His father owned and operated a local garage repairing automobiles. In the summer of 1921, Cullen's life nearly ended when he was stricken with polio. An interesting note is that Cullen's bout of polio hit him the very same summer that future President Franklin Roosevelt was stricken with the disease. Cullen recovered from the attack, but was left with a permanent limp in his left leg that affected his ability to walk normally.

> *Ann Cullen (Bill's widow: March 2006 telephone interview):*
> "He walked fairly well. He was not that handicapped. He had the typical polio walk, but his upper leg was very strong and his upper body was very strong. When we made reservations on trips, I would be careful that we wouldn't go to a hotel with 15 flights of stairs and we didn't go out dancing. Other than that, he was so good about it that I was never aware that he was handicapped. I know that's hard to believe because he had a definite limp. He was such a regular person and he never used it in any way."

Cullen the Athlete

Cullen wore a brace on his left leg until he was 10 years old by which time he was strong enough to walk without it. The limp knocked him out of playing sports at South High School in Pittsburgh, but he played sandlot baseball for fun. Cullen also played football and competed as a midget race car driver. In fact, he had begun driving at the age of 10 for his father's garage and obtained his driver's license by the age of 14. He also took boxing lessons from future world welterweight champion Fritzie Zivic.

Cullen pondered his future and decided to be a doctor. He graduated from high school and enrolled in the University of Pittsburgh as a premedical student in 1938. A shortage of funds forced him to withdraw from college, so he worked at his father's garage as a mechanic and tow truck driver.

Planes, Microphones, and Automobiles

At the garage, Cullen, always a ham, imitated local radio announcers to entertain his co-workers. One day, an executive for WWSW, a local 250 watt radio station, brought his car to the garage. Cullen asked about a radio job and offered to work for nothing. The man hired him initially as an unpaid announcer working six hours per night seven days a week on WWSW. Within two months he was earning $25 a week. Cullen later moved across town to KDKA where he worked as a disc jockey, sports announcer, and hosted a variety show. By 1943 he was making $250 a week.

With better finances, Cullen went back to the University of Pittsburgh, but decided to follow a broadcasting career and earned his degree in fine arts. He was ineligible for military service during World War II. because of his physical limitations. Always fascinated by airplanes, Cullen had been flying since he was 15 years old. He flew as a patrol pilot for the Civilian Air Defense and worked as a civilian flight instructor in Allegheny County, Pennsylvania.

New York, New York

By 1944 Cullen felt that it was time to try his luck in a larger radio market. With no job possibilities, Cullen moved to New York City. He walked into the offices of CBS radio and found that they needed announcers due to a wartime shortage. Within a week Cullen was a CBS staff announcer.

Most of his early announcing assignments were commercials and CBS drama shows. By 1946 he was the announcer for *Winner Take All*, a popular radio quiz. When the show's host took ill and resigned, Cullen stepped in as a substitute. Before long he won the post as full-time emcee. For the remainder of the 1940s, Cullen hosted *Hollywood Jackpot*, *Catch Me If You Can*, *Hit the Jackpot*, and *Quick as a Flash*. He also announced for the mystery series *This is Nora Drake*.

In February 1949 Cullen hosted his first television series, *Act It Out*, for WNBT-TV in New York City (later to become WNBC-TV). This game show employed a group of actors who performed a scene. A home viewer was telephoned and asked to describe the nature of the scene in one word. If successful, the viewer won a prize. *Act It Out* lasted only six months.

Flying for a Living

Although now a full time broadcaster, Cullen took his passion for flying and opened Appointment Airlines in 1949. He purchased three small airplanes and rented four others for the venture, but bit off more than he could chew. By 1953 the business had dwindled from seven airplanes to only one plane. Cutting his losses, he dissolved Appointment Airlines, but never lost his passion for flying. He maintained a four-seat Beachcraft Bonanza and piloted other small planes through the mid 1970s.

What They Don't Know Won't Hurt Them

Cullen feared that his limp would make him unattractive to television viewers so he avoided the medium. In early 1952, when NBC revived *Winner Take All* for television, Cullen got the nod to host. His limp was never a problem for viewers because many people were never aware of it. Until Cullen's retirement in the 1980s, directors on all of his game shows took pains to conceal his limp.

Ira Skutch (TV producer & director: February 2006 telephone interview):
"You never saw him walking on camera. He would stand or sit on the edge of things. He [usually] stood, but he was standing behind a podium and he didn't have to walk anywhere."

A Winner Takes All

Cullen's first major TV show, *Winner Take All*, was a simple game. Two contestants answered general knowledge questions. One player had a bell while the other had a buzzer. The first person to ring the bell or sound the buzzer answered the question. Correct answers earned one point and three points won the game. *Winner Take All* was the first game show to use lock out signaling devices that later became known simply as "buzzers," which were later used on countless game shows.

A Coast to Coast Host

In the summer of 1952, Cullen began a 15-year stint as a panelist on CBS's *I've Got a Secret*. Hosted by Garry Moore, a panel of four celebrities questioned contestants to guess secrets held by them. Cullen's relaxed style made him a popular television star.

By 1954 his workload spanned a variety of shows on two networks. On the television front, he hosted *Place the Face* for CBS, *Bank on the Stars* for NBC, and *Professor Yes 'n' No*, a filmed 15 minute quiz show seen in syndication. He also served as a panelist on *I've Got a Secret*. His hectic schedule in the summer of 1954 had him flying back and forth between New York City and Los Angeles to cover his assignments. On Wednesday evenings at 8:00 p.m., he hosted *Walk a Mile*, a radio quiz for NBC. At 9:30 p.m. he appeared on CBS with *I've Got a Secret*.

After the show, he boarded the 11:25 p.m. flight for Los Angeles at Idlewild Airport. On Thursday evenings, he hosted *Place the Face*, which originated from the newly constructed CBS Television City complex in Los Angeles. Fridays were spent flying back to New York. On Saturday afternoons, he hosted NBC radio's *Road Show*, a combination of music, news, weather, driving tips, and contests. On Saturday evenings, he hosted *Bank on the Stars*, a game where contestants answered questions based on film clips.

I Hate a Rut

When asked by *The New York Times'* Fred Rayfield why he worked such a crushing schedule, Cullen merely replied that he was bored when he received the job offer. He also said that he hated a rut, disliked working, and could never be an actor where constant rehearsal was in order.

By the fall of 1954, Cullen's schedule looked like this: Wednesday nights he hosted *Walk a Mile* at 8:00 p.m., then appeared on *I've Got a Secret* at 9:30 p.m. On Thursday evenings he hosted *Name That Tune* over CBS at 10:30 p.m. Immediately after the show, Cullen boarded a plane for Los Angeles where he arrived early Friday morning. Saturday at 8:00 p.m. he hosted *Place the Face*. By Monday he was back in New York recording five minute segments of the radio show *It Happens Everyday*. Finally, on Tuesday, he hosted *Stop the Music* for CBS radio and presided over *Professor Yes 'n' No*.

On-the-Go

For all of his activities, Cullen earned more than $150,000 a year. While he thrived on his constant on-the-go schedule, his marriage disintegrated and he and Carol Ames divorced. In the fall of 1954 while commuting to California to host *Place the Face*, Cullen met Ann Roemheld at a house party given by her sister and brother-in-law, Mary Lou and Jack Narz.

> *Ann Cullen:*
> "Jack was the announcer on *Place the Face*. Jack wanted to bring Bill out to the house. Bill didn't want to get involved in parties, but he finally came. Bill was actually kind of shy. You wouldn't think that he was, but with strange people, he was until he got to know them. My father and I were sitting together on the couch and Bill asked my sister Mary Lou, 'Who's that lovely young lady over there sitting with that old man?' Mary Lou said, 'The lovely young lady is my sister and the old man is my father.' (Laughing) Bill had eyes right away."

Bill and Ann began dating the following summer and finally married on December 24, 1955. The couple took up residence in an apartment in Manhattan.

Morning Radio

In 1956 he began a new radio series for WRCA in New York called *The Bill Cullen Show*. From 6:00–10:00 a.m. every weekday morning and for two hours on Saturdays, Cullen played records, read news and weather reports, and ran contests for prizes. The show later changed its title to *Pulse*.

The Actual Retail Price

In November 1956, Cullen began hosting his longest-running series and the program most identified with him: *The Price Is Right*. Four contestants guessed the actual retail prices of various prizes. After seeing a prize, the four players took turns bidding. The idea was to be the closest to guessing the price without going over. The successful player won the merchandise. Several rounds were played throughout the show in a similar manner with some variations to the bidding. Some prizes were one-bid items meaning that everyone could only make one guess on the price. Other prizes were open-bid items where everyone in turn made multiple guesses until a buzzer signaled the end of bidding.

A player could freeze their bid at any time if they felt that bidding any higher would put them over the price. Bidding continued through the panel until all four players froze their bids. In the final round, the players bid on a large showcase of merchandise and the contestant with the most winnings in prizes returned on the next day's program.

NBC bought *The Price Is Right* and scheduled the show for 10:30 a.m., which became a minor problem.

> **Bob Stewart (TV producer: April 2005 telephone interview):**
> "When we auditioned various emcees for *The Price Is Right*, the fellow that I liked the most was Bill. The problem was that he got through working on the radio at 10:00 a.m. and he was probably about eight or ten blocks away from the TV studio, which was not in the NBC building. It was in the Hudson Theater. It would take him 15 minutes to come down from the building, get a cab, and get over there which meant that he never had any rehearsal. NBC was concerned about that, but we talked them into having Bill without rehearsal and to use somebody else for the rehearsal."

The producers filmed a pilot episode to iron out any kinks in the game.

> **Bob Stewart:**
> "It was a pretty lousy pilot. When it was finished, NBC looked at it and they came over and said, having committed to 13 weeks, that the pilot was so bad, they offered to give us six weeks of money as if the show had been on the air and then call the whole contract off. I sort of convinced the Goodson-Todman people not to do that. While NBC was offering that [deal], we went over to CBS, who also liked the idea, but they did not have a time spot [on their daytime schedule]. They wanted to give us some holding money for six to nine months to see if there would be a spot for us."

The Price Is Right ended up on NBC and premiered November 26, 1956. By the time its 13 week contract was up, the show was soundly beating its competition. NBC immediately renewed *The Price Is Right*. At the end of 1956, NBC moved the show to 11:00 a.m. where it thrived. NBC added a nighttime version in September 1957.

Covering Sports

Along with his game show duties, Cullen served as a sportscaster covering the Army football games on radio during the 1956 and 1957 seasons. He also did play-by-play for hockey and

Associate producer Beth Hollinger, producer Bob Stewart, model Toni Wallace, Bill Cullen, model June Ferguson, and announcer Don Pardo on the set of *The Price Is Right* (Ann Cullen, courtesy Bob Stewart).

basketball games and provided color commentary for the Pittsburgh Steelers. At one point in 1958, Cullen was offered the chance to purchase 18 percent of the Cleveland Browns football team for $50,000 cash and a $150,000 note. As much as he loved sports, Cullen refused the offer fearing that getting involved in sports as a business would take the fun out of the passion.

A Day in the Life of Bill

By 1958 Cullen was one of the successful entertainers in the business earning around $300,000 a year. *The Price Is Right* mopped up the ratings in daytime and the nighttime version was a top ten attraction. His work schedule was not quite as complex as it was just four years earlier. Cullen arose at 4:15 a.m. each weekday and smoked for 20 minutes. At 6:00 a.m. he went on the air at WNBC with his radio program *Pulse*. At 10:00 a.m., Cullen went by taxi to The Hudson Theater where he rehearsed for *The Price Is Right*.

> *Bill Cullen (**Look** magazine July 8, 1958):*
> "Between *Pulse* and *Price*, I have a costume change. I straighten my tie."

At 11:00 a.m. *The Price Is Right* aired live. Cullen spent less than an hour rehearsing for the show, because most of the show was ad-libbed. Cullen's biggest challenge was learning where the large array of prizes used on the show would be positioned on stage.

By noon, Cullen was home for lunch and afternoons were spent taking a four-hour nap. That extra sleep was necessary for on Wednesday evenings he returned to the studio to sit on the panel of *I've Got a Secret*. On Thursday evenings he hosted the nighttime version of *The Price Is Right* from 10:00 to 10:30 p.m. Working such a bazaar schedule, Cullen relied on his ability to sleep in shifts.

> *Bill Cullen (**Look** magazine July 8, 1958):*
> "I'm the only man I know who has to wake up 12 times a week instead of seven."

> *Ann Cullen:*
> "He could nap, I could never nap. He would come home in the afternoon and sleep for a couple of hours and wake up just bright and fresh. He was always bright and wonderful right off the bat. He got his eight hours [of sleep] one way or the other."

Through it all, Cullen never lost his razor-sharp sense of humor and his ability to think quickly on his feet.

> *Bob Stewart:*
> "I remember a time [on *The Price Is Right*] when, for some reason, the show was going too quickly and we finished all our prizes and had time left on the air. This was live television and we couldn't stop. All I could do was look across at Bill and say, 'We have no more prizes to give away.' I held up my wallet and he knew right away what I meant. He said to the contestants, 'Okay, the next thing we're going to bid for is the contents of my wallet. Whoever comes closest to the amount of money that I'm carrying gets the money.' He just did that right there without blinking an eye. He was very quick and very clever."

On another occasion, an elephant was used as a gag prize to a contestant who won a piano. The joke was that when the original ivory in the piano's keys wore out, the elephant would provide ivory for new keys.

> *Bob Stewart:*
> "The elephant, who had come out in rehearsal when there was nobody in the theater, behaved okay. When the elephant came out on the show, the theater was packed with 500 people. He came out and the audience began to scream and applaud which scared the hell out of the elephant who crapped all over the floor. The whole floor was covered and the audience was hysterical. Bill didn't say a word. Every time we put the camera on him, he was just looking on smiling and the director was capturing these shots. The show was literally out of control. Finally when it began to slow down a bit, we got a shot of Bill with that mischievous smile on his face and he turned to the camera and said, 'Next week we're going to give the Democrats equal time.'"

Slowing Down

Cullen maintained a busy schedule through 1961 when he hosted his last radio edition of *Pulse*. Both versions of *The Price Is Right* were canceled by NBC in September 1963. ABC snapped up the show for its daytime and nighttime schedules. Unfortunately the show never performed as well on ABC and the nighttime version fizzled out after one year. Executive producer Bob Stewart left *The Price Is Right* in October 1964 to start his own production company and Cullen took over as the new executive producer. The daytime version continued for one more season until it expired on September 3, 1965, after a nine year run.

Eye Guess

By the fall of 1965, Cullen was reduced to his weekly chores on *I've Got a Secret*. But he took the loss of *The Price Is Right* in stride. The show's cancellation actually paved the way for his next big break. Cullen's good friend, Bob Stewart, created *Eye Guess* and hired Cullen as host. *Eye Guess* bowed over NBC on January 3, 1966, and became another hit for Cullen.

The game was a true test of memory and the rules were simple: two contestants faced a game board concealing answers to questions. The players were shown eight answers and given 10 seconds to memorize their location on the board. Cullen asked a question and the players in turn called out one of the eight numbers they believed concealed the answer. Correct answers yielded 10 points in round one and 20 in round two. The first player to score 100 points won the game.

The twist that made *Eye Guess* a hit was the comedy that resulted when a player called out a wrong number for an answer. For example, the eight answers shown might be 1) In the gas tank, 2) On the brake pedal, 3) On the bumper, 4) On the roof, 5) In the ash tray, 6) On the steering wheel, 7) In the trunk, and 8) In the back seat. The question is, "When your mother-in-law joins you for a drive, where do you put her?" The player could mistakenly call out number 1 (in the gas tank) or number 7 (in the trunk). By the way, the correct answer for those who get along with their mother-in-law is number 8 (in the back seat). *Eye Guess* left the air in September 1969.

Picking Up Steam

That same month, Cullen began a nine year run as a panelist on a syndicated revival of *To Tell the Truth*, a popular panel show of the 1950s. He returned to the host's chair in August 1971 with *Three on a Match*. Three contestants answered true or false questions and used the money they earned to purchase squares on the game board. Each square concealed a prize, and players won the game by matching the same prize in all three columns of the board.

Ubiquitous

In September 1974 Cullen began a five year run hosting *The $25,000 Pyramid*. This was a weekly syndicated version of ABC's *The $10,000 Pyramid* hosted by Dick Clark. Two celebrity-contestant teams guessed words from a series of clues given by their partners. The winning team advanced to the "winner's circle" where they guessed six subjects in 60 seconds to win $10,000. If the player won a second game, the bonus round was worth $25,000.

Many of Cullen's shows during this period were short-lived. Nevertheless, he stayed active because he frequently went from one show to the next in a matter of weeks. While he was regularly seen on *To Tell the Truth* and *The $25,000 Pyramid*, Cullen frequently hosted a third show during the 1970s. Between 1974 and 1978, Cullen hosted *Winning Streak*, *Blankety Blanks*, *I've Got a Secret*, and *Pass the Buck*. By 1978 Cullen was one of the few hosts who still lived and worked in New York.

Bill Cullen says you can be a top prize winner on *The $25,000 Pyramid* (Bob Stewart).

Ann Cullen:
   "Bill wanted to come out to California. Every vacation we took, we almost always came out to California because he just loved it out here. We used to come out here and go to Palm Springs and Los Angeles. But he kept getting shows in New York and he had to stay there."

Fortunately for Cullen, most game shows were now produced in Los Angeles, so he and Ann moved where the work beckoned. His first show after moving to California was *The Love Experts*, a radical departure from anything he had done. Contestants on this show had problems pertaining to love and romance. A panel of four celebrities gave advice to the lovelorn players. At the end of the show, the panel voted for the contestant they thought had the most interesting problem. *The Love Experts* disappeared after one season.

A Chain Reaction

Four months later, Cullen returned to host NBC's *Chain Reaction* in January 1980. Two teams battled it out to guess a series of eight associated words comprising a chain. The teams scored one point for every letter in the word correctly guessed. The first team to rack up 50 points won the game and played a bonus round for $10,000.

Meanwhile, Cullen substituted for Allen Ludden as host of *Password Plus* from April to May 1980. Ludden had taken ill with cancer and underwent surgery causing him to miss four weeks of tapings. Ludden returned to the show in May 1980.

A Blockbuster

Cullen was back in the Goodson-Todman fold in October 1980 with NBC's *Blockbusters*. One contestant played against a team of two related contestants to answer questions and connect a chain of hexagons across the game board. The solo player represented the color red while the two family members represented the color white.

The solo player formed a chain of hexagons from top to bottom on the board while the family pair worked from side to side. The family pair could cross the board in five moves while the solo player could do it in only four. The first team to win two games collected $1,000 and played the gold rush round for an additional $5,000. *Blockbusters* lasted until April 1982 when NBC cleaned out most of the game shows on its schedule.

Hosting Is Child's Play

The fall of 1982 brought CBS's *Child's Play*. As the title suggests, children ranging in age from five to nine appeared via pre-recorded sequences. The object of the game was for contestants to guess a series of words from definitions given by three children. The first player to win two games earned $500 and played the "Triple Play" bonus round.

In a July 1990 letter to *The Los Angeles Times*, Marla Schram Schwartz, a contestant on *Child's Play* in 1983, told the poignant story of how Cullen was instrumental in helping her fairly win $5,000. During the "Triple Play" bonus round, Schwartz was guessing word clues in 30 seconds when the producer accidentally gave her credit for a wrong answer. The producer stopped the taping when he realized his mistake. There was still 13 seconds remaining on the clock. Schwartz was given the choice of continuing the round with the remaining 13 seconds or starting a new bonus round. Unsure of what to do, Schwartz pondered for a moment until Cullen looked at the new set of word clues and encouraged her to start a new bonus round. Schwartz took his advice and asked for a new game where she nailed the $5,000.

A Quiet Exit

After *Child's Play* left the air in 1983, Cullen was looking to hang it up as far as game shows were concerned. However, an unexpected offer to host NBC's *Hot Potato* brought him back to work in January 1984.

When *Hot Potato* left the air in June 1984, producer Dan Enright called on Cullen one last time to take over *The Joker's Wild* after the death of its host Jack Barry. Cullen hosted *The Joker's Wild* until it folded in 1986. Without fanfare, he retired from hosting at the age of 66 after a spectacular 40 year run. In all he had appeared in more than 30 different television programs as a host or panelist and nearly two dozen radio shows. Cullen brought his career full circle when he returned to radio in a series of short programs on parental advice sponsored by Johnson and Johnson.

Cullen spent his remaining years retired with his wife Ann. One of Cullen's favorite pastimes was swimming in the pool at his Bel-Air home. He also tried to take care of his health by watching his diet. A pancreatic condition in 1968 had forced him to give up drinking, but Cullen continued to be a heavy smoker until quitting in the mid 1980s. In the summer of 1989, x-rays taken during an examination showed a tiny speck in one of Cullen's lungs. It turned out to be lung cancer. He spent the next year fighting the disease but never entered the hospital. Even during his illness, Cullen maintained his sense of humor.

> *Bob Stewart:*
> "The doctor recommended to Bill that he might want to consider chemotherapy. Bill said to the doctor, 'If I take chemotherapy, would I lose my hair?' And the doctor said, 'I'm afraid you would.' Bill said, 'Well, I'll have to turn down chemotherapy because I promised to leave my hair to Bob Stewart (who is bald)."

Despite the cancer, Cullen actually lived a normal life until his last month.

> *Ann Cullen:*
> "We went out for my birthday on June 6. That was the last time he went out."

Over the next month, Cullen's health rapidly declined as the cancer spread. Ann was by Cullen's side holding one of his hands while Bob Stewart held the other as Cullen died of heart failure on July 7, 1990, at the age of 70.

In an industry that relies so heavily on good looks and pretty faces, Bill Cullen often asked himself how he managed to last so long. With thick glasses, a bad complexion, and his limp as a result of polio, Cullen was not your typical television personality.

> *Ira Skutch (TV producer & director, February 2006 telephone interview):*
> "There's nothing bad you could say about Bill. I've never heard anyone say anything bad about him. He was absolutely a consummate, professional emcee. He had a marvelous sense of humor, very quick on his feet and quick witted."

JOHN DALY

Birth Name: John Charles Daly, Jr.
Born: February 20, 1914, in Johannesburg, South Africa
Died: February 25, 1991, in Chevy Chase, Maryland
Marriages and Children: Margaret Neal (1937–1960) (Divorced) 2 sons, 1 daughter; Virginia Warren (1960–1991) 2 sons, 1 daughter
Radio Career: Announcer (WRC-AM, Washington, D.C.) 1937; White House Correspondent (WJSV-AM, Washington, D.C.) 1937–1941; *Report to the Nation* (CBS) December 7, 1940–January 1943; *Spirit of '41/Spirit of '42* (CBS) June 29, 1941–January 1943; *World Today* (CBS) November 1941–January 1943; War Correspondent (CBS News) January 1943–Fall 1944; *Report to the Nation* (CBS) 1944–1945; *World Today* (CBS) 1944–1946; *The Continental Celebrity Club* (CBS) December 8, 1945–June 29, 1946; *CBS Is There/You Are There* (CBS) July 7, 1947–March 19, 1950; ABC News Commentator (ABC) 1950–1953; *What's My Line?* (NBC) May 20, 1952–August 27, 1952, (CBS) September 3, 1952–July 1, 1953
TV Career: HOST—*Riddle Me This* (CBS Primetime) December 5, 1948–March 13, 1949; *What's My Line?* (CBS Primetime) February 2, 1950–September 3, 1967; *We Take Your Word* (CBS Primetime) June 9, 1950–January 23, 1951; *The News and It's Meaning* (CBS Primetime) August 27, 1950–September 24, 1950; *The March of Time Through the Years* (ABC Primetime) February 23, 1951–August 27, 1951; *It's News to Me* (CBS Primetime) July 2, 1951–September 12, 1953; *America's Town Meeting* (ABC Primetime) April 1952–July 1952; *John Daly and the News* (ABC Primetime) October 12, 1953–December 16, 1960; *Open Hearing* (ABC Primetime) February 1954–July 1954; *Who Said That?* (ABC Primetime) February 2, 1955–July 26, 1955; *Voice of Firestone* (ABC Primetime) September 1958–June 1959; *Critique* (WNDT-TV, New York City) December 4, 1968–January 1, 1969; *Modern Maturity* (PBS) 1984–1989 ACTOR—*The Front Page* (CBS Primetime) September 29, 1949–January 26, 1950
Stage Work: Narrator: *"A Tribute to Rosalind Russell."* Ford's Theatre, Washington, D.C. (1974–1975)
Other Careers: Actor, The Peabody Players (1933–1934); Clerk for a Wool Factory (1933–1935); Schedule Engineer, Capital Transit Co. Washington, D.C. (1935–1937); Director, Voice of America (1967–1968); Forum Moderator, Sound Economy for Citibank, New York (1971–1986); Forum Moderator, American Enterprise Institute (1971–1986)

John Daly (Fred Wostbrock)

Picture this scenario: a man anchoring a nightly major network newscast while also hosting a game show. Now picture this: he is anchoring the news for one network and hosting the game show for a different one. John Daly did that, combining two vastly different careers as a news reporter/anchor and a game show host. Imagine Dan Rather or Tom Brokaw doing that. During the 1950s, Daly anchored ABC's network news each weeknight, while hosting the game show *What's My Line?* on CBS Sunday evenings. John Daly had a rare opportunity to display both his serious and humorous side to viewers.

John Charles Daly Jr. was born in Johannesburg, South Africa on February 20, 1914, as the second son born to John Charles and Helene Grant Tennant Daly. His father worked as a geologist and mining engineer in Johannesburg who was originally from Boston, Massachusetts, before uprooting to South Africa. Daly began his schooling while in Africa attending the Marist Brothers College from 1921 to 1923. That year, his father died of tropical fever, so his mother took him and his 11-year-old brother John Grant to the United States and settled in Boston.

A Social Outcast

Daly completed his elementary and high school education at a prep school called the Tilton Academy in Tilton, New Hampshire. His growing years were difficult and he told *TV Guide* in 1960 that he was a social outcast with his British accent and Eton jackets. After graduating, he enrolled in Boston College in 1931 as a mathematics major and supported himself by working part-time as a switchboard operator in a medical building.

A shortage of funds forced him to quit college before graduating. Daly then joined an acting troupe known as the Peabody Players. His first taste of acting came in a production of "Captain Applejack." The Peabody Players performed at the Boston Little Theater where Daly played the villain. Unfortunately, during the first performance his nervousness caused him to foul up his big line. The audience was said to have heard Daly utter, "I've got you caught like a trap in a rat," according to *TV Guide* in 1953. Throwing in the towel, Daly decided that acting was not his cup of tea and he took a job with a wool factory.

The Young Lady from Washington

While living in Boston, Daly began courting a young lady from Washington, D.C. named Margaret Neal. After awhile, Daly found that paying $15 a week to visit Margaret in the nation's capital was straining his finances. In 1935 he chucked his wool factory job and became a schedule engineer for the Capital Transit Company in Washington, D.C. He and Margaret finally married on January 7, 1937. Their first son John Neal was born in 1938 while second son John Charles was born in 1940. Daughter Helene arrived in 1945.

Not Scared of a Challenge

During the summer of 1937 when Washington, D.C. radio station WRC needed a summer replacement announcer for two weeks, Daly earned the job. From that day, he was hooked on a broadcasting career. After finishing his two-week stint at WRC, he snatched a job at WJSV, the CBS affiliate in Washington. It was here that Daly the reporter was born. Assigned as the White House correspondent, Daly also worked as a regular reporter. Besides covering presidential happenings, Daly reported a fence whitewashing contest, called the play by play for a boys' marble title game, and dressed in a white tie and tails to report penguins hatching their eggs in a zoo. Once, Daly was sent to Oklahoma City to cover a speech by President Franklin Roosevelt. When the president was late in arriving, Daly was forced to ad-lib to the radio audience for 35 minutes! After the incident, he told *Newsweek* in July 1952 that there was "no point in ever being scared again."

In the News

Daly's diverse reporting skills earned him a solid reputation as a correspondent. Working his way up to a CBS news correspondent, he covered the Windell Wilkie presidential campaign tour in 1940. He also covered both the Democratic and Republican conventions.

In January 1943, he was sent to the London Bureau of CBS news. There he narrated the overseas program *Transatlantic Call*, which was produced in cooperation with the BBC (British Broadcasting Corporation). In July 1943 Daly went to Italy to cover the North Africa campaign and landed in Sicily with the first Allied troops.

Returning to the United States in the fall of 1944, CBS News reassigned him to the program *World Today*. On April 12, 1945, while preparing for his *World Today* show, Daly broadcasted the first report of President Franklin D. Roosevelt's death of a cerebral hemorrhage earlier that day.

In 1947 Daly hosted *CBS Is There*, a program that took a trip back into time to report famous historical events of the past. Each week Daly and several reporters from CBS News covered an historic event as if it were the latest news of the day. On the first show, Daly was stationed with a microphone at Ford's Theater on April 14, 1865, the day Abraham Lincoln was assassinated. Sound effects brought the event to life and listeners "witnessed" the shooting while Daly was supposedly at the scene.

Riddle Me This

By the late 1940s, television was rapidly displacing radio as the dominant entertainment medium and Daly was uncertain about his future. Yearning to use his journalistic skills, Daly tried to find work with a newspaper. However, when a friend urged him to appear as a panelist on the CBS quiz show *Riddle Me This*, Daly took the job and was hooked on television. *Riddle Me This*, with host by Conrad Nagel, was a battle of the sexes game that featured male and female celebrity teams. The game used a simple question-and-answer format with clues to the questions provided through film clips and short skits performed on the stage. It was on *Riddle Me This* that the fun side of John Daly emerged. He always had a humorous side, but he was unable to show it during his news programs.

For his next television job, Daly played newspaper editor Walter Burns in the CBS dramatic series *The Front Page*. The series began on September 29, 1949, but died a quick death four months later on January 26, 1950. The following week on February 2, Daly turned up on CBS with the quiz show *What's My Line?* This program became his trademark show for which he was best remembered.

What's My Occupation?

What's My Line? was a simple guessing game involving four panelists who appeared each week on the show trying to guess the occupation of a contestant. Daly began each round by asking the contestant to "sign in please." The guest wrote his/her name on a blackboard and took a seat beside Daly at his podium. The four panelists took turns asking yes or no questions of the contestant to determine his/her occupation. As long as the contestant answered "yes," the panelist could continue questioning. Whenever the guest answered "no," he/she earned $5 and the next panelist asked questions. A total of 10 "no" responses ended the game and the contestant stumped the panel. The top prize was $50. If any of the four panelists guessed the contestant's occupation, the player won whatever amount they had accumulated.

The final round of each show featured a well-known person who was called the mystery guest. For this round, the panelists wore blindfolds to keep from identifying the person. Over the years, *What's My Line?* featured such mystery guests as Eleanor Roosevelt, Carl Sandburg, Frank Lloyd Wright, and Supreme Court Chief Justice Earl Warren. Many actors and actresses appeared including Sean Connery, Clint Eastwood, Bob Hope, Jackie Gleason, Liberace, Groucho Marx, Ronald Reagan, Diana Ross and the Supremes, and Walt Disney.

A Winning Panel

What's My Line? took time to develop into a major hit. It finally settled into a Sunday night slot airing live at 10:30 p.m. The program remained there for the next 17 years. In the show's first three years, there was a fair amount of turnover in the panel. The three panelists best known to viewers were newspaper columnist Dorothy Kilgallen, actress Arlene Francis, and book publisher Bennett Cerf.

The fourth panelist varied from year to year. Comedian Steve Allen filled the spot during the 1953-1954 season. He is credited with coining the phrase that became *What's My Line's?* trademark. While questioning a contestant on one game he asked, "Is it bigger than a bread box?" Radio comedian Fred Allen filled the fourth position from 1954 until his sudden death from a heart attack on March 17, 1956. After his death, a different guest panelist filled the fourth position for the rest of the show's run.

Anchor

Although John Daly enjoyed the fun and relaxed atmosphere of *What's My Line?* he also retained his serious desire to be a newsman. After leaving CBS News in 1950, Daly moved to ABC and anchored a weekly newscast for its radio network. By the summer of 1952 he was anchoring a Monday through Friday newscast. To keep his job on *What's My Line?* Daly inserted a clause in his ABC contract allowing him to work with other networks.

In October 1953 Daly was promoted to vice president in charge of news, special events, public affairs, religion, and sports of the ABC network's radio and television divisions. He became the anchor for ABC's nightly newscasts which were titled *John Daly and the News*. Instead of sitting behind a desk like the anchors on CBS and NBC, Daly stood behind a podium while reading the news. This idea later became popular with all three networks in the 1990s.

Panelists Arlene Francis, Bennett Cerf, and Dorothy Kilgallen wonder what host John Daly is thinking on *What's My Line?* (Fred Wostbrock).

As a newsman, Daly was a firm believer in researching every aspect of a story. He was not content to simply read something written for him. Daly would get the facts for himself and spend long hours putting the stories together. He read eight newspapers a day to stay on top of the world happenings. Much of his leisure time was spent reading histories and biographies.

Quizmaster vs. Newsman

Of all the shows that Daly hosted or anchored in his long career, none of them came close to the success of *What's My Line?* While most of Daly's other ventures such as the quiz show *Who Said That?* and the variety series *Voice of Firestone* came and went, *What's My Line?* continued. The show drew as many as 20 million viewers each week, which was far more than the ratings attained by his ABC newscasts. Though Daly liked being a newsman, the label of quizmaster did not seem to bother him. He told *TV Guide* in 1960 that more people knew him as a TV host than as a network anchorman.

Personal and Professional Struggles

Meanwhile, at ABC, a personnel struggle over control of news and public affairs programs was slowly undermining the network's news division. For a time, Daly had been fighting the network over the low budget and low priority given to the news department. With higher budgets at CBS and NBC's news departments, those networks could afford to send correspondents on location to film actual news happenings. ABC's news division was forced to rely heavily on the independent INS Telenews service for its on-the-spot filmed reports.

By 1960 Daly's personal life was unraveling as well. His 23-year marriage to wife Margaret had fallen apart and in February of that year, they obtained a divorce in an Alabama court. Daly plunged himself into a busy schedule throughout the year. In July he anchored ABC's coverage of the 1960 Republican Presidential Convention in Chicago.

The internal problems at ABC News grew much worse in the fall of 1960 as the presidential election approached. *John Daly and the News* was the lowest rated of the newscasts on all three networks with a 10.1 rating. NBC's *The Huntley-Brinkley Report*, ranked first with a 29.2 rating while *CBS Evening News* with Douglas Edwards garnered a 21.7 rating.

The Fur Hits the Fan

On election night, November 8, 1960, ABC opted to take an hour from its primetime schedule to air its regular programming instead of covering the presidential election. From 7:30 p.m. to 8:30 p.m. ABC viewers saw *Bugs Bunny*, which immediately followed Daly's newscast and *The Rifleman* at 8:00 p.m. Losing an hour of election coverage angered Daly, who was by then fed up with the network.

The straw that broke the camel's back came the following week when ABC's president, Leonard Goldenson, decided to preempt a documentary produced by Daly to air a documentary produced by Time Inc. As the Vice President of News and Special Events, Daly was never consulted about hiring Time Inc. to produce the film. He claimed that ABC violated the policy that all news and public affairs programs be prepared by the network and not by outside companies. When he learned that ABC planned to hire Time Inc. to produce four additional documentaries, Daly angrily resigned on November 14, 1960, but remained with the network for another month. He anchored his last network newscast on December 16, 1960.

At the time of his resignation, Daly was earning around $100,000 a year from ABC, but Daly had become disgusted with the direction that news and public affairs programming had taken at the network. In a 1960 *Time* magazine story, Daly complained that current public service programming paled in comparison to the older shows set earlier in his career.

Although he lost his high profile position at ABC, Daly hardly had to worry about money.

He was still earning $4,000 a week hosting *What's My Line?* on CBS. Since he had not taken a vacation in four years, Daly decided that now was the time to take it easy.

The Good Life

He also started a new life. On December 22, 1960, Daly married Virginia Warren, the 32-year-old daughter of United States Chief Justice Earl Warren. Daly and his bride honeymooned for a week in Hawaii. Since his chores on *What's My Line?* only took up his Sunday evenings, Daly spent much of his time golfing and playing tennis.

The urbane John Daly that viewers saw on television differed greatly from the private John Daly according to an April 1961 *TV Guide* story. Daly loved to socialize with his celebrity friends at baseball games and at New York night clubs. Describing himself as a very moderate drinker, Daly could drink Scotch for hours without any noticeable effect. He also loved good food and could really pack it away while remaining trim and fit.

When asked by *TV Guide's* Richard Gehman in 1961 what he planned to do for work in the future, Daly responded that he would return to work when he felt "itchy." He devoted a great deal of his break to raising a new family. He and his wife Virginia had three children, John Warren, John Earl, and Nina Elizabeth. Daly carried on a family tradition that had lasted for four generations to give each son the first name John.

The Line Continues

What's My Line? continued through the 1960s breaking all records as the longest-running game show in television history. Daly virtually hosted the show cold and required very little rehearsal. He arrived at the studio at 10:00 p.m. usually with a touch of indigestion from overeating before the show. The program aired at 10:30 p.m. and after going off the air, Daly left the studio and headed to Toots Shor's restaurant in New York City for a midnight snack.

The program experienced a sudden change on November 8, 1965, when longtime panelist Dorothy Kilgallen died of a medication overdose just hours after her appearance that night. The producers searched for someone to replace her on the panel, but ultimately decided to fill the position with another guest panelist each week. Only Arlene Francis and Bennett Cerf remained from the original panel.

End of the Line

By 1967 *What's My Line?* was showing its age. The show had dropped to 79th place in the Nielsen ratings according to producer Gil Fates in his book *What's My Line?* For some time, Fates had suggested changes to make the show's format more flexible. Daly opposed any changes and was adamant about tampering with a format that had worked for so many years.

CBS announced the program's cancellation in June 1967. Mark Goodson, the packager of the show, was angered by the way CBS announced the decision. Instead of telling Goodson himself, the word leaked out to *The New York Times*. A reporter from the *Times* caught up with show panelist Bennett Cerf at the Kennedy International Airport to get his opinion of the cancellation. Cerf promptly called Goodson to find out what was going on only to learn that Goodson knew nothing about it.

On September 3, 1967, *What's My Line?* aired for the 876th and last time on CBS. On the final show three contestants who had appeared on the first show in 1950 returned and Daly paid tribute to departed panelists Dorothy Kilgallen and Fred Allen.

As the show came to the last "mystery guest" segment, the panelists blindfolded themselves as usual. When John Daly said "sign in please," he promptly signed the board himself. Using a high-pitched voice to disguise his identity, he proceeded to act as the mystery guest and the host

Diana Ross and the Supremes, mystery guests on *What's My Line?* in 1966, share a laugh with host John Daly. (Fred Wostbrock).

of the show altering his voice between the two identities. The result was hilarious, but the panel had the last laugh, however, since Bennett Cerf eventually guessed his identity. Arlene Francis said, "I like your falsetto, John. Is that the new Voice of America?"

America's Voice

Francis was referring to Daly's new job that awaited him after finishing his run on *What's My Line?* In September 1967 Daly became the new director of the Voice of America (VOA), a

Washington, D.C.–based organization that broadcasted news and government policies of the United States to countries around the world.

Unfortunately Daly faced similar personnel problems with the VOA as he did at ABC News a decade earlier. According to *Newsweek* in 1968, Daly continually clashed with the United States Information Agency (USIA), which was the parent organization to the VOA. In June of 1968 while Daly was on a global tour, the USIA director Leonard Marks transferred a longtime VOA executive to a lower job in the agency without consulting Daly.

Upon learning what Marks had done, Daly promptly resigned as director of the VOA. In fact Daly was so angry that he only gave a 24-hour notice of his resignation before cleaning out his desk and leaving. *Newsweek* also noted that three previous Voice of America directors had resigned over similar fights with the United States Information Agency since 1964.

Critiquing TV

In December 1968, Daly returned to television on WNDT-TV in New York hosting *Critique*. A panel of three critics critiqued current books, movies, and music. While taping *Critique's* third episode, WCBS radio personality David Goldman, who was one of the three critics that evening, uttered a remark that Daly considered obscene. After completing the episode, Daly demanded that Goldman's remarks be edited from the tape.

However, Goldman's remarks remained and the episode ran as scheduled. WNDT told *The New York Times* in January 1969 that the station had received no complaints from viewers about the broadcast. Daly was not happy with the decision, so again he resolved the matter of principle by resigning from his job. Daly's last *Critique* episode aired on New Year's Day 1969.

After two years in retirement, Daly joined Citibank and The American Enterprise Institute as a forum moderator in 1971. He conducted public forums on economic and public policy around the country and published numerous magazine articles on these subjects.

Back in Line

On May 28, 1975, Daly appeared on the ABC primetime special *What's My Line? At 25*, a 90 minute retrospective celebrating the game show's 25th anniversary. Also appearing in the special was Arlene Francis, the only surviving member of the show's original panel, and creator Mark Goodson. Producer Gil Fates recalled in his book *What's My Line?* that the budget for the special was so tight that all 31 of Daly's scenes with Francis and Goodson were taped in two hours.

Retirement

Daly worked with Citibank and The American Enterprise Institute into the 1980s. In 1984 he returned to television as narrator of the PBS series *Modern Maturity*. Ill health brought on by emphysema prompted him to retire in 1989. Two years later on February 25, 1991, just five days after celebrating his 77th birthday, Daly died suddenly of cardiac arrest at his home in Chevy Chase, Maryland. He was survived by his second wife Virginia and six children.

The Man with the Velvet Whip

As a man who would not, and could not, be pushed around, John Daly was a powerful and popular figure. Whether he was hosting a game show, anchoring the news, directing the Voice of America, or conducting forums on public policy, Daly's urbane and smooth manner was highly respected. With two distinct sides to his personality, he easily mixed a polished and educated side with a fun-loving attitude. Television creator and producer Mark Goodson summed it up best to *TV Guide* in 1955 by calling Daly, "The Man with the Velvet Whip."

Richard Dawson

Birth Name: Colin Emm

Born: November 20, 1932, in Gosport, Hampshire, England

Marriages and Family: Diana Dors (1959–1967) (Divorced) 2 sons; Gretchen Johnson (1991–Present) 1 daughter

TV Career: HOST—*The Mike Stokey Show* (KCOP-TV, Los Angeles) September 1961–September 1962; *Lucky Pair* (KNXT-TV, Los Angeles, CA) September 1969–September 4, 1970; *Masquerade Party* (Syndicated) September 9, 1974–September 1975; *The Numbers Game* (Unsold ABC Game Show Pilot) 1975; *Family Feud* (ABC Daytime) July 12, 1976–June 14, 1985, (Syndicated) September 19, 1977–September 13, 1985; *All-Star Family Feud* (ABC Primetime Specials) May 8, 1978–May 25, 1984; *Bazaar* (Unsold ABC Variety Show Pilot) March 30, 1979; *You Bet Your Life* (Unsold NBC Game Show Pilot) August 1988; *Family Feud* (Syndicated) September 12, 1994–September 8, 1995   ACTOR—*Hogan's Heroes* (CBS Primetime) September 17, 1965–July 4, 1971; *Rowan and Martin's Laugh-In* (NBC Primetime) September 1971–May 1973; *Keeping an Eye on Denise* (Unsold CBS Sitcom Pilot) June 19, 1973; *The New Dick Van Dyke Show* (CBS Primetime) September 1973–September 1974   PANELIST—*Can You Top This?* (Syndicated) January 26, 1970–September 1970; *I've Got a Secret* (Syndicated) September 11, 1972–September 1973; *Match Game '73–'78* (CBS Daytime) July 2, 1973–August 23, 1978; *Match Game P.M.* (Syndicated) September 8, 1975–August 1978; *I've Got a Secret* (CBS Primetime) June 15, 1976–July 6, 1976

Theatrical Movies: *Promises, Promises* (1963); *King Rat* (1965); *Munster Go Home* (1966); *The Devil's Brigade* (1968); *The Running Man* (1987)

Made-for-TV Movie: *How to Pick Up Girls* (ABC) November 3, 1978

Other Careers: British Merchant Marine (1947–1950); Resort Waiter on Isle of Wight (1950); Actor, The Barry O'Brien Players (1950–1952); Nightclub Comedian, England (1952–1958); The Diana Dors Show Nightclub Act (1958–1959); Nightclub Comedian, U.S. (1959–1965)

Richard Dawson (Fred Wostbrock)

Of the many game show hosts who have dominated the small screen, there has never been one quite like Richard Dawson. Some people think of game show hosts as cheesy and phony. As a rule, game show hosts are not supposed to be controversial and should always be polite. Richard Dawson broke the mold of the old school of emcees who were always polite even when confronted with oddball contestants.

Dawson was not afraid to speak his mind even if that meant losing a sponsor. If he felt that a contestant was being rude or stupid, he would tell them in such a manner that sometimes the offending player did not realize that he or she had been had. Viewers came to expect the unexpected on Dawson's shows. To some, Dawson was cocky and smarmy. To others, he was a breath of fresh air.

Arriving in the world as Colin Emm, Dawson was born in Gosport, Hampshire, England on November 20, 1932. His father, Arthur Emm, drove a moving van for a living while his mother, Josephine, worked in a munitions factory. They were a poor family, but according to Mary Ann Norbom's book *Richard Dawson and Family Feud*, they had enough to eat, a home, and clothes on their backs. The start of World War II in September 1939 made Dawson's childhood rougher. The family lived only 70 miles southwest of London, which was bombed every day and night by Germany. Dawson's parents sent Richard and his older brother John to live with friends in a small rural town farther away from the bombing.

Since their guardians were financially secure, the boys could attend school. Two years later, however, when their guardians hit Richard and John, they ran away and went back to live with their parents in Gosport. The move back to Gosport also meant the end of Richard and John's formal schooling. Eager to find a better life, Richard ran away in 1947 at the age of 14.

Seeing the World

Lying about his age Dawson became a merchant seaman. Though he was only 14 years old, he was strong enough to endure the many fistfights he got into with the other tough sailors. He became a star attraction in the ship's boxing matches earning close to $5,000 in the ring during his three years at sea. In 1950 Dawson left the sea and worked as a waiter at a resort on the Isle of Wight. His interest in show business began when he and his brother saw a notice outside a theater calling people to audition for a repertoire company called the Barry O'Brien Players.

Having no experience in acting, Dawson decided the only way to have a shot at the stage was to wing it for the audition. He ad-libbed a series of lines using occasional Shakespearean words he learned during his brief schooling career. The company manager decided to hire Dawson when he realized how much the young man wanted to act. Dawson spent two years traveling with the Barry O'Brien Players doing five plays a week.

A Tricky Idea

He wrote an English talent agency telling them he was a famous Canadian comedian and was in England on a holiday looking for a vacation engagement. He received a six week contract to play at a music hall in Plymouth. His opening act was a bomb, but the theater manager decided to take a chance with him and referred him to 90-year-old comedian Billy Bennett. Under Bennett's tutelage, Dawson became a hit with audiences for the rest of his six-week engagement. For the next year, he worked as a comedian in nightclubs writing his own material. In 1954, he was invited to perform at the London Palladium, the most famous theater in England.

While appearing at London's The Stork Room in the summer of 1958, Dawson met actress Diana Dors, a beautiful blond who was Britain's answer to Marilyn Monroe. Dors had lived in Hollywood for a short time in the mid 1950s, but her career was going nowhere. Returning to Britain, she was planning to tour the country with a live musical/variety stage show called *The Diana Dors Show*. She spotted Dawson at The Stork Room and booked him as a comedian for her act. At the time, Dors was separated from her husband/manager, Dennis Hamilton.

Romance

It was not long before she and Dawson fell in love while on tour. In January 1959, they brought the show to the United States, giving Dawson his first crack at the American audiences. When Dennis Hamilton died of a heart attack later that month, Dors and Dawson decided to get married. On April 12, 1959, the couple tied the knot at the apartment of singer Fran Warren in New York. Richard and Diana continued their nightclub act in England and America and later had two sons, Mark and Gary.

The couple finally settled in a ranch house near Benedict Canyon in Beverly Hills, California. Richard and Diana tried to break into acting and Diana soon appeared in the movie *On the Double* with Danny Kaye. In September 1961, she made a guest appearance on *The Mike Stokey Show*, a new late-night television talk show on Los Angeles station KCOP-TV. Dawson met Stokey through Dors' appearance on the program and ended up joining the show as co-host.

After one season, Stokey left to host *Stump the Stars* on CBS. Dors became a regular weekly panelist on the new show. Except for her appearances on *Stump the Stars*, Diana Dors was not making any headway in Hollywood. She began making lengthy trips back to England to find acting work leaving Dawson alone in Hollywood with the two boys and their nanny. In 1964 Dors filed for divorce but she soon dropped the suit and they attempted to reconcile. After only a few months, Dors was again off to England to find work. Dawson and Dors saw very little of each other over the next three years.

Strong Career, Lost Marriage

Dawson's career finally took off in September 1965 when he began a six-year stint on the CBS sitcom *Hogan's Heroes*. Set during World War II. Dawson played a captured English soldier named Peter Newkirk, who was one of five prisoners of war who lived in a Nazi prison camp called Stalag 13. Colonel Robert Hogan, played by actor Bob Crane, was the leader of the small group that virtually had control of the prison camp. *Hogan's Heroes* became a top-10 hit on CBS during the 1965-1966 season and propelled Dawson to prominent fame.

While his career was blooming, his marriage was wilting. In June 1967, the Inland Revenue Service, which is England's equivalent to the Internal Revenue Service, gave Dors a hefty tax bill that left her virtually broke. Since she owned the Benedict Canyon home that she and Dawson shared, there was a possibility that the IRS would take the house leaving the family homeless. Richard and Diana discussed the situation and decided to have Richard file for divorce in America and seek custody of their two boys and possession of the house. When the court settled the case, Diana was freed from much of her tax burden and Richard and the boys remained in Los Angeles.

The breakup of his marriage left Dawson emotionally shattered. For years afterward he kept Dors' pictures on display in his Benedict Canyon home. Nevertheless, Dawson did not let this ruin his life. With two sons to raise, he set out as a single parent to give the boys a normal childhood.

It Wasn't Pure Luck

In 1969 Dawson took over as host of the game show *Lucky Pair* for Los Angeles station KNXT-TV. Two teams composed of a celebrity player and a contestant took turns calling out numbers on a board to find hidden words. The show was similar to the game show *Concentration* because the players had to remember where the hidden words were located. The players took the words and made them into short phrases to win the game.

Lucky Pair and *Hogan's Heroes* both left the air in 1971, but that fall Dawson moved to NBC for a two year stint on *Rowan and Martin's Laugh-In*. He also made frequent appearances as a panelist on *I've Got a Secret* during the 1972-1973 season. In the summer of 1973, Dawson secured two jobs. One was a panelist spot on the CBS game show *Match Game '73*. The second was on the CBS sitcom *The New Dick Van Dyke Show*. Here he played Richard Richardson, the next door neighbor to Van Dyke's character Dick Preston. It was on *Match Game '73* that Dawson's career really boomed.

On *Match Game*, two contestants matched answers to hilarious double-entendre questions with a panel of six celebrities. Dawson became very popular with the viewers and contestants alike. He was the celebrity most often selected by contestants for the Super Match bonus round. Here the contestant chose a celebrity for one final matching question. Players could win up to

$5,000 if they succeeded. Dawson alone was responsible for contestants winning around $3 million during his five-year association with *Match Game*.

While he was an excellent game show panelist, Dawson had a burning desire to be a game show host. During the 1974-1975 season he hosted *Masquerade Party*, a game where celebrities questioned a mystery guest disguised with heavy make up to guess the person's identity.

Let's Start the Family Feud

Nineteen seventy-six was a big year for Dawson. For the previous two years, Mark Goodson and his staff had spent countless hours developing a new game show called *Family Feud*. The game was based on the bonus round of *Match Game*, but with some twists. Dawson's manager, Leonard Granger, went to Mark Goodson and urged him to give Richard an audition. Goodson was reluctant at first, but when *Match Game* producer Ira Skutch pulled for Dawson, Goodson relented.

One reason for Goodson's reluctance was the fact that Dawson's personality did not fit the pattern of a regular game show host. At the same time, Goodson thought that having a different kind of host instead of the cliché type would benefit the show. July 12, 1976 was opening day for *Family Feud*. The show immediately outdrew the soap operas *As the World Turns* on CBS and *Days of Our Lives* on NBC.

Let's Play the Feud

There had never been a game show like it! *Family Feud* called for two teams composed of five members of a family. At the start of the show, the families sat in poses reminiscent of old-time family portraits while announcer Gene Wood read their names. The introductions were backed with fast-paced fiddle music since the game was based on an old-fashioned country fam-

Richard Dawson says that it's time to play *Family Feud* in 1976 (Fred Wostbrock)

ily feud. The families broke out of their poses and lined up at the top of the steps leading to their podiums on the set. Gene Wood announced, "On your marks! Let's start the *Family Feud*," and the families bounded to their podiums on the stage.

Dawson posed survey questions asked of 100 people. The idea was to guess the most popular answers given by the survey. One member from each team went to the face-off podium while Dawson read the question. A sample question: "Name a vegetable used in salads besides lettuce." The first contestant to buzz in and match an answer on the board (for example: tomato) earned the right to play the question or pass it over to the opposing family. The family winning the question guessed the remaining answers. Points were awarded based on the number of people out of 100 that gave an answer. The answer "tomato" for example may have been said by 60 of the 100 people. These numbers translated into dollar amounts so the answer was worth $60.

A scoreboard on top of the main board kept track of the accumulated money during each round. If a contestant gave an answer not on the survey, they received a "strike." Three "strikes" meant that the opposing family could win all the money in the bank by naming one of the remaining answers on the board. The first family to amass 200 points (later 300) won the game and played the Fast Money bonus round.

Two family members played the Fast Money round. One member went offstage out of earshot while the second player remained. Dawson asked the onstage contestant five survey questions and the player had 15 seconds to guess the most popular answers. After revealing the point values for the answers, the other contestant came out to play. Dawson asked the same five questions and the player had 20 seconds to answer. Scoring 200 points netted the family $5,000.

Are You on Narcotics?

As previously mentioned, Dawson was not your typical game show host. He once said in a 1994 *People Weekly* article that the appropriate word to describe him was "smarmy." As a game show host, Dawson did things that broke the unwritten rules dictating a host's behavior. Two months into the run on *Family Feud*, he started kissing the female contestants on the lips during his opening banter with each family.

He also was not afraid to say exactly what was on his mind. A 1979 *Newsweek* magazine once reported Dawson asking a contestant if he was on narcotics upon getting a weird answer from the man. After receiving an off-the-wall answer on another episode he told the player to stop watching television and "read some books." It was rare for a game show host to insult the contestants.

Dawson frequently made jokes against former President Richard Nixon, who had resigned from office in 1974 after facing impeachment charges for his role in the Watergate scandal. When one of the show's sponsors complained to ABC about the Nixon jokes, Dawson went on the air and told the sponsor to take its business elsewhere. When ABC decided to cut Dawson's remarks out of the tape, he threatened to quit the show. Mark Goodson supported Dawson 100 percent and pointed out to ABC the potential violation of freedom of speech by cutting out the remarks. The network quickly changed its mind and the show aired intact.

Dawson's kissing of the female contestants began drawing negative mail in protest of the action. In fact the volume of mail was so large that the producers and Dawson decided to do something about it. Mark Goodson appeared on *Family Feud* and asked the viewers to write in their comments and vote "yes" or "no" on whether or not the kissing should continue. The producers received thousands of responses and the viewers overwhelming approved of the kissing.

Number One

With all of this commotion, *Family Feud* quickly became the number-one rated daytime show on television. The show won an Emmy for Outstanding Game Show in May 1977. That fall, a syndicated nighttime version began airing once a week. The top prize for winning Fast

Money in the syndicated version doubled to $10,000. In May 1978 ABC began airing *All-Star Family Feud* specials four or five times a year on their primetime schedule.

The specials actually originated from a week of episodes on the daytime version using the casts of ABC's daytime soaps who played for charity. At the time, ABC's soaps were foundering in the ratings and the shows needed a boost. When ABC saw the spectacular ratings from the special soap opera stars week, they immediately asked *Family Feud*'s producers to do a series of specials for primetime using the cast members of ABC's nighttime shows as contestants to play for charity.

This idea helped boost ABC's primetime ratings during the 1978-1979 season. When they continued the *All-Star Family Feud* specials for the 1979-1980 season, the producers began using cast members from CBS and NBC programs. Among the shows featured were *The Waltons*, *The Dukes of Hazzard*, *Dallas*, *Three's Company*, *The Jeffersons*, *Eight Is Enough*, *The Love Boat*, and *Benson*.

Things just kept getting better for *Family Feud* and for Richard Dawson. In April 1977 ABC moved the show to 11:30 a.m. where it successfully competed with the second half hour of *The Price Is Right*. In June 1978 Dawson won an Emmy for Outstanding Game Show host. Then, in January 1979, the syndicated version of *Family Feud* expanded to two nights a week in most markets. Finally in September 1980 the syndicated version expanded to five nights a week. Dawson's success on *Family Feud* and *Match Game* made him one of the most recognized television stars. He used the opportunity to guest on other television shows working his acting muscles in episodes of *Love Boat* and *Fantasy Island*.

Dawson also frequently guest-hosted *The Tonight Show* when host Johnny Carson took vacations. When Carson talked of quitting the program in 1979, Dawson was considered as a possible replacement, but Carson changed his mind and stayed with the show.

The Ego Is Wild

To the viewers, Dawson was a huge favorite between hosting *Family Feud* and serving as a panelist on *Match Game*. Backstage, things were not the way they appeared.

> *Ira Skutch (Goodson-Todman producer/director, February 2006 telephone interview):*
> "After he became the emcee of *Family Feud* and became very successful, I guess he got tired of working on *Match Game*. He became very, very difficult. It finally got the point where he was hardly contributing anything [to the show.]"

Dawson quit *The Match Game* in August 1978. A 1984 *TV Guide* article by Mary Murphy revealed a side of Dawson not seen by the viewers. One executive who worked on *Family Feud* noted that Dawson became angry over things such as burned out light bulbs or broken microphones. Another Goodson-Todman executive stated that Dawson frequently ran the show five to six minutes past its allotted 30 minutes. He would tell jokes and stories that had to be cut from the tape every week. Dawson also frequently clashed with *Family Feud* producer Howard Felsher over the rulings of contestants' answers during the game.

> *Howard Felsher (***Family Feud*** producer, June 2006 telephone interview):*
> "In the beginning for the first four or five years, we got along very well. Then he began to become a big star. That's when he became difficult and we stopped getting along. He was the boss. It was his show."

Things reached the boiling point in 1983 when Dawson barred Felsher from the set. Mark Goodson kept Felsher on the show as the executive producer. Therefore, Felsher could still retain some control of the show without having to be present on the set. Dawson's daughter-in-law, Cathy, became the new producer.

> *Howard Felsher:*
> "I was the best producer that show had and Dawson knows it. He won't even talk to me these days. I can pass him on the street and he'll look the other way."

The Feud Unravels

Family Feud remained popular during the early 1980s. ABC moved the show to 12:00 p.m. in June 1980 where it was virtually indestructible for the next four years. The nighttime version remained the number one-rated syndicated game show. That is, until a syndicated version of *Wheel of Fortune* began beating *Feud* by 1984.

The 1984-1985 season brought some changes to *Family Feud*. Teams now had to score 400 points in the front game to play the fast money round. The show ran at a faster pace to cram more questions into each game, but the humor that had sustained *Family Feud* was gone. With falling ratings on both versions of the show, *Family Feud* left ABC on June 14, 1985, after a spectacular nine-year run. The syndicated version pulled out in September 1985.

Dawson was out of work for the first time in 20 years. He had come a long way from his days as a struggling nightclub comedian in England. Since there were no jobs in the offering, and being financially secure, Dawson retired. He spent his time with his girlfriend, Gretchen Johnson, whom he met on *Family Feud* in April 1981.

Life After the Feud

According to a 1994 *People Weekly* story, Gretchen first appeared with her family as a contestant on April 6, 1981. Dawson took an instant liking to Gretchen, a 26-year-old San Diego education major in college. After the Johnson family left the show with $12,659, Gretchen accepted an invitation from Dawson to a home-cooked gourmet dinner. They soon began dating.

Dawson's career picked up in 1987 when he played a sleazy game show host in the futuristic Arnold Schwarzenegger film *The Running Man*. Set in the year 2019, Schwarzenegger played a police officer in a society run by dictatorship. He was imprisoned for refusing to kill unarmed civilians. As punishment, he was forced to appear on the game show *The Running Man* where he was released and hunted down by stalkers who were instructed to kill him if captured. With Dawson presiding, the studio audience watched the proceedings via a large monitor.

In 1988 Mark Goodson Productions revived *Family Feud* for CBS and syndication. Since Dawson was not popular with the folks at Goodson Productions, he was never considered to host the new version. The job went to a young comedian named Ray Combs. Dawson, in the meantime, focused on other projects.

In August 1988 he hosted an NBC pilot for a revival of Groucho Marx's game show *You Bet Your Life*. The network passed on that venture. The next year, Dawson auditioned to host *Trump Card*, but lost out to former football player Jimmy Cefalo. Meanwhile, Dawson's home life changed in 1991 when he married Gretchen Johnson and she gave birth to a daughter, Shannon. Dawson was now a truly happy man with a new family life.

Home Again

By the fall of 1993 CBS had canceled *Family Feud* leaving only the syndicated version. The ratings had gone south and the show's producers seriously considered replacing host Ray Combs. Mark Goodson had recently passed away and his son Jonathan Goodson was now running the company. Late in 1993, Dawson was asked to return as host of the syndicated version of *Family Feud* to see if he could breathe new life into the flagging property. Dawson quickly agreed. He loved *Family Feud* and the opportunity to return to the show was a dream come true.

With Dawson's return, several changes took place. Longtime producer Howard Felsher, who had come back to produce during the Ray Combs era, was replaced by Dawson's son Gary. The show expanded to one hour and featured two complete games. The winning team of the first game returned to face a family that had competed on the 1976–1985 version of the show.

The most drastic changes were the set and theme music. The 1976 and 1988 versions of

Family Feud featured a bright and colorful set with a bouncy theme song. The set was redesigned with dark blue and red colors and no flashing lights. The original board with the answer slats was replaced with a computerized image that revealed the answers. The theme song was re-recorded with a slower and jazzier touch. Gone was the old fiddle music used to give the show a country flavor. *Family Feud* began the 1994-1995 season with 138 stations airing the show.

Dawson Changes

Dawson had gained considerable weight during his nine year retirement so *Family Feud's* producers insisted that he slim down before coming back to work.

> *Howard Felsher (June 2006 telephone interview):*
> "He was so anxious to get the show that he guaranteed to lose 50 pounds before it got on the air. He didn't lose half a pound. The stations had already bought the show based on his being there and that was that."

Once on the air, Dawson considerably toned down the wisecracks he once aimed at the contestants. Also noticeable was the fact that Dawson no longer kissed the female contestants. On the first episode in 1994, he talked about his marriage to Gretchen and the birth of his daughter Shannon. He had promised Shannon that he would not kiss any other women besides her mom. Dawson simply shook their hands or gave hugs as a substitute. All of these changes failed to save the show and by the spring of 1995, the game was over.

Retirement

Since 1995 Dawson has enjoyed retirement with his family in Beverly Hills, California. He made occasional television appearances on the Game Show Network in interviews and specials. On one special in late 1995, he and Ray Combs appeared together for the first time to reminisce about their years hosting *Family Feud*. In the spring of 2000, Dawson narrated a Fox Network special, *World's Funniest Game Shows*.

In September 1999, *Family Feud* hit the airwaves once again as a syndicated series with comedian Louie Anderson as host. He was replaced by actor Richard Karn in 2002 who in turn was succeeded by John O'Hurley in 2006. Of the five people who hosted *Family Feud* through the years, Dawson remains the most popular and recognized one. Love him or hate him, there is no denying that Dawson had wide appeal as a television star. Despite the stories of Dawson's ego, off camera he remains a devoted family man.

Mark Goodson told *The Washington Post* in 1978 that Dawson's appeal lied in the fact that he usually said the unexpected, was open with his feelings, and could take all of that and work it in a largely structured format. Goodson seasoned his assessment of Dawson by adding the descriptive words "naughty" and "dangerous."

GEOFF EDWARDS

Birth Name: Geoffrey Bruce Owen Edwards
Born: February 15, 1931, in Westfield, New Jersey
Marriages and Family: Suzanne Weaver (Divorced) 2 sons, 1 daughter; Michael Feffer (1984–Present) 2 stepsons
Military Career: United States Air Force (1954–1956)
Radio Career: Announcer/Disc Jockey (WOKO-AM, Albany, NY) 1957–1958; Announcer/Disc Jockey (WEAT-AM, West Palm Beach FL) 1958–1959; Program Director/Disc Jockey (KFMB-AM, San Diego, CA) 1959–1963; Program Director/Announcer (KHJ-AM, Los Angeles, CA) 1963–1966; Disc Jockey (KFI-AM, Los Angeles, CA) 1966–1967; Disc Jockey (KMPC-AM, Los Angeles, CA) 1967–1979; Announcer/Program Host (KFI-AM, Los Angeles, CA) 1987–1989; *The Touring Company* (KPCC-FM, Pasadena, CA) 1996–2000, (Syndicated) 2000–2001; Travel Editor (KION-AM, Monterrey CA) 2000–2005; Program Host (KSUR-FM, Los Angeles, CA) 2003; Travel Correspondent (KABC-AM, Los Angeles, CA) 2005–Present
TV Career: HOST—News Anchor (WEAT-TV, West Palm Beach, FL) 1958–1959; *Lucky Pair* (KNXT-TV, Los Angeles, CA) September 3, 1968–September 1969; *The His and Her of It* (Syndicated) November 16, 1969–September 1970; *Says Who?* (Unsold Game Show Pilot) May 28, 1971; *Cop-Out!* (Unsold Game Show Pilot) February 15, 1972; *Hollywood's Talking* (CBS Daytime) March 26, 1973–June 22, 1973; *The New Treasure Hunt* (Syndicated) September 10, 1973–September 1977; *Jackpot* (NBC Daytime) January 7, 1974–September 26, 1975; *Shoot for the Stars* (NBC Daytime) January 3, 1977–September 30, 1977; *Bargain Hunters* (Unsold Game Show Pilot) 1979; *Play the Percentages* (Syndicated) January 7, 1980–September 12, 1980; *Treasure Hunt* (Syndicated) September 14, 1981–September 1982; *Starcade* (Syndicated) September 1983–September 1984; *Mid-Morning L.A.* (KHJ-TV, Los Angeles, CA) January 1984–February 1986; *$50,000 a Minute* (Unsold ABC Game Show Pilot) 1985; *Big Spin* (California State Lottery) November 28, 1985–December 10, 1994; *Chain Reaction* (USA) December 29, 1986–December 27, 1991; *Mid-Morning L.A.* (KHJ-TV, Los Angeles, CA) 1989–1991; *Jackpot* (Syndicated) September 18, 1989–March 16, 1990   ACTOR—*Petticoat Junction* (CBS Primetime) January 6, 1968–December 14, 1968; *The Bobby Darin Amusement Company* (NBC Primetime) July 27, 1972–Sept. 7, 1972; *The Bobby Darin Show* (NBC Primetime) January 19, 1973–April 27, 1973   PANELIST—*The Love Experts* (Syndicated) September 18, 1978–September 1979
Theatrical Movies: *Penelope* (1966); *The Comic* (1969); *WUSA* (1970); *Thelma and Louise* (1991)
Made-for-TV Movies: *Three on a Date* (ABC) February 17, 1978; *The Outlaws* (ABC) July 9, 1984

Geoff Edwards (Fred Wostbrock)

Business Interests: Partner: Smith-Edwards Productions (1979–1981)
Other Careers: Member, The Duke Ambassadors Band (1949–1953); Dixieland Band Combo Musician (1949–1953); Western Electric Company (1956)

If you were searching for a hidden treasure worth $25,000 or answering a tricky riddle, or even playing a video game, then look no further. The man you want is Geoff Edwards. Whether you were selecting a gift box on *Treasure Hunt*, guessing a riddle on *Jackpot* or blowing up a villain in a video game on *Starcade*, Edwards was there to root for you. These shows are only a small sample of his varied career.

One of two sons born to Edwin and Winifred Edwards, Geoffrey Bruce Owen Edwards came into the world on February 15, 1931, in Westfield, New Jersey. As a child, Edwards showed a flair for the drums. He began playing drums at age 11 and by the time he was 14, he was playing in bands.

> *Geoff Edwards (March 15, 2004 telephone interview):*
> "I got a drum set and my parents took me to see Tommy Dorsey and Buddy Rich at a place called the Meadowbrook in New Jersey. We got home probably around 11 o'clock at night and they would let me sit and pound away on the drums for about an hour. I don't know what the neighbors thought."

The "Duke" of Dixieland

He considered a career in music and after high school was offered a job with Louis Prima's band. Edwards' parents, however, wanted him to go to college first and get a good education. In 1949 Edwards enrolled at Duke University in North Carolina. He discovered that the university had a 15-piece band called The Duke Ambassadors, so he joined the group as a drummer. Edwards soon formed his own combo and began playing gigs around North Carolina. He also ran a Dixieland club on Saturday afternoons called the Turnages.

> *GE:*
> "I think in four years of college, I had one Saturday night where I wasn't working."

Having spent four years in the Air Force ROTC during college, Edwards enlisted in the United States Air Force as a 2nd Lieutenant where he was stationed on an island about 50 miles west of Okinawa.

> *GE:*
> "There was no getting into anything, not even trouble."

Upon his discharge in 1956, Edwards set out to pursue his musical ambitions, but he was in for a disappointment. At the Union Hall in New York, he bumped into Phil Urso, a tenor with Woody Herman's band.

> *GE:*
> "It was kind of sprinkling. And he walked up to me in his overcoat with his collar turned up and he said, 'Hey man, do you know where I can get a gig for the weekend?' This guy is really good and he's looking for work!"

Greener Pastures

Pressured by his parents to get a good job, Edwards worked for about three months at The Western Electric Company in New York, but was unhappy there. He enrolled at the School of Radio and Television and graduated in 1957. His first job was a disc jockey position at WOKO-AM in Albany, New York. As the morning man, Edwards opened the station each day and had to work the first hour of his shift in an overcoat and gloves since there was no heat until all the transmitting equipment warmed up the room.

After nine months at WOKO, Edwards grew tired of the cold weather in New York, not to mention the cold weather inside the station each morning. He wrote several radio stations along the coast of Florida seeking a job in 1958. Two weeks later he was off to West Palm Beach, Florida working for WEAT and the station's television wing WEAT-TV. There he worked a split shift as a disc jockey in the mornings and again from 2–4 p.m. At 6:00 p.m. he anchored the station's local television newscast.

A year later, Edwards still yearned for greener pastures and set his sights on the west coast. In December 1959 he landed a job with KFMB-AM in San Diego, California and from then on was a converted Californian. At KFMB, Edwards worked as a disc jockey and program director. He used his piloting skills learned from the Air Force by flying KFMB's traffic airplane giving reports on San Diego's traffic conditions.

Climbing up in the ranks, Edwards moved to Los Angeles in 1963 as Program Director for KHJ-AM. However, a hang-up in the station's programming department forced Edwards to take a temporary position as the man in charge of special events. That temporary job put Edwards in the position to witness one of the most spectacular and tragic events in United States history.

History in the Making

On November 22, 1963, KHJ sent Edwards to Dallas, Texas to cover the proceedings after President John F. Kennedy was killed by an assassin's bullet. The accused killer, Lee Harvey Oswald, was soon captured and taken to the Dallas City Jail. During that weekend following Kennedy's murder, Edwards reported from the Dallas police station.

> *GE:*
> "I had the run of the police station. I walked in on Oswald talking to his mother one time. I was in the police captain's office using his phone to report on telegrams they got. I never had to show any identification until [Sunday] morning."

On Sunday, November 24, 1963, Edwards was among the many reporters in the underground parking garage under the Dallas police station covering Oswald's transfer from the city jail to the Dallas County Jail. While television cameras covered the event live, Oswald was escorted by police officers and detectives. Suddenly a 52-year-old Dallas nightclub owner named Jack Ruby jumped out of the crowd of reporters and shot Oswald point blank in the abdomen. Oswald soon died of the wound.

> *GE:*
> "I was probably about ten yards away from him when he got shot. When all of a sudden this pop goes off and the flash, it was unbelievable! The immediate thing my mind said was, 'That idiot threw a firecracker!' I mean you just couldn't imagine that he would be shot there in front of everybody and all the police on television."

Edwards immediately ran for a telephone and broke the big scoop to KHJ in Los Angeles. Shortly after returning to California, Edwards assumed the position of Program Director for KHJ. He remained there until 1966 when he moved to KFI-AM as the morning disc jockey from 6–9 a.m. His program soon became the number one rated radio show in Los Angeles. His success at KFI soon attracted the attention of the much larger station KMPC-AM, who hired him in 1967.

TV Acting and Hosting

While working in radio during the late 1960s, Edwards dabbled in acting. His first acting job was a small role in the 1966 theatrical movie *Penelope*. He then played reporter Jeff Powers in six episodes of the CBS sitcom *Petticoat Junction* between January and December of 1968. The fall of 1968 brought his first game show hosting gig called *Lucky Pair*, which was produced and owned by Bob Barker. *Lucky Pair* aired on Los Angeles television station KNXT.

GE:

(Laughing) "In order to get an audience for that [show], they had a page go out into the street and try to pull people inside."

He left *Lucky Pair* in 1969 to co-host a one season talk show with his first wife Suzanne Weaver called *The His and Her of It*.

What a Cop-Out!

In May 1971 Edwards hosted an ABC game show pilot for Bob Stewart called *Says Who?* but it never became a series. Edwards tried again in February 1972 with the Chuck Barris pilot *Cop-Out*. The game featured two contestants and a panel of eight celebrities. The contestants guessed if an answer given by a celebrity to a personal question was the truth or a "cop out" (a false statement). Behind the celebrities and Edwards was a large wall of lights. Whenever a celebrity answered a question, Edwards asked if the answer was honest or a cop out. The wall either lit up the word "honest" or "cop out." The pilot was a big fiasco.

GE:

"These were all like 250 watt spotlight bulbs. The idea behind it was that they (the lights) were all lit and the ones that weren't part of the spelling would go out. We had to pause every ten minutes because everybody's back was burning."

While taping the pilot, the machine that was supposed to spell out the words in the lights quit working. When it was time for the words "honest" or "cop-out" to flash on the wall, the taping stopped while the stage hands unscrewed the bulbs by hand that were not part of the spelling until either the words "honest" or "cop-out" were left in the lights. Then taping would resume.

GE:

"It was so hard to get any timing off of that show. It was almost impossible."

Needless to say, *Cop-Out* failed to become a regular series.

With Bobby Darin

During the summer of 1972, Edwards joined the cast of *The Bobby Darin Amusement Company*, a comedy variety series that served as the summer replacement for *The Dean Martin Show* on NBC. The show featured an assortment of comedy skits and musical numbers by Darin and guest stars. The program drew decent ratings during its summer run, so NBC brought it back as *The Bobby Darin Show* in January 1973.

Sadly, Darin became ill with an old heart ailment that had plagued him since he was stricken with rheumatic fever as a child.

GE:

"I would go into the dressing room where he and I would go over some comedy bits and he'd be on oxygen."

Whenever Edwards said something funny, Darin would have to take off the oxygen mask to laugh. *The Bobby Darin Show* ended its run in April 1973. Darin passed away eight months later at the young age of thirty-seven following surgery to correct a malfunctioning heart valve.

Hollywood's Talking

On March 26, 1973, Edwards finally got his first network game show with CBS's *Hollywood's Talking*. The show was created and produced by veteran host Jack Barry. On *Hollywood's Talking*, three contestants watched film clips of famous celebrities who talked about people, places, and things without identifying the subject. The object was for the players to guess what subject the celebrity was talking about in the film clip.

Early in the show's run, Edwards clashed with its creator, Jack Barry.

GE:

"He walked into my dressing room one day, maybe the second week we were taping. And he said, 'You know, you have a really annoying voice. Can you do something about that?' I said, 'Jack, I have a contract for 13 weeks. At the end of 13 weeks, don't renew it and don't ever come into my dressing room again.'"

Edwards did not have to worry because the ratings were mediocre, and CBS pulled the show on June 22, 1973.

GE:

"I never worked for Jack Barry again. I think Barry had a difficult time having anyone be an emcee and get any attention away from him."

Finding His Treasure

Three months later, Edwards began hosting *The New Treasure Hunt*, an update of a 1956–1959 game show hosted by comedian Jan Murray. Chuck Barris bought the rights to the show and launched this new version in syndication. On *The New Treasure Hunt*, contestants won money and prizes by choosing a box from 30 numbered boxes on the stage. The boxes contained small props used to illustrate the prizes.

Two rounds were played per show, and Edwards chose the contestants from the audience. After the contestant selected a box, Edwards peeked inside and milked all the suspense he could out of the situation. The prizes on the show ranged from appliances and trips. One box contained a check for $25,000. There were also worthless prizes called "klunks" which increased the suspense of the game. Before seeing the prizes, players had the option to take a cash payoff in exchange for the box.

30 Boxes, 30 Acts

Each box of prizes featured a short "skit" to go along with it. To keep contestants from prematurely finding out what they had won, there were no cue cards for Edwards to read. Each act was scripted and Edwards memorized the scripts before taping began.

GE:

"We would stop tape because we had to load the area where the prizes were going to be. There would be about a 15 minute stop down and I'd go to a trailer. Production staff would be there and they'd say, 'Okay this is bit so and so,' and I'd look at the script again and they'd say, 'the music cue is here and so on.' I only had to [say] the things that would cue particular effects [during the act]."

Aside from his scripted cues, Edwards was free to ad-lib during the game. On one show, a skit ran too short and Edwards found himself with four extra minutes to fill. Thinking quickly, he had the contestant choose a box and then excused himself for a couple of minutes to eat lunch leaving the woman standing alone on the stage.

GE:

"She'd start looking [at] the box and getting nervous, and it was a very funny couple of minutes."

While backstage, Edwards conveniently found half of a sandwich that someone on the crew had left, so he picked it up and walked back on the set eating it and the game resumed.

King of the Hill

In January 1974 Edwards began hosting *Jackpot* for NBC daytime. *Jackpot* featured 16 contestants who solved riddles for cash and prizes. One contestant became "King of the Hill" and stood behind a podium at center stage. The "King of the Hill" answered riddles posed by the other 15 contestants. If the "King of the Hill" missed a riddle, he or she switched places with the contestant who stumped them.

"What should I do?" A contestant ponders a decision on *The New Treasure Hunt* **as Geoff Edwards looks on (Fred Wostbrock).**

Edwards enjoyed his greatest career success during 1974 and 1975. In addition to hosting *The New Treasure Hunt* and *Jackpot* on television, he was a popular daily radio personality on KMPC in Los Angeles. His taping schedule for both game shows kept Edwards jetting back and forth across the country since *The New Treasure Hunt* taped in Los Angeles one weekend while *Jackpot* taped in New York the next weekend.

In the spring of 1975, when *Jackpot* lagged in the ratings, the format switched from answering riddles to a standard question and answer contest.

> *GE:*
> "It was just bad. It just ruined the show and it died."

Close Call to a Hit

In the spring of 1976, Edwards was offered an audition to host *Family Feud* for ABC. When Edwards first heard about *Family Feud*, he thought the show was going to be similar to a low-rated, critically panned ABC game show called *The Neighbors*, which had just gone off the air.

> *Geoff Edwards (May 3, 2004 telephone interview):*
> "The title *Family Feud* made it sound like *The Neighbors*."

His fear that *Family Feud* would be a flop, coupled with the fact that he had just taped a pilot called *Shoot the Works* for producer Bob Stewart, prompted Edwards to turn down *Family Feud*. Richard Dawson became the host and the show went on to a nine year run.

Meanwhile, *Shoot the Works* became *Shoot for the Stars* and premiered on NBC in January 1977 with Edwards hosting. By that fall, both *Shoot for the Stars* and *The New Treasure Hunt* had left the airwaves. Edwards hung in with his daily radio show for KMPC. During the 1978–1979 season, he worked as a celebrity panelist on the syndicated game show *The Love Experts*, hosted by Bill Cullen.

Winding Down in Radio

In late 1979, KMPC radio management offered to expand Edwards' daily three hour show to four hours, but he declined it. Tired of the radio routine, Edwards decided to quit KMPC and work on new television projects. One of the TV activities was a new game show called *Play the Percentages*. He also made a deal to develop new game shows for Warner Brothers. With his business partner Mark Smith, they formed Smith & Edwards Productions. After 13 years at KMPC, Edwards hosted his last radio show on December 15, 1979.

"Could You Change the Cue Card Please?

His new gig on *Play the Percentages* returned Edwards to the host's spot for the first time in three years. On *Play the Percentages*, two husband and wife teams heard a general knowledge question previously asked of a survey group. The teams guessed what percentage of the people correctly anwered the question. The team guessing the closest earned points based on the percentage number. The couple could answer the question for additional points. The first team to score 300 points won the game and played a bonus round for $25,000.

Instead of hiring someone to hold the cue cards Edwards used on the show, Executive Producer Dan Enright opted to handle the cards himself. One day while Edwards was explaining the rules of the game, someone on the crew distracted Enright from the cue cards.

> *Geoff Edwards (March 17, 2004 telephone interview):*
> "He just didn't bother to change the cue cards and he got into this conversation. I'm looking over and I said, 'Dan, could you change the cue card please?' So in the next show, each time he changed the card he handed it off to somebody else and they handed it to somebody else until it went all around the studio. It was very funny. He had a great sense of humor."

On another show, a section of the game's set malfunctioned. The bonus round of the show used a large circular-shaped board with a percentage sign on it. During the main game when the board was not in use, it served as part of the floor design. As the game went to the bonus round, the huge board raised from the floor into an upright position. On one occasion, as the board was rising for the bonus round, it started to pull the floor up with it and nearly destroyed the set. Needless to say, the board was never used again.

Play the Percentages also went through at least two formats during its run.

> *GE: (Laughing)*
> "They kept changing the rules about every two shows."

With all of these problems, *Play the Percentages* could not attract a large audience and was pulled after eight months.

A Second Treasure

Meanwhile, Edwards and Mark Smith developed an NBC game show pilot that never sold. Subsequent ideas for shows never got off the ground and Smith & Edwards Productions closed in 1981. That fall Edwards returned to host *Treasure Hunt* as a five-a-week syndicated show. The game was practically identical to the 1973–1977 version except that the number of boxes on the stage increased from 30 to 66. The cash jackpot started at $25,000 and increased by $1,000 for each day it was not won. This second version of *Treasure Hunt* fizzled out after one season.

Bring on the Video Games

The popularity of video arcade games in the early 1980s provided Edwards with his next big break. In 1982 producers James Caruso and Mavis Arthur created the game show *Starcade*, which was billed as "TV's first video arcade game show." Two teams of fathers and their sons competed. A toss-up question was asked and the first team to correctly answer played one of five video games on the stage. Each contestant played the game against the clock to rack up as many points as possible. The team with the highest score played the "Name the Game Board" where they identified four video games from pictures of the game's graphics. The team with the highest score after three rounds took home a video arcade game.

Starcade originated on Ted Turner's WTBS superstation in Atlanta, Georgia as a weekly series with Mark Richards as host in December 1982. When the show went national in September 1983, Edwards became the new host. As a real-life fan of video games, he was a natural as host. Edwards still plays video games on occasion and says that his current favorite is "Unreal Tournament."

Talking with Meredith MacRae

In early 1984, Edwards teamed with actress Meredith MacRae to co-host *Mid Morning L.A.* for station KHJ-TV. Edwards won a local Emmy for his chores on the show. However when the show's producers declined to syndicate the show nationally, Edwards quit in 1986, though he later returned to the show for another two years.

In November 1985, Edwards took over as host of the California Lottery television game, *Big Spin*. The show originated every Saturday evening from Sacramento, California. In a 1987 *Los Angeles Times* interview, Edwards noted that for years he only wanted to have one weekly TV series and nothing else. With *Big Spin*, he finally got his wish.

Hectic Taping Schedules

Before long, Edwards was bored by the inactivity. In late 1986 when the opportunity came to host the game show *Chain Reaction*, he readily accepted the job. The show taped in Montreal, Canada to cut production costs. The pace was hectic since as many as eight episodes were taped in one day. Normally five episodes (one week's worth) are taped per day on half hour game shows.

This stressful schedule turned out to be nothing compared with Edwards' next assignment. In the fall of 1989, Edwards emceed a syndicated revival of *Jackpot*. Although the show taped in Glendale, California and Edwards did not have to leave town to host it, the producers decided to cut production costs by taping 10 shows at a time over a three-day period. A total of 130 episodes were produced in 13 days.

> *GE:*
> "We would stop one show and I would go to change wardrobe and in 15 minutes they started [again]. If I was there, fine. If I wasn't, they were on their way. More than once I had the opening music playing and John [Harlen] would say, 'And now here's the host,' and I'm running down the hall [to the studio]."

Jackpot drew respectable ratings, but the program's syndicator went bankrupt and the show was withdrawn in March 1990.

Back in Radio

During his television renaissance, Edwards came back to Los Angeles radio in October 1987 as an afternoon personality on KFI-AM. His new show was a mixture of music, interviews, comedy bits, news, and commentary. Things took an interesting turn in February 1989 when Edwards found himself mixed up in a controversy involving former singer Cat Stevens. According to a February 1989 *Los Angeles Times* article, singer Cat Stevens, who had converted to the Islamic faith, supported Iranian leader Ayatollah Khomeini's order to kill author Salman Rushdie because of his book called *Satanic Verses*. Khomeini felt that the book was an insult to Islam. Cat Stevens told Muslim students in England that the reason he supported Khomeini's order to kill Rushdie was because the Koran says anyone who defames the [Islamic] prophet (Muhammad) must die.

Tom Leykis, a talk show host on KFI, critiqued the situation on his February 23, 1989, program. Leykis denounced Stevens' support of Khomeini, so when a caller on the show suggested burning Cat Stevens' records, Leykis jumped at the idea. Leykis promptly launched a record burning campaign, and after clearing the idea with KFI management, suggested that listeners bring their Cat Stevens records and tapes to the station for a mass burning.

"I'm Out of Here"

The next day on February 24, 1989, Edwards criticized Leykis' record burning campaign on his radio show. He threatened to resign if a promotional spot for the record burning aired during his program. KFI management did not object to Edwards' opinion on the record burning but took offense at his stand on running a promotional spot for the record burning during his program.

> *GE:*
> "I told them, 'Book burning and stuff like that was a long time ago.' If [Leykis] wanted to talk about that on his show, fine, but not on my show."

On February 27, 1989, Edwards was suspended by KFI for an indefinite period. According to Edwards, KFI had the opportunity to pick up Rush Limbaugh's nationally syndicated talk show for the station.

> *GE:*
> "We made a deal. They bought out my contract. They had a chance to get [Limbaugh] for free. I was getting paid a lot of money so they were really happy to get [Limbaugh's show]."

With the deal in place, Edwards said goodbye to KFI on March 3, 1989.

Calling It a Career

Meanwhile *Big Spin* and *Chain Reaction* kept Edwards busy into the 1990s. In January 1991 *Chain Reaction* upgraded its format to include a larger prize budget and a tournament of champions. The show was re-titled *The $40,000 Chain Reaction*, but the changes failed to lift the sagging ratings. *Chain Reaction's* cancellation on December 27, 1991, marked the end of Edwards's national television career. He remained with *Big Spin* for three more years and finally called it a career in late 1994.

"My Life Is My Hobby"

Now freed from his broadcasting chores, Edwards and his second wife Michael Feffer, whom he married in 1984, spent their time traveling. Edwards had always enjoyed traveling, but now had all the time he wanted to indulge in this pastime. In January 1996, Edwards was lured back to radio when he and his wife agreed to co-host *The Touring Company*, a weekly two hour travel show for station KPCC-FM in Pasadena, California. *The Touring Company* featured commentary by Edwards and his wife along with co-hosts Paul Lasley and Elizabeth Harryman about the many places they had visited around the world. Sometimes they hosted the show on location while traveling. After four years on KPCC, *The Touring Company* was syndicated nationally for one more season through Cypress Radio from Palm Springs and later Los Angeles. After the death of Cypress Radio founder Dan Moschetti, the company folded and *The Touring Company* left the air.

In 2000 Edwards became the travel editor for KION-AM in Monterrey, California. Rather than broadcasting his travel reports from a studio, Edwards hosted the weekly program from home using a Comrex broadcasting unit that relayed the program to the station. He also hosted a morning show for station KSUR for nine months during 2003.

In 2005 Edwards and his wife became traveling correspondents for KABC-AM in Los

Angeles. Even though he considers himself retired, he continues working. Today, Geoff Edwards enjoys a life of traveling and writing articles for magazines about his experiences. He does not miss the daily grind of broadcasting and is content with his travel reporting chores for radio, which do not take up much time. That leaves him with ample opportunities to spend time with his wife, children, and grandchildren.

GE:

   "My life is my hobby. I have so many different interests."

BOB EUBANKS

Birth Name: Robert Leland Eubanks

Born: January 8, 1938, in Flint, Michigan

Marriages and Family: Irma [surname unavailable] (1960–2002) (Deceased) 2 sons, 1 daughter; Debra [surname unavailable] (2003–Present) 1 son

Radio Career: Disc Jockey (KACY-AM, Oxnard, California) 1958–1960; Disc Jockey (KRLA-AM, Pasadena, California) 1960–1967; *Hesston Rodeo Commentary* (Syndicated) (1981–1983)

TV Career: HOST—*POP/Pickwick Dance Party* (KTLA-TV, Los Angeles, CA) February 1962–June 1962; *Hollywood Dance Time* (KTTV, Los Angeles, CA) April 13, 1963–September 7, 1963; *The Newlywed Game* (ABC Daytime) July 11, 1966–December 20, 1974, (ABC Primetime) January 7, 1967–August 30, 1971; *The Diamond Head Game* (Syndicated) January 6, 1975–September 1975; *Rhyme and Reason* (ABC Daytime) July 7, 1975–July 9, 1976; *Tournament of Roses Parade* (KTLA-TV, Los Angeles, CA) January 1, 1976–Present; *The Newlywed Game* (Syndicated) September 5, 1977–September 1980; *Hollywood Christmas Parade* (KTLA-TV, Los Angeles, CA) Nov. 1977–Nov.

Bob Eubanks (Bob Eubanks, courtesy Fred Wostbrock)

1997; *All Star Secrets* (NBC Daytime) January 8, 1979–August 10, 1979; *Dollar a Second* (Unsold Game Show Pilot) 1981; *Atlantic City Alive* (TBS) July 5, 1981–September 1982; *Dream House* (NBC Daytime) April 4, 1983–June 29, 1984; *Trivia Trap* (ABC Daytime) October 8, 1984–April 5, 1985; *The New Newlywed Game* (Syndicated) September 16, 1985–December 9, 1988; *Card Sharks* (CBS Daytime) January 6, 1986–March 31, 1989; *Celebrity Secrets* (Unsold Game Show Pilot) 1988; *The Name Game* (Unsold ABC Game Show Pilot) 1989; *Gambit* (Unsold ABC Game Show Pilot) 1990; *Infatuation* (Syndicated) September 14, 1992–September 1993; *Family Secrets* (NBC Daytime) March 15, 1993–June 11, 1993; *Prime Time Country* (TNN Primetime) April 22, 1996–May 3, 1996; *The Newlywed Game* (Syndicated) September 8, 1997–September 1999; *Powerball: The Game Show* (State Lottery Game) October 7, 2000–Sept. 28, 2002 EXECUTIVE PRODUCER—*The Captain & Tennille* (ABC Primetime) September 20, 1976–March 14, 1977; *All Star Secrets* (NBC Daytime) January 8, 1979–August 10, 1979; *The Guinness Game* (Syndicated) September 17, 1979–September 1980; *You Bet Your Life* (Syndicated) September 8, 1980–September 1981; *The Toni Tennille Show* (Syndicated) 1980–1981

Theatrical Movies: *Out of Sight* (1966); *Roger and Me* (1989); *Payback* (1990) (Producer); *Home Alone 2: Lost in New York* (1992); *Forced to Kill* (1993) (Producer)

Business Interests: The Cinnamon Cinder Young Adult Clubs (1962–1967); Prestige Promotions (Music Promotion Company) (1965–1967); Concert Associates (Music Promotion Company) (1967–1968); Owner & Operator, Calabasas Saddlery (1968–1969); Concert Express (Music Promotion Company) (1972–1982); Partner with Michael Hill: Hill-Eubanks Group (1976–1982); *The $25,000 Game Show* (Live Game Show) (1994–1998); Motivational Speaker, Bob Eubanks Enterprises (1999–Present); Spokesman, NeWave (2004–Present)

Book: *It's in the Book, Bob!* (2004)

Other Careers: Assembly Line Worker: Lockheed Aircraft, Burbank, Ca. (1956); Usher/Doorman: Egyptian Theatre, Hollywood, Ca. (1956–1958)

"Where is the weirdest place that you had the urge to make whoopee?" There is only one place in all of television where that question could be heard. Give yourself 25 points if you guessed *The Newlywed Game*. Through four decades, *The Newlywed Game* and its host, Bob Eubanks, have been as synonymous as bread and butter. Although Eubanks hosted a number of game shows in his 40 year career, he is so closely identified with *The Newlywed Game* that many viewers either forget or are not aware that Eubanks has been a radio disc jockey, concert producer, manager, movie and television producer, businessman, motivational speaker, and a cowboy all rolled into one.

Robert Leland Eubanks first saw light on January 8, 1938, in Flint, Michigan, as the only child of John Eubanks and Gertrude McClure. In Michigan, Eubanks' father worked as a barber, but in 1939 he moved the family to California to work at an aircraft plant. As a child, Eubanks enjoyed roller skating. He practiced through his teenage years and won fourth place in the National Championships in Melrose Park, Illinois in 1956.

Urged by his mother to get into show business, Eubanks appeared as a model for the J.C. Penny catalogue advertisements at the age of ten. He also appeared in a print advertisement with Gene Autry for one of Autry's clothing companies. Along with his interests in skating and show business, Eubanks developed a love for horses and enjoyed horseback riding. Upon graduation from Pasadena High School in 1955, Eubanks studied broadcasting at Pasadena City College. To help pay for his college costs, Eubanks worked at Lockheed Aircraft in Burbank, California, assembling radar racks.

Never Looked Back

He quickly discovered that mechanical work was not for him and spent two miserable days learning the ropes. According to Eubanks' autobiography, *It's in the Book, Bob!* on the morning of his third day at work, a man collapsed and died from a heart attack right in front of him. That was it for Eubanks and he promptly quit. Following his show business ambitions, Eubanks worked as an usher and doorman at the Egyptian Theatre in Hollywood opening limo doors for movie and television stars. Disenchanted with Pasadena City College, Eubanks switched to a nine month program of study at the Don Martin School of Broadcasting.

He finally got his start in radio in 1958 when he was hired as a disc jockey for KACY-AM in Oxnard, California. Eubanks enrolled in California State University at Northridge to study Broadcasting, but dropped out after moving to the larger rock and roll radio station KRLA-AM in 1960.

Bob Eubanks (September 2004 telephone interview):
"I was working at the number one rock and roll station in Los Angeles at the time. I was making too much money to continue in college. I was majoring in radio and [working] in radio so it didn't make any sense."

A Powerful Station

At KRLA, he worked the unenviable overnight shift, but later moved to mornings and from there to a 6–9 p.m. shift. Gradually Eubanks became one of the most popular disc jockeys on California radio during the 1960s.

> *BE:*
>
> "We didn't know how powerful we were because there were only two rock and roll stations in southern California. We didn't really have any idea of the strength of the station as you look back on it now."

Capitalizing on the popularity of rock and roll music with the younger generation, Eubanks launched a series of young adult nightclubs called The Cinnamon Cinder. For entertainment at the clubs, Eubanks booked such acts as The Beach Boys, The Righteous Brothers, Ike and Tina Turner, and Stevie Wonder. In 1962 Eubanks moved to television when he took over from Wink Martindale as host of *POP Dance Party* on KTLA in Los Angeles.

POP Dance Party originated from the Pacific Ocean Park in Santa Monica and like *American Bandstand*, the show featured big-name and up-and-coming music stars. The show later moved to the Pickwick Recreation Center in Burbank and was renamed *Pickwick Dance Party*. Never very comfortable working on this show, Eubanks was fired after four months. In 1963 he tried again, with more success, on *Hollywood Dance Time* for KTTV in Los Angeles.

Concert Promoter

Eubanks' success with music in radio and television primed him for one of the most unforgettable experiences of his life. On February 9, 1964, Eubanks was one of millions of viewers who saw the Beatles as they made their American television debut on *The Ed Sullivan Show*. Eubanks was so taken with the group's popularity with the teenagers that he decided to figure out a way to bring them to Los Angeles for a concert. To get the necessary money for luring the group into town, Eubanks tried to get a loan, but was turned down by several banks. Putting everything on the line, he mortgaged his recently purchased Hidden Hills, California, house for $25,000. If the Beatles concert was a flop, Eubanks stood to lose his home.

Any worries of a Beatles concert failing were unfounded. The concert took place at the Hollywood Bowl on August 23, 1964, playing to a sold-out audience of 18,000 people. The Beatles netted $58,000 for their 30 minute concert while Eubanks paid off his mortgage and saved his home, but only made a $1,000 profit. Despite the meager income, Eubanks formed Prestige Promotions to produce concerts for rock groups and handle public relations demands. Through the 1960s, Eubanks worked with The Rolling Stones, Bob Dylan, the Supremes, and the Who. By the late 1960s, he was managing the careers of Dolly Parton, Barbara Mandrell, and the Lennon Sisters.

Here Come the Newlyweds

Life for Eubanks was going well. By the time he was 28 years old in 1966, he was one of the most popular disc jockeys on Los Angeles radio and had rubbed elbows with some of the biggest names in the music world. When he won the hosting job for ABC's *The Newlywed Game* that year, he had no idea that he was about to embark on a career as a game show host for the next four decades. *The Newlywed Game*, which was created by Nick Nicholson and Roger Muir and produced by Chuck Barris Productions, featured four couples who had been married less than two years.

The couples were asked a series of questions to see how much they really knew about each other. In the first round, the wives were secluded backstage while the men were asked three questions about their wives. The wives then returned to the stage and tried to match their husbands' answers. Each match scored five points for the team. In round two, the husbands left the stage

Bob Eubanks makes his entrance during an early episode of *The Newlywed Game* **(Bob Eubanks, courtesy Fred Wostbrock).**

while the wives answered questions about their mates. Matching answers in this round earned 10 points for the teams. The final question of the day was worth 25 points. The couple with the most points won the game and a prize "selected especially for you," as Eubanks always reminded his contestants.

The Newlywed Game was not your typical game show. The questions were mostly of the double-entendre variety and designed to embarrass the contestants. Typical questions were "Where is your husband clumsiest: the restaurant, the dance floor, or the bedroom?" "If your wife were a car, what would need to be repaired most, her fenders or transmission?" "When it comes to making whoopee, would your husband say that he has what it takes or it takes everything he's got?" The only serious questions asked on the show were the 25 point bonus questions which gave couples who were trailing in the game one last chance to catch up for the win.

A Winner from the Start

The day *The Newlywed Game* premiered on July 11, 1966, was fortuitous. It aired at 2:00 p.m. against two popular shows: the game show *Password* on CBS and the NBC soap opera *Days of Our Lives*. However, on that July 11, CBS and NBC pre-empted their regular programs at 2:00 p.m. to air an address from the United States Secretary of Defense Robert McNamara concerning Vietnam. ABC elected to run *The Newlywed Game* instead of the address so the program drew a large audience right from the starting gate. A few months into the run, *The Newlywed Game* topped *Password* in the ratings and knocked the long-running show off the air in 1967.

Eubanks got off to a terrible start as the host. He recalled in *It's in the Book, Bob!* that during the first episode, he was so nervous that he went the entire half hour without blinking his eyes. After nearly two weeks on the show, he was still having problems adjusting to his role, and producer Chuck Barris considered replacing him. But suddenly one day, Eubanks finally hit his stride and became a seasoned host.

By his second year on *The Newlywed Game* in 1967, Eubanks had given up his radio chores at KRLA and closed the Cinnamon Cinder nightclubs. His love of horses and western-related activities led him to open Calabasas Saddlery, a store selling western products in Calabasas, California. He soon grew restless with retail business and, after racking up a $40,000 debt, sold the store in 1969. Eubanks had also grown weary of the music world so he sold his share of Concert Associates and temporarily left the concert business.

Back in Music/Game Over

Since *The Newlywed Game* only taped 35 days per year, Eubanks had plenty of time to pursue other interests. After spending three years working his newly purchased ranch in Santa Ynez, California, Eubanks was itching to get back into music promotions and management. Shifting his focus to country music, he launched Concert Express and produced concerts for Merle Haggard, George Jones, Tammy Wynette, and Marty Robbins.

During 1974 the ratings for *The Newlywed Game* dropped to the point of no return. Eubanks blamed the show's demise on the Watergate scandal and low marriage rates. On December 20, 1974, an emotional Eubanks presided over *The Newlywed Game* for the last time on ABC. On the final episode, four couples who had previously appeared on the show played for charity.

Off to Hawaii

Two weeks later, Eubanks was back with *The Diamond Head Game.* Taped on the beach near the Kuilima Hotel in Oahu, Hawaii, the show had two major hooks to attract the viewers: the beautiful outdoor scenery and the large glass booth called "Diamond Head." The booth contained a wind machine that blew around dollar bills of various denominations and slips of paper with prizes written on them. Contestants played a series of question and answer rounds and the winner entered "Diamond Head." The player was given 15 seconds to stuff a treasure bag full of money and prizes.

Eubanks pulled up to 10 bills out of the bag one at a time. Any money and prizes pulled from the bag was awarded to the contestant unless a $1 bill was drawn which meant that all winnings were lost. The pleasant Hawaiian scenery and the unique bonus round were not enough to entice the viewers and the show was pulled from syndication in September 1975.

> *BE:*
> "Just because God is your set designer doesn't mean that you have a hit show. The format was pretty weak."

Rhyme Time

Eubanks moved on to *Rhyme and Reason*, a game involving open-ended rhyming couplets. Players secretly filled in the blanks with rhyming words and tried to guess which of the six celebrity panelists used the same rhyming words. For each match, the contestant scored points and the winner played a bonus round for $5,000. *Rhyme and Reason* left the air in July 1976 after one season. On the last episode, celebrity guests Charlie Brill, Pat Harrington, Jr., Mitzi McCall, and Jaye P. Morgan surprised Eubanks and the viewers by destroying the show's set. They pulled up the carpet, broke lights, and knocked down Eubanks' podium.

Urban Legend

The fall of 1977 brought Eubanks back in front of the camera to host *The Newlywed Game* for three years in syndication. It was on this version of *The Newlywed Game* that Eubanks asked the infamous question, "Where is the weirdest place that you had the urge to make whoopee?" The contestant replied, "In the a**." The answer was bleeped but the episode aired in 1977.

For years the incident became an urban legend and Eubanks repeatedly denied that it ever happened. The episode was never seen on television again until the clip aired on an NBC game show bloopers special in 2002. How could Eubanks forget such an incident? He noted in *It's in the Book, Bob!* that after hosting shows for nearly 40 years, everything tends to "blur together."

Hill-Eubanks Group

Eubanks and his business partner Michael Hill formed Hill-Eubanks Group to develop new game shows. None came to fruition until January 1979 when they finally scored a hole-in-one with *All Star Secrets* for NBC. Eubanks doubled as the host and co-executive producer. *All Star Secrets* was a game of celebrity gossip. A secret was read about one of the five celebrities playing the game. The contestants guessed which celebrity was the holder of that secret. *All Star Secrets* left the air after seven months.

During the 1979-1980 season, Hill and Eubanks produced *The Guinness Game* with Don Galloway as host. Each week, *The Guinness Game* presented four attempts to break a world's record in some fashion. If successful, the record breakers were included in the Guinness Book of World Records. A revival of *You Bet Your Life* with comedian Buddy Hackett as host followed during the 1980-1981 season. Another project was a daily syndicated talk show hosted by singer Toni Tennille. By the fall of 1981, Hill and Eubanks had no shows on the air and the company folded.

Keeping Up Appearances

Eubanks then took the reigns of *Atlantic City Alive*, a low-budget weekly variety series for the TBS superstation in July 1981. He commuted from Los Angeles each weekend to Atlantic City, New Jersey, where the show aired on Sundays. Eubanks also flew to shopping malls around the country staging non-televised versions of *The Newlywed Game*. He had begun making the rounds of malls after the syndicated version of the show left the air in 1980. Over a seven year period, Eubanks staged approximately 300 shows to the delight of shoppers across the nation.

Eubanks also did radio and television Rodeo commentary for the syndicated Hesston Rodeo Series. During his long run as a game show host through the 1970s, Eubanks had continued working as a concert promoter and manager, but by 1982 had burned out dealing with the big egos of the music stars and the financial demands of the industry. The constant travel for his work was wrecking his marriage and keeping him away from his children. He left the music business permanently and never looked back.

Dreaming of Success

A pair of short-lived game shows, *Dream House* and *Trivia Trap*, returned Eubanks to the spotlight in the mid 1980s. He cited these shows as two of the weakest ones in his career. *Dream House*, which premiered on NBC in April 1983, featured two married couples competing in question and answer rounds for the right to win a house. Couples received furniture for each game they won and played a bonus round for their "dream house." To win the house, the couple guessed a three digit combination that opened the golden doors on the stage.

Midway through *Dream House's* run, the rules were changed.

> **Richard Reid (Dream House *executive producer, June 2006 telephone interview):***
> "When I came to everybody and said, 'Here's how we're going to do it,' Bob said, 'I don't see how that's going to work.' He said, 'I'll do it,' but the unspoken part was, 'You don't know what you're talking about.' We started to do the new stuff and to his surprise it was working. We went to a commercial break and he was talking to the writers going over something. I was sitting in the audience and he said, 'Hey Richard that was pretty good. It worked like a charm.' From that time on we had a terrific relationship."

The rule changes came too late as *Dream House* left the air in June 1984.

Bob Eubanks:
"We had so much trouble giving a house away. We gave away a ton of furniture. It should have been called 'Dream Furniture.'"

Caught in a Trap

His next game show, *Trivia Trap* for Mark Goodson Productions, was even less successful. *Trivia Trap* pitted two teams of three players in a fast-paced game of trivia questions. The unique aspect of this show was the first round where the teams viewed two rows of four answers. The team in control selected a group of answers and Eubanks read the question. The players had to eliminate all of the wrong answers leaving the one correct answer on the board. If someone cut the correct answer, they hit the "Trivia Trap" and lost control to the opposing team.

BE:
"I thought *Trivia Trap* had a format flaw."

The flaw, in his opinion, was the very hook that made the show different. He pointed out that if the audience knew the correct answer after seeing the four selections, eliminating the three wrong answers to get to the right one was a waste of time.

BE:
"Mark Goodson didn't agree with us. The whole staff tried to tell him but he couldn't buy it."

Two months into *Trivia Trap's* run, Goodson had a focus group from the American Film Institute examine the show. When the group reached the same conclusion about the format flaw, Goodson altered the game to having contestants simply pick the correct answer from four possible choices on each question. *Trivia Trap* left the air after six months on ABC.

A Winner Again

In the fall of 1985, Eubanks entered a career renaissance when he returned to front *The New Newlywed Game* for syndication. Armed with a flashier set, an updated recording of the original theme song, and racier questions, *The New Newlywed Game* became a hit. In January 1986 he popped up on CBS to host a revival of *Card Sharks*, a popular late 1970s game show once hosted by Jim Perry.

In December 1988 Eubanks and his former partner Michael Hill sold the game *Celebrity Secrets* for syndication. With *The New Newlywed Game* sliding in the ratings, Eubanks exited the show. He was replaced by comedian Paul Rodriguez for the remainder of that season. Meanwhile, Casablanca IV, the syndicating company for *Celebrity Secrets*, suddenly went out of business and the show was left without any distribution. Unable to find another distributor, *Celebrity Secrets* died before production commenced. Eubanks was dealt another blow when *Card Sharks* was canceled by CBS in March 1989.

A TV Drought

In the summer of 1989, Eubanks was one of six people considered to host the daytime version of *Wheel of Fortune* when it moved from NBC to CBS. The network auditioned Eubanks, John Davidson, Pat Finn, Bob Goen, Chuck Henry, and Marc Summers before settling on Goen as the new host.

In the early 1990s Eubanks hosted two pilots, *The Name Game* and *Gambit*, but neither became a series. He then turned to movie work producing the 1990 action movie *Payback* and the 1993 release *Forced to Kill*, both of which starred his son, movie and television stuntman Corey Eubanks. While Bob Eubanks stayed away from the cameras in these movies, he appeared in the 1992 release *Home Alone 2: Lost in New York*.

Infatuated

After a three year absence, Eubanks returned to television in September 1992 with *Infatuation*, a new relationship-oriented game show. Michael Hill got the idea for the show after watching an episode of *Sally Jessy Raphael* where the guests had a secret crush on someone and confided it to the person on national television.

Hill took the idea to Eubanks and they crafted a game show where contestants told their stories about a secret crush. The object of their affection was brought out and the enamored contestant made a plea to win over their secret crush. Coming at a time when relationship-oriented game shows like *Love Connection* and *Studs* were at their peak, *Infatuation* seemed a natural addition to the growing trend. Instead, the show was canceled after one season.

Family Secrets

In a drastic departure from *Infatuation*, Eubanks turned up in an NBC game show in March 1993 called *Family Secrets*. Promoted as a wholesome family show, *Family Secrets* pitted two teams composed of a father, mother, and a child between the ages of 9–12. Played in a similar fashion to *The Newlywed Game*, Eubanks asked the family members questions to see how much they much they knew about each other. The difference was that the questions on *Family Secrets* contained none of the sexual innuendo that dominated *The Newlywed Game*. NBC hoped that *Family Secrets* would help revive its sagging daytime schedule, but the wholesome concept faded after 12 weeks.

During its brief run, *Family Secrets* was the subject of controversy when one team competing on the show turned out not to be a real family. Identifying themselves as the Hansen family, the team actually consisted of a father, his 10-year-old daughter, and his live-in girlfriend posing as the daughter's mother. According to a May 1993 *Chicago Tribune* story, the team won $6,000 in prizes, but the girl's real mother discovered the deception. She called NBC and Dave Bell Associates, the packagers of *Family Secrets*, to get the episode pulled before its May 27, 1993, air date. Officials at both companies agreed, so the episode was pulled and replaced with a rerun. Ironically, the father and his girlfriend married on June 11, 1993, the same day that *Family Secrets* left the air.

Going for $25,000

In the fall of 1993, Eubanks and Michael Hill developed *The $25,000 Game Show*, a non-televised project combining the formats of different games. *The $25,000 Game Show* opened on March 31, 1994, from the Moe Bandy Americana Theatre in Branson, Missouri. Each day, 42 contestants selected from the audience competed in a series of games with the winner going for the cash jackpot. Eubanks hosted most of the daily shows, but also hired fellow emcees Dennis James, Jim Lange, and Peter Marshall along with actors Jamie Farr and Dick Van Patten to substitute for him on occasion.

Nashville, Newlyweds, and Powerball

In April 1996 Eubanks moved back before the television cameras as substitute host on The Nashville Network variety series *Prime Time Country*. Eubanks was one of many substitute hosts seen during the spring and summer of 1996 while the producers sought a permanent emcee. Ultimately, the job went to Gary Chapman, the onetime husband of singer Amy Grant.

In 1997 Eubanks returned to host *The Newlywed Game* for two additional seasons. Then in the fall of 2000 he hosted *Powerball: The Game Show*, a state lottery program seen on select stations around the country. The show originated from Los Angeles, but when it moved to Las Vegas in September 2002, Eubanks withdrew from the show to pursue a different career.

Speaking Out

Eubanks embarked on a new chapter in 1999 when he became a motivational speaker. Aiming specifically at the corporate world, Eubanks travels the country offering workshops on bet-

Play your cards right and Bob Eubanks could reward you with a new car on *Card Sharks* (Bob Eubanks, courtesy Fred Wostbrock).

ter communication skills in the workplace. His presentations include anecdotes of his years in show business, video clips of *Newlywed Game* segments, and tips on how to improve communication between co-workers. As part of his presentation, Eubanks chooses people in his audience to play *The Not So Newlywed Game*.

On May 22, 2002, Eubanks along with Jim Lange, Peter Marshall, Wink Martindale, and Ben Stein hosted a primetime special for NBC called *Most Outrageous Game Show Moments*. The show was so well received that NBC ordered four more specials that aired between February and May 2003. Eubanks hosted the second and third episodes solo, but was joined by Chuck Woolery as co-host for the final two shows. As a testament to the wide appeal of game shows, the five specials were rerun on NBC during the 2003-2004 season and later on VH-1 and Game Show Network.

When he is not working, Eubanks spends his time at his Peppertree Ranch in Santa Ynez, California. Eubanks purchased 20 acres of the ranch in 1970 for his family and two years later added another 26 acres to the property. The spread of his ranch enabled him and his family to raise horses and work the land. One of Eubanks' favorite hobbies is horseback riding and roping cattle. He has been a member of the Professional Rodeo Cowboy's Association for more than 35 years and has competed in many rodeos. One year he won the buckle at the Hall of Champions in Colorado.

Peppertree Art

In 1976 Eubanks' wife Irma, an avid art buff, got the idea to host an art show at their Peppertree Ranch. At first the family was not too receptive of the idea according to a 2004 *Santa Ynez Valley Magazine* story. With the family's eventual support, Irma had the barn on the ranch renovated into an art gallery and invited artists to display their paintings and wood carvings.

Since it began in 1976, the Peppertree Art Show has thrived with people coming to Eubanks' Santa Ynez ranch to purchase works of art. The show originally took place twice a year in May and November until Irma's health declined in the mid 1990s. She reluctantly cut the show back to once a year in 1998, but lost her battle to cancer in 2002.

After some discussion, Eubanks and his son Trace decided to continue the project. Since Trace had worked with his mother on the show from its beginnings, he had developed an eye for spotting good art. Using a hand-built lighting system, the art work is displayed with care. With Trace working full time on the project, the art show has returned to its twice-a-year schedule. Bob handles the promotions, the business accounts, and keeps the barn in shape.

Just a Good Ol' Cowboy

Now with ample time to share with his family, Eubanks spends time with his second wife Debbie and their young son Noah, who was born in 2004. Eubanks also devotes much time to his sons Trace and Corey, his daughter Theresa, and his five grandchildren. In October 2004, his autobiography, *It's in the Book, Bob!* was published by Benbella Books. With his work as a motivational speaker, the Peppertree Art Show, the occasional television appearances, and raising a new family, Bob Eubanks is busier than ever and has no plans to retire.

With an enormous resume listing his occupations as a game show host, radio announcer, music promoter and manager, and professional speaker, Eubanks is happy to consider himself just a good old cowboy. He put it best in the last line of his autobiography by noting that he was "born a cowboy" and would "die a cowboy."

ART FLEMING

Birth Name: Arthur Fleming Fazzin
Born: May 1, 1924, in New York, New York
Died: April 25, 1995, in Crystal River, Florida
Marriages and Family: Peggy Ann Ellis (1947–1971) (Divorced) 1 son, 1 daughter; Rebecca Lynn (July 4, 1977–April 25, 1995)
Military Service: Air Corps, United States Navy (1941–1945)
Radio Career: Disc Jockey (WEED-AM, Rocky Mount, NC) 1945–1947; Disc Jockey (WPTF-AM, Raleigh, NC) 1947–1948; Disc Jockey (WAKR-AM, Akron, OH) 1948–1950; Staff Announcer (ABC Network) 1950–1954; *The College Bowl* (CBS) October 1979–September 1982; Announcer (KMOX-AM, St. Louis, MO) 1980–1992; *When Radio Was* (Syndicated) January 1990–April 1995
TV Career: ACTOR—*Man Against Crime* (NBC Primetime) 1953–1954; *The Californians* (NBC Primetime) September 1958–August 27, 1959; *International Detective* (Syndicated) September 1959–September 1960   HOST—*Doctor I.Q.* (ABC Primetime) November 4, 1953–October 17, 1954; News Anchor, WNBC-TV, New York, NY (1961–1963); *Jeopardy!* (NBC Daytime) March 30, 1964–January 3, 1975, (Syndicated) September 9, 1974–September 7, 1975; *The All-New Jeopardy!* (NBC Daytime) October 2, 1978–March 2, 1979; *The National Science Test* (PBS) October 1984–October 1987; *Biff America* (Buffalo Flats, Colorado) 1988–1989; *Senior America* (Florida Regional) September 1994–April 1995

Theatrical Movies: *The Last Outpost* (1951); *The Prime Time* (1960); *A Hatful of Rain* (1961); *MacArthur* (1977); *Airplane II: The Sequel* (1982); *Twilight Zone* (1983); Plus 42 additional movies

Book: *Art Fleming's TV Game Show Fact Book* (1979)

Other Careers: Assistant Manager, Roxy Theater, New York City (1937–1941); State Ambassador, Pennsylvania Lottery; Television Stuntman (1954–1958)

Art Fleming (Art Fleming, courtesy Fred Wostbrock)

The answer is, "He presided over TV's first answer and question game show," (note that we said "answer and question," not "question and answer"). The question is, "Who is Art Fleming?" For 12 years and nearly 3,000 episodes, Art Fleming hosted a unique concept in game shows. That show was *Jeopardy*, which has remained a bonafide hit with a new generation of viewers under host Alex Trebek. But who is this man Art Fleming? Many people who are too young to remember or were not yet born do not know about the man who started *Jeopardy!*

Born as Arthur Fleming Fazzin on May 1, 1924, in New York City, Fleming was first of two children of William Guy and Marie Volk Fazzin. His parents were a European dance team who moved from Austria to New York City hoping to capture American audiences. They gave up their dancing careers when Arthur was born.

Following in his parents' footsteps, Arthur made his stage debut in a Broadway musical at the age of four. A stint as assistant manager of the Roxy Theater in New York City during his high school years helped nurture his growing interest in show business. His younger sister, Marie, caught the acting bug as well. She appeared on the Broadway stage under the name Marie Foster.

Fleming enlisted in the United States Navy the day after Pearl Harbor was attacked in December 1941. He was assigned to the Navy's V-5 program and sent to Colgate University where he played football. He later transferred to Cornell University and graduated with a Bachelor of Science degree in 1944. He finished his Navy hitch piloting a PBY patrol bomber in the South Atlantic searching for U-boats.

A Mixed Bag Career

Following his discharge in 1945, Fleming took a job as the early-morning disc jockey for WEED-AM in Rocky Mount, North Carolina. He later moved to WPTF-AM in Raleigh, North Carolina in 1947. While hosting the station's *Saturday Night Dance Party*, he met Peggy Ann Ellis, one of the show's singers. They later married and had a son and a daughter. In 1948 Fleming moved to Akron, Ohio, to work for the larger station WAKR-AM. Finally in 1950 ABC hired Fleming as a staff announcer for both its radio and television divisions. He became the first announcer for the R.J. Reynolds Tobacco Company to voice the popular slogan, "Winston tastes good like a cigarette should."

In 1953 he became one of the five roving announcers for the ABC primetime quiz show *Doctor I.Q.* The announcers walked around the audience with microphones looking for potential contestants. When one of them found a willing participant they might tell the host Jay Owen (later James McClain), "I have a lady in the balcony Doctor!" The "doctor" asked questions of the players and winners were paid with silver dollars.

While working on *Doctor I.Q.*, Fleming appeared as Ralph Bellamy's stunt man in the NBC drama series *Man Against Crime*. For the next three years, Fleming worked as a stunt man on a variety of TV shows until he joined the cast of the NBC western *The Californians* in 1958 playing lawyer Jeremy Pitt. Following its cancellation in 1959, Fleming won the starring role as Detective Ken Franklin on the syndicated series *International Detective*. The show was based on actual files of the William J. Burns Agency and filmed in England.

According to *TV Guide* in 1974, Fleming lived in England during the show's one year in production and became interested in British military history. He started a collection of English relics consisting of swords, medals, regimental histories, a flint-and-lighter set made of cannonballs from the Battle of Balaclava, and even a tin of mummified chocolates that Queen Victoria gave to her troops. Television producer Bob Rubin, who worked with Fleming on *Jeopardy*, told *TV Guide* in 1974 that he believed if Fleming could be reincarnated, he would come back as a Victorian England lancer.

What's the Question?

After *International Detective* stopped production in 1960, Fleming returned to the United States where he resumed an undistinguished movie career with minor roles in *Prime Time* and *A Hatful of Rain*. He also anchored the eleven o'clock news for WNBC-TV in New York and appeared in commercials. In early 1963 when Merv Griffin was developing a new television game show for NBC called *What's the Question?* he spotted Fleming in a TWA commercial.

When Fleming's agent told him that Griffin wanted to meet with him about hosting the show, Fleming was reluctant. A meeting with Griffin and a run-through of the game changed his mind, however. After months of work, Griffin changed the show's title to the catchier name *Jeopardy!* Fleming beat out two other competitors for the job and *Jeopardy!* moved to NBC daytime on March 30, 1964.

This Is Jeopardy!

The show's format was different from any other game show in history. The game could be summarized in one sentence: we give you the answers and you give us the questions. Three contestants faced a board containing thirty squares. There were six different categories with five answers in each row. In the first round, the dollar amounts for the answers ranged from $10 to $50. The questions increased in difficulty with higher dollar amounts. One contestant chose a category (example: State Capitals) and a dollar amount. Then the answer was revealed (example: Atlanta). The first player to buzz in received the chance to guess the correct question that corresponded to the answer (in our example, the question would be, "What is the capital of Georgia?").

All guesses had to be phrased in the form of a question or the contestants did not win the money. The player who guessed the correct question won the corresponding dollar amount and selected the next clue from the board. If the contestant answered incorrectly, the dollar amount was deducted from their score. Players often found themselves with negative scores if they continually missed questions. A player kept control of the board until another contestant buzzed in with the correct question.

Round two was called "Double Jeopardy" and the dollar amounts ranged from $20 to $100. Six new categories were revealed and the questions increased in difficulty in this round. At the end of the "Double Jeopardy" round all three contestants participated in "Final Jeopardy" where they wagered any part of their winnings on one last question. If any of the three players ended with a negative score at the end of the "Double Jeopardy" round, they could not play "Final Jeopardy" since they had no money with which to bet. When the "Final Jeopardy" clue was revealed, the contestants had thirty seconds to write down their response. The player with the most money won the game and the right to return and face two new challengers on the next program. The other two players kept their winnings (if any) and left the show.

Viewers Put Their Lives in Jeopardy!

Jeopardy! was an instant hit with its unusual, fast-paced format. Fleming finally became a household name. In 1965 *Jeopardy!* moved to 12:00 p.m. where it remained a fixture for the next decade. The game was particularly a hit with college students because of its convenient midday time slot. Many college students cut classes and high school students came home during their lunch periods to see the show.

Jeopardy! was more than just a popular quiz show. On one occasion, the show was indirectly responsible for saving one viewer's memory. In his book *Art Fleming's TV Game Show Fact Book*, Fleming stated that he received a letter from a cadet at the United States Military Academy who had seriously injured himself when he fell headfirst onto a cement floor. After a long surgery, the man's life was saved, but he had lost his memory.

Several months later while a nurse was wheeling the cadet along the hospital corridor, the man heard the audio portion of *Jeopardy!* coming from a television in one of the rooms on the hall. When the man suddenly answered one of the questions out loud, the nurse rushed the patient back to his doctor. Upon hearing what had happened, the doctor gave the young cadet a prescription: a daily dose of *Jeopardy!*

Game show hosts Art James, Bill Cullen, and Peter Marshall join Fleming for a special *Jeopardy!* anniversary show (Art Fleming, courtesy Fred Wostbrock).

The cadet spent the next six months watching the show every day and slowly, he began answering more questions correctly. Even more important was that he began to recall events from his own past. The man completely recovered and returned to the academy in time to start his fourth year as a cadet.

It Can't Last Forever

Jeopardy! remained a popular lunchtime favorite with viewers until NBC moved the show to 10:30 a.m. in January 1974. According to Maxine Fabe's 1979 book *TV Game Shows*, the ratings at noon had decreased slightly from a 33 share (33 percent of the audience) to a 29 share. At the time, *Jeopardy!* ran against CBS's *The Young and the Restless* and the long-running *Password* on ABC.

Meanwhile at 10:30 a.m., the show's ratings dropped from a 29 to a 22 share during the spring of 1974, although it still managed to hold its own. Another time change to 1:30 p.m. in July 1974 put *Jeopardy!* against ABC's *Let's Make a Deal* and the top-rated *As the World Turns* on CBS. The ratings dropped to a 12 share during the fall of 1974.

To jazz up the show, a weekly syndicated version was offered to local stations in September 1974. The show retained the format from the NBC version with a bonus round added after the "Final Jeopardy" round. The winning contestant chose one of 25 squares and won the prize concealed behind it. One square contained a $25,000 jackpot. The game's set was updated with flashing lights and Fleming began wearing gaudy-looking tuxedos.

These efforts were all in vain. *Jeopardy!* still had another year left on its contract, but its creator, Merv Griffin, had developed a new game show called *Wheel of Fortune* for NBC. The network made a deal with Griffin that *Wheel of Fortune* could go on the air if NBC could buy out the remaining year on *Jeopardy's* contract. With this deal secured, the daytime version left NBC on January 3, 1975, after an impressive 11 year run. The syndicated version remained until September 1975.

Think Positive

Fleming returned to acting with an appearance in the 1977 movie *MacArthur*. Some years after his first marriage ended in divorce, Fleming met Rebecca Lynn and married her just three weeks after their first date. The couple married on July 4, 1977, at the estate of Dr. Norman Vincent Peale. Fleming, who was a deacon at Peale's Marble Collegiate Church in New York, was a devout believer in Peale's optimistic approach to life.

One of Fleming's characteristics was his unflappable positive attitude. A genuine and openly sentimental man with a chivalrous heart, he told *TV Guide* in 1974 that people everywhere were too uptight and that life was too short to dwell on the negative. Fleming knew that life could be difficult (he had gone through a divorce in the early 1970s), but he pointed out that the best way to deal with the punches was to roll with them. In the same manner, Fleming's positive attitude carried him through the loss of *Jeopardy!* as he stayed busy with a number of projects.

An All New Experience

On June 3, 1978, Fleming hosted a televised special of the quiz show *College Bowl*. Teams representing various colleges and universities competed in a game of general knowledge questions. *College Bowl* aired from 1959 to 1970 with Allen Ludden, and later Robert Earle, as host. The 1978 syndicated special, which originated from Miami Beach, Florida, featured students representing Yale, Oberlin, Stanford, and Cornell (which was Fleming's alma mater).

A few months later, Fleming was called to host a revival of *Jeopardy!* for NBC. Sporting a brand new set and a new taping location in Los Angeles, *The All-New Jeopardy!* premiered on October 2, 1978, with several changes in the game. After the first round, the low-scoring contestant was eliminated and only two contestants played the "Double Jeopardy" round. The low-scoring player at the end of round two moved on to "Final Jeopardy" where they attempted to answer five questions in a row for a jackpot of $5,000.

Slotted at 10:30 a.m. against *The Price Is Right*, it lagged in the ratings. In January 1979 it was moved to 12:00 p.m. (its original time slot in the early 1970s). *The All-New Jeopardy!* competed for the second time against *The Young and the Restless* on CBS. Predictably, the show failed to draw an audience, and left the air again on March 2, 1979. In all Fleming hosted 2,858 episodes of *Jeopardy!* and he never missed a show.

Off to College Bowl

Fleming returned to the airwaves in October 1979 hosting a new version of *College Bowl* for the CBS radio network. This was an unusual move since quiz shows had long since disappeared from radio. *College Bowl* traveled to different college campuses around the country taping the games for later airing during its three year run.

> **Richard Reid (College Bowl** *producer: June 2006 telephone interview):*
> "Art was as beloved as any host I've ever worked with. Wherever we went with *College Bowl*, people were dying to talk to him. [The college students] just couldn't get enough of him and they had profound respect for him. Wherever we went, they wanted to talk to him about *Jeopardy!* He didn't want to talk about *Jeopardy!* because he kept saying, 'I'm doing *College Bowl* now. I did *Jeopardy!* and it was terrific, but I'm here to do *College Bowl*. Let's talk about that.' [The students] couldn't get away from asking him questions about *Jeopardy!*"

Meet Me in St. Louis

In 1980 Fleming and his wife moved to St. Louis where they lived for the next 12 years. There he hosted a two-hour morning talk show for KMOX-AM. Two more movie appearances followed with the first coming in 1982's *Airplane II: The Sequel*, in which Fleming played himself hosting a mock version of *Jeopardy!* Again he played himself in the 1983 theatrical release *Twilight Zone: The Movie*, which was produced by Steven Spielberg.

A Year's Supply of Lip Gloss

In 1983 when Merv Griffin revived *Jeopardy!* as a syndicated series, Fleming was invited to return as host. He turned down the offer when he discovered that the show would be easier than the original version and that it would tape in Los Angeles. Having lived in Los Angeles on four occasions in the past, Fleming had no desire to move back to California. In 1989 Fleming told *Sports Illustrated* that New Yorkers were more intellectually stimulated than people in California. In the search for a new host, Alex Trebek won the job.

> **Richard Reid:**
> "Alex has done a terrific job of making *Jeopardy!* his own. Those two guys (Art and Alex) are distinct eras in that program."

Fleming was not terribly unhappy about passing up the show for a variety of reasons. Because the new version used a computerized game board instead of the pull-card system used on the original show, Fleming felt that the program was too glitzy. He pointed out to *Sports Illustrated* that the show was part of Hollywood and not the real world.

He disliked the new ruling that contestants could only buzz in after Trebek finished reading the clue. In the previous versions, players could buzz in with their guess while Fleming was reading the clue. In Fleming's opinion, the show changed from being a game about superior knowledge to one of superior reflexes.

Fleming was also unhappy with the new ruling that only the winners kept the cash and the runners-up received consolation prizes. As he put it to *Sports Illustrated*, a player finishing only one dollar from first place ended up with a year's supply of lip gloss instead of their money.

When the new *Jeopardy!* started a trivia craze in the United States during the mid 1980s, the game was widely touted as an educational show. Fleming brushed off the game's educational label. He told *Sports Illustrated* that to him *Jeopardy!* was merely a party game and an entertaining way to pass the time for 30 minutes.

Take a Science Test

In October 1984 Fleming hosted *The National Science Test*, a segment of PBS's *Nova* series. The special featured a celebrity panel that competed against the studio audience in answering scientific questions. The audience had taken the test prior to the special. Fleming asked multiple choice questions and the celebrities selected answers. These were compared with the answers given by the studio audience. Fleming hosted sporadic *National Science Test* segments for *Nova* through 1987.

Busier Than Ever

By the late 1980s, Fleming was co-hosting a three hour quiz show for KMOX-AM in St. Louis called *Trivia Spectacular* with radio personality David Strauss where listeners could call in and play along. He commuted once a week to Breckenridge, Colorado, where he hosted *Biff America*, a local television talk show that featured a game segment similar to *Jeopardy!* He also owned a restaurant in Breckenridge called Art Fleming's Buffalo Flats Saloon & Grill. Along with these activities, Fleming found time to travel the country hosting as many as 80 mock *Jeopardy!* games for business conventions each year.

In 1990 Fleming began hosting the syndicated nostalgia radio program *When Radio Was*. Produced by 26-year-old Carl Amari, a radio buff who made a career out of his passion for old time radio programs, Amari secured broadcasting rights to air *The Shadow*, *Lights Out*, *Sherlock Holmes*, *Lum and Abner*, and *Fibber McGee and Molly*.

Amari wrote commentary to be wrapped around the individual episodes of the show and mailed the scripts to Fleming in St. Louis, who recorded the material and added his own comments. Fleming sent the taped commentary back to Amari, who edited the material into the finished program. The appeal of these classic radio programs was obvious since *When Radio Was* aired on approximately 100 stations nationwide.

Off to Florida

In September 1992 while visiting Florida, Fleming and his wife Rebecca stopped at a welcome center in Lake City and found some brochures about a community called Crystal River. They spent four days vacationing in Crystal River and fell in love with the area. Tired of big city life in St. Louis, the Flemings bought a two bedroom home near the Indian River and to Crystal River where they enjoyed fishing and boating.

Fleming emceed a number of events for local civic groups in Citrus County and programs at the Seven Rivers Presbyterian Church where he and Rebecca attended. They also volunteered their services for the Citrus Abuse Shelter Association, an organization that helped abused spouses. In September 1994 Fleming returned to television one last time co-hosting *Senior America*, a news magazine for Florida retirees.

By early 1995, Fleming was not feeling like his usual self. He continued working on *Senior America* despite his poor health until the show took a short hiatus in the spring of 1995. Fleming planned to return to the show when it resumed taping that July, but during the second week of April, doctors finally discovered that he was suffering from pancreatic cancer. Unfortunately the cancer had spread to the point of no return. Fleming retained his cheerful outlook until he passed away in his sleep at home in Crystal River on April 25, 1995, just

Art Fleming: TV's Answer Man (Art Fleming, courtesy Fred Wostbrock).

six days short of his 71st birthday. He was survived by his wife Rebecca, his son Timothy Bryan, daughter Kim Renee Woodring, and four grandchildren.

Always Jeopardy!

Today, the show made famous by Art Fleming lives on as one of the longest running programs in American history. *Jeopardy!* continues to entertain and educate viewers with its fun and simple format. For Fleming, it was a rewarding experience. He continued to receive letters, birthday cards, and holiday greetings from the fans long after the original *Jeopardy!* left the air.

> *Richard Reid:*
>
> "He was so inseparable from that [show]. We used to laugh about it on a regular basis. He said, 'You know, if I do [*College Bowl*] for 50 years, Allen Ludden [the original host] will always be *College Bowl* and I will always be *Jeopardy!*'"

MONTY HALL

Birth Name: Monte Halparin
Born: August 25, 1921, in Winnipeg, Manitoba, Canada
Marriage and Family: Marilyn Doreen Plottel (September 28, 1947–Present) 2 daughters, 1 son
Military Career: Canadian Officers Training Corps Reserve (1940–1945)
Radio Career (Canada): Announcer (CKRC-AM, Winnipeg, Manitoba) 1945–1946; Announcer/Program Host (CHUM-AM, Toronto) 1946–1948; *The Auctioneer* (CFRB-AM, Toronto) 1947–1948; Announcer/Program Host (Canadian Broadcasting Corporation) 1948–1949; *Who Am I?* (Syndicated) 1949–1959; Colgate Carnival (CBC) early 1950s; *Find Your Fortune* (CBC) early 1950s; The Wrigley Show (CBC) early 1950s
TV Career (Canada): *Floor Show* (CBC) June 22, 1953–July 13, 1953; *Matinee Party* (CBC) October 11, 1953–May 25, 1954
TV Career (United States): HOST—*The Sky's the Limit* (WNBC-TV, New York City) December 30, 1955–June 30, 1956; *Cowboy Theater* (NBC Saturdays) September 15, 1956–September 15, 1957; *Bingo-at-Home* (WABD-TV/WNEW-TV, New York City) February 17, 1958–December 12, 1958; *Keep Talking* (CBS Primetime) July 8, 1958–October 28, 1958; *Twenty-One* (NBC Primetime) August 11, 1958–September 1, 1958; *By-Line Monty Hall* (WNEW-TV, New York City) January 5, 1959–April 24, 1959; *Video Village* (CBS Daytime) September 19, 1960–June 15, 1962; *Junior Video Village* (CBS Saturday Morning) September 30, 1961–June 16, 1962; *Let's Make a Deal* (NBC

Monty Hall (Hatos-Hall Productions)

Daytime) December 30, 1963–December 27, 1968, (NBC Primetime) May 21, 1967–September 3, 1967, (ABC Daytime) December 30, 1968–July 9, 1976, (ABC Primetime) February 7, 1969–August 30, 1971, (Syndicated) September 13, 1971–September 1977; *Take My Word* (Unsold Game Show Pilot) 1965; *The Big Money* (Unsold NBC Game Show Pilot) January 20, 1966; *Talking Pictures* (Unsold ABC Game Show Pilot) May 11, 1976; *It's Anybody's Guess* (NBC Daytime) June 13, 1977–September 30, 1977; *The Courage and the Passion* (Unsold NBC Drama Pilot) May 27, 1978; *The All New Beat the Clock* (CBS Daytime) September 17, 1979–February 1, 1980; *Let's Make a Deal* (Syndicated) September 22, 1980–September 1981; *The Joke's on Us* (Unsold Game Show Pilot) 1983; *The All New Let's Make a Deal* (Syndicated) September 17, 1984–September 12, 1986; *For the People* (Unsold Human Interest Show Pilot) 1986; *Split Second* (Syndicated) December 15, 1986–September 1987; *I Predict* (Unsold CBS Game Show Pilot) September 1987; *Let's Make a Deal* (NBC Daytime) October 8, 1990–January 11, 1991 PRODUCER—*Your First Impression* (NBC Daytime) January 2, 1962–June 26, 1964; *Let's Make a Deal* [see "Hosting Career" above] 1963–1977, 1980–1981, & 1984–1986; *Chain Letter* (NBC Daytime) July 4, 1966–October 14, 1966; *Split Second* (ABC Daytime) March 20, 1972–June 27, 1975; (Syndicated) December 15, 1986–September 1987; *It Pays to Be Ignorant* (Syndicated) September 10, 1973–September 1974; *Masquerade Party* (Syndicated) September 9, 1974–September 1975; *The McLean Stevenson Show* (NBC Primetime) December 1, 1976–March 3, 1977

Stage Career: *High Button Shoes* (Musical Comedy Tour) Summer 1978
Business Interests: Partner: Stefan Hatos-Monty Hall Productions (1962–Present)
Book: *Emcee Monty Hall* (1973)
Charity Work: Member of Variety Clubs International (1947–Present); International President of Variety Clubs International (1975–1977); Chairman of the Board for Variety Clubs International (1977–1981); International Chairman of Variety Clubs International (1981–Present)

Monty Hall and his longtime business partner Stefan Hatos once had a sign in their office that read, "You could learn a lot more about America from half an hour of *Let's Make a Deal* than one year of Walter Cronkite." For nearly three decades, Monty Hall hosted that enormously successful game show, which he co-produced with Stefan Hatos. Airing on daytime and primetime television at one time, this show made him a household name. He became so closely identified with this program that many people overlook all the other accomplishments of his career.

Monty Hall was born as Monte Halparin in Winnipeg, Manitoba in Canada on August 25, 1921, the older of two boys born to Maurice and Rose Halparin. According to Hall, he had a rather tough childhood.

> *Monty Hall (March 2000 telephone interview):*
> "I was in a scalding accident, and then I came down with double pneumonia. And that was in a time before they had proper drugs. It was very touch and go for a couple of weeks."

The bout of pneumonia knocked him out of school for a year. In the meantime his parents tutored him at home. When he returned to school, he began skipping grades so rapidly that he graduated from high school at the age of 14 in 1935.

Having no money to attend college, Hall tried to get a job. Because he was so young, he had difficulty finding anything until his father hired him to work in his meat market as a delivery boy. By 1938 Hall had earned enough money to enroll at the University of Manitoba but was forced to withdraw after one year when he ran out of money. He returned to college in 1940 when a benefactor provided the funds for him to finish his education. While at the University of Manitoba, Hall was a member of the Canadian Officers Training Corps, similar to the ROTC programs in the United States. In his 1973 autobiography, Hall wrote that he volunteered for the regular Army when Canada entered World War II, but was rejected. He graduated with a Bachelor of Science degree in Chemistry in 1945.

Hall wanted to enroll in medical school to become a doctor, but was rejected three times. During his last year in college he worked for radio station CKRC as a disc jockey. After graduating he remained with the station as announcer for music, drama, quiz, and sports shows. In February 1946 he moved to Toronto to work at radio station CHUM. It was here that he legally changed his name from Monte Halparin to Monty Hall at the advice of his boss.

Who Am I?

On September 28, 1947, Hall married Marilyn Plottel, whom he had met shortly after moving to Toronto. Plottel worked as an actress while attending the University of Toronto. The couple had three children, Joanna, Richard, and Sharon. After a brief honeymoon, Hall began hosting a radio quiz program called *The Auctioneer* on CHUM. This show became the basis for *Let's Make a Deal* nearly 20 years later. "We did certain things like going into the audience and asking for crazy things," Hall explained.

In 1949 he formed his own production company and created the quiz show *Who Am I?* Its format was simple: over a period of weeks Hall gave clues to a mystery person in the form of rhymes. Listeners called in with their guesses. The prize for correctly guessing the mystery person increased in value with each new clue. Unable to get the Canadian Broadcasting Corporation (CBC) to buy the show, Hall sold it to an advertising agency in Toronto. The program was then syndicated by a tape network to stations around Canada. *Who Am I?* proved to be a durable quiz show lasting 10 and a half years.

In 1953 Hall moved into Canadian television with *Matinee Party* on CBC. After two years, however, the television assignments dried up and Hall was unable to find a job. He was still hosting *Who Am I?* on the radio, but the income was barely adequate for his family. After spending a year searching for a television job in Canada, Hall finally decided to try American television. In the summer of 1955 he went to New York City while his family remained in Canada.

The Memo from Monty

For six long months he auditioned for producers in New York while traveling back and forth to Toronto. He taped several episodes of *Who Am I?* during his visits to Toronto on weekends and then headed back to New York for more auditions and interviews. Hall began writing a newsletter detailing his daily activities called "The Memo from Monty," which he sent to New York producers with whom he could not get an audition or interview. By November 1955, Hall felt he was beating his head against a brick wall and stopped writing the newsletter. Shortly afterward, his luck changed.

> *MH:*
>
> "I called Steve Krantz at WNBC-TV and before his secretary could get rid of me he got on the phone. [Krantz] said 'where's The Memo from Monty this week? It didn't come this past week.' I said, 'You read it?' He said, 'Every week. I look forward to it.' I was flabbergasted. He said, 'I'd like to meet the man who wrote that. How about having lunch with me?' That started a series of good things for me."

Krantz was looking for someone to replace Gene Rayburn as host of the local WNBC quiz show *The Sky's the Limit.* Hall became the new host on December 30, 1955. In early 1956, he was hired by NBC radio as a weekend host of the *Monitor* series, a program of music, news, interviews, comedy bits, and live remote broadcasts. Hall remained with this show for five years. *The Sky's the Limit* faded in June 1956, but three months later, he turned up on a weekend NBC series in which he introduced old western movies called *Cowboy Theater.* On the strength of his network jobs, Hall finally moved his family to New York. Unfortunately, *Cowboy Theater* was canceled after one season, and Hall was again without a television show.

In February 1958, Hall was hired by New York City station WABD-TV to host *Bingo-at-Home.* This show was a pioneer in interactive game playing. There were no studio contestants, but instead the home viewers played the game. Viewers used the last five digits of their telephone numbers to form a Bingo card. Hall called out the numbers from the studio as in a regular Bingo game. Anyone completing five in a line on their Bingo card called the station to confirm their victory. During the first show so many viewers called the station and jammed the telephone lines that the rules were quickly changed. Thereafter, viewers sent their winning cards to the station by mail.

"What Is This About?"

In July 1958, Hall came back to network television with CBS's *Keep Talking.* He was bounced from the show after three months when it failed to generate good ratings. The only controversial program of his career came in August 1958 when he was called in to substitute for Jack Barry on the rigged quiz show *Twenty-One* on NBC.

> *MH:*
>
> "I was called in to replace [Barry] as he went off on a nightclub tour. After four weeks of doing that show, I was called in and they said, 'You can't do the show this week. There's been a big inquiry into it and Jack Barry has to come back from Chicago to front the show again.' I said, 'What is all this about?' They said, 'Well a guy went to the D.A. and said that the show is fixed.' Of course I knew nothing about it. I was just the innocent patsy who emceed the show believing that these guys were brilliant."

Hall put together a new interview program, *By-Line Monty Hall*, for WNEW-TV in New York. That show was canceled after three months. He still had a contract with WNEW-TV, so he did some sports announcing in the New York area: hockey games for the New York Rangers, wrestling at the Sunnyside Gardens, and international soccer at the Polo Grounds.

Video Village

In September 1960 he was called at the last minute to replace Jack Narz as host of *Video Village*, a popular CBS daytime show. *Video Village* played like a home board game with contestants rolling a large die and moving as playing pieces around a game board that took up the entire studio. When the show moved to Los Angeles in March 1961, Hall went with it and moved his family to Beverly Hills, California. *Video Village*, lasting until 1962, gave Hall his first real television success.

Hall ventured into producing when he sold his first game show, *Your First Impression*, to NBC. The show debuted in January 1962 with Bill Leyden as emcee while Hall produced and occasionally substituted as host. Hall hired Stefan Hatos to help produce the game in June 1962, and that year the duo formed Hatos-Hall Productions.

TV's Big Dealer

In 1963 Stefan Hatos and Monty Hall found their bonanza when they created *Let's Make a Deal*. NBC purchased the concept, and *Let's Make a Deal* premiered on December 30, 1963, with Hall as the host and co-producer with Hatos. On this show 33 contestants sat in the section of the audience known as the trading area. Hall selected a few players from the group to participate in the day's program. Using a variety of trading games and lots of prizes which included appliances, automobiles, and money, contestants were given a prize and then offered a chance to trade it away for something else that may or may not be worth more in value.

The catch was that the newer prizes were hidden from view behind doors and curtains, so players never knew what they were getting until they made the trade. Worthless nonsense prizes called "zonks" were tossed into the mix to add yet another angle to the game. Many times, the contestants' greed got the best of them and they ended up trading a large, expensive prize for something like a cow or a broken-down car. Any of the players could participate in the Big Deal of the day at the end of each program. There were no "zonks" in this part of the game and players could trade their previous winnings for even larger prizes.

Shortly after the show's premiere in 1963, contestants in the trading area began dressing in loud and crazy costumes in order to attract Hall's attention and ensure their chances of being selected. This new twist gave *Let's Make a Deal* the formula for which it has become famous. From May to September 1967, *Let's Make a Deal* also aired as a summer replacement series on NBC's primetime schedule in addition to the daytime series. However, when NBC refused to give the program a permanent berth on its nighttime schedule, Hatos and Hall took their business to ABC, who gladly gave the show spots on both its daytime and primetime schedules.

On December 30, 1968, *Let's Make a Deal* officially moved to ABC where it clobbered its competition on NBC. During the 1968-1969 season it became the number one-rated daytime game show. The primetime version, which began in February 1969, rated just as well at night as it did during the afternoons. When ABC canceled the nighttime series, Hatos and Hall persuaded the network to finance a weekly syndicated edition that went on the air in September 1971.

Hall described his hosting job on *Let's Make a Deal* as dangerous.

> *MH:*
> "I suffered plenty of shocks. People with football helmets jumped up to kiss me, and the face guard would give me a smack in the head. Others wearing boxes put together rapidly at their home with pins sticking out would scratch me, or people jumped up and knocked me down the aisle. It's a pretty good obstacle course."

The cast of *Let's Make a Deal*: Announcer Jay Stewart, host Monty Hall, and model Carol Merrill in the 1970s (Hatos-Hall Productions).

Of the 4,700 episodes of *Let's Make a Deal*, Hall missed about 30 or 40 shows by his own estimate. He pointed out that his rare absences were not from injuries but from bouts of the flu or some other illness.

Branching Out

In 1972 Hatos and Hall packaged *Split Second* for ABC. Game show veteran Tom Kennedy hosted this rapid-fire question and answer game. During the show's run, Hall and *Split Second* producer Stu Billet clashed over Billet's rulings on the contestants' answers to the questions.

> *MH:*
> "I used to come into the office and say, 'Don't be so hard on these people.' The difference between Stu and myself was that if someone asked a question and the answer was 'Marie Antoinette' and the contestant answered 'Maria Antoinette,' Stu ruled them wrong. I was furious. I said, 'This is not life or death. This is a quiz show.' If someone knew enough to say,

'Maria Antoinette,' who is going to rule them wrong because there was a letter wrong in the first name, but the intent of the answer is absolutely right? We used to have fights about that. Even on *Jeopardy!* today, they rule people out if they get a syllable wrong and they shouldn't be that way."

During the 1970s while *Let's Make a Deal* was burning up the ratings, Hall branched out into acting, appearing in guest roles on the sitcoms *That Girl, The Odd Couple*, and *Love, American Style*. He also headlined a nightclub act in Las Vegas, but met only limited success. On August 24, 1973, Hall received his star on the Hollywood Walk of Fame. That same year, he published his autobiography, *Emcee Monty Hall,* coauthored with Bill Libby. Hall also served as honorary mayor of Hollywood from 1969 to 1979.

Deal Me Out

Let's Make a Deal continued on ABC until July 1976, when falling ratings led to its cancellation. The syndicated edition continued for another season after moving its tape location to the Las Vegas Hilton Hotel. By now Hall had grown tired of the show and wanted to work on other projects. After 14 years, *Let's Make a Deal* went off the air in September 1977. During the 1976-1977 season he served as executive producer of the short-lived NBC sitcom *The McLean Stevenson Show*. From June to September 1977, Hall produced and hosted the NBC game show *It's Anybody's Guess*, in which two contestants tried to guess whether five members of the studio audience would come up with the answers to a series of questions.

Returning to acting, Hall appeared as General Sam Brewster in the television movie *The Courage and the Passion* on May 27, 1978. The movie was a pilot for a proposed NBC drama series, but the network passed on the concept. During the summer of 1978, he toured with the musical comedy production *High Button Shoes* in theaters across the country.

"I Hated It with All My Heart"

More game show stints followed. In September 1979, Hall found himself hosting *Beat the Clock*, the CBS revival of its 1950s stunt show, in which contestants tried to complete stunts in an allotted amount of time. Titled *The All New Beat the Clock,* the show failed to draw an audience. In November 1979, the contestants were replaced with celebrities who competed in the stunts and won money for members of the studio audience. The changes did not help, and the show was canned in February 1980.

> *MH:*
> "I hated it with all my heart. The people were asked to do stupid stunts and so on. I just didn't care for it. I'm so glad it wasn't successful."

More Revivals

His next project was a revival of *Let's Make a Deal*. The program's format remained the same, but production shifted to Vancouver, Canada. The revival lasted only one season. Another game show, *The Joke's on Us*, did not make it past the pilot stage in 1983. In the fall of 1984 Hall returned with *The All New Let's Make a Deal* for two additional years. In December 1986, Hall brought back *Split Second* and doubled as the show's host. After *Split Second* left the air in September 1987, Hall retired from hosting.

Another Deal

This was not quite the end, however. In the summer of 1990, NBC brought out another version of *Let's Make a Deal* for its daytime schedule. Hall was not interested in returning as emcee. After hosting 4,700 episodes of the show, he decided that was enough, but did agree to help search for a new host. After auditioning people by tape and in person for three months, game show announcer Bob Hilton was selected as host. The revival taped in Orlando, Florida, at Disney World where a large studio had been built just for the show.

The new version never caught on, and NBC told Hall that unless he returned as host, the show would be canceled.

> *MH:*
> "It was a very, very sad blow to Bob Hilton and one that I did not want to do because I didn't want to do the show again. But to save the show, I went down to Orlando and did the next three months."

Ratings failed to improve despite his return, and much to Hall's relief, NBC axed the show in January 1991. This marked the end of Hall's hosting career. His business partner Stefan Hatos died of a heart attack in March 1999 at the age of 78.

Variety Clubs

Many people associate Monty Hall only with *Let's Make a Deal*, but there is much more to this man than just handling people dressed up as chickens that jump up and down in excitement. For almost 60 years, Hall has been an active member of Variety Clubs International, a charity that helps underprivileged children around the world by raising money to build hospital wards for the sick and camps for the disabled. Since he joined the Toronto, Canada chapter in 1947, Hall has raised more than $800 million for Variety Clubs International and other charities worldwide.

Each year Hall makes approximately 60 unpaid appearances as host on telethons, auctions, and other shows to raise the money. His travels around the world have taken him to Mexico, France, Israel, Great Britain, Ireland, the Channel Islands, and Australia. There are 36 chapters of Variety Clubs International in the United States, and Hall has visited most of them. Each chapter picks its own children's charity to sponsor.

> *MH:*
> "It's a marvelous organization because we are very scrupulous about the money we raise and how it's raised and the cost of raising it. Everybody is a volunteer and our international board pays their own expenses to attend meetings. I love this charity because all the money goes to the kids."

For his charity work, Hall has received more than 500 awards. These include three honorary doctorates from the University of Manitoba, Haifa University, and Hahnemann Medical College in Philadelphia. The children's wings at the Hahnemann Hospital, the Mount Sinai Hospital in Toronto, Canada, and at the UCLA Medical Center are named for him. In May 1988, the Canadian government presented him with the Order of Canada, the highest award offered by that country.

Hall currently serves as International Chairman for Life of Variety Clubs International, a position he has held since 1981. He became International President in 1975 and was promoted to Chairman of the Board in 1977. When it was time for Hall to retire in 1981, the organization did not want to lose him, so it created the new role of International Chairman for Life.

> *MH:*
> "That means you don't stop raising money."

Despite being remembered mainly for his television career, he noted that television made his charity work possible.

> *MH:*
> "If I did not have the stardom on television, I would have never been asked to do all these things. I wouldn't have had the money to do all of this. Television and *Let's Make a Deal* made it all possible. In my family, we don't laugh at people dressed up like chickens."

"It's Stuff That Warms My Heart"

At one point in 1986, Hall combined his television and charity work with a pilot called *For the People*. The pilot spotlighted a man who worked in Cincinnati while his wife had to take their daughter to Chicago for medical treatment. The show arranged for the man to leave his job as a McDonald's assistant manager and take a new job in Chicago to be closer to his family.

> *MH:*
> "Putting that on TV was just an extension of my life. It's stuff that warms my heart and makes me feel good."

Unfortunately, station managers at the NATPE convention in New Orleans were not so warm to the show's idea.

> *MH:*
> "I was astounded to find the station managers coming up to me and saying, 'Well, we don't believe in stuff like this. We like *Let's Make a Deal*. Bring that back.' So I said, 'This is something great. It's helping people.' The station managers looked at it with jaundiced eyes. They said, 'Who really cares. Give them a refrigerator.' I said, 'Well, if nobody cares, I'm out of here.' That kind of comment just soured me. As a matter of fact, I left the convention after the second day. I never tried to sell the show again. I just put it away and forgot about it."

Hall made an interesting observation about the current wave of talk shows.

> *MH:*
> "If you take a look at shows on the air today, it's not for the good of people. It's Jerry Springer's people fighting and kicking each other. It's all these other talk show people emulating him with all the dirty laundry being hung out to dry."

Recalling the sign that once hung in his office that said, "You could learn a lot more about America from half an hour of *Let's Make a Deal* than one year of Walter Cronkite," Hall used that example again for the talk shows.

> *MH:*
> "All these terrible things that are happening get on television. Something like mine that was for the goodness of people didn't get on. So you could learn more about that than you could from Walter Cronkite!"

Family

For Monty Hall, however, the most important part of his life is his family. He ranks his charity work second and his television work third. All of his family has participated in the entertainment industry in some way. His wife Marilyn is an award-winning producer of TV movies, including *Do You Remember Love?* a drama about Alzheimer's Disease. His oldest daughter Joanna Gleason won a Tony Award on Broadway for Best Actress in a Musical, and has been a regular cast member in the CBS sitcoms *Love and War* and *Bette* starring Bette Midler. His son Richard has won many awards as a television producer and documentarian, and youngest daughter Sharon is a television director. Her husband co-produced the ABC drama series *The Practice*. To this day all the talented members of Hall's family remain very close.

"When You Put Your Pants On, Sit Down"

His busy schedule temporarily halted in June 2002 when he broke a hip during a physical examination.

> *Monty Hall (February 2004 telephone interview):*
> "I was in the hospital for routine x-rays. I went without breakfast and went in and had my x-rays. I went back into a little cubicle to put my clothes back on and when putting my pants on, I was a little groggy I guess from having not eaten. I put my foot into the middle seam [of the pants] instead of the hole where the leg goes in and down I went tumbling and broke my hip. And that was a thrill."

After several weeks of recuperation, Hall slowly resumed his normal activities which included playing golf and tennis.

> MH:
> "My legacy now all over the world is when you put your pants on sit down." (Laughing)

One More Deal

Late in 2002 NBC approached Hall about reactivating *Let's Make a Deal* for primetime. The network commissioned five one hour episodes to air beginning in January 2003. Once again, Hall did not return as host, choosing instead to work behind the scenes. Billy Bush, who hosted the magazine show *Access Hollywood*, was selected to fill Hall's shoes as "TV's Big Dealer."

> MH:
> "Billy came out and I had exactly three days to work with him. Then we had to do five one hour shows in three days. We had all kinds of problems doing it because no one was really prepared in that space of time."

After taping the five shows in a rush, NBC delayed the show's premiere until March 2003.

> MH:
> "I could have had two more months to work with everybody. And on top of that instead of putting us on Saturday night like they said they would, they put us on Tuesday night against *American Idol*."

Let's Make a Deal premiered on March 4, 2003. Longtime viewers of the show were shocked to find that the new version had a racy edge to it. Hall found that he took on more than he bargained for when he agreed to do the series. At NBC's prompting, the show's staff of producers and writers tried to model it along the lines of reality shows. Hall protested that those kinds of changes did not fit in with the format of the show.

The opening deal on the first episode involved three female contestants and three men who dressed in different outfits. The first man wore a kilt, the second a toga, and the third a grass skirt. Each man had a small prize hidden inside his garment and the female contestants were given the option of reaching up the men's legs to get the hidden prize or taking a $500 payoff. Hall reluctantly agreed to let this setup go on the air.

> MH:
> "I was offended. I turned down about 19 out of 20 suggestions [that were brought to me] and I let that one go through. I was not happy with it. I was disgusted with it. But you should have seen the stuff they tried to put past me."

NBC canceled *Let's Make a Deal* after three episodes and never aired the remaining two shows. The question remained: Would NBC ever air the other episodes?

> MH:
> "I don't care! I don't want to do a *Deal* like that ever again!"

Still Going Strong

Although he has experienced some career disappointments in recent years, Hall has shown no signs of slowing down. He still travels around the United

Monty Hall today (Hatos-Hall Productions)

States hosting *Let's Make a Deal* for conventions and organizations. More than 40 years after its debut, the show most associated with Hall is still very much alive. His schedule is filled almost daily with meetings, speaking engagements, and performances for his charities. This keeps him busy all year long. As long as he is able, Monty Hall will continue working and helping the needy children around the world through Variety Clubs International. All of this is possible because of his long broadcasting career and because of the strong support of his family.

ART JAMES

Birth Name: Arthur Simeonovich Efimchik

Born: October 15, 1929, in Dearborn, Michigan

Died: March 28, 2004, in Palm Springs, California

Marriages and Family: Jane Hamilton (1957–1981) (Divorced) 1 daughter, 1 son; Sandy Pietron (1991–2004)

Military Service: United States Army: Armed Forces Network, Frankfurt, Germany (1952–1954)

Radio Career: Disc Jockey (WKNX-AM, Saginaw Michigan) 1951; Disc Jockey (WKMH-AM, Detroit, Michigan) 1951–1952; Disc Jockey (WKNX-AM, Saginaw, Michigan) 1954–1955; Disc Jockey (WJR-AM, Detroit, Michigan) 1956–1958

TV Career: HOST—Staff Announcer/News Anchor (WKNX-TV, Saginaw, Michigan) 1954–1955; Staff Announcer/News Anchor (WWJ-TV, Detroit, Michigan) 1955–1956; *Say When!!* (NBC Daytime) January 3, 1961-March 26, 1965; *Tricky Triangle Bowling* (Unsold Game Show Pilot) 1961; *It's Academic* (WNBC-TV, New York) 1961–1965; *Fractured Phrases* (NBC Daytime) September 27, 1965-December 31, 1965; *Matches 'N' Mates* (Syndicated) March 20, 1967-September 1968; *Temptation* (ABC Daytime) December 4, 1967-March 1, 1968; *Pay Cards!* (Syndicated) September 9, 1968-September 1969; *The Who, What, or Where Game* (NBC Daytime) December 29, 1969-January 4, 1974; *Blank Check* (NBC Daytime) January 6, 1975-July 4, 1975; *The Magnificent Marble Machine* (NBC Daytime) July 7, 1975-June 11, 1976; *Moneywords* (Unsold Game Show Pilot) 1976; *Word Grabbers* (Unsold Game Show Pilot) 1977; *Pot 'o' Gold* (Unsold Game Show Pilot) 1977; *Get It Together* (Game Show Run-through) 1978; *It's Who You Know* (Game Show Run-through) 1978; *Mismatch* (Unsold Game Show Pilot) 1979; *Super Pay Cards!* (Syndicated) September 14, 1981-April 23, 1982; *Catch Phrase* (Syndicated) Sepember 16, 1985-January 10, 1986 ANNOUNCER—*Concentration* (NBC Daytime) August 25, 1958-December 30, 1960; *Face the Music* (Syndicated) Spring 1981; *Tic Tac Dough* (Syndicated) 1981 (Substitute for Jay Stewart); *The Joker's Wild* (Syndicated) 1981 (Substitute for Jay Stewart); *NFL Trivia Game* (Syndicated) September 11, 1989-December 25, 1989; *Tic Tac Dough* (Syndicated) 1991 (Substitute for Larry Van Nuys); *Classic Concentration* (NBC Daytime) July 1991-August 1991 (Substitute for Gene Wood)

Off-Broadway & Summer Stock Theatre: *The Buttered Side* (Actor & Producer); *Charlie Was Here and Now He's Gone* (Actor & Producer); *Mr. Roberts* (Actor); *Sunday in New York* (Actor)

Theatrical Movie: *The Mallrats* (1994)

Made-for-TV Movie: *The Gridlock* (NBC) October 2, 1980

Business Interests: President: Art James Productions (1975–2004)

Art James (Art James, courtesy Fred Wostbrock)

"A woman came up to me before I came on stage and said, 'Don't you ever get nervous?' I said, 'No, gosh. Years ago maybe, but why do you ask?' and she says, 'What are you doing in the ladies room?'" This joke was one of the many effective ways that Art James won over his audience. His sense of humor and polished speaking skills along with his relaxed style carried him far in his career. Through the years as a host, announcer, producer, businessman, writer, lecturer, and teacher, James was a well-rounded host on the tube.

Art James was born as Arthur Simeonovich Efimchik in Dearborn, Michigan, on October 15, 1929, to Russian immigrant parents Sam and Olga Efimchik. One of his early ambitions was to pursue a career in baseball, so in 1946 at the age of 17, he tried out for the New York Yankees as a pitcher. According to James, he had a good chance to make it in baseball, but that was not to be the case.

Art James (March 1999 telephone interview):
"I was a pretty good sandlot pitcher in Detroit, and a Yankee scout came around and took a handful of us to try out. The scout's name was Burly Grimes. I remember he always had a cigar in his mouth and he was burly. I pitched two innings for him and I struck out five guys. He looked at this 140-pound kid and they're looking for raw meat at the time to throw the ball 100 miles an hour. I was fast, but I had a great curve ball. Anyway, I guess I was too small because he looked at me and said, 'Okay kid, you can go home now.' I was crushed."

Action and High Spirits

After high school, James attended Wayne State University and, after a few interruptions, graduated in 1952 with a degree in business administration. While in college, James got his first taste of acting during his junior year when he auditioned for Moliere's play *The Miser*. The action and high spirits of the theater appealed to him and he landed one of the leading roles. From that day, he started hanging around the theater.

James began his broadcasting career in 1951 spinning country music records for WKNX-AM, a Saginaw, Michigan radio station. After college, he worked his way up to a bigger station in Detroit, WKMH-AM. He interrupted his career in 1952 when the U.S. Army drafted him during the Korean War. Stationed in Frankfurt, Germany Hoechst, James was assigned to the Armed Forces Network. After his discharge in 1954 James returned to Michigan, but was unable to get back his Detroit radio job. Starting over again in Saginaw at WKNX radio and television, he was back in Detroit six months later working for WWJ-TV.

Oops!

Once while doing the local news for WKNX-TV, there was an evening when the cameraman was forced to answer the call to nature during a live newscast.

Art James (February 2004 telephone interview):
"It was a one-camera operation. The cameraman and I were the only ones there at the station because it was the night shift."

When the cameraman could not wait any longer, he carefully framed the camera shot on James and left the studio to go to the restroom. Unfortunately he neglected to fix the latch that locked down the camera to prevent it from tilting up or down. While the man was out of the studio the camera slowly began tilting upward.

AJ:
"The camera kept rising up and I kept rising up [behind the desk] with it until the camera was shooting the lights in the [studio] ceiling."

Without missing a beat, James kept reading his news copy until the cameraman returned to the studio and quickly moved the camera back into its proper position.

Concentrating on Success

James' big break came in 1958 when an old Army buddy, who had gone to New York as an NBC executive, told him about a new game show. Jack Barry and Dan Enright produced *Concentration* with Hugh Downs as host and the show needed an announcer. James promptly recorded a demo tape by taking the audio recording from the opening of a game show and dubbing his own voice over the announcer's words. Not long after submitting his demo tape, the Barry-Enright offices called him in for an audition. However, his audition got off to a rough start.

> *AJ (March 1999):*
>
> "I was supposed to do an audience warm-up on the game show *Tic Tac Dough* in 10 or 15 minutes, but I was so nervous that it took me only three or four minutes. They had to run and get Jack Barry, the host of the show, out of the men's room because I finished so early. Luckily, the audience laughed at a few jokes I told and the producers saw a new face. I was hired as the announcer for *Concentration*."

Concentration debuted over NBC on August 25, 1958. It was a huge ratings success and soon became the number one game show on daytime television. Contestants on the show faced a game board containing 30 squares. Behind each square was a prize (each prize was located behind two separate squares on the board). The object was to pick two squares and match prizes for the chance to see part of a rebus puzzle hidden behind the board.

Are You Related to Dennis James?

As the announcer for *Concentration*, part of James' job was to do the audience warm-up prior to show time. During the warm-ups, James frequently took questions from the audience members. One question he was often asked was whether or not he was any relation to game show host Dennis James.

> *AJ (February 2004):*
>
> "They asked [that question] so many times that Hugh Downs and I cooked up this thing where whenever it was asked of Hugh or me, we would say that Dennis James was my father. That went on for quite awhile. Maybe five years after that after I was long gone from *Concentration* and hosting *Say When*, I met Dennis James for the first time at a press party that NBC organized. The first thing that Dennis James said to me was, 'You S.O.B! You know how many people think I'm your father?' (Laughs) It was all said in good humor."

Say When!!

While announcing for *Concentration*, James began auditioning as a host for other producers on game show run-throughs. In late 1960 he auditioned to host Goodson-Todman's *Say When!!* and won the job. James announced his last *Concentration* show on December 30, 1960. *Say When!!* debuted over NBC the following Tuesday on January 3, 1961. Two contestants were shown a group of prizes. Each player selected a prize and its value was added to that contestant's pot. Players continued selecting prizes, but the catch was to not go over a predetermined total. Players could freeze anytime forcing their opponent to select more prizes to get closer to the total or go over in the attempt to win.

"Mama Told Me There Would Be Days Like This"

James was the victim of a blooper on *Say When!!* in 1964 while doing a commercial for Peter Pan peanut butter. The bottom of the jar cracked open causing the peanut butter to leak out. Playing it cool, he continued with the commercial until he finally broke down laughing. James said, "Mama told me there would be days like this!" For years the blooper remained hidden in the vaults. Then during a 1975 episode of *The Magnificent Marble Machine*, the producers surprised James by playing the blooper for the first time in a decade. Since then, the flub has become a favorite on several blooper specials.

It's Academic

Say When!! aired live from 10:00 to 10:30 a.m. weekday mornings out of New York until the show switched to videotape around 1963. James also hosted, *It's Academic,* a syndicated quiz show that pitted high schools from local cities against each other. The show was produced in Washington, D.C., but was sold to stations in Chicago, New York, Los Angeles, Philadelphia, and Boston. Each station purchased the idea from the producers and selected its own host. James emceed the New York and Boston versions of *It's Academic* until 1965.

Say When!! folded in 1965 and James moved on to NBC's *Fractured Phrases*. In this game, two teams of contestants guessed familiar phrases from phonetic clues. The show was so terribly received that James recalled a letter written by one viewer. It read, "Dear NBC: I am an invalid, and it is very difficult for me to get out of my chair, but your show made me do it to change the channel."

This Is Inhuman. I Won't Do It.

By now, the practice of videotaping programs in advance was common in most television shows. No longer was there just one show per day done live. Now long tape sessions completed several shows in one day. James found himself in a conflict with the tape days for *Fractured Phrases* and *It's Academic.*

AJ (March 1999):

"We were taping two *It's Academic* and two *Fractured Phrases* at a time, so I threw up my hands and said 'four shows a day, this is inhuman. I won't do it.' I quit *It's Academic* for that season. A year later, we were taping five or six shows a day as a matter of course. It takes tremendous concentration because you're keeping track of so many things and a very high energy level. I would be tired after one show. Normally we do three shows and take a lunch break. I always had to shut the dressing room door and get in a recliner chair and nap for maybe five or ten minutes just to break the surface tension."

During 1966, James was temporarily without a TV program. He did the run-throughs for *The Newlywed Game,* which was created by Nick Nicholson and Roger Muir. Production of the show was turned over to Chuck Barris and sold to ABC. The hosting job went to Los Angeles disc jockey Bob Eubanks. James wound up hosting another Nicholson-Muir creation, *Matches 'N Mates,* beginning in March 1967. This game involved two married couples answering questions for the right to guess a series of mystery words.

A Not-So Tempting Job

In December 1967, James hosted ABC's *Temptation.* Three contestants secretly selected a prize from among three choices. Players won the prize only if neither of their opponents picked the same item. The player with the highest prize total after five rounds won the game.

AJ (February 2004):

"It was a weak show. It was murder because there were a lot of prizes [used in the game] and they had to be arranged just right. We would be taping until two or three o'clock in the morning."

Temptation was anything but tempting to the viewers and it vanished after 13 weeks. In September 1968 James popped up on *Pay Cards!* the first game show to use Poker in its format. Three contestants selected cards from a 20 card game board to build the best Poker combination. It lasted only one season.

Who, What, or Where

Finally in 1969 James hit pay dirt again with NBC's *The Who, What, or Where Game.* At the beginning of each round, a category was revealed accompanied by three questions (a "who," "what," and a "where") which were worth varying amounts of money. Contestants each started the game with $125 and secretly chose one of the three questions bidding any amount up to $50 on their ability to answer it. If only one contestant chose a particular question ("who" for example) they automatically got the chance to answer it.

If more than one player chose the same question, the highest bidder answered it. If two or three contestants bid the same amount for a question, James auctioned it off to the highest bidder. In the final round, the $50 betting limit was waived and contestants could risk any amount of their pot on the last question. *The Who, What, or Where Game* enjoyed a four year run.

A Taste of Acting

During the early 1970s, James' early acting ambitions led him to produce and star in the off-Broadway comedy *The Buttered Side*. He also produced the play *Charlie Was Here and Now He's Gone* with future television star Robert Guillaume in the cast. Because of low budgets for the plays, the actors were only paid $75 a week. James also acted in summer stock doing the comic plays *Mr. Roberts* and *Sunday in New York*.

AJ:
"It was just something I wanted to do. I'm pretty good at light comedy, but I could never do serious acting. I don't really go deep into myself."

Receiving a Blank Check

On January 6, 1975, James returned to television with NBC's *Blank Check*. Billing itself as "TV's First ESP game," *Blank Check* called for six contestants to appear on a week's worth of shows. The object was to complete a four-digit check using five pre-selected numbers. One player was designated the "check writer" and secretly selected one of the five numbers as the last digit for the check. The other five players answered riddles for the right to guess which number the writer had picked. If the player correctly guessed the number, they became the new "check writer." The writer who completed the final digit in a check won the four figure amount in cash.

A "Magnificent" Game

Running at 12:00 p.m. against the red hot CBS soap opera *The Young and the Restless*, *Blank Check* quickly sank in the ratings. It was canceled on July 4, 1975, but the following Monday on July 7, James appeared again with *The Magnificent Marble Machine*. Two celebrity-contestant teams competed for the right to play a huge pinball machine that took up most of the studio. Each team member worked a flipper on the machine and tried to keep the ball in play to score 15,000 points.

*Robert Noah (*MMM *producer: June 2006 telephone interview):*
"The studio audience used to go nuts. They loved it, but [the show] never did much on the air."

An effort to boost the ratings with all-celebrity teams beginning in January 1976 failed to help. Until now, James was still living in New York and commuting to Los Angeles to tape his shows. He moved his family to California in early 1976, but *The Magnificent Marble Machine* was canceled that June and James did not host another game show for five years. During the interim, he created, produced and hosted the game show pilots *Pot 'o' Gold*, *Get It Together*, *It's Who You Know*, *Mismatch*, and *Moneywords*. James also served as the commercial spokesman for J.C. Penney for five years.

Tongue-In-Cheek Writing

In 1977 while taking a nonfiction writing course at the U.C.L.A. extension, James submitted, as he called it, "a tongue-in-cheek" article looking at the loss of live television shows, which included stories of his own experiences. The class instructor encouraged him to submit the arti-

Could you play pinball on a machine this big? Art James dares you try on *The Magnificent Marble Machine* (Art James, courtesy Fred Wostbrock).

cle to *TV Guide*. The magazine published the article in its June 11, 1977, issue. Between 1977 and 1981, James authored seven game show related articles for *TV Guide* and became a guest lecturer for the writing course at U.C.L.A.

In the spring of 1981, James substituted as announcer for *Face the Music*. That fall he returned to the host's podium with *Super Pay Cards!* a revival of his 1968 game show. The format remained the same as the original version with the winning contestant playing a bonus round for a possible $5,000. The show bit the dust after 26 weeks in April 1982.

Full Circle

During the next three years, most of James' work consisted of filling in as a game show announcer, including the Barry-Enright shows *Tic Tac Dough* and *The Joker's Wild*. In 1985 he hosted his last game show, *Catch Phrase*. Using puzzles consisting of animated drawings, contestants answered questions for the right to see one of the nine parts of the "catch phrase puzzle." The first player to guess the catch phrase won the money accumulated in the pot. The show only lasted half a season leaving the air on January 10, 1986.

For 13 weeks in the fall of 1989, James announced for ESPN's *NFL Trivia Game*. In the early 1990s, he occasionally substituted for Gene Wood as announcer on *Family Feud*. He brought his career full circle during the summer of 1991 when he filled in for one month as announcer on NBC's revival of *Concentration*, which was now called *Classic Concentration*.

> *AJ (March 1999):*
> "They made a big deal of it because 30 years ago, I was the announcer and there I am again."

Games for Corporate America

Besides his long and successful game show career, Art James developed a unique idea that served as his livelihood for more than 25 years. In 1975 a soap company that sponsored one of his game shows asked him to stage a game show for one of its corporate meetings, James happily obliged. That meeting resulted in a new career. Forming Art James Productions, James and his crew traveled around the country staging game shows for corporations using company employees as the contestants for the shows.

> *AJ (March 1999):*
> "My producer and I hit the road to a sales meeting, convention, or a conference. We learn the client's business and the game is based on product knowledge and what they should have learned over a training period. We divide the audience into teams and the players on stage represent the teams. It's a lot of fun and really noisy, but we're really reinforcing job skills and putting these guys on their toes to show off what they should know about their work."

Art James Productions used about 1,200 pounds of equipment that included a large set, podiums, lights, and sound system equipment. The company staged more than 200 game shows for such companies as IBM, AT&T, Dow Chemical, Motorola, Sony, and Apple Computer to name a few. At first, this was only a side job for James when he was working steadily on television. After his television career stalled in the mid 1980s, he began devoting full time to Art James Productions. The company was first based in Santa Cruz, California and later in San Diego, California, Philadelphia, Pennsylvania, and finally in Minneapolis, Minnesota.

"I Love a Client with a Sense of Humor"

James had some funny stories to tell about the corporate game shows he staged over the years.

> *AJ (February 2004):*
> "I love a client with a sense of humor. I did [a show for] a huge financial advisory firm in Los Angeles. When I had my first meeting with them they said, 'What are we going to call

the game.' Just to be funny I said, 'How about *You Bet Your Assets?*' They loved it! They bought it!"

At another corporate game staged for a law firm, the lawyers showed they could be funny too.

> *AJ:*
> "I asked them to come up with clever names for their teams. Well, they certainly did. One of the names was 'The Well-Hung Jury.'"

In later years, however, Art James Productions suffered a decline in business due to the United States economic recession in 2000. Budget cuts led many corporations to cut back on their conferences and meetings. As a result, James staged fewer game shows for businesses.

> *AJ:*
> "My game show was always a tough sell. When you mention game shows to people, sometimes what comes to mind is *Let's Make a Deal* and people dressed up in costumes and jumping up and down. It's always been a hard sell getting [the corporations] to realize the educational value of what I'm doing even though it's couched in a very popular entertainment format."

Speak Well, Do Well

While looking for ways to increase business, James unexpectedly found a new calling. Over the years while flying around the country staging his corporate game shows, James had become increasingly annoyed by many flight attendants botching up the in-flight announcements made to the passengers on the airplanes.

> *AJ:*
> "There were mispronunciations and sloppy diction. It just struck me that these [people] sounded uneducated and poorly trained and this could reflect the quality of the company itself for the people listening to them."

James wrote a letter to the head of in-flight services for Northwest Airlines explaining the problem and found that the airline was interested in training its flight attendants in public speaking. James designed a speech course that became part of the Northwest Airlines training program. Art James Productions began recording the trainees going through the exercise of reading flight announcements and offered written critiques. James also taught coaching techniques on voice quality.

The speech course was so well received by Northwest Airlines that James decided to take it to the corporate world. He offered it as regular workshop called "Speak Well, Do Well." Joining the National Speakers Association in October 2003, James discovered that fellow television host Bob Eubanks was also a member, and was touring the country with a workshop of his own as a motivational speaker. He called Eubanks to learn more about marketing and promoting himself.

Art James Productions offered the "Speak Well, Do Well" workshop along with the corporate game shows. The fact that corporations had the option of taking one or both of the workshops increased business for Art James Productions. James also lectured at high schools and colleges in Minnesota teaching the students techniques on public speaking.

> *AJ:*
> "I just found that this whole thing of effective speaking and doing research into language and linguistics has been a fascinating study for me."

Art James: The Man

On his personal side, Art James married actress Jane Hamilton in 1957 and had two children, a son Jeffrey and a daughter Jennifer. Jeffrey James ran the offices for his father's company while it was based in California. Art and Jane's marriage ended in divorce in 1981. Then in 1986 while on a flight, James met Sandy Pietron, a flight attendant for Northwest Airlines. They struck up a friendship that became a commuting romance since James lived in Los Angeles and Pietron lived in Minneapolis.

AJ (March 1999):

"I would go to Minneapolis and she would arrange for her flights to lay over in Los Angeles. We did that for five years before deciding to get married."

After marrying Pietron in 1991, James moved to Minneapolis.

AJ:

"This is a great state other than the cold winters. I have friends who say, 'Geez it's 50 below wind chill. How do you deal with that?' I told them it's the only place where you could lock your car with a bucket of water and clean up after your dog with a nine iron."

In his spare time James was an avid golfer and listened to classical music. He also enjoyed flying, yoga, reading, writing, singing, and speaking Russian. In 1997 James began teaching English to Russian immigrants and said that his knowledge of Russian increased as most of his instruction to them was spoken in Russian.

AJ:

"They are warm, wonderful people and serious students anxious to become American citizens."

On March 28, 2004, Art James died suddenly of natural causes at the age of 74 while in Palm Springs, California, on a business trip. His sudden death was a mere five weeks after his February 2004 interview for this book. From his beginnings as Arthur Simeonovich Efimchik, the potential baseball player to Art James, the radio and television host, announcer, producer, and teacher, he left his mark on millions of people.

He mentioned once about how he changed his name from the Russian name Arthur Simeonovich Efimchik in the early 1950s.

AJ:

"One of my Russian relatives said that Efim, the root of the name, means James. So I went to court and had my name legally changed. It turned out that they didn't know what they were talking about at all. It doesn't mean James, but here I am."

Dennis James

Birth Name: Demie James Sposa
Born: August 24, 1917, in Jersey City, New Jersey
Died: June 3, 1997, in Palm Springs, California
Marriages and Family: ???? (Divorced) 1 son; Mildred "Micki" Crawford (1950–1989) (Deceased) 2 sons
Military Career: United States Army Air Force (1942–1945)
Radio Career: Announcer and Disc Jockey (WAAT-AM, Jersey City, NJ) 1937–1938; *Lawyer Q* (MBS) April 3, 1947–June 29, 1947; *Original Amateur Hour* (ABC) September 29, 1948–September 18, 1952
TV Career: HOST—*Television Roof* (W2XWV-TV, New York City) 1938–1939; *Dennis James Sports Parade* (W2XWV-TV, New York City) 1938–1939; Sports/News Commentator & Commercial Announcer/Salesman (W2XWV-TV, New York City) 1938–1942; *DuMont Beepstakes* (DuMont Test Program) May 29, 1946; *Cash and Carry* (DuMont Primetime) June 20, 1946–July 1, 1947; *Okay Mother* (DuMont Daytime) November 1, 1948–July 6, 1951; *The Dennis James Show* (ABC Daytime) September 24, 1951–February 15, 1952; *Chance of a Lifetime* (ABC Primetime) May 8, 1952–August 20, 1953, (DuMont Primetime) September 11, 1953–June 24, 1955, (ABC Primetime) July 3, 1955–June 23, 1956; *Turn to a Friend* (ABC Daytime) October 5, 1953–December 31, 1953; *On Your Account* (CBS Daytime) October 4, 1954–March 30, 1956; *The Name's the Same* (ABC Primetime) October 25, 1954–April 4, 1955; *High Finance* (CBS Primetime) July 7, 1956–December 15, 1956; *Club 60* (NBC Daytime) March 1957–September 27, 1957; *What Makes You Tick?* (Unsold Game Show Pilot) 1957; *Haggis Baggis* (NBC Daytime) February 9, 1959–June 19, 1959; *Beat the Odds* (KTLA-TV, Los Angeles, CA) July 1962–August 23, 1963; *People Will Talk* (NBC Daytime) July 1, 1963–December 27, 1963; *Chain Letter* (Unsold Game Show Pilot) 1964; *PDQ* (Syndicated) August 30, 1965–September 26, 1969; *Your All-American College Show* (Syndicated) September 1968–September 1970; *The Price Is Right* (Syndicated) September 11, 1972–September 1977; *Name That Tune* (NBC Daytime) July 29, 1974–January 3, 1975 ANNOUNCER—*Ted Mack's Original Amateur Hour* (DuMont, NBC, ABC, & CBS Primetime) January 18, 1948–September 26, 1960; Boxing Coverage (DuMont Primetime) July 1948–July 1950; Wrestling Coverage (DuMont Primetime) July 30, 1948–May 1951 PANELIST—*Your First Impression* (NBC Daytime) January 2, 1962–June 26, 1964

Dennis James (Fred Wostbrock)

Theatrical Movies: *Mr. Universe* (1951); *The One and Only* (1978); *Rocky III* (1982); *The Method* (1997)
Commercial Work: Spokesman, Old Gold Cigarettes; Spokesman, Kellogg Cereals (1950–1961); Spokesman, Physicians Mutual Insurance Co. (1970–1997)
Business Interests: President: Dennis James Productions (1950–1997)
Charity Work: United Cerebral Palsy Foundation (1950–1997); ChildHelp USA; The American Cancer Society; The American Heart Association

Dennis James claimed many firsts in the world of television. He appeared in the very first television commercial, the first sports commentary show, the first program recorded on videotape, and emceed the first audience-participation show. Nevertheless, these are only a few of this television pioneer's claims to fame. It was also just the beginning of a career that lasted for nearly six decades.

Dennis James arrived in this world as Demie James Sposa on August 24, 1917, in Jersey City, New Jersey. After graduating from high school and St. Peter's College, he passed up medical school over his parents' wishes to become an actor. He enrolled in the Theater School of the Performing Arts at Carnegie Hall in New York where he graduated in 1937. His first job after theater school was not in acting, but in selling dog supplies at Abercrombie and Fitch. Later in 1937 James joined the staff of WAAT-AM, a small radio station in his hometown of Jersey City, New Jersey.

Change Your Name

In Jeff Kisseloff's book *The Box*, James mentioned that the manager of WAAT was Italian. The manager suggested that James, whose own name was Italian, adopt a new handle. James protested, but went along with the idea when the manager threatened to fire him. James' older brother, Lou Sposa, suggested that he use his first two names. His first name was Demi, which came from his father's name Demitriou. With a few adjustments, Demi James Sposa became Dennis James.

Meanwhile, his brother, Lou was working as a technician in the DuMont Laboratories in New York City. The company's founder, Allen B. DuMont, planned to venture into the new and undeveloped medium of television with an experimental station called W2XWV. DuMont needed a performer for his two programs that would inaugurate the new television station. Lou immediately suggested his brother Dennis and DuMont hired him.

Up on the Roof

On a Tuesday evening in September 1938 in a 5-by-10 feet studio on the 42nd floor at 515 Madison Ave. in New York City, James appeared to a handful of New Yorkers who were fortunate enough to own a television set. In a 1963 *TV Guide* interview, James noted that New York City had 300 television sets in 1938 but 200 of them failed to work. The first show was a half hour called *Television Roof*, which James later described as "like Ed Sullivan without the acrobats."

Using only two cameras, the show opened with a shot of an elevator going up a New York skyscraper. In reality, the "skyscraper" was only a scale model about two feet tall. After the elevator reached the top of the model, the other camera cut to a shot of James who introduced a famous performer (maybe famous by New York City standards). Two of these acts included Dick Haymes and the Pied Pipers, who were both accompanied by a three-piece orchestra.

Though these early television cameras only broadcast black and white images, James still had to wear brown lipstick because the cameras were sensitive to the color red. Since the hot lights brought the studio temperature up to 140 degrees and caused James to sweat profusely, he was a strange sight to the early television viewers. On Fridays James emceed a second half hour program called *The Dennis James Sports Parade*. These two shows made up the entire schedule of television station W2XWV. James was paid $50 for each show.

A Knockout

The Dennis James Sports Parade had an interesting format: James interviewed a sports figure for five minutes and then joined the athlete in playing the sport. Each week James could be seen boxing, wrestling, and playing baseball among other things. With *The Dennis James Sports Parade* airing live, anything could happen.

One Friday, the featured guest was wrestler Bibber McCoy, who was showing various wrestling holds and maneuvers. McCoy mentioned that a particular hold could put a man out in 10 seconds. When James did not believe him, McCoy demonstrated the choke hold and knocked the poor host out. After smacking James around to snap him out of his unconscious state, he revived and the show continued.

Time Out for a Commercial

James also worked as a sportscaster and news commentator appearing in the first on-the-spot live TV newsreel in the early 1940s. He also did an unpaid 30 minute advertisement for Wedgwood china, the first television commercial. Television executives eventually discovered that by selling advertising time on their schedules to companies, stations could turn a profit and use the money to expand their operations.

When local stations later became affiliates of the ABC, CBS, DuMont, and NBC networks in the late 1940s, the practice of selling commercial time continued on a much larger scale at the national level. Dennis James joined the ranks of television pioneers in commercial development. Besides hosting, he worked in advertising as a performer, announcer, and salesman selling commercial time.

Working for DuMont

James interrupted his career in 1942 to enlist in the United States Army during World War II. After his discharge in 1945, he rejoined DuMont, which by now had expanded to become a national television network. His game show career began with a live test show for DuMont on May 29, 1946, called *DuMont Beepstakes*. The game was a simulated car race from New York to Los Angeles with DuMont network executives acting as the players. The game board consisted of a large map of the United States. Starting with their "cars" in New York, the contestants answered a series of questions that allowed their "cars" to advance one state at a time across the board. The first player to reach Los Angeles won the game.

Three weeks later on June 20, 1946, James hosted his first regularly televised game show, *Cash and Carry*. Seen Thursday nights at 9:00 p.m., the show's set resembled a grocery store that was lined with shelves of the sponsor's products, Libby's Foods. The products all had questions attached to them worth $5, $10, and $15. The game also consisted of stunts such as a man imitating a woman taking off her clothes for a bath and a blindfolded woman feeding her husband ice cream. Another regular feature each week allowed home viewers to call the show and guess what was under a large barrel.

Practical Jokes

James' entrance to each *Cash and Carry* episode varied from week to week. Sometimes he would be sitting in a barber chair or a bath tub. *TV Guide* noted in 1963 that the show's crew members used this as an opportunity to play practical jokes on James. When getting into the bathtub just before airtime, James discovered that the crew had filled it with ice cubes. When he was seated in the barber chair, he found that the crew had wired it. The crew turned on the juice sending James jumping in the air. On another show, a cash register was rigged so that the drawer shot out across the studio. James took all of the jokes as good fun but finally drew the line when the crew cut a sand bag from the ceiling and it just missed hitting him.

James also announced for *Ted Mack's Original Amateur Hour* on the DuMont network. Thousands of people from across the United States auditioned for the show and if successful were given a chance to do their stuff on national television. Old Gold Cigarettes was the sponsor and James began his long association with the company as their spokesman. James remained with *Ted Mack's Original Amateur Hour* for the next 12 years.

Learning How to Wrestle

By the late 1940s James was an established television star. DuMont discovered that wrestling and boxing matches were inexpensive forms of programming and the network began saturating its primetime schedules with both sports beginning in July 1948. The network assigned James the task of announcing the wrestling and boxing matches from the Jamaica, Jerome, Columbia Park, Sunnyside Gardens, and Dexter Arenas.

Of the two sports, James had the most fun with wrestling since it was played more for entertainment. Having absolutely no experience with wrestling, James bought himself a book on the subject. Whenever he saw a wrestling maneuver he did not know, he thumbed through the book right on camera.

"Look At the Suet on Hewitt"

James never took the fights seriously and his commentary was often comical. His catchphrase "Okay Mother" when addressing the lady viewers became a popular expression. Adding to the fun was James using sound effects to punctuate the different wrestling moves.

When one wrestler had another one in a headlock or some painful hold, James cracked walnut shells or pieces of wood to give the illusion of bones breaking. If the wrestlers pulled on each other's trunks, he tore a lamp shade. He even resorted to playing waltz music during some fights. During a bout staged in an outdoor arena, James had the show's director focus one camera on the fighters while the other camera aimed at the moon. On the air the two shots were superimposed to give the illusion of the wrestlers fighting on the moon.

His lighthearted approach to the sport did not always endear James to the wrestlers. According to *TV Guide* in 1954, one wrestler named Tarzan Hewitt objected when James ad-libbed a poem during the fight saying, "Look at the suet on Hewitt." When the two met after the fight, Hewitt grabbed James' arm and almost broke it.

Wrestling Loses Favor

For three years, James announced wrestling for the DuMont network on a regular basis Monday, Thursday, Friday, and Saturday nights. His boxing chores usually took place Monday, Tuesday, Wednesday, and Thursday evenings during the months when DuMont did not air wrestling matches. As television began growing in the early 1950s and more viewers began seeing the wrestling matches, there were many complaints to stop the violence.

The Athletic Commission imposed several restrictions on the sport that all but eliminated the fun atmosphere created by James. He finally hung up his boxing microphone in September 1950 when DuMont quit airing the bouts and gave up the wrestling chores in May 1951. That same year, James portrayed a boxing announcer in the theatrical movie *Mr. Universe*.

Okay Mother

On November 1, 1948, James started what is said to be the first daytime audience participation/variety show. Telecast on DuMont, the program was called *Okay Mother*, a popular phrase used by James. The show ran for three years until July 6, 1951. He then moved to ABC hosting *The Dennis James Show*, a daytime variety series, until February 1952.

James also created and hosted *Chance of a Lifetime*. During the first half of each show, two contestants competed performing various acts ranging from singing, telling jokes, and playing musical numbers. Audience applause determined the winner. The second half of the show pitted that night's winner against the winner from the previous week. The winner of the second round earned $1,000 and a week's engagement at the prominent New York's Latin Quarter. The runner-up received a booking at a lesser known nightclub.

As was often the case with *Ted Mack's Original Amateur Hour*, very few of the contestants on *Chance of a Lifetime* went on to successful show business careers. One discovery, however, was comedian Dick Van Dyke, who went on to a Broadway career before starting his highly successful sitcom *The Dick Van Dyke Show* in 1961. In more recent years, Van Dyke was seen as Dr. Sloane on the CBS detective series *Diagnosis Murder*.

Roll Out the Games

By the mid 1950s, James focused more and more on game shows. In October 1954, he replaced Win Elliot as host of *On Your Account*. Contestants answered questions for money that went to the player's favorite charity or to a person they wanted to reward for doing a good deed. The format later changed to a straight question-and-answer game involving three competitors with the winner playing for a $1,500 jackpot.

James also added the hosting duties of *The Name's the Same*. A panel of four celebrities guessed the identities of contestants sharing the same names of famous people, places, or common objects (for example: A. Mattress).

With game shows now giving away huge sums of money to winners, James, along with his *Chance of a Lifetime* colleague Robert Jennings, created their own entry in the big money sweepstakes, *High Finance*. In this game, contestants "invested" their accumulated money through a series of question rounds to win prizes and stay on the show. The top prize was $75,000.

High Finance debuted on July 7, 1956, but the show never built much of a following and left the air that December. During its five months on the air, nobody won the $75,000 top prize, but many contestants left the show with winnings near $25,000. Of all the big money quiz shows that aired during the mid 1950s, there has never been any evidence or mention of rigging practices taking place on *High Finance*. While shows such as *The $64,000 Question*, *The $100,000 Big Surprise*, *Twenty-One*, and *Tic Tac Dough* fell under fire, *High Finance* escaped the trap.

Turning Down Tonight

James went to Chicago in March 1957 to host *Club 60*, an NBC daytime variety series. Broadcast live, *Club 60* was one of the few regularly scheduled television programs to air in color. After six months, James was dropped as host and replaced by Howard Miller.

During his run on *Club 60*, James was offered the spot as host of NBC's *The Tonight Show* but he turned it down. *The Tonight Show* aired live and James disliked the idea of putting in long hours he felt would be necessary to do the show each night. The job went to comedian Jack Paar, and *The Tonight Show* soared in the ratings under his guidance. James never regretted turning down the show even after seeing it make a star out of Jack Paar.

Fewer Activities

By the late 1950s, James' activities were restricted to his weekly announcing chores on *Original Amateur Hour* and as Kellogg's Cereals spokesman on CBS's *What's My Line?* He also filled in for Jan Murray as substitute host for the game show *Treasure Hunt*. In February 1959 he replaced Fred Robbins as host of *Haggis Baggis*, a game that offered contestants the choice of two sets of prizes. One group consisted of luxury items called the "haggis" prizes. The second group contained utilitarian items labeled "baggis" prizes. *Haggis Baggis* was the last game show that James hosted from New York. He stayed with the show until it left the air in June 1959.

Falling in Love with California

In late 1961, Monty Hall asked James to come to California to work as a panelist on a new show called *Your First Impression*. James agreed to work on the show for 13 weeks, but upon arriving, he fell in love with the warm weather and California sunshine. He moved his family to the west coast and his initial 13 week commitment on *Your First Impression* turned into a stay of more than two years.

Meanwhile, he remained busy moonlighting as host of *Beat the Odds*, a word game broadcast over Los Angeles television station KTLA during the 1962-1963 season. From July to December 1963, James hosted NBC's *People Will Talk*, a game where two contestants predicted how a panel of 15 people composed of a cross-section of the American public would answer yes or no questions.

PDQ

James resurfaced in August 1965 with *PDQ*. The title of the show stood for "Please Draw Quickly." Two teams, one composed of a celebrity and contestant and the other with two celebrities, played the game. One member from each team entered the two soundproof booths on stage. One team played first while the sound in the opponent's booth was eliminated. The contestant was shown a word or phrase and had to get his/her celebrity partner to guess it by gradually adding

It's the first tape day on *PDQ* in 1965. Celebrity guests Morey Amsterdam, Rose Marie, and Gisele MacKenzie join Dennis James and a contestant to start the festivities (Fred Wostbrock).

letters. The opposing team then played the same phrase. The team using the least number of letters to guess the phrase won points. *PDQ* ran four seasons until September 1969.

James devoted much of his time to commercial work and hosting his annual United Cerebral Palsy telethons. James had begun his work for United Cerebral Palsy in 1950 when the telethons began airing on television. He traveled around the United States on behalf of the organization raising millions of dollars each year to help thousands of Americans suffering from Cerebral Palsy. In 1970 he became the commercial spokesman for Physicians Mutual Insurance Company, a position he held for 27 years.

Deal Me in Because the Price Is Right

One day in January 1972 while golfing at a Los Angeles country club, James received a call to host *Let's Make a Deal* when its host Monty Hall took ill. One of the people who saw that show was game show producer Bill Todman. At the time, Goodson-Todman Productions was looking for someone to host a revival of *The Price Is Right*. After Goodson and Todman viewed a tape of James hosting *Let's Make a Deal*, they immediately signed him to host a syndicated nighttime version of *The Price Is Right*.

CBS also picked up the show for its daytime schedule and it looked as if James might also host that version. He noted in a 1982 *Miami Herald* interview that because the nighttime *Price Is Right* aired mainly on NBC owned and operated stations across America, CBS considered James an NBC personality, and thus did not want him on their version. The daytime hosting duties went to Bob Barker.

Both editions of *The Price Is Right* hit the air in September 1972 and became huge hits. James' five year stint with *The Price Is Right* was memorable. On one episode, his microphone cable became twisted around a camera and he could not move. When a female contestant came out of contestant's row, she ran up the steps to the stage too fast and crashed into James. Needless to say, both the host and contestant tumbled to the floor.

Naming That Tune

In the summer of 1974, James' career received another boost. Game show producer Ralph Edwards purchased the rights to a 1950s game show called *Name That Tune* and launched a daytime version on NBC and a weekly nighttime syndicated edition. James was selected to host the daytime version while Tom Kennedy took the nighttime series. Debuting in July 1974, *Name That Tune* featured a series of musical guessing games and was divided into three rounds. The winner advanced to the Golden Medley and named seven songs in 30 seconds for a possible $2,500.

While Tom Kennedy's version of *Name That Tune* enjoyed high ratings, the daytime series floundered. James was never comfortable as the show's host. To his chagrin, Lin Bolen, the head of NBC daytime programming, insisted on making James look like a young stud by dressing him in leisure suits, bell-bottoms, and asking him to grow longer hair. The sight of a 57-year-old man trying to look about 30 years younger was embarrassing. He was not sorry when *Name That Tune* faded from view on January 3, 1975.

Giving Back

James hosted the nighttime version of *The Price Is Right* until the fall of 1977 when he handed the reins over to Bob Barker. Although no longer a regular television performer, James remained a fixture on the small screen through the 1980s and 1990s with the annual Cerebral Palsy telethons and by producing and appearing in scores of commercials through his company Dennis James Productions Inc.

He also raised money off camera hosting a number of charity golf tournaments and campaigning for the children's charities ChildHelp USA and Variety Club. In his lifetime, James was responsible for raising more than $1 billion for his charities, of which $700 million came from the United Cerebral telethons.

After suffering a heart attack in 1987, James spoke on behalf of the American Heart Association and the American Cancer Society. He traveled the country speaking at seminars on the diseases and how they related to aging. In 1992 the entertainment world saluted him with a star on the Hollywood Walk of Fame and in 1993 he received an individual achievement award from the American Heart Association.

Laboring to the End

James worked right up to the very end of his life. He was still doing commercials for Physicians Mutual Insurance when he was diagnosed with lung cancer in January 1997. Although James had smoked for a number of years, he quit in the 1960s when the surgeon general announced that smoking could cause cancer. Despite his illness, James continued golfing every day and working on commercials until shortly before passing away at his Palm Springs home on June 3, 1997, at the age of 79.

Even after his death, James could still be seen by movie goers in his last motion picture performance as a university dean in *The Method*, which was released in the summer of 1997.

Strive for Realism

One of Dennis James' secrets for his long success, whether it was hosting a game show, promoting a product on a commercial, or raising money for charity, was that he came across as a sincere and warm person. He genuinely cared about the people for whom he raised money to fight cerebral palsy, heart disease and cancer. He rooted for the contestants on his game shows and firmly believed in all of the products he endorsed.

Instead of heavily turning on the charm or going to the other extreme by talking down to people, James aimed for the middle road in sincerity. His secret, according to a 1982 *Miami Herald* story, was that he "always strived for realism," and that he worked hard to never appear condescending or fake.

TOM KENNEDY

Birth Name: James Edward Narz

Born: February 26, 1927, in Louisville, Kentucky

Marriage and Family: Betty Gevedon (1952–Present) 3 daughters, 1 son

Military Career: United States Army Air Force Pilot Training (1944–1945); United States Navy (1945–1946)

Radio Career: Announcer/Engineer (WLOU-AM, Louisville, KY) 1949–1950; Announcer/Engineer (WGRC-AM, Louisville, KY) 1950; Announcer/Engineer (WKLO-AM, Louisville, KY) 1950; Announcer/Engineer (KFRU-AM, Columbia, MO) 1950–1951; Announcer/Engineer (WVLK-AM, Lexington, KY) 1951; Announcer/Engineer (WKLX-AM, Lexington, KY) 1951–1952; Disc Jockey/Announcer (KPOL-AM, Los Angeles, CA) 1952–1957

TV Career: ANNOUNCER—Spokesman (Plymouth Corporation) 1957–1958; *The Gisele MacKenzie Show* (NBC Primetime) January 18, 1958–March 29, 1958; *About Faces* (ABC Daytime) January 4, 1960–June 30, 1961   HOST—*Big Game* (NBC Primetime) June 13, 1958–September 12, 1958; *Doctor I.Q.* (ABC Primetime) December 15, 1958–March 23, 1959; *Temptation* (KTLA-TV, Los Angeles, Ca.) 1962; *Sundown* (KABC-TV) February 4, 1963–March 29, 1963; *You Don't Say!* (NBC Daytime) April 1, 1963–September 26, 1969, (NBC Primetime) January 7, 1964–May 12, 1964; *The Real Tom Kennedy Show* (Syndicated) July 11, 1970–September 1970; *It's Your Bet* (Syndicated) March 1971–March 1972; *Split Second* (ABC Daytime) March 20, 1972–June 27, 1975; *$100,000 Name That Tune* (Syndicated) September 9, 1974–September 1981; *You Don't Say* (ABC Daytime) July 7, 1975–November 28, 1975; *Break the Bank* (ABC Daytime) April 12, 1976–July 23, 1976; *50 Grand Slam* (NBC Daytime) October 4, 1976–December 31, 1976; *Name That Tune* (NBC Daytime) January 3, 1977–June 10, 1977; *To Say the Least* (NBC Daytime) October 3, 1977–April 21, 1978; Arthritis Foundation Annual Telethons 1979–1984; *Whew!* (CBS Daytime) April 23, 1979–May 30, 1980; *Password Plus* (NBC Daytime) October 27, 1980–March 26, 1982; *Body Language* (CBS Daytime) June 4, 1984–January 3, 1986; *The Price Is Right* (Syndicated) September 9, 1985–September 5, 1986; *Wordplay* (NBC Daytime) December 29, 1986–September 4, 1987; *Star Play* (Unsold Game Show Pilot) 1988   CREATOR—*Joker in the Pack* (BBC) (Great Britain) 1991–1992, (Germany, Portugal, Spain) 1992–1993

Made-for-TV Movie: *Having Babies* (ABC) October 17, 1976

Summer Stock: *The Odd Couple* (1966); *Tunnel of Love* (1967); *There's a Girl in My Soup* (1968)

Tom Kennedy (Tom Kennedy, courtesy Fred Wostbrock)

"It's not important what you say. It's what You Don't Say." "I have a lady in the balcony doctor." "I can name that tune in four notes." "Whew!" "The actual retail price is…" Do you recognize these catch-phrases? They all have one thing in common. These words were all said on game shows hosted by Tom Kennedy. Third only to Bill Cullen and Wink Martindale in the most game shows hosted by one person, Kennedy helmed 15 nationally televised game shows in almost three decades.

Born as James Edward Narz in Louisville, Kentucky on February 26, 1927, Kennedy enjoyed a happy childhood with his brother and sister. While he was in high school, the United States entered World War II. with the attack on Pearl Harbor. His older brother, Jack Narz, joined the Army Air Force in early 1942. Since Kennedy was not old enough to join the military, he followed in his brother's footsteps and joined a pilot training program offered by the Army Air Force for people under the age of 18.

> *Tom Kennedy (October 2004 telephone interview):*
> "I'd go out to the air field on weekends and they would put us in uniform and take us up and teach us about flying. But all they were doing was training us how to look at airplanes and to figure out what they were and how they operated. They never got around to teaching us how to fly."

Upon graduation from high school in 1945, he planned to become a fighter pilot, but the Japanese surrender and the end of the war in August 1945 prompted the military to eliminate all pilot training programs.

> *TK:*
> "We had V-J (Victory in Japan) Day while I was in boot camp. That was the end of it right there. All they did was try to figure out what to do with us guys that were late comers, so they put us in various schools until we were discharged."

Kennedy transferred from the Army Air Force to the U.S. Navy and went to radar school in Boston, Massachusetts.

Mechanical Engineer

After his discharge in 1946, Kennedy returned to Louisville, Kentucky, but was unsure of what kind of career to pursue. On a lark, he enrolled at the University of Louisville and majored in Mechanical Engineering.

> *TK:*
> "I had no idea what it really meant, but I signed up as a guy who was going to become a Mechanical Engineer."

While in college, Kennedy corresponded with his brother Jack Narz, who had gone to California after the war and had become a radio announcer. Narz encouraged him to try his luck in the broadcasting business. Using money from the GI Bill, Kennedy moved to California to attend The Don Martin School of Radio Arts in 1948.

> *TK:*
> "I just wanted to see what the west coast looked like. I had never been to the west. I came out to that school and fell in love with not only that school, but with the industry."

He took a combination course in announcing and engineering and received his first class radio/telephone operator's license to operate a radio station transmitter. After graduating in 1949, Kennedy's first radio job was in, of all places, Louisville, Kentucky. He joined the staff at WLOU-AM as an announcer and engineer.

Professional Dropout

During the summer months, Kennedy worked at two other Louisville stations, WGRC-AM and WKLO-AM, as a substitute announcer. Soon he learned of a better job at KFRU-AM in Columbia, Missouri, and after securing the job, he enrolled at the University of Missouri majoring in journalism. However, when his GI Bill ran out, he was forced to withdraw from the University of Missouri, quit his job at KFRU, and return to Kentucky.

Moving to Lexington, Kentucky, Kennedy worked for WKLX-AM and enrolled in the University of Kentucky. He dropped out after a short time.

> *TK:*
> "I was a professional dropout. I never got enough credits [with] all of that jumping around. I never got a diploma. I went to three different universities."

"If It Doesn't Work Out, We'll Come Back Home"

While at the University of Kentucky, Kennedy fell in love with Betty Gevedon, a student at the school. After dating for close to a year, they eloped in 1952 and soon headed for the west coast seeking greener pastures.

> *TK:*
> "We went out there with our agenda being, we will go out there and we'll try it for two to five years and if it works, fine. If it doesn't, we'll come back home."

Not long after arriving in Los Angeles, he landed a job as a disc jockey playing polka records for KPOL-AM where he remained for five years. He also worked part time at KGIL-AM in the San Fernando Valley.

By now Kennedy was anxious to spread his wings and try television. Since KPOL was a daytime station and signed off at sunset, Kennedy had the evenings to shop for television work. He got his foot in the door doing commercials for Los Angeles television stations. At the time, with very few exceptions, all the local commercials were done live since videotape did not yet exist and stations could not afford film.

> *TK:*
> "In those days, there were only five [television] stations in Los Angeles. So if you were on the air with any frequency at all, you received a depth of recognition."

On the strength of his commercial work, Kennedy started getting calls to host benefits, luncheons, dinners, pageants, and fashion shows.

> *TK:*
> "The combination of doing live television and emceeing those events, I didn't realize it, [was] training me to be a TV game show host."

Jim Narz or Tom Kennedy?

By 1957 Kennedy was making a name for himself in Hollywood. Until now, he was still going by his real name Jim Narz. He was about to sign a contract to be a television spokesman for Plymouth Motor Company when the agency suggested that he change his name. Jim's brother, Jack Narz, was already a nationally known television personality as an announcer on game and variety shows.

The problem was that people frequently confused the two brothers. The Plymouth agency suggested that Jim Narz take the last name of Kennedy since he looked Irish and the name seemed to fit. For the first name, Jim suggested "Rick," but someone else said that it sounded like "Rock." Finally someone suggested "Tom" and the name stuck. Jim Narz became Tom Kennedy, though he never legally changed his name. To this day, among his family, Tom Kennedy is still called Jim Narz.

Hunting for Big Game

While working in the trenches in Los Angeles television, Kennedy started auditioning as a game show host. He did run-throughs for game show ideas conjured up by producers, but the shows either never made it to the air or someone else became the host. Finally on June 13, 1958, Kennedy became the host of NBC's *Big Game*, which was seen on Friday evenings. *Big Game* was based on the children's game "Battleship." Two contestants each had a game board containing 25 squares, which their opponent could not see. Each player secretly placed three magnetic animal pieces anywhere on their board. Contestants answered questions for the right to call out numbers and "shoot" their opponent's animals. The first player to knock out all three of their opponent's animals won $2,000 and faced a new challenger.

Big Game was the first regularly scheduled game show to be telecast in color, but that was not without its problems.

> *TK:*
> "In those days, since we were in color, the [studio] lights were intense. They had two boards with animals on them instead of battleships. [The squares] would light up [on the board] when you had a hit and then they wouldn't light up when you didn't have a hit. On camera in the studio, we could see some of those lights, but at home you couldn't tell which lights were on. There was so much light [in the studio] that your screens at home just sort of glazed over it."

The fact that most viewers in those days still owned black and white televisions only exacerbated the problem.

> *TK:*
> "People at home couldn't really follow [the game] and so that was one of our major technical blocks."

Big Game bit the dust after 14 weeks.

"I Have a Lady in the Balcony"

Three months later, Kennedy was back with his second game show, *Doctor IQ*. As "Dr. IQ," Kennedy asked questions to contestants selected from the studio audience. Players were paid in the form of silver dollars for correct answers. *Doctor IQ* faded after three months.

Kennedy stayed afloat doing commercials in Los Angeles. In January 1960, he became the announcer for ABC's *About Faces*, a game show hosted by actor Ben Alexander, formerly of the police series *Dragnet*. In 1962 Kennedy hosted a game show called *Temptation* for KTLA-TV in Los Angeles. He followed up in February 1963 with a talk show for KABC-TV called *Sundown*, which he co-hosted with tennis star Gussie Moran.

You Don't Say!

In the meantime, KTLA-TV launched the game show *You Don't Say!* in late 1962 to test the waters for a possible major network run. Kennedy and veteran television host Jack Barry took turns hosting the show on a short-term basis. When NBC picked up the series in the spring of 1963, Kennedy became the host. When offered the job, Kennedy had to decide whether to continue with *Sundown* on KABC-TV or take *You Don't Say!* on NBC since the network would not let him host both shows. Kennedy gave it a lot of thought before going with *You Don't Say!*

The simple word game featured two celebrity-contestant teams who guessed the names of famous people and places using a series of clues. One member of the team was given the mystery name and tried to get his or her partner to guess it. The clues were given in the form of incomplete sentences with the last word of the sentence being left blank, hence the show's name: *You Don't Say!* The first team to correctly identify three names collected $100 and played a bonus game.

The show became a popular fixture on NBC's daytime schedule for more than six years. By the 1967-1968 season, *You Don't Say!* was the top-rated daytime game show on television. With a hit series on the air, Kennedy stretched his legs and appeared in an off–Broadway version of the play *The Odd Couple* in Michigan. He later appeared in the plays *Tunnel of Love* and *There's a Girl in My Soup*. He also did occasional guest spots on television sitcoms and dramas during the 1960s through the 1980s including *That Girl*, *Cannon*, and *Hardcastle and McCormick*. He found that acting was quite different from hosting a game show.

> *TK:*
> "I'm a slow learner. It takes a long time to learn a play. I don't have very good retention."

Going from Game to Talk

A sudden blow hit Kennedy when NBC canceled the still highly-rated *You Don't Say* in September 1969. This was one of several mistakes NBC made in the late 1960s that ultimately cost the peacock network the top spot in the daytime ratings. NBC had just canceled *Let's Make a Deal*, which was a ratings monster for the network. ABC promptly snatched the show and started beating NBC in the ratings.

> *TK:*
> "NBC went into the dumper and it took them a long while to recover from that. It wasn't the brightest move they've ever made."

For Kennedy and his family, losing *You Don't Say!* could not have come at a worse time. The family had just purchased a house in Toluca Lake near Hollywood and was moving in when Kennedy got his cancellation notice from NBC.

> *TK:*
> "There I was without a job and it was a big gap in our lives."

After spending nearly a year out of work, he returned to television in the summer of 1970 to helm *The Real Tom Kennedy Show*. The hour-long talk-variety series featured guests George Carlin, Carol Burnette, and Vicki Lawrence. Interspersed with the chatting were musical numbers by guest bands and singers. *The Real Tom Kennedy Show* only lasted nine weeks because there were not enough stations across the nation carrying the series to give it a large audience.

In a Split Second

Kennedy's next break came in the spring of 1971 when he took over as host of *It's Your Bet*, a celebrity guessing game. Finally in 1972 Kennedy scored again with ABC's *Split Second*. Three contestants played a series of three lightning fast question and answer rounds. To start the game, Kennedy revealed a three-part question in the form of three clues. Each player had a lock out button and tried to buzz in before their opponents. The first to buzz in chose one of the three clues and Kennedy asked a question. If the player was correct, the player who buzzed in second chose from one of the two remaining question clues. The third player automatically had to answer the one remaining question.

The payoffs for round one were $5 apiece if all three players answered correctly, $10 if only two were right and $25 if one was correct. In round two, the stakes increased to $10, $25, and $50. The winner chose one of five automobiles on the stage and started it. Only one of the cars could start. If successful, the contestant won the car and retired from the game. If not, they returned on the next show. Contestants winning five days in a row automatically received a car.

To keep four of the cars from starting, a mechanic disconnected the ignition coil. As insurance that no one would know which car would start, ABC insisted that the mechanic work under a blanket. A January 1980 *TV Guide* article by Art James revealed that one day, the mechanic accidentally disconnected a spark plug instead of the ignition coil on one of the cars. During the show, the winner naturally chose the car with the disconnected spark plug. When the player started the engine, the car sputtered and started, then died, then started again, then stopped. All of this time, smoke poured from the car's exhaust pipe filling the studio. The producers ultimately awarded the car to the contestant.

Name That Tune

In 1974 Kennedy became the host of the syndicated nighttime version of *Name That Tune*. Two contestants played a series of musical guessing games for cash and prizes. The contestant with the most points after three rounds played the "Golden Medley" bonus round where they identified seven tunes in 30 seconds for a cash jackpot.

In the fall of 1976, the show was renamed *The $100,000 Name That Tune* and the producers instituted a new tournament of champions format where weekly winners returned to play for $100,000. The show went on to a phenomenal seven year run. Kennedy related a story from *The $100,000 Name That Tune*. One day while members of the studio audience selected to play the game were called to the stage, one particular lady got a little too excited as she made her way down the aisle.

> *TK:*
> "This one lady had on a pair of slacks. When they called her name, she was so excited that she jumped up [from her seat], jumped over the rail and came running up to me. When she gave me a hug, she said in my ear, 'Oh my goodness my pants are coming down.' She had those buttons on the side of the slacks and they gave [away]. It was either buttons or a zipper. I don't remember which one. They didn't really fall down, but they stood a chance of falling down. I remember that she was a very spry lady and she was a grandmother. You wouldn't think she was over 21."

Kennedy took off his suit coat and gave it to the lady to wrap around herself and the show went to a commercial. During the break, a seamstress fixed the slacks and the show continued.

Working for ABC and NBC

During his tenure on *Name That Tune*, Kennedy also hosted a string of network game shows. From July to November 1975, he hosted a revival of *You Don't Say!* on ABC. Then in the spring of 1976 he hosted the comedy game show *Break the Bank* for 15 weeks. Kennedy then signed a contract with NBC and hosted three game shows for the network between 1976 and 1978.

His first assignment was *50 Grand Slam*, a tough question and answer show that offered a $50,000 prize. Two contestants were placed in isolation booths on stage and asked four-part questions on a given subject. The contestant who correctly answered the most parts of the question received $200. Succeeding questions were worth $500, $1,000, $2000, $5,000, $10,000, $20,000, and finally $50,000.

A Wrong Answer

A mishap occurred on one show where the subject of the question was "Musical Comedy." Both contestants responded "Cole Porter" to the question, but Kennedy's card said the answer was Irving Berlin. Suddenly Kennedy and the producers realized that the contestants may have been right. The taping stopped immediately while the producers tried to reach a representative with the NBC Standards and Practices Department in New York. At first the man could not be located.

> *TK:*
> "We had a live audience and they tried to keep the audience [in the studio]. But after a couple of hours we had to let them go. They couldn't find this guy [from Standards and Practices]. When they finally did, he insisted on getting a lawyer first before he would [make a decision] because there was $50,000 involved."

It took almost six hours to resolve the issue, but when taping finally resumed, the episode was completed without a studio audience by using canned applause. Kennedy explained to the viewers that both of the contestants answered correctly and that his question card contained the wrong answer.

Tom Kennedy stands in front of the Melody Roulette wheel on *Name That Tune* **(Tom Kennedy, courtesy Fred Wostbrock).**

After 13 weeks, *50 Grand Slam* was replaced by a daytime version of *Name That Tune* with Kennedy working double duty as host. Although the nighttime edition of the show was still burning up the ratings, the daytime version failed to capture that same spirit and was dropped on June 10, 1977. That fall, Kennedy turned up in NBC's *To Say the Least*, a game where two teams composed of a contestant and two celebrities tried to guess subjects from clues given in the form of short sentences. *To Say the Least* left the air in April 1978.

Whew!

In the spring of 1979, Kennedy jumped to CBS to host *Whew!* (pronounced ph-ew). This ultra fast game show was created by Jay Wolpert, who had previously produced *The Price Is Right*. Players on *Whew!* answered questions from a board containing five rows of five boxes and a sixth row with three boxes. The contestant answering the questions was called the "charger" while the other player was called the "blocker." The "blocker" secretly placed six blocks on the board concealed behind the boxes. The "charger" had 60 seconds to pick one box on each of the five rows and answer questions to win money.

If the "charger" picked a box containing a block, they lost five seconds off the clock. If the "charger" succeeded in answering one question in each of the six rows in less than a minute, they won the round and the money. Otherwise, the "blocker" won. Players switched roles in round two and the winner played a bonus round for $25,000.

> *TK:*
> "It was a good show that just went too fast. To me it was a show written at 33 and a third [revolutions per minute] that we played at 78 [rpms]. That show on paper was a very entertaining and very cleverly written show, but we did it so fast that people at home only got half of it."

Whew! drew dismal ratings and in November 1979, the format was altered to include celebrity players. The ratings stayed in the cellar and the show was laid to rest on May 30, 1980.

An Unhappy Time

In October 1980, Kennedy received an unexpected call to host NBC's *Password Plus*, a show emceed by Allen Ludden. Ludden, who was suffering from stomach cancer, had been sidelined by a stroke. Ludden and Kennedy were close friends, so Ludden specifically requested that Kennedy take his place on the show. Ludden kept the details of his illness a secret and Kennedy thought he would only host the show temporarily. He had no idea that Ludden would not be coming back.

> *TK:*
> "I thought he was merely indisposed, that he was ill with something, but I didn't know what it was. If he wasn't doing the show, I knew it had to be something rather serious that he couldn't overcome at the moment. But I had no idea, not even an inkling, that it was terminal. I used to talk to him on the phone even while I was doing the show. We would talk about the goofs I made. When I finally learned that it was terminal, well, it's like when you hear about your own brother."

Ludden's death in June 1981 was a huge blow to Kennedy, but he remained with *Password Plus* until it faded from view in 1982. Over the next two years, he devoted his time to hosting telethons for the American Arthritis Association, a task he had begun in 1979.

The Games Continue

Kennedy returned in June 1984 with CBS's *Body Language*, a celebrity-driven game based on charades. During its one and a half year run, *Body Language* attracted several big name celebrities in the business.

TK:
"It was good enough to entice Lucille Ball on stage, so you know it had to be fairly good."

In 1985 a syndicated nighttime edition of *The Price Is Right* went on the air. The show had been running on CBS for 13 years with Bob Barker as host. Barker was not interested in hosting two versions of the show so the nighttime gig went to Kennedy. Of all the shows he hosted in his career, this one year entry turned into a challenge.

TK:
"It was a very tough assignment. It was one that I was privileged to do, and I was flattered that they asked me, but to be honest, I never did that show the way I liked to see me do it. I was so wrapped up in trying to memorize all of those pricing games. It's remarkable what [Bob] Barker does. He's got 100 games in that noggin of his. A professional makes a difficult job look easy, and that's what he does."

In December 1986, Kennedy launched *Wordplay*, his 15th nationally televised game show. Players on this game guessed which of three celebrities was giving the correct definitions to obscure words.

TK:
"I thought it was the kind of show that once it became established would go on and on and on. But it didn't."

Wordplay left the air in September 1987. Although it was not known at the time, this turned out to be Kennedy's last show.

Creator

In 1988 Kennedy created *Star Play*, a show based on charades that he co-produced with comedienne Carol Burnett, but the game never made it to the air. He then developed *Tom Kennedy's World of Humor*, a show where people told their favorite funny stories or jokes. In the pilot episode, Kennedy showed up at a farmer's market, a fire station, a beauty shop, and a department store. To give the show some structure, the jokes and stories were divided into categories.

The show never aired in the United States, but a group called Action Time bought the series from Kennedy and sold it to the BBC Network in Great Britain. The format was retooled and the name changed to *Joker in the Pack*, which ran on BBC during the 1991-1992 season. The show later aired on stations in Germany, Portugal, and Spain through 1993. Kennedy did not host the overseas versions of the show, but he received licensing fees while it was on the air.

"No One Really Cares"

By the mid 1990s, Kennedy was no longer in demand so he retired from show business. In his spare time, he developed *Wonderful World of Game Shows*, a live presentation with Kennedy narrating the history of game shows. His narration was accompanied by large quantities of pictures and video clips illustrating game shows past and present.

Kennedy presented *Wonderful World of Game Shows* to a test audience, but found the project a tough sell.

TK:
"No one really cares. The only people to whom it had any interest whatsoever were people I would say 55 or older who remembered some of the old game shows and knew what I was talking about. The younger group from ages 20 to 50 just sat there and stared at me. They thought it was quite boring so I just wrapped it up and put it on the shelf."

Life Today

Despite a number of disappointments in the last decade, Kennedy has remained active with guest appearances on talk shows such as *Donahue* and *The Late Show*. In November 2003, he appeared as a celebrity player on a special game show host week of *Hollywood Squares*. Today, Kennedy lives with his wife Betty in Oxnard, California in a house they built in 1994 along the beach overlooking the Pacific Ocean. The location gives Tom and Betty a good view of the Channel Islands.

TK:

"We just absolutely love it here because we sit and stare at the ocean and forget there's a world behind us."

Describing himself as a "do-it-yourselfer," he putters around the house working on projects such as *The Wonderful World of Game Shows* for his own amusement. Kennedy occasionally plays golf and also enjoys skiing in the mountains during the winter.

TK:

"I don't know what it is but the mountains really beckon me."

Tom Kennedy has come a long way from James Edward Narz, the would-be mechanical engineer from Louisville, Kentucky. He once mentioned how he and his wife Betty had come to California in the early 1950s with the understanding that if things did not work out, they would go back to Kentucky. Now 55 years later, Kennedy is a bonafide Californian.

TK:

"We're going to try for another 55 years and if it doesn't work, the hell with it, we're going to go home."

Jim Lange

Birth Name: James John Lange

Born: August 15, 1932, in St. Paul, Minnesota

Marriages and Family: Fay Madigan (1953–1975), (Divorced) 2 sons, 1 daughter; Nancy Fleming (1978–Present) 1 step son, 1 step daughter

Military Career: United States Marine Corps (1954–1957)

Radio Career: Disc Jockey/Announcer (WMIN-AM, St. Paul, MN) 1949–1951; Disc Jockey (KGO-AM, San Francisco, CA) 1958–1960; Disc Jockey/Sports Announcer (KSFO-AM, San Francisco, CA) 1960–1970; Disc Jockey (KMPC-AM, Los Angeles, CA) 1970–1971; Disc Jockey/Sports Announcer (KSFO-AM, San Francisco, CA) 1971–1983; Disc Jockey (KMPC-AM, Los Angeles, CA) 1984–1990; *Encore* (Syndicated) 1987–1989; Disc Jockey (KFRC-AM, San Francisco, CA) 1990–1993; Disc Jockey (KKSJ-AM, San Jose, CA) 1994–1996; Disc Jockey (KABL-AM/FM, San Francisco, CA) 1997–2005

TV Career: ANNOUNCER—*The Tennessee Ernie Ford Show* (ABC Daytime) April 2, 1962–March 26, 1965   HOST—*Captain 11* (WTCN-TV, St. Paul, MN) 1953–1954; *Bright and Early* (KGO-TV, San Francisco, CA) 1959–1960; *Oh My Word* (KGO-TV, San Francisco, CA) March 20, 1965–January 1970, (Syndicated) September 1966–September 1967; *The Dating Game* (ABC Daytime) December 20, 1965–July 6, 1973; (ABC Primetime) October 6, 1966–January 17, 1970, (Syndicated) September 10, 1973–September 1974; *Bowling for Dollars* (KTTV-TV, Los Angeles, CA) 1970–1971; *A.M. San Francisco* (KGO-TV, San Francisco, CA) 1974–1975; *Spin-Off* (CBS Daytime) June 16, 1975–September 5, 1975; *Give-N-Take* (CBS Daytime) September 8, 1975–November 28, 1975; *The Hollywood Connection* (Syndicated) September 5, 1977–March 1978; *The Dating Game* (Syndicated) September 4, 1978–September 1980; *Bullseye* (Syndicated) September 29, 1980–September 24, 1982; *Twenty-One* (Unsold Game Show Pilot) 1982; *Take My Word for It* (Syndicated) September 13, 1982–September 1983; *The New Newlywed Game* (ABC Daytime) February 13, 1984–February 17, 1984; *$100,000 Name That Tune* (Syndicated) September 10, 1984–September 1985; *$1,000,000 Chance of a Lifetime* (Syndicated) January 6, 1986–September 11, 1987; *Triple Threat* (Syndicated) October 8, 1988–October 1, 1989; *The Puzzle Game* (Unsold Game Show Pilot) October 1989; *Top Dog* (Unsold CBS Game Show run-through) 1989

Non-Broadcast Show: Host, *The $25,000 Game Show* (Branson, MO & Nashville, TN) 1995–1996

Theatrical Movies: *Shoot the Moon* (1982); *Confessions of a Dangerous Mind* (2003)

Jim Lange (Fred Wostbrock)

Most television hosts are noted for one particular show, even if they emceed several different game shows. For Jim Lange, that one show was *The Dating Game*. Although Lange hosted 11 different game shows and has worked as a radio disc jockey and sports announcer for many years, most people identify him as the man who hosted *The Dating Game*. Though this was the show that gave him great fame, Lange found his identity with the game a double-edged sword.

James John Lange was born on August 15, 1932, in St. Paul, Minnesota. He was the oldest of three children born to John and Catherine Lange. As a teenager, his primary interest was to be a sportswriter, but as it happens to many, a twist of events steered him in another direction.

> *Jim Lange (September 2006 telephone interview):*
> "I was out one night with a friend and we saw this line of young people in front of a radio station. We asked, 'What's going on?' They said, 'We're auditioning for this show. If you get the show, you get a trip to Chicago and you get a weekly radio show.' My friend dared me because he knew I was taking a speech course [in high school]. I tried it and I qualified for the finals and obviously I won finally (Laughs)."

Lange and a teenage girl won the co-hosting spot on WMIN-AM. It aired every Friday night between 1949 and 1951.

> *JL:*
> "She would talk about what was going on in high school dances and socials. I would talk about what was going on in high school sports. Then we would play music. We had to write our own scripts and it was a good way to break into [the business]."

Lange was not initially sold on being a radio announcer after winning the radio job. However, he also won a trip to Chicago as part of the prize for his successful audition. After the trip he changed his tune.

> *JL:*
> "While we were there, we got to see some live big time network radio stuff. One of the shows we saw was the *Bell Telephone Hour*. There was a full symphony orchestra that played music. There was an announcer up there wearing a tuxedo on radio. He said, 'This is the NBC radio network.' I asked a page, 'How much does he make for this?' He said, 'Probably around $500.' I said, 'Now I've found my career. That's what I ought to do. Just stand up there and talk and they pay you. I think that's really a good deal.'"

After high school, Lange studied Radio and Television Speech at the University of Minnesota. During his junior and senior year, he hosted *Captain 11*, a daily children's television show, for WTCN-TV in St. Paul/Minneapolis. Known to viewers as "Today's man of the future," Lange dressed in a space suit for the part. For the rest of the show, he played old episodes of the movie serials *Buck Rogers* and *Flash Gordon*.

Lange's senior year in college also found him marrying his girlfriend, Fay Madigan, in 1953. Shortly after graduating in 1954, Lange joined the United States Marine Corps and was stationed in Hawaii. He served as an Infantry Platoon Leader and was discharged with the rank of Second Lieutenant. During his occasional free time in the service, Lange worked part time at a radio station near his base.

The All-Nite Mayor

Upon his discharge in November 1957, Lange returned to Minneapolis, but was restless for other ventures. A friend who had gone to San Francisco as a disc jockey for KGO-AM told Lange to call the station and inquire about a job. Lange took his friend's advice and was soon working for KGO as the all-night disc jockey. He was such a popular radio personality that the San Francisco city government named him "The All-Nite Mayor." Lange also hosted a morning television series for KGO-TV called *Bright and Early* during the 1959-1960 season.

In January 1960, Lange moved to KSFO-AM just across town where he remained for the next 23 years except for a brief period in the early 1970s. Lange not only played music, but developed a repertoire of comedy bits, a segment where he said "hello" to a variety of listeners and friends once a week, and contests where listeners could receive "Lange Gang" and "Early Riser" cards. One of his characters he played was Captain Show Biz, whose trademark line was shouting "Yet-THIR."

In 1961 Lange and KSFO morning personality Don Sherwood competed in a 23.8 mile footrace. The highly publicized race ran from Stinson Beach to the Ferry Building in San Francisco. As an ex–Marine, Lange was still in top form, and he beat Sherwood to the delight of 10,000 fans that turned out for the race.

Hello Pea Pickers

Lange enjoyed his newfound radio fame in San Francisco, but he found a new calling in April 1962 when ABC television hired him as the announcer/sidekick to Tennessee Ernie Ford for a daily afternoon variety show. Lange played the urbane straight man to Ford's country homespun sense of humor.

> *JL:*
> "[Ford] called me and said, 'We're having an interview on such and such day,' and I said, 'Gee I can't do it. My dad is not well. I have to go back to Minnesota to see him.' And Ford said, 'Well, I'm sorry about that.' When I finally returned [to San Francisco], I got a call from his manager and he said, 'You got the job.' I didn't have to audition. It was just a matter of being in the right place at the right time."

Initially titled *The Tennessee Ernie Ford Show* and later *Hello Pea Pickers*, the venture lasted three years until March 1965.

The Word Is Piddock

That same month, Lange began hosting *Oh My Word* for KGO-TV in San Francisco. He named *Oh My Word* as his all-time favorite of the many shows he hosted. Two celebrities guessed the definitions of obscure words. A word was displayed and four panelists each gave a definition for that word. Three of the definitions were bluffs while one was correct. All the two celebrities had to do was guess which panelist was giving the correct definition.

This was by no means easy to do because the words were very obscure. On the premiere episode, one of the words was "piddock." The definitions given by the panel ranged from "the runt in a litter of pigs" to "a tender cut of venison." By the way, a "piddock" according to *Webster's Dictionary* is "a bivalve mollusk that bores holes in wood, clay, and rocks."

From Hollywood, the Dating Capital of the World

In late 1965 Chuck Barris hired Lange to host ABC's *The Dating Game*. A bachelorette questioned a group of three bachelors who were hidden behind a wall and selected one of the men for a date. The idea of having the bachelors hidden behind a wall added a measure of suspense because the audience and viewers could see them while the bachelorette could not. It also added fairness to the game since the bachelorette was forced to make her decision based on personality and not just by appearance. In succeeding rounds, the roles reversed and a bachelor was brought out to question three women and select a date.

The questions on *The Dating Game* were often of the double-entendre variety and allowed for unlimited comedy. The classic exchanges between the men and women carried the show. On one episode, a bachelorette said, "One of my worst subjects is spelling. Tell me, how do you spell relief?" The bachelor paused, looked at the audience, grinned, and said, "F-A-R-T." As the camera cut to a shot of Lange, he just sank his head down on the podium.

December 20, 1965, was opening day for *The Dating Game*. It became an instant hit, especially with the younger viewers. During the show's long run, many future television and movie celebrities appeared before they were stars. Some of them included Farrah Fawcett, Michael Jackson, John Ritter, Arnold Schwarzenegger, Tom Selleck, and Suzanne Sommers.

Dating Around

Lange kept his day job at KSFO in San Francisco and commuted to Los Angeles for *The Dating Game*. Before long Lange was hosting four television shows. In October 1966 ABC added a nighttime version of *The Dating Game* to its schedule. In addition, *Oh My Word* continued on KGO-TV while a nationally syndicated version of that show was seen during the 1966-1967 season.

In 1970 Gene Autry, the owner of KSFO radio, transferred Lange to another of his stations, KMPC-AM in Los Angeles. During the 1970-1971 season, Lange replaced sports announcer Chick Hearn as host of *Bowling for Dollars* for KTTV in Los Angeles.

> *JL:*
> "[Chick Hearn] was delighted to get rid of it. That was, far and away, the hardest show I ever did. We did five shows a night and the contestants were not selected in the way of a normal game show where they are really screened for the very best, most excitable person. They were just drawn out of a hat. All they had in common was that they bowled. Each time they bowled, there was a five to eight minute interview and it was just like pulling teeth. And every one of them seemed to have the same interests."
> Lange: 'What do you do for fun?'
> Contestant: 'Uh, nothing.'
> Lange: 'Well, have you ever traveled?'
> Contestant: 'Well, I've got Winnebago and we've gone to the lake.'

No Right or Wrong Answers

In 1971 Lange was transferred back to KSFO radio in San Francisco. He also remained with *The Dating Game* and was forced to resume his regular Los Angeles commute. Although he enjoyed the show, Lange felt restricted as a host. Unlike many game shows, *The Dating Game* was not a typical question-and-answer show. Lange found the different kind of format challenging.

> *JL:*
> "In a way, it was a bit harder. *The Dating Game* was not a right or wrong answer show. There was no right answer. My job was, if something got a little slow, to try and pull something out of the bachelors or straighten out [any confusion]. It was really a little more difficult than a straight game show. It was basically a reality show. It was probably the first reality show."

Producers so identified Lange with *The Dating Game* that they would never consider him for anything else. Although Lange saw the show as an obstacle to other challenges, he continued to preside over the shenanigans that frequented most episodes.

When stripper Gypsy Rose Lee won a date on the show with a 6-feet-4 blonde man, Lange found himself in an interesting predicament. When the date put his arm around Lee, he touched her in an inappropriate place.

> *JL:*
> "She whacked her date in the mouth. She just slapped him and he started to bleed a little bit. I had to keep going. I didn't know what to do. The camera was not on them when she hit him. I was telling them where they were going on their date. I think it was Europe. It was a beautiful date. While they were taking beauty shots of Europe to cover my voice-over, she whacked him. I just kept going and when they came back they took a shot and he was still smiling, but he had a little blood coming down his mouth. That was on camera. I'm sure the people at home thought, 'What the heck is happening?' He just smiled away like nothing had happened."

Fortunately Lee and the man went ahead with their date and, according to Lange, they really liked each other. The nighttime version of *The Dating Game* left the air in 1970. After nearly

It's *The Dating Game*. A bachelorette questions three potential dates as Jim Lange looks on (Fred Wostbrock).

3,000 dates, ABC dropped the daytime version in July 1973. It returned two months later as a weekly syndicated offering but that version lasted one season.

Polish Sausage and Sauerkraut Makes a Match

The mid 1970s brought personal troubles as Lange's 22 year marriage ended in divorce. However, a stint as co-host of *A.M. San Francisco*, a morning talk show for KGO-TV in San Francisco, teamed Lange with his future second wife, Nancy Fleming. He and Fleming had met once in 1961 when she was Miss America. At first, Lange and Fleming only had a professional relationship and after his stint on *A.M. San Francisco*, he and Fleming went their separate ways.

Sometime later when he returned as a guest co-host on *A.M. San Francisco*, Lange asked Fleming out. For their first date, Fleming invited Lange to her home where she served Polish sausage and sauerkraut. Lange was not only impressed by her cooking skills, but he was also very taken with Fleming. They finally married in 1978.

Two Short Games

Back in his career track, Lange spent 1975 hosting a pair of short-lived CBS game shows: *Spin-Off* and *Give-N-Take*. On *Spin-Off*, two couples played an automated version of poker. Answering questions afforded players the right to activate a machine containing five spinners. Each spinner contained the numbers 1–6 and spun at a rate of 17 numbers per second. The object was to spin five numbers and make a better hand than your opponent as in the card game of poker. Contestants could spin full houses (three of one number and two of another), four of a kind, three of a kind, and so forth. The players were paid in cash according to the hand they spun.

Spin-Off sank after ten weeks on September 5, 1975, but Lange returned the following Monday in the same time slot with *Give-N-Take*. Here, four female contestants answered questions to earn prizes determined by a computerized spinning arrow. The object was to collect enough prizes totaling as close to $5,000 without going over. *Give-N-Take* also failed to make the grade and vanished after 10 weeks.

From Network to Syndication

Although Lange would no longer host a regular network game show, he found a gold mine through syndication. Starting in 1977, he hosted a string of syndicated game shows for the next decade. First up was *The Hollywood Connection*, a game where six celebrities answered questions designed to reveal aspects of their personalities.

In 1978 Lange returned to host *The Dating Game* for two more seasons. After this version folded, Lange took on a series of new game shows that finally allowed him to stretch his legs.

Hitting the Bullseye

September 1980 brought *Bullseye*, a cross between two popular Barry-Enright shows: *The Joker's Wild* and *Tic Tac Dough*. On *Bullseye*, two contestants answered a designated number of questions in a given category called a "contract." A large board with three windows concealed the categories. The windows were covered by computerized swirls and one contestant pushed a plunger to stop the spinning swirls. The first two windows revealed categories and dollar amounts while the third window revealed the number of questions (1–5) required to complete the contract. Sometimes the third window revealed a bullseye. In this case, the contestant could answer as many questions as they wanted. The player chose a category and earned the corresponding dollar amount for every correct answer.

If the player answered all of the questions, he or she could bank the money accumulated and pass control to their opponent. Their other option was to leave the money and continue playing to build a larger bank. If, however, the player missed a question, their opponent could steal the contract with a correct answer and win the money. The first player to bag $2,000 won the game.

After two years on *Bullseye*, Lange turned up in *Take My Word for It*, an update of *Oh My Word*. Unlike his other shows, this one taped in San Francisco during the 1982-1983 season so for once, Lange did not have to leave town for work.

I Left My Heart in San Francisco

Television had been very rewarding both financially and personally for Lange, but his radio stint at KSFO in San Francisco was where he truly felt at home. In December 1983 the station was sold by Gene Autry's Golden West Broadcasting Company to the Seattle-based King Broadcasting Company. KSFO's new management immediately dismissed the entire station staff. History repeated itself, however, because Lange immediately hooked up with KMPC radio in Los Angeles, where he had worked in the early 1970s. He began broadcasting for KMPC on January 2, 1984.

His return to Los Angeles coincided with a return to television. ABC produced a new version of *The Newlywed Game* with Lange taking over for Bob Eubanks as host. Before ABC committed to a long-term series, the network opted to run one week of shows to test the audience reaction. *The New Newlywed Game* test week aired from February 13–17, 1984, but the network scrapped plans for the revival.

From $100,000 to $1,000,000

Lange then signed with Sandy Frank Productions to host *The New $100,000 Name That Tune*, which premiered in September 1984. This was an update of the 1974–1981 series where contestants competed in several rounds of different musical guessing games. Like its predecessor, Lange's version incorporated a monthly tournament of champions where the daily winners were eliminated until someone took home the $100,000 prize. The new show faded after one year.

Lange popped up again in January 1986 hosting *The $1,000,000 Chance of a Lifetime*, the first game show to offer a million dollar payoff. Two teams of couples guessed puzzles from clues provided by Lange. The players stood before a large keyboard with all 26 letters of the alphabet. The letters used in the puzzle were lit on the keyboard and players selected letters. For every letter that appeared, the value of the puzzle increased. One extra letter called "the stinger" was on the keyboard. Contestants who chose "the stinger" lost control of the game to the opposing team. The winners played a bonus round of guessing six puzzles in one minute for $5,000.

The couple could take the $5,000 and quit, or risk it by returning to compete on the next show. If they lost the next game, they lost their $5,000. However, if they won the second day, they earned $10,000 and could keep that or risk it all to play one more game. Winning the third day in a row netted the $1,000,000 prize.

The $1,000,000 Chance of a Lifetime started off with high ratings and was renewed for a second season, but the million dollar craze fizzled out in 1987. Not until the premiere of *Who Wants to Be a Millionaire?* would a game show ever again give away such a large prize.

End of the Games

On the radio side, Lange was running strong at KMPC. The Los Angeles listeners voted him Favorite DJ in 1988. In October of that year, he hosted his last game show, *Triple Threat*. This weekly syndicated effort pitted two teams of three players from different generations answering questions on music, television, and movies. After *Triple Threat* was canceled in October 1989, Lange hosted one more failed game show pilot, *The Puzzle Game*, where contestants solved video puzzles.

Moving out of game shows, Lange joined ESPN as a reporter for the network's golf coverage in February 1990. Lange also hosted a nationally syndicated series called *Encore*, where he played music from different years. One of the stations carrying *Encore*, KFRC-AM in San Francisco, invited Lange to guest host a program locally. Lange enjoyed the station's big band format and asked about a job. KFRC found a spot for him so in September 1990, Lange left Los Angeles and returned home permanently to San Francisco.

> JL:
> "I enjoyed [Los Angeles] a lot. I lived within five minutes of the station so I didn't have to contend with the horrendous freeway traffic. [I also lived] about one minute from my golf course. It certainly is the 'Mecca of Show Biz,' but I was glad to return home to the Bay area near my children and grandchildren and the more laid back existence that it affords."

Hang On!

Although KFRC enjoyed high ratings as the number four ranked station in the Bay Area, KFRC continued to lose money each year because it attracted mostly listeners over the age of 50 and not the 25 to 54 crowd that most advertisers try to lure. KFRC continually struggled to attract advertisers willing to spend the big bucks.

With the financial problems came a change in the station's format to include more up-to-date music mixed with the older pop standards. There was also considerable turnover in the disc jockey line-up as DJ's were hired and fired. With each change, Lange held on to his job, but it was only a matter of time before he became another victim to the changes. In August 1993,

KFRC was purchased by Alliance Broadcasting and the company immediately fired 49 of the 60 employees at the station, including Lange.

Full Circle

He spent the next year playing golf and working on his house while searching for another radio job in the Bay area. In August 1994 he started a weekend show playing big band standards on KKSJ-AM in San Jose while waiting for a more permanent position. The next year Lange became one of three hosts of *The $25,000 Game Show*, a live production in Branson, Missouri. The game selected 42 contestants from the audience to compete for cash and prizes. The show later moved to Opryland in Nashville, Tennessee in June 1996, with Lange, Bob Eubanks, and actor Jamie Farr taking turns as host.

Finally in January 1997, Lange got the radio position he had long sought when the newly reorganized San Francisco station KABL-AM hired him for the early morning shift. Playing a variety of nostalgia music including big band hits and pop tunes from the 1940s and 50s, Lange's show was heard from 6–10 a.m. each weekday. When KABL was sold in the summer of 2005, Lange retired from full time broadcasting. Happy that his career came full circle, Lange is content to leave television behind.

Life Today

Lange turned up periodically in television guest appearances on *The Super Mario Brothers Super Show* and *Parker Lewis Can't Lose* during the early 1990s. In May 2002, he joined Bob Eubanks, Peter Marshall, Wink Martindale, and Ben Stein in the NBC television special *Most Outrageous Game Show Moments*. In November 2002 he appeared on a special game show host week of *Hollywood Squares* as a celebrity guest.

He also appeared in the 2003 theatrical movie *Confessions of a Dangerous Mind*, which was based on the 1984 autobiography of Chuck Barris. In the book, Barris claimed that while he created and hosted game shows during the 1960s and 1970s, he worked for the CIA on the side as an operative and killed 33 people in Europe.

Today, Jim Lange can usually be found on a golf course or working his vegetable and flower gardens at his home. Although retired, he still freelances with commercial and voice-over work, but takes full advantage of his immense free time to travel with his wife Nancy. Their travels have taken them to Sicily, Sardinia, South America, Turkey, and Tahiti. Whatever he does or wherever he is, Jim Lange knows how to make the most of things as evidenced by his simple quote:

> *JL:*
> "I kind of enjoy life wherever I am."

ALLEN LUDDEN

Birth Name: Allen Ellsworth
Born: October 5, 1917, in Mineral Point, Wisconsin
Died: June 9, 1981, in Los Angeles, California
Marriages and Children: Margaret McGloin (1943–1961) (Deceased) 2 daughters, 1 son; Betty White (June 14, 1963–June 9, 1981)
Military Service: United States Army (1942–1946)
Radio Career: Announcer (KEYS-AM, Austin, TX) 1942; Announcer/Program Executive (WTIC-AM, Hartford, CT) 1947–1953; *New Talent U.S.A.* (NBC) June 1953–September 1953; *College Bowl* (NBC) October 10, 1953–May 6, 1955; *Monitor* (NBC) 1955–1956; Program Director (CBS Radio) 1956–1961
TV Career: HOST—*Mind Your Manners* (NBC Saturday Mornings) June 24, 1951–March 2, 1952; *Inside Our Schools* (WNBT-TV, New York City) 1952–1953; *On the Carousel* (WCBS-TV, New York City) December 5, 1953–February 1954; *Good Morning* (WABC-TV, New York City) July 5, 1954–August 27, 1954; *Dance Time* (WPIX-TV, New York City) July 5, 1954–April 8, 1955; *Sentimental You* (WNBT-TV/WNBC-TV, New York) August 30, 1954–February 25, 1955; *G.E. College Bowl* (CBS Sunday Afternoons) January 4, 1959–June 17, 1962; *Password* (CBS Daytime) October 2, 1961–September 15, 1967. (CBS Primetime) January 2, 1962–September 9, 1965, (CBS Primetime) December 25, 1966–May 22, 1967; *Talking Pictures* (Unsold CBS Game Show Pilot) February 1968; *Win with the Stars* (Syndicated) September 18, 1968–September 1969; *The Joker's Wild* (Unsold CBS Game Show Pilot) April 1969; *Allen Ludden's Gallery* (Syndicated) May 19, 1969–September 1969; *The Pet Set* (Syndicated) September 1970–September 1971; *Password/Password All-Stars* (ABC Daytime) April 5, 1971–June 27, 1975; *Stumpers* (NBC Daytime) October 4, 1976–December 31, 1976; *Liar's Club* (Syndicated) March 1977–September 1979; *Holly-*

Allen Ludden (Allen Ludden, courtesy Fred Wostbrock)

149

wood Smart-Alecks (Unsold Game Show Pilot) 1978; *Password Plus* (NBC Daytime) January 8, 1979–October 24, 1980
Theatrical Movie: *Futureworld* (1976)
Made-for-TV Movie: *The Gossip Columnist* (Syndicated) March 21, 1980
Business Interests: Partner: Eltee Productions, Los Angeles, CA (1968–1981)
Other Careers: Teacher: Austin High School, Austin, TX (1941–1942); Business Manager: Maurice Evans (1946–1947); Consultant for Creative Services: CBS News (1956–1961)
Books: *Plain Talk for Men Under 21* (1954); *Plain Talk for Women Under 21* (1956); *Roger Thomas, Actor* (1959); *Plain Talk About College* (1963); *Plain Talk for Young Marrieds* (1964)

Allen Ludden was a rare one in the world of game show hosts. Possessing a master's degree in English and sporting horn-rimmed glasses, he was a classy, high-brow intellectual who also possessed a great sense of humor. His winning personality put people at ease. In his long career, Ludden worked his way from a Texas high school teacher to hosting one of television's most popular game shows of all time. Although he never planned to become a TV star, several twists of events propelled him to greater fame.

Allen Ludden was born as Allen Ellsworth in Mineral Point, Wisconsin on October 5, 1917, the only child of Elmer and Leila Ellsworth. His father died during the influenza epidemic in 1919 and Allen's mother later remarried. He then took his stepfather's surname and legally changed his name to Allen Ludden. At the age of nine, he moved with his mother and stepfather to Corpus Christi, Texas and went through public school. After high school he enrolled in the University of Texas in 1937 and graduated Phi Beta Kappa in 1940. He also earned a Master of Arts degree in English in 1941.

Duty Calls

Ludden taught English at Austin High School in Texas during the 1941-1942 school year. When the United States entered the Second World War, Ludden enlisted in the Army. His previous acting and directing experience from college plays landed him an assignment with the Army's Central Pacific Base Command. He worked as a production officer in the Special Services group headed by English actor Maurice Evans, with whom Ludden became good friends.

During a brief rest leave in 1943, Ludden married his high school sweetheart, Margaret McGloin. He received the Bronze star and was honorably discharged in 1946. After the war, Maurice Evans offered Ludden a job as his manager for the actor's theatrical productions and lecture tours. Ludden occasionally filled in for Evans as lecturer and, without knowing it, had taken the first step in a new career.

Mind Your Manners!

In 1947 while lecturing in Hartford, Connecticut, Ludden was so well-received that radio station WTIC offered him a job. He hosted *Mind Your Manners*, a show where teenagers discussed current events and tips on how to properly behave. In June 1951 *Mind Your Manners* moved to NBC television.

After the show left the air in March 1952, the New York City Board of Education hired Ludden to produce and host two educational shows: *Inside Our Schools* for WNBT-TV and *On the Carousel* for WCBS-TV.

The College (Bowl) Graduate

One Sunday afternoon in the summer of 1953, Ludden's friend Grant Tinker, who worked as an NBC producer, dropped by Ludden's home in Hartford, Connecticut with an idea for a radio quiz called *College Bowl*. According to Tinker's autobiography *Tinker in Television*, the idea originated from Don Reid several years earlier. Reid had come up with the basic idea for a quiz competition between colleges, but had not yet worked out the details of the game. When Tinker presented the idea, Ludden took a yellow legal pad and sketched out the entire format that became *College Bowl*. Tinker hired Ludden to host the show so he moved his family to Dobbs Ferry, a small community outside New York City. *College Bowl* premiered over NBC radio on October 10, 1953.

Ludden hosted the show from the NBC studio in New York while the two student teams played from their school campuses by means of a three-way hookup. Four undergraduate students comprised each team. Ludden read a toss-up question and any of the team members from both sides could buzz in to answer. The buzzer signal was accomplished by a lock out device devised by NBC engineers. When a member of one team pushed their buzzer, the other team's button went dead. A correct answer was worth 10 points and the team could answer additional questions worth 20 to 40 points. The team scoring the most points won scholarship grants for their school.

Grant Tinker served as *College Bowl's* producer and kept score for the teams on a blackboard in the studio with Ludden. According to his book, Tinker said he frequently botched up the task since the game moved fast and the scores constantly changed. Ludden was often forced to ad-lib until the scores were correct. Although Ludden did much of the creative work developing *College Bowl*, Don Reid, who originated the idea, became the owner of the series.

New York Television

In the summer of 1954, Ludden supplemented his income working on three local television shows. His day began at 6:00 a.m. when he left his Dobbs Ferry home for New York City to host *Good Morning* on WABC-TV. The show was a combination of news, weather, and special features with guests. Ludden made his entrance each morning on the street while a camera, positioned outside the studio, captured him coming around the corner and entering the building to appear as if he were on his way to work.

Producer Grant Tinker recalled one morning when Ludden, who was waiting around the corner, missed his cue. Since the show was live, the camera was forced to stay on the street action outside the studio until Ludden appeared. On that particular morning, there was no one around except a dog walking down the sidewalk. Local New York viewers were treated to the sight of the dog stopping to take his morning dump.

After *Good Morning* ended at 9:00 a.m., Ludden hustled to WNBT-TV to co-host the talk show *Sentimental You* at 1:00 p.m. At 5:00 p.m., he popped up on WPIX-TV with *Dance Time*, a music show where high school students danced to current hits. Saturday nights were reserved for hosting *College Bowl*.

With little time to see his wife and three children, Ludden quit *Good Morning* in August 1954. He remained with *College Bowl*, *Sentimental You*, and *Dance Time* until they were canceled in 1955. Ludden moved to CBS as a radio program director and as Creative Services Consultant for the network's television news.

The National Spotlight

When CBS developed *College Bowl* for television, Ludden returned as host. Under the sponsorship of General Electric, *The G.E. College Bowl* premiered on January 4, 1959. The format remained the same as the radio version. The scholarship money for the winners on the television version was $1,500 while the runners-up received $500. *The G.E. College Bowl* followed the pattern of school schedules by starting each television season in September and going off the air in June for the summer.

In 1960 *The G.E. College Bowl* became the first television game show to win a Peabody Award for excellence in broadcasting. The show became so popular that many high schools staged their own versions of the game.

The Password Is...

In 1961 Ludden's wife, Margaret, became seriously ill with lung cancer, an illness she had battled for the past four years. With a family of two girls and one boy to support, the increasing hospital bills for Margaret's cancer treatment strained the family's finances. Then one day, the offer came to host *Password*, a new CBS daytime game show. Show packagers Mark Goodson and Bill Todman were willing to pay Ludden far more than he was making with his duties at CBS News and *College Bowl*.

Ludden consulted with his wife Margaret and their children David, 14, Martha, 13, and Sarah, 9. The family frowned on Ludden taking the *Password* offer, but he knew that Margaret did not have long to live. Already deluged with a string of medical bills coupled with upcoming funeral expenses, Ludden accepted Goodson-Todman's offer and resigned his creative consultant position at CBS.

Password debuted on October 2, 1961. Two celebrity-contestant teams competed. A password was shown to the audience and the home viewers. One member from each team used one word clues to get his/her partner to say the word. Teams received 10 points if the player guessed the word after one clue. If the contestant failed to guess the word, the opposing team had a crack at the word for nine points and so on.

Game play alternated between the teams until someone guessed the word or until ten clues had been given after which no one scored for that round. The first team to score 25 points won the game. In the "lightning round," the celebrity conveyed five passwords to their partner in 60 seconds. The player scored $50 for each word for a maximum of $250.

Password was a monster hit and spawned a nighttime version in January 1962. Ludden continued hosting *G.E. College Bowl* Sunday afternoons giving him six days a week of television exposure. In the spring of 1962 CBS decided to move the nighttime *Password* to Sunday evenings at 6:30 p.m. General Electric, the sponsor of *G.E. College Bowl*, which aired from 5:30 to 6:00 p.m., did not like the idea of Ludden appearing in both shows on the same night. He was told to quit one of the shows. After much thought, Ludden stayed with *Password* and departed *G.E. College Bowl* on June 17, 1962. Robert Earle replaced Ludden as host and remained with the series until 1970.

Meanwhile, Margaret Ludden's condition became critical in early October 1961. Allen spent most of his time with her in the hospital, leaving only long enough to tape episodes of *Password*. Four weeks later, Margaret Ludden died on October 31, 1961. Allen was devastated, but he made it through the tough times by throwing himself into work and taking care of his three children. In a twist of events, *Password* ended up being the place where Allen met his second wife.

"I'm Going to Marry That Woman"

During the third week of *Password* just before Margaret died, actress Betty White appeared as one of the celebrity players. This was Allen's first meeting with Betty, but at the time, Margaret was dying and he was in no mood to socialize. Betty returned to play *Password* again in early 1962.

> **Bob Stewart (Password** *executive producer, April 2005 telephone interview):*
> "Before all of these game shows, we did a little rehearsal in the studio to give the celebrities a feel for what the show was going to be when they went on the air. Allen Ludden came out to greet the two celebrities and do this little rehearsal. When that rehearsal, which was 10 or 15 minutes, was over, Allen went [in for] makeup and Betty went to her makeup. I walked into Allen's dressing room just to give him a couple of notes about the show. As I walked in, he turned to me and said, 'I'm going to marry that woman!' That's an actual quote. Allen's wife had just passed away maybe five or six months before and I said, 'Allen, you're just kind of reacting to the situation.' He said, 'No, No. I'm going to marry that woman!'"

Persistence Pays Off

Allen did not see Betty again until May 1962 when he took a role in a Massachusetts summer theater production called *Critic's Choice*. In her book *Here We Go Again*, Betty said that Allen had decided to do the play to get his children away from their house for the summer following Margaret's death. Ironically, Betty had also signed to do *Critic's Choice* and was cast as Ludden's wife.

As Allen and Betty rehearsed together for the play during the summer of 1962, their professional interest in each other slowly developed into a romance. They shared their first kiss on stage during *Critic's Choice* since the script called for their characters to kiss at the end of the play. On the play's opening night, Allen held the kiss with Betty much longer than usual.

Betty White recalled in *Here We Go Again* that Allen proposed marriage to her several times but she always refused. Allen spent his vacations flying from New York to see Betty in California. Finally in early 1963, Allen gave her a gold wedding ring containing a circle of diamonds. Betty still refused to accept his proposal, but this did not stop the persistent Allen. Instead of taking the ring back to the jewelers, he put it on a chain and wore it around his neck, refusing to take it off until Betty said "yes."

Allen wore the ring around his neck for three months, but never referred to it when they were together. Just the sight of the ring around his neck was enough to give her the message. Allen even wore it on days he taped *Password*. Since the sight of the ring would be a distraction from the game, Allen concealed it behind his necktie and the microphone which he wore around his neck. Finally during the Easter weekend in April 1963, Betty accepted Allen's proposal and the two were married in Las Vegas on June 14, 1963.

A New Life

Allen and Betty were unable to take a honeymoon trip since Allen had used up all of his vacation time from *Password* the previous winter. According to Betty's book *Betty White: In Person*, she and Allen flew to Las Vegas on Friday June 13 and took the required blood test to obtain the marriage license. The day after their marriage, they flew back to New York to resume taping for *Password* on Monday. Allen and Betty settled with his three children in a 100-year-old farmhouse in Chappaquer, New York.

After their marriage, Betty became a frequent celebrity player on *Password* for the rest of its CBS run. Allen dabbled briefly in the record business by cutting *Allen Ludden Sings His Favorite Songs* for RCA in 1964. During the mid 1960s, Allen and Betty went to Columbus, Ohio to demonstrate QUBE-TV, a new state-of-the-art television system that gave viewers an unprecedented 32 channels to watch. The QUBE-TV system was given a test run in the Columbus area, but it was way ahead of its time and died quickly. Several years later, the idea of multiple channel cable TV systems became commonplace in most American homes.

The Password Is...Cancellation

Password thrived during the 1960s, and the daytime version pulled ratings of more than 50 points! The nighttime edition slowly lost its steam and was canceled in September 1965 but returned briefly from December 1966 to May 1967. The daytime version remained popular until competition from ABC's *The Newlywed Game* slowly eroded *Password's* ratings from 50 points to 34 points during the 1966-1967 season. CBS canceled *Password* on September 15, 1967, in favor of a new soap opera, *Love is a Many Splendored Thing*. According to *Saturday Evening Post* in 1975, *Love is a Many Splendored Thing* never even reached *Password's* lowest rating of 34 points!

Since most game shows now taped in Los Angeles, Allen and Betty decided to move to California where the work existed, so in August 1968 the family packed up and moved. Allen soon landed the hosting job of a syndicated weekly game show called *Win with the Stars*. This musical game called for two celebrity-contestant teams to identify as many songs as possible in a 45-second time limit. The players then sang the first two lines of lyrics scoring five points for identifying the song and one point for each word they sang correctly. *Win with the Stars* only lasted the 1968-1969 season.

Producing

Allen and his longtime friend Grant Tinker formed Eltee Productions with the intent to create and produce new game shows. In 1969 Allen produced and starred in what Betty said was his all-time favorite show in his career. The project was *Allen Ludden's Gallery*, a combination variety and talk show. The variety portion gave Allen a chance to show off his singing talents. One feature of the show called "Ludden's Gallery" introduced two or three well-known entertainment columnists who compared their notes on a star they had all interviewed at an earlier date. *Allen Ludden's Gallery* was canceled after only a few months on the air.

Betty put together her own syndicated show in 1970 called *The Pet Set* with Allen serving as producer and announcer. *The Pet Set* spotlighted celebrities who brought their pets on the show ranging from dogs to horses. Burt Reynolds, Jimmy Stewart, Carol Burnett, Vincent Price, and Merv Griffin were among the guests. *The Pet Set* was canceled after 39 weeks.

Back in the Action

Allen returned to the game show circuit in April 1971 when ABC revived *Password* for daytime. The basic game remained intact with a new feature called "Betting Word" after the bonus round. Contestants were given a password and could bet any portion of their bonus round winnings on their partner's ability to guess the word in 15 seconds.

Password prospered until ABC moved it from late afternoons to 12:00 p.m., which put it in direct competition to NBC's *Jeopardy!* Because both shows were so popular, the head-to-head competition hurt their ratings. Despite the ratings decline, *Password* won an Emmy for Outstanding Game Show in May 1974. By that summer, the show had slipped to the point that ABC almost canceled the program.

However, a month of summertime specials, among them a week where Allen and Betty played the game while Monty Hall hosted, boosted ratings. ABC renewed the show for an additional six months and changed the format to include all celebrity teams. The show was renamed *Password All-Stars* in November 1974, but the new format did not sit well with viewers. In February 1975, the show returned to its original celebrity-contestant format, but the change came too late. *Password* played its final ABC show on June 27, 1975. For his hosting duties on *Password,* Allen Ludden won an Emmy Award as Best Host in a Game Show in May 1976.

Stumped

He returned to television in October 1976 hosting NBC's *Stumpers*. Two teams composed of two players and a celebrity guessed phrases from a series of three possible clues. Teams scored points according to how many clues they needed to solve the phrase. The game was very similar to *Password*, but *Stumpers* failed to match the popularity of the former show and was canceled after 13 weeks.

In the spring of 1977, Ludden replaced Bill Armstrong as host of *Liar's Club*, a syndicated game show with four celebrities and four contestants. A strange-looking object was displayed at the start of each round and the celebrities took turns explaining its function. The four contestants bet up to half of their initial stake of $100 on which of the four celebrities was telling the truth. Spotlighting such celebrities as Betty White, Dick Martin, Fannie Flagg, Larry Hovis, and David Letterman, *Liar's Club* remained a popular weekly attraction.

Celebrity guest Elizabeth Montgomery gives a clue to her partner on *Password* as Allen Ludden and Bill Bixby look on (Allen Ludden, courtesy Fred Wostbrock).

It's More Than Password...It's Password Plus!

In January 1979, NBC revived *Password* for another daytime run with a totally restructured format. The two celebrity-contestant teams still took turns guessing passwords from one-word clues. Each password served as a clue to the "Password Puzzle." A maximum of five words were played in each round and the first team to guess the puzzle won $100 in the first two rounds and $200 in all succeeding rounds. The first team to reach $300 advanced to the new "Alphabetics" bonus round. The celebrity conveyed 10 passwords in 60 seconds to their partner for a jackpot of $5,000. *Password Plus* premiered on January 8, 1979, with Ludden again steering the action.

Illness

In late 1979, Allen and Betty decided to build a second home in Carmel, California, one of their favorite vacation spots. During all of the preparation work, Allen began feeling feverish and occasional pain in his stomach. According to Betty's autobiography, *Here We Go Again*, Allen had days where he felt ill and then bounced back and felt good again. This went on for about two months while Allen sought medical help. After getting two opinions and two CAT scans, Allen entered Los Angeles' Good Samaritan Hospital in March 1980 where a gallium scan revealed stomach cancer. Allen was immediately scheduled for surgery since the doctors believed that the cancer was treatable.

Surgery meant that Allen had to miss tape days on *Password Plus* for an indefinite amount of time. The show's producers and NBC hired Bill Cullen to substitute during Allen's absence. At the time, Cullen was hosting *Chain Reaction*, which aired at noon right before *Password Plus* on NBC. The public was informed that Allen was ill but no details were given about his condition. Allen came through the surgery, but the doctors were unable to remove all of the cancer. Told that he had only months to live, Allen decided to forgo any radiation or chemotherapy treatments.

On a positive note, the surgery helped Allen feel much better than he had felt in months. He made a quick recovery and returned to host *Password Plus*. Allen still did not want the public to know about his condition reasoning that viewers would be watching him closely to notice any changes in his health. He returned to the show on May 13, 1980, and Bill Cullen appeared on that week's worth of shows as a celebrity player along with actress Susan Richardson. Allen thanked the viewers for their cards and letters he received during his absence and thanked Bill for holding down the fort.

Though Allen knew he was dying, he did not let that stop him from enjoying the next several months. He and Betty continued overseeing the construction of their new vacation house in Carmel during the summer of 1980. Allen took time from his busy schedule to guest on the ABC series *Love Boat* and rode a horse for that episode. In September 1980, Allen appeared on a special game show host week of *Card Sharks* with fellow emcees Bill Cullen, Gene Rayburn, and Wink Martindale.

Collapse

On October 7, 1980, just two days after his 63rd birthday, Allen collapsed while in Carmel with Betty and was rushed to Monterey Community Hospital. Lying in a coma, he was not expected to live out the day. Allen remained in the coma for six days before finally beginning a slow recovery. After two weeks, he had recovered enough to be taken back to Los Angeles to the Good Samaritan Hospital. It was later determined that Allen had experienced a stroke-like reaction to steroid medication he was taking to treat the cancer. The illness spelled the end of Allen's working career and his last *Password Plus* episode (taped just prior to his collapse) aired on October 24, 1980. NBC elected to continue the show and, at Allen's suggestion, his good friend Tom Kennedy replaced him as host.

Fortunately Allen suffered no paralysis or speech impairment and he recovered sufficiently to return home on November 15, 1980. With the news of his cancer now public, viewers sent him cards and letters by the thousands wishing him well. The outpouring of public support kept Allen's spirits up during those last few months.

He returned to the airwaves one last time to tape some radio commercials for Southern California Gas Company in early 1981. Allen and Betty finally settled into their new house in Carmel in March 1981. They spent two nights there before Allen had to reenter the hospital. At 1:30 a.m. (Pacific Time) on June 9, 1981, Allen Ludden died quietly in the Good Samaritan Hospital at the age of 63. In addition to Betty, Allen was survived by his three children. The game show most associated with Ludden lived on however. *Password Plus* continued on NBC until its cancellation on March 26, 1982. It returned to NBC under the title *Super Password* with Bert Convy as host from 1984 to 1989.

Betty White: In Person

After years as a celebrity panelist on game shows, Betty White made her debut as a game show hostess on NBC's *Just Men* in January 1983. On this game, two female contestants predicted how a panel of seven male celebrities would respond to various personal questions. This marked a rare occasion where a female hosted a television game show.

Unfortunately *Just Men* was canceled that April after a mere three months, but Betty won her fourth Emmy Award from that show in June 1983 (she won a fifth and sixth Emmy in 1986 and 1987 for her role in *Golden Girls*). After *Just Men*, Betty returned to acting with appearances on the NBC sitcom *Mama's Family*. In September 1985, she began a seven year stint on NBC's *Golden Girls* playing the widow Rose Nylund. After the show left the air in 1992, she continued this role in the spin-off series *Golden Palace* through 1993.

Number One

Reruns of *Password* and *Password Plus* made their way to the Game Show Network in 1994 where they drew sizeable ratings. This has enabled older viewers to remember Allen Ludden and his contributions to television and allowed young viewers to get acquainted with him. One of the most polite and congenial emcees ever to grace the airwaves, nearly 20 years after his death, Allen Ludden had the honor of being the number one pick in a January 2001 *TV Guide* poll of the top ten "Hosts We Love the Most."

HAL MARCH

Birth Name: Harold Mendelson
Born: April 22, 1920, in San Francisco, California
Died: January 19, 1970, in Los Angeles, California
Marriage and Children: Candy Toxton (February 18, 1956–January 19, 1970) 3 sons, 2 daughters
Military Service: United States Army (1942–1943)
Radio Career: Announcer (KYA-AM Radio, San Francisco, CA) 1943–1944; *The Story of Sandra Martin* (CBS) 1944; Disk Jockey (WJZ-AM, New York, New York) 1945–1946; *Something New* (CBS) 1945–1946; *Sweeney & March* (CBS) August 31, 1946–October 1, 1948, (ABC) April 1, 1951–May 11, 1951; *The Alan Young Show* (NBC) January 11, 1949–July 5, 1949; *Young Love* (CBS) July 4, 1949–May 13, 1950; *December Bride* (CBS) June 8, 1952–September 6, 1953; *That's Rich* (CBS) January 8, 1954–September 23, 1954; *The $64,000 Question* (CBS) October 4, 1955–November 29, 1955

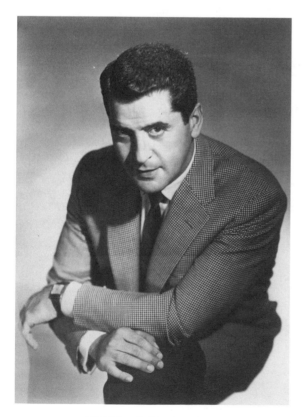

Hal March (Fred Wostbrock)

TV Career: ACTOR—*The Burns & Allen Show* (CBS Primetime) October 12, 1950–December 28, 1950; *The RCA Victor Show* (NBC Primetime) October 1952–June 1953; *My Friend Irma* (CBS Primetime) October 1953–June 1954; *The Imogene Coca Show* (NBC Primetime) February 19, 1955–June 25, 1955; *The Soldiers* (NBC Primetime) June 25, 1955–September 3, 1955; *I Married a Dog* (Unsold NBC Sitcom Pilot) 1961 HOST—*The $64,000 Question* (CBS Primetime) June 7, 1955–November 2, 1958; *What's It For?* (NBC Primetime) October 12, 1957–January 4, 1958; *Laughs for Sale* (ABC Primetime) October 20, 1963–December 22, 1963; *It's Your Bet* (Syndicated) September 29, 1969– January 1970 DIRECTOR—*Camp Runamuck* (NBC Primetime) 1965–1966; *It's About Time* (CBS Primetime) 1966–1967
Theatrical Movies: *Outrage* (1950); *Ma & Pa Kettle Go to Town* (1950); *Combat Squad* (1953); *The Eddie Cantor Story* (1953); *The Atomic Kid* (1954); *Yankee Pasha* (1954); *My Sister Eileen* (1955); *It's Always Fair Weather* (1955); *Hear Me Good* (1957); *Send Me No Flowers* (1964); *Guide for the Married Man* (1967); *Nobody Loves an Albatross* (1968)
Broadway Career: *Two for the Seesaw* (1959–1960); *Come Blow Your Horn* (1961–1963)
Other Career: Welder, San Francisco Shipyards (1940–1942)

In the 1950s, game shows, or quiz shows as they were then called, began something new and exciting. They started giving away thousands of dollars as prizes to lucky winners. Since then, winning big bucks has become a tradition. Hal March has the distinction of hosting the first big money quiz show in television history. Between 1955 and 1958, *The $64,000 Question* broke records in ratings and monetary winnings to set the standards for modern game shows.

Hal March was born as Harold Mendelson in a run-down section of San Francisco, California, on April 22, 1920, as the only boy of four children. His father, Leon Mendelson, ran a grocery store and delicatessen. Harold grew up in a rough neighborhood where getting into fights with the other kids was a typical day.

> *Hal March (***Look** *magazine September 18, 1956, interview):*
> "The kids were tough and you figured to have two or three fights a day. I changed my name to Hal after about 150 fights. The kids thought Harold was a sissy name."

From this experience, March fought 25 amateur bouts as a welterweight boxer in his teens but decided not to make this a career.

> *HM (***Look** *magazine):*
> "I was never much of a fighter. I didn't have the killer instinct."

March worked in his father's grocery store and entertained customers with imitations of the neighborhood dialects.

A Variety of Jobs

In high school, the lead in the operetta *Melinka of Astrakham* encouraged March to pursue acting. When his father died in 1939, he headed for Hollywood with around $200 in his pocket. After working the rounds of the movie studios, he organized a nightclub act with four boys and a girl called The Hollywood Rioteers. March went back to San Francisco in 1940 where he was hired to be the straight man in a burlesque act with Smoky Wells.

By the end of the year, March had switched to the San Francisco Shipyards where he made better money as a welder. After America entered World War II. in December 1941, March tried to enlist in the Army, but was rejected due to flat feet. He worked in the shipyards until he was accepted by the Army for limited service in November 1942. His battery commander asked him to put on a Christmas show so March wrote the entire act and put on two performances. Hoping to get a transfer to Special Services to pursue acting, he instead was given radar duty. March was discharged when his limited service time ended in November 1943.

"Hal Marches On"

Heading back once more to San Francisco, March met Bob Sweeney, the chief announcer at KYA-AM. Hired by Sweeney, the two began a local comedy show called *There's Always the Guy*. March played all types of characters such as a talkative barber or a pest at the movie theater. At the advice of KYA's manager, March adopted his stage name. He told *Saturday Evening Post* in 1957 that he came up with the name Hal March while working on a slogan to advertise his show. The slogan "Hal Marches on at Six Tomorrow Morning" was the result and the name Hal March stuck.

In 1944, March went back to Hollywood and played the male lead on the radio soap opera *The Story of Sandra Martin* for $90 a week. A year later, Bob Sweeney joined March in New York to become disk jockeys for WJZ-AM. They also hosted *Something New*, an afternoon radio show on CBS. In August 1946 they opened their new comedy show *Sweeney and March* for CBS. Their characters were two radio comedians sharing an apartment who got themselves into one mishap after another. After the show was canceled in 1948, Sweeney and March went their separate ways, although they briefly reunited in the spring of 1951 for a revival of *Sweeney and March* for ABC radio.

The Small and the Big Screen

March remained in New York to work in television. In October 1950, he began a regular stint on the *George Burns and Gracie Allen Show* for CBS television. March was the first of four actors to play George and Gracie's neighbor Harry Morton. He left the show after two months and became a freelance actor. He turned in guest appearances on NBC's *The Colgate Comedy Hour* and *All Star Revue* and appeared in a pair of movies: *Outrage* and *Ma & Pa Kettle Go to Town*.

Back on the small screen, he landed regular roles as Dennis Day's neighbor in the *RCA Victor Show* in 1952 and the character Joe Vance on the sitcom *My Friend Irma* the next year. Early 1955 found March co-starring with Imogene Coca for the last few months of her first solo TV show. He also worked with actor Tom D'Andrea in a series of skits called *The Soldiers*, which had been featured on *The All Star Revue*. NBC commissioned *The Soldiers* as a weekly series for its fall 1955 lineup.

Not Sold on the Show

Meanwhile in April 1955, Louis G. Cowan, an advertising man at CBS, called March about hosting a new quiz show called *The $64,000 Question*. The game was an inflated variation of the 1940s radio quiz *Take It or Leave It* where the top prize was a mere $64.

March was unenthusiastic because, as he put it to *Saturday Evening Post* in 1957, he thought that quiz shows were "hokey." He was already making good money as a freelance actor and building a solid reputation. Besides, he had already signed to do *The Soldiers* for NBC and already had enough on his plate. March said that he argued with Cowan for three weeks about hosting *Question* and never once was the subject of money discussed. March was simply was not sold on the game.

March finally agreed to host *The $64,000 Question*, but only for the summer of 1955 since *The Soldiers* was set to begin on NBC that fall. CBS unveiled *The $64,000 Question* on June 7, 1955. There had never been a quiz that offered the big money and suspense as did *Question*. The premise of the show was simple, although the questions were not.

Contestants, playing one at a time, answered a series of questions from a category of their choosing worth from $1 and doubling in stakes to $64,000. When a player reached the $4,000 level, they went home and came back to answer just one question per week to the $64,000 level. Because there was so much money involved, and to avoid any help from the studio audience, players entered a sound-proof isolation booth for questions beginning at the $8,000 level.

Players had the option of quitting any time and keeping their winnings because missing one question cost them everything. Each show featured several contestants, some who were just starting their climb from $1 and others who had been on for weeks and were now in the higher plateaus. Since the show aired live, the suspense was very real for viewers. Contestants who missed a question after reaching the $8,000 plateau won a new Cadillac as a consolation prize.

Big Money, Big Ratings

March's career went through the roof as a result of *The $64,000 Question*. His decision to only do the show for that summer changed quickly when NBC moved the premiere date for *The Soldiers* up to June instead of September. *The Soldiers* broadcast live from Los Angeles on Saturdays while *Question* originated from New York City on Tuesday nights. March was forced to fly between the two cities in what turned out to be a hectic summer.

His commute ended rather suddenly when NBC discharged *The Soldiers* after three months. March was now free to remain with *The $64,000 Question* on a permanent basis. The game shot to the top of the ratings, replacing *I Love Lucy* as the number one primetime show for the 1955-1956 season, averaging a 47.5 rating. In the fall of 1955, a simulcast of *The $64,000 Question* aired for nine weeks over CBS's radio network.

No pressure! Hal March asks *The $64,000 Question* **while a contestant sweats it out in the isolation booth (Fred Wostbrock).**

A Human Host

One of the reasons March succeeded in his new role as a game show host was that he was not a typical emcee. He was quite versatile as an actor playing every type of role, but not quite polished as a host. His low key style was a perfect fit on *The $64,000 Question*, yet he knew how to build suspense without dominating the game. His occasional tendencies to make mistakes on the air only enhanced his appeal with the viewers. He came across as human. One evening on *The $64,000 Question*, March mixed up his cards and forgot to ask the contestant the $32,000 question.

He was really on a roll one night according to *TV Guide* in 1956: he scratched a jazz record used to illustrate a question, let too much time elapse for one contestant pondering a question in the isolation booth, and nearly forgot to do the final commercial before signing off the broadcast. True to form, March always laughed off his blunders and the audience laughed with him.

Big Winners

The big money craze swept the country and millions of viewers tuned in to watch ordinary people sweat it out answering complicated multiple-part questions in an isolation booth. Churches canceled their Tuesday night services, and ballparks and movie theaters flashed the results of the winners to keep their audiences. Ratings and publicity increased when Marine Captain Richard McCutcheon became the first $64,000 winner in September 1955.

Ordinary people became national celebrities overnight. New York City policeman Redmond O'Hanlon won $16,000 in the category of Shakespeare. Bronx shoemaker Gino Prato won $32,000 for his knowledge of Opera, and a housewife, Catherine Kreitzer, won $32,000 in the Bible category. Before long, the big money quiz craze spawned a round of new shows including *The $100,000 Big Surprise*, *Twenty-One*, *Tic Tac Dough*, and a spin-off from the producers of *Question* called *The $64,000 Challenge*. The latter show featured the top winners from *Question* who competed against each other for another $64,000. Many older game shows jacked up their top prizes to compete in the ratings.

Candy

Up to now, March had remained a bachelor and work was his way of life. That changed on February 18, 1956, when he married Candy Toxton Torme, a former model and ex-wife of singer Mel Torme. March met her while commuting to Los Angeles in 1955 to do *The Soldiers*. Candy had a three-year-old son (singer Steve Torme) and a one-year-old daughter, and March lost no time adapting to his new family life.

This surprised many of his friends, who advised him against the marriage, because they were not sure how March would feel about being a husband and stepfather so quickly. This was not the only factor: March was Jewish and Torme was Catholic. They surprised everyone and made the marriage work. On June 7, 1957, the couple had their first baby, Peter Lindsey March, who was born on the anniversary of *The $64,000 Question*'s debut. The couple later had another son and daughter.

Fixed!

The popularity of *The $64,000 Question* declined sharply during the spring of 1958 as rumors spread that the big money quizzes were rigged. Magazine and newspaper stories in which contestants admitted that the producers had given them answers to questions in advance greatly damaged the integrity of the shows. As rumors turned into truths during the fall of 1958 when reports from the shows *Dotto* and *Twenty-One* hit the papers, the roof collapsed on the big money quiz empire. CBS executives investigated *The $64,000 Question*, but March maintained that the show was clean. After Revlon Cosmetics pulled out as sponsor, CBS canceled the show on November 2, 1958.

According to Joseph Stone's 1992 book *Primetime and Misdemeanors*, investigations indeed turned up evidence of rigging on *The $64,000 Question*. One of the earliest players affected was Richard McCutcheon, the show's first big winner. Prior to each game, McCutcheon was given a warm up session of questions to help him relax. Once in the isolation booth on the show, he was surprised to find some of the questions asked were the same ones used in the warm up. McCutcheon later revealed that the final $64,000 multi-part question, where he named the five dishes and two wines from a royal banquet given in 1939 by King George VI of England for French President Albert Lebrun, had already been asked during a warm up session.

Despite feeling guilty for winning the money, McCutcheon reluctantly went along with the setup, but later admitted the deception. Another contestant, the Reverend Charles Jackson, also testified that many of his questions and answers came from pre-show sessions with producers.

Driving Him Crazy

In many ways, Hal March was relieved by the cancellation of *The $64,000 Question* saying that the show was beginning to drive him crazy. Subsequent investigations of the show resulted in Louis G. Cowan resigning his position as president of CBS. No one involved with *The $64,000 Question* was charged with a crime. However, quiz shows were never the same again. Producers scaled back the prizes considerably and big money games virtually disappeared.

Changing the Rules

Game show executives of the early 1960s took measures to ensure that rigging could never take place on their shows. One way was to make the questions easier thus beginning the popular phrase of "dumbing down the show." Networks developed Standards and Practices Departments and always had members present when game shows aired live and later when many switched to videotape. It would be years before big money game shows became popular again.

Escaping the Rigging Trap

March was never implicated in the rigging scandal and his career was far from finished despite his quiz show's suspicious demise. Television appearances were cut to a minimum during 1959 as he concentrated on Broadway. During the year, he toured in the play *Two for the Seesaw*.

In the spring of 1961, NBC announced plans for a nighttime version of its popular daytime game show *Concentration*. Not only would the nighttime show give away larger prizes than its daytime counterpart, but it would broadcast in color, a rarity in television at that time. NBC wanted March to host the show while the sponsor wanted Hugh Downs, the host of the daytime version of *Concentration*. The sponsor won the battle and Downs hosted the primetime version, which lasted only five months.

March then embarked on a 19-month stint in the Neil Simon comedy *Come Blow Your Horn*. He also toured with the play for six months. When the play closed in 1963, March returned to series television as the host of *Laughs for Sale*, an ABC comedy show. Well-known comedians formed a panel that judged comic material submitted to the show by inexperienced comedy writers. *Laughs for Sale* was thrown together as a replacement for *100 Grand*, the first big money quiz show to air on television since 1958. That show had been axed after three weeks and *Laughs for Sale* was rushed on the air in its place. *Laughs for Sale* never found its audience and was canceled in December 1963.

TV Is Predictable

March moved his family to Los Angeles where he continued his acting career. Most of his 1960s television work encompassed multiple guest appearances on *Burke's Law*, *Mr. Broadway*, *Trials of O'Brien*, *Gidget*, *The Lucy Show*, and *The Monkees*. He also appeared as a celebrity guest on the game shows *Password*, *I've Got a Secret*, and *You Don't Say*.

In a 1966 *Newsweek* interview, March was unhappy at the direction television had taken since the 1950s. His opinion was that television was "less inventive" and "predictable" but that one day there would be pay TV giving the public more viewing variety.

Away from television, March continued his movie career with appearances in *Send Me No Flowers* (1964), *Guide for the Married Man* (1967), and *Nobody Loves an Albatross* (1968). March also tried his hand at television directing in episodes of the sitcoms *Camp Runamuck* and *It's About Time* between 1965 and 1967.

It's Your Bet

In September 1969, he returned to the game show arena hosting *It's Your Bet*, an update of the 1965 NBC game show *I'll Bet*. This game featured celebrity couples who played for members of the studio audience. One member from a team predicted whether or not their mate could answer general knowledge questions correctly.

Before making the prediction, the player bet from 25 to 100 points on their mate's ability to answer. If the mate answered correctly, that team won the points wagered. If incorrect, the opposing team scored the points. The first team to rack up 300 points won the game and played a bonus round to win prizes for the audience.

Twilight

For March, however, this was the twilight of his career and his life. Shortly after starting *It's Your Bet*, he was diagnosed with cancer in one of his lungs. A two-pack-a-day smoker for many years, March had quit smoking in 1968, but resumed within a year. He entered the hospital in November 1969 where the affected lung was removed. While at home to recuperating, pneumonia set in and March reentered the hospital shortly after Christmas. With only one lung remaining, he was too weak to fight the pneumonia and he passed away on January 19, 1970, at the age of 49. March was survived by his wife Candy and their five children. His show *It's Your Bet* continued until 1973 with Dick Gautier, Tom Kennedy, and Lyle Waggoner doing stints as host.

The Return of the Big Money Shows

After his death, March's legacy lived on. In the fall of 1976 a revival of *The $64,000 Question* appeared with the top prize doubled to $128,000. The new series was appropriately titled *The $128,000 Question* with Mike Darrow, and later Alex Trebek, hosting. It lasted two years in syndication.

Big money game shows made a comeback in 1999 with the success of ABC's *Who Wants to Be a Millionaire?* All of the major networks trotted out big money creations with each one trying to top the others in the size of prizes. NBC brought out a revival of *Twenty-One* while the Fox Network rolled out *Greed*, whose top prize was $2 million. CBS entered the fray with *Survivor*, which put people through a series of physical competitions to see who could survive the longest for a top prize of $1 million.

The big money quiz fever spread across America during the 1999-2000 season as it did in Hal March's day in 1955. Game shows have been giving away so much money that it is easy to take them for granted and to forget that they were not always this generous. Early quizzes on radio and television only gave away a few dollars for the prize. Even *The $64,000 Question's* radio counterpart, *Take It or Leave It*, handed out $64 as the big prize. The current trend of big money and big prizes on game shows came only after Hal March and *The $64,000 Question* started it all.

PETER MARSHALL

Birth Name: Ralph Pierre LaCock

Born: March 30, 1927, in Clarksburg, West Virginia

Marriages and Family: Nadine Teaford (1947–1974) (Divorced) 2 sons, 2 daughters; Sally Carter Ihnat (1979–1982) (Divorced) 2 stepchildren; Laurie Stewart (1989–Present)

Military Service: United States Army (1944–1946)

Radio Career: Singer & Program Host (WQAM-AM, Miami Beach, FL) 1946–1947; *The Music of Your Life* (Syndicated) 2000–Present

TV Career: HOST—*Let There Be Stars* (ABC Primetime) September 21, 1949–November 27, 1949; *Two of the Most* (ABC Daytime) October 24, 1955–December 30, 1955; *Stimulus* (KTLA-TV, Los Angeles, CA) October 9, 1964–December 4, 1964; *The Hollywood Squares* (NBC Daytime) October 17, 1966–June 20, 1980, (Syndicated) November 1, 1971–September 1981; *Storybook Squares* (NBC Saturday Mornings) January 4, 1969–August 30, 1969; *NBC Action Playhouse* (NBC Primetime) June 24, 1971–September 1971, (NBC Primetime) May 1972–September 5, 1972; *The Peter Marshall Variety Show* (Syndicated) September 1976–March 1977; *Fantasy* (NBC Daytime) September 13, 1982–October 28, 1983; *All-Star Blitz* (ABC Daytime) April 8, 1985–December 20, 1985; *Yahtzee* (Syndicated) January 11, 1988–September 1988; *3rd Degree* (Game Show Pilot) 1988; *Reel to Reel* (PAX) August 31, 1998–November 27, 1998   ACTOR—*Shore Leave* (Unsold NBC Sitcom Pilot) August 18, 1961   PRODUCER—*Skeedaddle* (Unsold Game Show Pilot) 1974; *The Numbers Game* (Unsold ABC Game Show Pilot) 1975

Non-Broadcast Game Show: *The $25,000 Game Show* (Branson, MO) 1994–1995

Theatrical Movies: *Holiday Rhythm* (1950); *FBI Girl* (1951); *The Forty-Ninth Man* (1953); *The Rookie* (1960); *Swingin' Along* (1961); *The Cavern* (1964); *Ensign Pulver* (1964); *Mary Jane* (co-writer with Dick Gautier) (1968); *Black Jack* (writer) (1973); *Americathon* (1979); *Annie* (1982)

Made-for-TV Movies: *Harold Robbins' "79 Park Avenue"* (NBC) October 16–18, 1977; *A Guide for the Married Woman* (ABC) October 13, 1978

Broadway Career: *How to Make a Man* (1961); *Skyscraper* (1965–1966); *La Cage aux Folles* (1986–1987)

London Shows: *Bye Bye Birdie* (1961); *HMS Pinafore* (1960s)

Stage Plays: *Tongue in Cheek* (1949) Anaheim, CA; *Last Frontier* (1952) Anaheim, CA; *All About Sin* (1958) Las Vegas, NV; *Panama Hattie* (1960s); *High Button Shoes* (1963–1964) Las Vegas, NV; *Anything Goes* (1963–1964) Las Vegas, NV; *Brigadoon* (1966) Houston, TX/ Anaheim, CA; *42ND Street* (1987) (1992–1993) Atlantic City, NJ/ Anaheim, CA

National Touring Company Shows: *La Cage aux Folles* (1984–1986); *Rumors* (1989–1991)

Other Careers: Usher: Paramount Theater, New York City (1941–1942); Page: NBC Studios, New York City (1942–

Peter Marshall (Peter Marshall (courtesy Fred Wostbrock).

1943); Singer: Bob Chester Band (1942–1943); Comedy Team Partnership: Noonan & Marshall (1949–1954) & (1958–1960)
Comedy Team Partnership: Tommy Farrell (1954–1958)
Book: *Backstage with the Original Hollywood Square* (2002)

Peter Marshall was born as Ralph Pierre LaCock in Clarksburg, West Virginia on March 30, 1927. Marshall's father was a pharmacist in Wheeling, West Virginia, but after his death in 1937, the rest of the family, including Marshall's mother and sister moved to Huntington, West Virginia.

Marshall's mother and sister later moved to New York while he remained in Huntington with his grandmother. His 14-year-old sister, Letitia, met a modeling agent named John Robert Powers, who hired her and changed her name to Joanne Marshall (later she changed her name to Joanne Dru). With the money she earned as a model, she and her mother brought Marshall up to live with them in New York.

Marshall began his show business career as an usher at the Paramount Theater when he was 14 years old. Within a year, he was working as a page at NBC and began singing with the Bob Chester Band. As a singer, he decided to change his name to something easier for people to remember. He adopted "Marshall" after his sister had used that name as a model. Marshall later returned to Huntington when he was 17 to finish high school. After graduation, he was drafted into the Army in 1944 and sent to Italy.

> *Peter Marshall (May 2005 telephone interview):*
> "I was in the artillery and there was an old radio act by the name of John Raby, who I used to help page [at NBC]. He was a dear man. I was walking in Naples when I hear my name, and he's the Captain. He was the head of I and E (Information and Education). He said, 'What are you doing?' I said, 'Well, they're shipping us to Manila. We're going to invade Japan I guess after Italy falls.' He said, 'No, no. I've got two job openings: *Stars and Stripes* as a reporter or a disc jockey here in Naples.'"

Since Marshall had learned to operate a sound board at NBC in New York, he chose the disc jockey position. Over the next 18 months, Marshall spun records and announced on a 50,000 watt station in Naples and was discharged in 1946 with the rank of Staff Sergeant. After the war, he moved to Fort Pierce, Florida where he landed a job as a singer on station WQAM. He also sang in bars in Miami, but his career was going nowhere. Meanwhile in 1947, he married Nadine Teaford, whom he met shortly after moving to Florida. They had two sons and two daughters during their marriage.

Get Your Act Together

By 1949 Marshall was in Los Angeles with no prospects of work. Fortunately, his sister's husband, John Ireland, had a brother named Tommy Noonan, who was a struggling comedian. Marshall needed money to pay a $78 dental bill so he and Noonan teamed up to play in nightclubs. With Noonan as the comedian and Marshall as the straight man, the duo soon made a name for themselves.

Noonan and Marshall were popular enough to join the cast of an ABC variety series, *Let There Be Stars*, in the fall of 1949.

> *PM:*
> "We were the first network show ever to [come] out of California broadcasting to New York."

The series only lasted a few weeks, but it gave Marshall his first national television exposure. During the 1950s, Noonan and Marshall performed in nightclubs with Chicago being one of the hot spots for the comedians. The team also appeared in a two theatrical movies: *Holiday Rhythm*, which Marshall described as "awful," and *FBI Girl*.

After Noonan and Marshall broke up their act in 1954, Marshall teamed with comic Tommy

Farrell. The duo starred in a five a week ABC variety series, *Two of the Most*, during the fall of 1955. He reunited with Tommy Noonan in 1958 and the pair signed with 20th Century Fox for the theatrical releases *The Rookie* in 1960 and *Swingin' Along* in 1961. Television again beckoned the duo's services with appearances on *The George Gobel Show*, *The Ed Sullivan Show*, and *The Garry Moore Show*.

Going Solo

By the early 1960s, Marshall was on his own again, but this time he wanted to try something besides nightclub work. In 1961 he appeared in his first Broadway show, *How to Make a Man*. He also went to London to appear in *Bye Bye Birdie* and *HMS Pinafore*. Back in the U.S. in 1963, he starred in *High Button Shoes* at the Thunderbird Hotel in Las Vegas. For his work, Marshall earned $1,750 a week. A month later, Marshall signed for a second play at the hotel, *Anything Goes*. Unfortunately he was only paid $1,500 per week for *Anything Goes*, which was less than he made from *High Button Shoes*.

Looking for a way to earn more money, Marshall was told to try daytime game shows. At the time, Marshall was working nights and sleeping during the day so he almost never watched television. Having virtually no exposure to game shows, Marshall took over as host of *Stimulus* in October 1964. Seen over Los Angeles station KTLA-TV, the show was canceled after 10 weeks.

In 1965 Marshall starred in a one hour episode of *Bell Telephone Hour* on NBC and returned to Broadway in the musical *Skyscraper* with Julie Harris. The show ran for one season, but ended one week before its intended closing date. The day after returning to Los Angeles, Marshall received a telephone call from producer Bob Quigley about hosting a new game show. Quigley and his partner Merrill Heatter had just created *Hollywood Squares* and NBC was interested in the series. For Marshall, the timing could not have been better.

The Master of the Hollywood Squares

The pilot for *Hollywood Squares* had been taped for CBS in 1965 with Bert Parks hosting, but the network turned down the series. Marshall got the job under some unusual circumstances. In his book, Marshall explained that after auditioning for *Hollywood Squares*, he was not really interested because of a possible acting job in the play *Breakfast at Tiffany's*. His agent told him that if he turned down the *Hollywood Squares* gig, the producers would hire comedian Dan Rowan as host. Marshall had a strong dislike for Rowan. He said that Rowan had taken comedy material from him and Tommy Noonan in the 1950s without their permission. Marshall changed his mind and took the job partly out of spite and as he put it mildly in his book, "To screw Dan Rowan out of a job."

Hollywood Squares earned good reviews when it debuted over NBC on October 17, 1966. After a slow start, the show gradually built its ratings until it was attracting up to 40 percent of the viewing audience in its time slot. The game utilized nine celebrities seated in a large tic tac toe board (three rows of three squares). Two contestants representing "X" and "O" tried to capture three squares in a row either across, up and down, or diagonally. When a player in turn chose a celebrity, Marshall asked a question and the star answered it. The contestant then had to correctly agree or disagree with the celebrity's answer to capture that square. The winner of each game collected $200. During the game, one of the celebrities was chosen as the "Secret Square" and if that star was picked, the contestant could win a prize package worth thousands of dollars. There were usually two "Secret Square" games played per show. The game continued until time ran out and the player with the most money won a large prize (usually a car).

What made *Hollywood Squares* such a hit was the comedy resulting from having so many celebrities in one setting. The stars usually gave funny replies before giving their real answers and many of the jokes were double entendres. A sample exchange between Marshall and celebrity George Gobel went as follows:

An early promotional still for *The Hollywood Squares*. Clockwise from top right: Cliff Arquette, Abby Dalton, Wally Cox, Morey Amsterdam, Rose Marie, and host Peter Marshall in the center (Peter Marshall, courtesy Fred Wostbrock).

MARSHALL: "True or False? A pea can last as long as five thousand years."
GOBEL: "Boy, sometimes it sure seems like it."

In another exchange with comedian Paul Lynde:

MARSHALL: "Pride, anger, coveting, lust, gluttony, envy, and sloth are collectively known as what?"
LYNDE: "The bill of rights."

The stars seemed to effortlessly rattle off the jokes, but in truth, the gags were all scripted. Using an elaborate system, the stars were given the jokes in advance, but never the questions. At the same time, Marshall did not know what the jokes would be during the show. Henceforth, the proceedings on *Hollywood Squares* looked spontaneous. In his book, Marshall explained that there were nine slots under his podium, one for each of the nine celebrities. After a contestant chose a star, Marshall pulled a question from that celebrity's slot.

Meanwhile, each of the nine stars had a list of joke answers in front of them that corresponded to the questions in their slot under Marshall's podium. When Marshall asked a question, the star inconspicuously looked at the corresponding joke answer and delivered the punch line.

Playing It Straight

Through the years, *Hollywood Squares* booked practically every big name celebrity in the business. Many stars appeared on a regular basis including Wally Cox, Rose Marie, Paul Lynde

Contestants on *The Hollywood Squares* enjoyed the funny answers from the celebrities as much as host Peter Marshall did (Peter Marshall, courtesy Fred Wostbrock).

(who became the star center square), Cliff Arquette (as Charley Weaver), George Gobel, Karen Valentine, and Vincent Price. Marshall presided over all of the comedy with an easy manner while also keeping a rein on celebrities who got out of hand. His years of playing the straight man with Tommy Noonan and Tommy Farrell were finally paying dividends as Marshall was flawless in his ability to make the stars funny.

In January 1969 NBC launched a Saturday morning version of the game called *Storybook Squares* that featured children as the contestants. The stars for this version dressed up as famous real and fictional characters such as Daniel Boone, Cinderella, Tarzan, Paul Bunyan, Snow White, and Little Boy Blue. *Storybook Squares* was expensive to produce, and that, coupled with low ratings cut the show's life to only eight months. The *Storybook Squares* idea was later seen on special occasions throughout the rest of the show's run. In November 1971 a weekly nighttime version premiered in syndication and became as big a hit as the daytime series.

Other Projects

As much as Marshall enjoyed hosting the show, he wanted to work on his singing and acting career. Since taping *The Hollywood Squares* took up little of his time, Marshall was free to pursue acting jobs in summer stock theatrical productions, movies, and to guest star on other television shows. In 1968 he co-wrote the movie *Mary Jane* with actor Dick Gautier. The story focused on the horrors of marijuana use in high school. During the 1970s, he popped up in guest spots on the television shows *Love American Style*, *The Love Boat*, *WKRP in Cincinnati*, and *CHIPS*.

Marshall and *Hollywood Squares* producer Bill Armstrong formed Marshall-Armstrong Productions and put together new television projects, including the game shows *Skeedaddle* and *The Numbers Game*, but none of them made it to the air. Then in 1976 he starred in *The Peter Marshall Variety Show*.

> PM:
> "It was an expensive show. We had music, comedy, and we were starting to do really well, but they wanted me to cut down on the orchestra and cut down on expenses. I said, 'I'd rather not do it. I want to do it this way or not do it.'"

Mounting production costs led to the show's demise after 19 weeks.

End of the Squares

Hollywood Squares thrived until 1976 when NBC moved it from 11:30 a.m. to 10:30 a.m. Then in 1978 the show moved again to 1:00 p.m., but many NBC affiliates ran local news at that hour and the show lost substantial ground. After enduring more time slot changes, NBC canceled the daytime series on June 20, 1980, after a run of 14 years. The weekly syndicated version of *Hollywood Squares* still had a sizeable audience, so the producers expanded the show to five days a week. For the 1980-1981 season, *Hollywood Squares* began taping in the Riviera Hotel in Las Vegas.

Problems surfaced immediately after the move to Vegas. The large set used on the show had to be constructed and torn down each tape day at the Riviera as opposed to the NBC days when the set remained standing between shows. In his book, Marshall noted that everyone associated with the show spent so much time gambling in the casinos that it affected the quality of the program. *Hollywood Squares* finally wrapped up in 1981.

May All of Your Fantasies Come True

Marshall returned to the small screen in the fall of 1982 co-hosting *Fantasy* with Leslie Uggams. The hour long series rewarded people by making their "fantasies" come true. Viewers sent in their requests to the show and those selected were brought on the air to have their wishes granted. A tape crew also traveled around the country surprising unsuspecting people. Some of the fantasies granted included reuniting long lost relatives, giving people the chance to wing walk or jump from an airplane, and repairing someone's broken down car.

The show received a number of monetary requests for various reasons, but those kinds of fantasies were refused. *Fantasy* only lasted one season, but the concept of making peoples' wishes come true lives on today.

> **PM:**
> "I loved it, it was a great show. They're doing a lot of "Fantasies" [on television] now. I was watching *Oprah Winfrey* and she was really doing the old *Fantasy* show [with] people wanting this or that."

Hitting the Stage

Late in 1984, Marshall returned to the stage as one of the leads in *La Cage aux Folles*, a popular Broadway musical comedy about the joys and heartaches of an aging homosexual couple on the French Riviera. The play toured the United States for two successful years and then returned to Broadway in New York for another season.

Blitzed

In the spring of 1985, Marshall signed to host *All-Star Blitz*, a new ABC game show. Two contestants and four celebrity guests answered questions to solve word puzzles. Contestants picked a star and Marshall asked a question. As in the days of *Hollywood Squares*, the celebrities often gave funny answers. The contestants then agreed or disagreed with the star's answer and if correct saw a portion of the word puzzle. The first player to solve the phrase won the game.

Marshall hosted the show while touring with *La Cage aux Folles*.

> **PM:**
> "I would fly into Los Angeles on my day off and tape *All-Star Blitz* on Monday. I would just fly in and do the show and get out and go back to wherever I was working."

His busy schedule of two shows ended when *All-Star Blitz* got the axe in December 1985.

Scoring a Yahtzee

Marshall was appearing in the play *42nd Street* in Atlantic City, New Jersey when he was hired for another game show. Producers Ralph Andrews and Larry Hovis brought the popular dice game *Yahtzee* to television as a syndicated series in January 1988. Two teams of three players each answered questions and tried to match answers with a panel of five celebrities. Two questions were asked in each round and the team who matched the most stars won the right to roll the giant dice.

The object was to roll five of the same number (known as a "Yahtzee") using five dice. The team coming the closet to scoring a yahtzee after several rounds won the game. A bonus game allowed the players to roll the giant dice for a large cash prize.

> **PM:**
> "They had some financial problems and the whole thing collapsed. That was a shame because it was a really good show."

"Be Straight with Me"

His next project turned into a legal nightmare. In the fall of 1988 Bert Convy asked Marshall to host a new show he had developed called *3rd Degree*. Marshall was reluctant to host, but Convy persuaded him. After taping the pilot, *3rd Degree* was slated to air in September 1989.

Meanwhile, Convy was dropped as the host of *Win, Lose, or Draw*, a show he co-owned with

Burt Reynolds. The game's syndicator felt that Convy was too old for the show and wanted a younger host. Now suddenly without a show, Convy decided to take over as host of *3rd Degree*. On June 30, 1989, Burt and Bert Productions told Marshall that his services were no longer needed. Marshall promptly filed a lawsuit against the company charging them with breaking the contract.

> *PM:*
>
> "If [Convy] wanted to do the show, he should have called me and said, 'Hey Pete, can I have lunch with you? Look, they just fired me from my own show. I want to do *3rd Degree*. I'll tell you what we'll do. We'll make a deal with you.' I would have said, 'Go ahead and do it, that's fine.' I didn't want to do it in the first place. I didn't think it was that good of a show, but they made me such a deal that it was almost impossible to turn it down. That's all [Convy] had to do was to be straight with me, but he wasn't."

Convy hosted *3rd Degree* during the 1989-1990 season, but the show was not renewed for a second year. When Convy took ill with a brain tumor in the spring of 1990, Marshall dropped the lawsuit.

> *PM:*
>
> "I didn't want to have to sue [Convy's] children and I didn't want to sue the estate."

Convy died in July 1991.

More Plays and Games

The early 1990s saw Marshall returning again to his roots as an actor. He joined the cast of the Neil Simon comedy, *Rumors*. The play toured through selected cities around the country for one season. After another touring engagement in *42nd Street* during the 1992-1993 season, Marshall accepted nightclub dates to perform one-man shows singing and dancing.

In 1994 he rotated as host of *The $25,000 Game Show*, a live program that originated from Branson, Missouri. Not intended for television, the show was produced by Bob Eubanks and designed as entertainment for tourists. Marshall shared the hosting duties with Eubanks and Dennis James, but left the show after a few months.

> *PM:*
>
> "I just didn't want to stay in Branson [Missouri]."

He hosted one more game show in 1998 when he was tapped as host of *Reel to Reel* for the cable channel PAX. Based on the popular board game "The Reel to Reel Picture Show" created by Sandy and Martin Cherry in 1993, the game pitted two celebrity/contestant teams in a competition on movie trivia. Teams alternated selecting categories and answering a series of questions worth from 100 to 500 points. The team with the most points after two rounds played a bonus game where they answered questions and solved a puzzle for a trip. *Reel to Reel* debuted on the first day of broadcasting for the new PAX network on August 31, 1998.

Reel to Reel gradually attracted a significant audience for the fledgling network. Plans were made to move the show from Orlando, Florida to Los Angeles since it was difficult flying the celebrities in from California to play the game. Then the production company went bankrupt and *Reel to Reel* abruptly stopped production after 13 weeks.

> *PM:*
>
> "I don't know why it went belly up. They owe me a ton of money. I never got paid and none of my stars were paid."

Music of Your Life

Marshall has not hosted any game shows since 1998, but he has remained active as a singer doing concerts around the country. In 2000 Marshall was singing in a concert with the Les Brown Band performing big band songs when the producers of *Music of Your Life*, a syndicated radio package, spotted Marshall. He was offered a daily two hour show to play Big Band Standards and was given creative control over his program. "I enjoy doing it," Marshall said.

> **PM:**
> "I get to play my records and I get to talk about the music. I know a lot about the music of the 1930s and 1940s."

Returning to the Squares

In his long career, Marshall has hosted six game shows and starred in countless musical comedies, but people always remember him as the host of *Hollywood Squares*. Since he last hosted the game in 1981, there have been three revivals, but Marshall was never asked to return. The first was in 1983 as part of *The Match Game–Hollywood Squares Hour* on NBC with actor Jon Bauman as host. A second revival from 1986 to 1989 featured former Squares panelist John Davidson in the host's chair. Another version ran from 1998 to 2004 with Tom Bergeron hosting.

After Marshall released his book, *Backstage With the Original Hollywood Square* in the summer of 2002, the producers of *Hollywood Squares* finally invited him back to play the game as the star center square.

> **PM:**
> "They asked me if I'd like to do the show. I had a book out and I said, 'If you'll plug the book everyday and let me host it one day, I'll do the show.' And they said, 'Sure.'"

On the December 13, 2002, episode, Bergeron and Marshall changed places, and for the first time in 21 years, Marshall once again was the master of *Hollywood Squares*.

Surprise! Look What We Found!

For years, the original episodes of *Hollywood Squares* were never seen on television after their initial run because NBC erased most of the tapes and used them to record other shows. Suddenly in April of 2002, the long lost episodes of *Hollywood Squares* began airing on Game Show Network. As it turned out, many of the episodes had been sitting in a Burbank, California warehouse for all of these years and nobody knew they were there. According to Marshall in his book, an executive named Jim Pierson was in the warehouse one day searching for episodes of the 1960s soap opera *Dark Shadows* when he discovered approximately 3,000 tapes of *Hollywood Squares* episodes dating from 1968 to the late 1970s.

How were 3,000 tapes overlooked all of these years? As it turned out, when *Hollywood Squares* had been owned by Filmways during the 1970s, the company made copies of the tapes before NBC erased the masters. Since then, Filmways had been absorbed by Orion Entertainment and later by MGM, but after more than twenty years, everybody had forgotten about the tapes. After Jim Pierson discovered that the shows still existed, he contacted Game Show Network and the rest is history.

Boy Singer

Today, Marshall resides in Los Angeles with his third wife Laurie, whom he married in 1989. Along with his daily radio series, Marshall continues singing and has released a number of albums over the years. His most recent recordings were *Boy Singer* in 2000 and *No Happy Ending* in 2003. The latter album is a tribute to singer Billie Holliday. Both CDs along with copies of Marshall's autobiography *Backstage with the Original Hollywood Square* can be purchased through Marshall's website *www.boysinger.com*. When he is not working, Marshall enjoys playing golf and has participated in many charity tournaments. One of his philanthropic efforts is the Peter Marshall Golf Classic which he started with his son, former baseball player Pete LaCock. He also enjoys gardening and spending time with his ten grandchildren and great grandson.

When looking back at his long show business career, Marshall has contributed so much as an actor on and off Broadway; one could easily think that he would be offended at being labeled a game show host. Not so. In a 1987 interview for the *Daily News of Los Angeles*, Marshall was quick to credit his 15 years as the master of *Hollywood Squares* with making his whole career possible noting that without that show, he would still be an unknown.

WINK MARTINDALE

Birth Name: Winston Conrad Martindale
Born: December 4, 1933, in Jackson, Tennessee
Marriages and Family: Madelyn Leech (1954–1971) (Divorced) 3 daughters, 1 son; Sandy Ferra (August 2, 1975–Present); Radio Career: Disc Jockey (WPLI-AM, Jackson, TN) 1951; Disc Jockey (WTJS-AM, Jackson, TN) 1951; Disc Jockey (WDXI-AM, Jackson, TN) 1951–1953; Disc Jockey (WHBQ-AM, Memphis, TN) 1953–1959; Disc Jockey (KHJ-AM, Los Angeles, CA) 1959–1960; Disc Jockey (KRLA-AM, Los Angeles, CA) 1960–1962; Disc Jockey (KFWB-AM, Los Angeles, CA) 1962–1967; Disc Jockey (KGIL-AM, Los Angeles, CA) 1968–1971; Disc Jockey (KMPC-AM, Los Angeles, CA) 1971–1979; Substitute Program Host (KABC-AM, Los Angeles, CA) 1982; Disc Jockey (KMPC-AM, Los Angeles, CA) 1983–1987; *The Wink & Bill Show* (KABC-AM, Los Angeles) January 3, 1989–Sept. 29, 1989; Disc Jockey (KJQI-AM, Los Angeles, CA) 1993–1994; *The Music of Your Life* (Syndicated) May 1, 1996–Present

TV Career: HOST—*Wink Martindale and the Mars Patrol* (WHBQ-TV, Memphis, TN) 1953–1956; *Top Ten Dance Party* (WHBQ-TV, Memphis, TN) 1956–1959; *Wink Martindale Dance Party* (KHJ-TV, Los Angeles, CA) July 25, 1959–Sept. 1960; *POP Dance Party* (KCOP-TV, Los Angeles, CA) September 1960–July 21, 1961, (KTLA-TV, Los Angeles, CA) July 24, 1961–February 1962; *Zoom* (KTLA-TV, Los Angeles, CA) July 8, 1963–September 30, 1963; *What's the Name of That Song?* (KTLA-TV) March 2, 1964–May 29, 1964; *Take It from Me* (KTLA-TV, Los Angeles, CA) June 8, 1964–September 7, 1964; *What's This Song?* (NBC Daytime) October 26, 1964–September 24, 1965; *Dream Girl of '67* (ABC Daytime) June 26, 1967–September 22, 1967; *How's Your Mother-in-Law?* (ABC Daytime) December 4, 1967–March 1, 1968; *Can You Top This?* (Syndicated) January 26, 1970–September 1970; *Words and Music* (NBC Daytime) September 28, 1970–February 12, 1971; *Gambit* (CBS Daytime) September 4, 1972–December 10, 1976; *Tic Tac Dough* (CBS Daytime) July 3, 1978–September 1, 1978, (Syndicated) September 18, 1978–September 6, 1985; *Headline Chasers* (Syndicated) September 9, 1985–September 5, 1986; *Banko* (Unsold Game Show Pilot) 1986; *High Rollers* (Syndicated) September 14, 1987–September 9, 1988; *Top Secret* (Unsold CBS Game Show Pilot) 1988; *The Last Word* (Syndicated) September 18, 1989–January 5, 1990; *Great Getaway Game* (Travel Channel) June 1, 1990–April 1991; *Trivial Pursuit* (FAM) June 7, 1993–July 14, 1995; *Trivial Pursuit—The Interactive Game* (FAM) June 7, 1993–March 4, 1994, (FAM) Sept. 5, 1994–Dec. 30, 1994; *Boggle—The Interactive Game* (FAM) March 7, 1994–November 18, 1994; *Shuffle–The Interactive Game*

Wink Martindale (Wink Martindale, courtesy Fred Wostbrock)

(FAM) March 7, 1994–June 10, 1994; *Jumble–The Interactive Game* (FAM) June 13, 1994–September 2, 1994, (FAM) November 21, 1994–December 30, 1994; *Debt* (Lifetime) June 3, 1996–August 14, 1998, (Syndicated) March 9, 1998–September 1998   ANNOUNCER—*Everybody's Talking* (ABC Daytime) February 6, 1967–June 23, 1967   EXECUTIVE PRODUCER—*Headline Chasers* (Syndicated) September 9, 1985–September 5, 1986; *Bumper Stumpers* (USA) June 29, 1987–December 28, 1990; *Second Honeymoon* (CBN) September 14, 1987–September 2, 1988; *Great Getaway Game* (Travel Channel) June 1, 1990–April 1991; *Why Didn't I Think of That?* (Syndicated) September 1992–September 1993; *Trivial Pursuit* (FAM) June 7, 1993–July 14, 1995; *Boggle—The Interactive Game* (FAM) March 7, 1994–November 18, 1994; *Shuffle—The Interactive Game* (FAM) March 7, 1994–June 10, 1994; *Jumble—The Interactive Game* (FAM) June 13, 1994–September 2, 1994, (FAM) November 21, 1994–December 30, 1994

Theatrical Movies: *Let's Rock* (1958); *The Lively Set* (1963)

Made-for-TV Movies: *Gridlock* (NBC) October 2, 1980; *Medusa* (*Dare to Be Truthful*) 1992

Business Interests: Owner, Wink Martindale's Restaurant (1982–1984); President, Wink Martindale Enterprises (1984–Present); Partner, Martindale-Hillier Entertainment (1992–1995)

Book: *Winking at Life* (2000)

Other Careers: Recording Artist: Dot Records, Los Angeles (1959–1966); Artist and Repertoire Agent: Dot Records, Los Angeles (February–August 1962); Television Spokesman: Orbitz (2005–Present)

The game show hosting fraternity is a small group. Since the beginning of game shows on radio in the 1930s, only a handful of people have succeeded in making a career out of hosting. Wink Martindale was one of those fortunate few to come back to the small screen year after year and show after show. In 35 years, he helmed 19 game shows, and is second only to Bill Cullen in the largest number of television game shows emceed.

Jackson, Tennessee was the birthplace to Winston Conrad Martindale on December 4, 1933. Wink was the fourth of five children born to James and Francis Martindale. Winston enjoyed an active childhood with odd jobs delivering newspapers and groceries. He also worked as a dishwasher and soda jerk, a term he despised according to his 2000 autobiography, *Winking at Life*.

One of his biggest interests as a child was listening to the radio, so Martindale soon began cutting out advertisements from *Life* magazines and pretending to be a radio announcer by reading them out loud. He later purchased a special microphone, which when connected to the back of a radio set, enabled him to talk into the microphone and hear himself through the speaker. Unfortunately the device never worked properly and Martindale succeeded in blowing out two of the radio's vacuum tubes.

Climbing the Ladder

In April 1951 at the age of 17, he began his climb on the broadcasting ladder. His Sunday School teacher Chick Wingate, who managed radio station WPLI-AM in Jackson, Tennessee, hired him to work the evening shift as announcer for $25 a week. Two months later, Martindale moved to WTJS where he did the play-by-play announcing for local high school football and basketball games along with the usual announcing chores. He later was invited to join the staff at WDXI-AM. On the air Winston Martindale was known as Winkie Martindale. The nickname "Winkie" had been given to him by a childhood friend who could never pronounce his real name Winston. During his tenure at WDXI radio Martindale enrolled in Lambuth College.

After 20 months of working in radio in his hometown of Jackson, Martindale tried his luck in a larger market by applying at WHBQ-AM in Memphis, Tennessee. His timing was right because the manager was looking for someone to take over the station's early morning shift. Martindale joined WHBQ in March 1953 and dropped out of college to move to Memphis. At the advice of WHBQ's manager Bill Grumbles, Martindale changed his nickname to "Wink."

In July 1954 Martindale eloped with his girlfriend Madelyn Leech, whom he had met while working at WDXI in Jackson. The couple had three daughters Lisa, Madelyn, and Laura, plus a son, Winston Jr. That marriage lasted until 1971. Meanwhile, Martindale enrolled in Memphis State University and graduated with a degree in Speech and Drama in 1957.

Blast Off!

At WHBQ Martindale hosted *Clockwatchers*, the early morning music show, weekdays from 6:00–9:00 a.m. and served as the station's record librarian. In September 1953, Martindale earned his first television gig, *The Wink Martindale Mars Patrol*. Sporting a turtleneck sweater designed to look like a space suit, Martindale interviewed some local Memphis children on a set resembling a space ship. Then the space ship "blasted off" and was followed by a short episode from the *Flash Gordon* movie series popular in theaters in the 1940s. At the end of the *Flash Gordon* episode, the space ship with the children "landed," and Martindale finished the show by giving some facts about the solar system and the planets.

Dancing with Success

After *Mars Patrol* was canceled in 1956, Martindale immediately moved over to *Top Ten Dance Party* for WHBQ. It was similar in format to the nationally televised *American Bandstand* series hosted by Dick Clark. *Dance Party* featuring a studio of teenagers who danced to records of current music hits. There were also live performances by artists such as Elvis Presley and Roy Orbison.

Martindale and Presley became good friends and kept in touch through the years. In 1956 Martindale convinced him to appear on *Top Ten Dance Party*. Since the show aired live, Martindale brought in a camera and hired someone to film Elvis' appearance. This became one of the first Elvis Presley interviews to be recorded.

Goodbye Tennessee, Hello California

By 1959 Martindale felt his career had reached its limit in Memphis. With the help of WHBQ's manager Bill Grumbles, Martindale won a spot at KHJ radio and television in Los Angeles. In March 1959 he moved his family to the west coast. On the radio he served as the weekday morning disc jockey and on weekends hosted *The Wink Martindale Dance Party* for KHJ-TV.

Shortly after his move, Martindale was approached by Dot Records about recording a narrative called "Deck of Cards." This was the story about a soldier describing how he used a deck of cards as a bible, almanac, and prayer book. The narrative had been a hit for T. Texas Tyler in 1948 and had been recorded by other artists. Martindale's recording peaked at number 7 on the Billboard Top 40 in September 1959. He soon recorded a full album with "Deck of Cards" as the leading piece.

Between 1959 and 1966, Martindale recorded a number of singles and three additional albums for Dot Records called "The Bible Story," "My True Love," and "Giddyup Go." None came close to the success of "Deck of Cards." These recordings led to two film appearances in *Let's Rock* (1958) and *The Lively Set* (1963).

Career Change

Back on the radio, Martindale moved from KHJ to become the morning disc jockey for KRLA in 1960. By then his interest in radio had diminished, and in February 1962 he accepted an offer to work as the A&R (Artists and Repertoire) man for Dot Records. According to his book, *Winking at Life*, he thought that working directly in the record business would allow him to have some impact on the type of music that hit the record shops and radio stations. Soon he discovered that the task was much harder than he thought, so he left Dot Records in August 1962, though he continued to record for the label.

Returning to radio as a disc jockey for KFWB-AM, one of the most popular stations in southern California, Martindale was still unhappy and considered other career options. His two theatrical movies had failed, so he put aside his acting ambitions. He had recorded a number of records with limited success, but a recording artist career was also out of the question. His television work in Memphis and Los Angeles had been limited to music-oriented programs. He needed a new kind of format.

A Great Living

When Martindale became a big fan of the game show *Password*, he was sold on the idea of being a game show host. In July 1963 his dream came true when he began hosting *Zoom* for Los Angeles station KTLA-TV. Two contestants identified an object that slowly came into focus as a camera zoomed closer to the object. The show only ran for 13 weeks, but it whetted Martindale's appetite for more game show gigs.

Early 1964 brought *What Is the Name of That Song?* Two celebrity-contestant teams identified songs earning 20 points for each correct answer. They could score an additional 20 points by singing the first two lines of the chorus without a mistake. The first team to amass 100 points won the game. The show was successful enough on KTLA to win a spot on NBC's daytime schedule. With the shorter title *What's This Song?* the game debuted on October 26, 1964. Martindale also shortened his own name for the series. In his book, *Winking at Life*, Martindale said that vice-president of NBC Daytime Programming Bob Aaron felt that the name "Wink" sounded too juvenile. By dropping one letter from his name, Wink Martindale became Win Martindale during the one year run of the show.

Three Shows in One Year

Martindale continued as a popular radio personality on KFWB until 1967 when he auditioned to host ABC's *Everybody's Talking*. He lost out to Los Angeles disc jockey Lloyd Thaxton, but the producers hired Martindale as the show's on-camera announcer.

Four months later, Martindale moved back to the host's circle with *Dream Girl of '67*, a daily beauty pageant. Three celebrity judges rated five female contestants based on poise, personality, and fashion. The weekly winners competed at the end of the year for the title of "Dream Girl of '67."

After three months, Martindale departed to take the reins of *How's Your Mother-in-Law?* According to Martindale in *Winking at Life*, audience response to the pilot for this show was through the roof. However, audiences tuned out once *How's Your Mother-in-Law?* took to the air in December 1967. Three celebrity comedians acted as defense attorneys in mock "court cases" for three mothers-in-law who were "on trial" for accusations raised by their sons-in-law. A jury of five bachelors and five bachelorettes then decided which mother-in-law was the best. The show quickly vanished from the tube in March 1968.

The Only Games of 1970

Martindale returned to radio with an adult contemporary music show on KGIL-AM in the San Fernando Valley area of Los Angeles. Two more game shows in 1970, *Can You Top This?* and NBC's *Words and Music*, failed to draw substantial ratings. A note of interest is that these two programs were the only new game shows introduced in 1970 and both of them were hosted by Martindale. In March 1971 he moved from KGIL radio to KMPC as the midday personality where he remained for almost nine years.

Deal Them Up

In 1972 Martindale scored his first successful game show with *Gambit*, which was based on the card game Blackjack. Two teams of married couples answered questions to earn cards from a standard deck of 52 oversized playing cards. The object of the game was to score as close as possible to 21 points without going over. The first team to win two games collected $200 and advanced to the "Gambit Board." The team selected prizes from the board and earned playing cards to score 21 points. Going over lost the couple their bonus prizes.

> **Robert Noah (Gambit producer, June 2006 telephone interview):**
>
> "Audiences love Wink because he is a delightful man and he doesn't have a phony bone in his body. He just loves talking to people. He always did the long [audience] warm-up himself because he loved doing it. In fact, you had a terrible time getting him out of the audience [to do the show] because he was enjoying himself so much."

Wink Martindale holds two winning hands on *Gambit* (Wink Martindale, courtesy Fred Wostbrock).

Riding High

The best event of 1972 in Martindale's opinion was meeting his second wife, Sandy Ferra. She worked as a talent coordinator for Bob Eubanks in his Concert Express enterprise with Dolly Parton, Merle Haggard, and Barbara Mandrell. Wink and Sandy dated for three years and married on August 2, 1975.

By the mid 1970s, Martindale was riding high with a successful radio show on KMPC and *Gambit* running five days a week on CBS. The bubble burst when *Gambit* lagged in the ratings against NBC's *Wheel of Fortune*, and bit the dust on December 10, 1976. Martindale continued on KMPC radio in the interim and hosted a 15-hour music salute to his friend Elvis Presley after Presley's sudden death in 1977.

X's and O's

In the summer of 1978 Martindale started his longest-running show, *Tic Tac Dough*. Based on the children's game "Tic Tac Toe," two contestants, one representing "X" and the other representing "O," competed. A player selected one of the nine categories from a board containing nine squares in three rows of three. Answering the question correctly allowed the contestant to put their "X" or "O" on the board. The categories were shuffled and the opponent selected one. The first player to get three "X's" or "O's" in a row across, up and down, or diagonally on the board won the game. Questions were worth $200 in the outer boxes while the tougher center box question was worth $300. The money for all the correct answers was placed in a pot, and the winner of the game collected all the money accumulated in that round.

The winner played a bonus round where the nine squares concealed various amounts of money ranging from $100 to $500. The player selected numbers and won the corresponding dollar amounts. One square contained the dragon and picking that box meant losing all bonus round winnings. If the player could bag $1,000 or more without hitting the dragon, they won the cash and a bonus prize. Contestants faced new challengers until defeated.

The most successful contestant on *Tic Tac Dough* during its eight-year run was Thom McKee, a 24-year-old Naval Lieutenant, who won 43 games in a row and racked up $312,700 and eight automobiles before his defeat in 1980. McKee held the record as the single biggest winner in game show history until the big money series *Who Wants to Be a Millionaire?* came on the scene in 1999.

Save Our Show!

Tic Tac Dough almost died as quickly as it had started. It first aired over CBS on July 3, 1978, with a syndicated version set to premiere that September. CBS yanked the show after just nine weeks before the syndicated version could get started. To save *Tic Tac Dough*, Martindale and his staff hit the road in a media blitz to assure station owners who bought the show that it would succeed. Once the syndicated version got underway in the 1978–1979 season, the ratings climbed through the roof.

In November 1979 Martindale resigned from KMPC radio to focus on television projects. He returned to host *Las Vegas Gambit*, a revival of his mid 1970s show. This version only lasted one year.

Wink Martindale asks the next question on *Tic Tac Dough* (Wink Martindale, courtesy Fred Wostbrock).

"Go Take a Cold Shower"

With *Tic Tac Dough* still running successfully, Martindale turned his attention to a new line of work. He and his younger brother David opened a restaurant and lounge called "Wink Martindale's" in Memphis, Tennessee in 1982. According to Martindale's autobiography, he and his brother planned to build the restaurant in their hometown of Jackson, Tennessee. Before construction got underway, they found a building in Memphis for a good price and decided to buy it to speed up the restaurant's opening.

For the next two years, Martindale and his wife Sandy flew back and forth from Los Angeles to Memphis to oversee the restaurant and lounge. The venture turned into a financial fiasco for Martindale, and he closed the restaurant in 1984.

> **Wink Martindale (February 2004 telephone interview):**
> "Everybody wants to be in the restaurant business and they don't know how people steal you blind. It's a stupid business. Anybody who wants to go into the restaurant business, I try to talk them out of it. Go take a cold shower."

Despite losing nearly half a million dollars in the venture, Martindale was far from ruined. He returned to his true forte by going back to KMPC radio as an afternoon personality.

A Heck of a Game Show

Through his years in game shows, Martindale had come up with ideas for programs of his own, but none of them ever came to fruition. One morning in 1984, a front page headline in *The Los Angeles Times* gave Martindale an idea.

He created a game show based on guessing famous newspaper headlines from past and present and titled it *Front Page*. He produced and hosted a 13-minute pilot and sold it to television mogul Merv Griffin, who bought the first show created by someone outside of his company in more than 20 years.

Griffin renamed the series *Headline Chasers*, and the game was syndicated to 128 stations. Since he would have to devote more time to *Headline Chasers* not only as the show's host, but also as executive producer, Martindale left *Tic Tac Dough* at the end of the 1984-1985 season. The show ran one more year with Jim Caldwell as host. On *Headline Chasers*, two teams of married couples answered questions that served as clues to a puzzle. The puzzle was a newspaper or magazine headline with missing letters. The value of the puzzle started at $500 and decreased by $100 for every clue. Guessing the headline won the couple the amount left in the pot. The couple with the most money after three rounds won the game.

From Host to Producer

Headline Chasers only lasted the 1985–1986 season, but Martindale was hooked as a game show producer. With his new production company, he totally immersed himself into the creation of new game shows. Martindale developed *Second Honeymoon* and *Bumper Stumpers* for a 1987 launch. Hosted by Wayne Cox, *Second Honeymoon* featured three teams of families who matched answers to hypothetical questions. *Bumper Stumpers* involved contestants deciphering personalized license plates for cash and prizes. Canadian personality Al DuBois hosted the show, which debuted on the USA cable network in June 1987. That fall Martindale went before the cameras to host *High Rollers*, a syndicated revival of the popular 1970s dice game.

Working on three television shows made it difficult for Martindale to squeeze the daily KMPC radio show into his schedule. He signed off from the station for the second time in March 1987. Of the three game shows Martindale had during the 1987-1988 season, only *Bumper Stumpers* was renewed for a second year.

A New Kind of Radio

In January 1989, Martindale teamed with former Los Angeles news anchor Bill Smith for *The Wink and Bill Show* on KABC radio. Martindale and Smith had worked together in 1982 when they filled in for Ken Minyard and Bob Arthur on KABC. Unlike Martindale's previous radio music programs, the 1982 show focused on news and talk and served as a model for his current project.

Becoming savvy about current events was no problem for Martindale, who regularly got up at 4:30 a.m. to read the newspaper and was a loyal fan of CNN. His partner Bill Smith called Martindale a "news junkie." *The Wink and Bill Show* only lasted eight months.

The Games Temporarily Fade

Martindale spent the 1989–1990 season hosting *Last Word*, which taped in Vancouver, Canada. He followed with a one season run of *The Great Getaway Game* for the Travel Channel during the 1990–1991 season. Both shows were word-association games. By now Martindale figured that his game show career was over since games were gradually being replaced by talk shows.

In 1992 Martindale, along with his business partner Bill Hillier and longtime friend Ron Hoffman, developed *Why Didn't I Think of That?* Inventors brought their original creations on the show for demonstrations to a studio audience. Another segment of the show had the inventors test their creations out in public places to gauge people's reactions. The weekly series was hosted by comedian Wil Shriner in syndication during the 1992-1993 season.

The Interactive Games

After several attempts by producers to put the popular board game "Trivial Pursuit" on the tube during the 1980s, Martindale and Bill Hillier acquired the rights and launched a daily version of *Trivial Pursuit* for the Family Channel in June 1993. The one-hour show began with a half-hour elimination game of 12 studio contestants (later reduced to nine) competing to answer a series of multiple-choice trivia questions.

The three highest scoring players moved to the second half of the show where they played a lightning fast game of answering questions in various categories. The first player to fill a "pie" consisting of 12 colored wedges won the game. Interactive segments of the game where home viewers played along by telephone were sandwiched between rounds of the studio game.

Trivial Pursuit captured a large audience during the summer of 1993, but attempts to syndicate the show were unsuccessful. *Trivial Pursuit* ceased production in March 1994, but reruns of the game remained on the air until July 1995.

The Family Channel commissioned Martindale-Hillier Entertainment to create three other interactive game shows. They obliged with *Boggle*, *Shuffle*, and *Jumble*. All three shows were based on popular word games, but none of them translated well to the small screen. In December 1994 Family Channel scrapped the entire interactive game block.

The Music of Your Life

In the spring of 1996, Martindale joined a syndicated radio music series called *The Music of Your Life*, which is the name of the format used by Jones Satellite Networks. Instead of hosting the series in a radio studio, Martindale records his daily three-hour show from his home in Calabasas, California. *The Music of Your Life* features a wide variety of music ranging from the 1940s to current hits depending on the artist.

Martindale wisely had maintained recorded copies of his many interviews with famous artists over his four decades in radio in Memphis and Los Angeles. He uses segments of these interviews along with the songs played during the show.

According to a 1996 *Billboard Magazine* story, Martindale spent three months transferring all of his recorded interviews from reel-to-reel tapes to the new DAT (digital audio tape) format for use on the show.

Going into "Debt"

Coinciding with Martindale's newfound success on the radio, he launched his 19th television game show, *Debt*, in June 1996 for the Lifetime Network. Three contestants, all of whom were in debt for various reasons, competed to wipe out their debts in a pop culture trivia game. All three players began with minus scores and chose categories and dollar amounts from a board. Correct answers to questions added money to the contestant's score. The winner advanced to the "Get out of Debt" bonus round where they answered 10 trivia questions in 60 seconds. If successful, their entire real-life debt was wiped clean and paid for by the show.

Far from Retired

Martindale has not hosted any game shows since 1998, but has continued to enjoy great success with *The Music of Your Life*. In 1999 he did a series of commercials for the Virginia State Lottery Association, and later that year donned a green tuxedo to host a music video with the rock group Everclear. In April 2002 he appeared on NBC's *Today Show* during a special week honoring game show hosts. One month later, he joined fellow emcees Bob Eubanks, Jim Lange, Peter Marshall, and Ben Stein on the NBC special *Most Outrageous Game Show Moments*. Most recently, Martindale gained fame as spokesman for Orbitz airline commercials. On June 2, 2006, Hollywood honored him with a star on its famous Walk of Fame.

Today Martindale resides with his wife Sandy and their Chihuahuas in a Tudor-style home they purchased in 1994 in Calabasas, California. In 2000 Martindale published his autobiography *Winking at Life* and recorded an accompanying CD featuring a selection of poems and stories called "Winking at Life: God, Country, Mom and Apple Pie." The CD also contains a new recording of his 1959 hit "Deck of Cards."

When not working, Martindale spends time with his family which includes seven grandchildren and one great-grandchild. Through the years he has devoted much of his spare time to charity work, hosting telethons for the West Tennessee Cerebral Palsy Center in his hometown of Jackson, Tennessee from 1977 to 1988, and working for the St. Jude Children's Research Hospital.

Retirement is definitely not a word in Martindale's vocabulary. "Retire from what?" is his usual answer to anyone who mentions the word. He still enjoys working and plans to keep going pointing out in *Winking at Life* that despite the pressures of age, the seasoned and experienced person can compete just as well as younger people in the broadcasting field.

GARRY MOORE

Birth Name: Thomas Garrison Morfit
Born: January 31, 1915, in Baltimore, Maryland
Died: November 28, 1993, in Hilton Head Island, South Carolina
Marriages and Family: Eleanor Little (1939–1974) (Deceased) 2 sons; Mary Elizabeth DeChant (1975–1993)
Radio Career: Writer and Announcer (WBAL-AM, Baltimore, MD) 1933–1938; News Announcer & Sports Commentator (KWK-AM, St. Louis, MO) 1938–1939; *Club Matinee* (NBC) 1939–1942; *Beat the Band* (NBC) January 28, 1940–February 23, 1941; *The Show Without a Name/Everything Goes* (NBC) July 1, 1942–November 20, 1943; *Camel Caravan* (NBC) March 25, 1943–October 28, 1943; *The Durante-Moore Show* (CBS) October 8, 1943–June 27, 1947; *Take It or Leave It* (NBC) September 14, 1947–September 4, 1949; *Breakfast in Hollywood* (NBC) May 10, 1948–August 20, 1948; *The Garry Moore Show* (CBS) September 12, 1949–August 25, 1950, (CBS) September 28, 1959–September 21, 1961; *New York, New York* (Voice of America Network) 1968–1971
TV Career: HOST—*The Garry Moore Show* (CBS Primetime) June 26, 1950–September 1950, (CBS Daytime) October 1950–June 27, 1958, (CBS Primetime) October 18, 1951–December 27, 1951, (CBS Primetime) September 30, 1958–June 14, 1964; *I've Got a Secret* (CBS Primetime) June 19, 1952–September 14, 1964; *The Garry Moore Show* (CBS Primetime) September 11, 1966–January 8, 1967; *To Tell the Truth* (Syndicated) September 8, 1969–September 1977
Theatrical Movie: *It Happened to Jane* (1959)

Garry Moore (Fred Wostbrock).

"To Tell the Truth, I've Got a Secret." That sounds like an unusual sentence, but these words have a common bond in a man named Garry Moore. By now you most likely have figured out that these are the names of Moore's two most famous game shows that he hosted in his career. Moore also proved his worth as a comedian by fronting his own variety show for more than a decade while hosting a popular game show at the same time.

Born as Thomas Garrison Morfit on January 31, 1915, in Baltimore, Maryland, Moore was the only child of Mason S. and Mary Louis Harris Morfit. His father was a prominent lawyer in Baltimore. From an early age, Moore showed a talent for comedy, although he did his best to hide that fact. He preferred that people think of him as the serious type. He fought his comedian image throughout grammar and high school, but his flair for comedy always came to the surface.

Boiled Ham and Parsley

In a 1948 *New York Times* interview, Moore told the story of an assembly he attended in high school when the principal addressed the students on the virtues of good citizenship. Moore thought that the principal's bald head resembled a "boiled ham surrounded by parsley." He whispered this to the student seated next to him and the joke made its way around the auditorium. Before long the entire student body was laughing leaving the poor principal wondering what was so funny.

During his last year in high school, Moore joined a Baltimore theater group called The Vagabonds as a comedy writer and actor. Writer F. Scott Fitzgerald happened to see the group perform and asked Moore to collaborate with him on a musical modeled after the *Grand Guignol* melodramas. According to Moore, the script was bad in quality and their partnership ended after three months.

Can I Be Serious?

Although his parents wanted Moore to attend either law or medical school, they eventually accepted his decision to go into radio. Offered a chance to attend the American Academy of Dramatic Arts, Moore instead made the rounds of Baltimore radio stations until WBAL hired him as an all-purpose staff announcer and writer in 1933. One day, the comic on WBAL's variety show collapsed in a nearby saloon just before airtime. Pressed by the station manager to do the show, Moore quickly won over the listeners and before long became a full-time comedian. Still not convinced that his talent was in comedy, Moore left WBAL in 1936 and moved to St. Louis to take a job as a sports and news announcer for radio station KWK.

Content with his more serious work, Moore kept his knack for comedy a secret. Then in 1938, a person who knew him from Baltimore happened to tell KWK management about Moore's previous comedy experience. Forced again to be a comedian Moore refused, but when the manager threatened to fire him, Moore quickly reconsidered.

In the middle of this job turmoil, Moore married Eleanor Little in St. Louis on June 5, 1939. Frustrated with his comedian image when he wanted to be a serious announcer, Moore quit his job at KWK. Two weeks later on June 17, 1939, he met a seedy-looking man named Sims at a hot dog stand in St. Louis. Moore could not remember the man's first name when recalling this story in his 1948 *New York Times* autobiography, but the man recognized him as Garry Morfit, the radio comedian from KWK.

Be a Comedian

Sims told him that he was the "funniest feller on the air." Asked why he was no longer on the radio, Moore told Sims the story of how everybody wanted him to be comedian while he wanted to do something serious. Sims pointed out that it was easy for anyone to be serious, but that not many people can be funny. He advised Moore to be a comedian since he had the talent.

Those words finally changed Moore's thinking. He readily accepted his talent for comedy and, with his new bride, headed for Chicago to get a network audition with NBC radio. The network executives told him that without any previous network experience, there was no place for him.

Learning the Ropes

Undaunted by this stumbling block, Moore learned that the popular radio quiz show *Doctor I.Q.* was broadcasting a special show from St. Louis. He went to the show's producers and won the job as one of the six roving announcers who walked through the program's audience with microphones looking for contestants. When one of the announcers found a potential player, they told host Lew Valentine, who was on the stage.

Valentine asked the player a question. The winners were paid off in silver dollars with the value depending on the difficulty of the question. With this one network appearance to his credit, Moore wired NBC in Chicago and told them of his experience. The network finally gave in and hired him to co-host *Club Matinee*, a weekday afternoon variety show. Working with the program's main host Ransom Sherman, Moore learned the ropes of network radio.

A New Name

In 1940 *Club Matinee* held a contest to pick a new stage name for Moore, who was still working under his real name Thomas Garrison Morfit. Moore once noted that the reason for the change was that that the name Morfit was hard for listeners to understand over the radio. A woman from Pittsburgh won the prize of $50 when she suggested the name Garry Moore. Moore kept this name for the rest of his career.

That same year, he hosted his very first quiz show called *Beat the Band*. A 14-member band was asked musical questions submitted by the listeners. The questions were posed as riddles with the answer being a song title. The listeners received $10 if they submitted a question used on the program and $20 if it stumped the band. When the band missed a question, they had to "feed the kitty," which meant that they tossed half-dollars onto a bass drum.

In the summer of 1942, Moore moved to New York to host *The Show Without a Name*. In early 1943, the show offered a $500 prize for an official name. Since the show's format was so flexible and full of spontaneous comedy, the name *Everything Goes* won the contest. NBC was impressed with the size of Moore's audience on *Everything Goes* and decided to put him in a summer replacement series for *The Abbott & Costello Show*. Titled *The Camel Caravan*, the program was rushed into production in March 1943 when comedian Lou Costello became ill with rheumatic fever and *The Abbott & Costello Show* stopped production.

"Dat's My Boy Dat Said Dat"

However, the sponsor of *The Camel Caravan* was reluctant to let Moore host the show on his own since he was relatively new to the business. The agency hired veteran comedian Jimmy Durante to share the billing with Moore. After a slow start, the program built a solid audience, and by the time *The Abbott & Costello Show* returned to the air in November 1943, *The Camel Caravan* moved to CBS as *The Durante-Moore Show*. The duo worked well together despite their age difference (Moore was 28 and Durante was 50 when the series began). They made the age difference part of the act with Durante often referring to Moore as "Junior" and saying the famous phrase, "dat's my boy dat said dat."

After four hit years, Moore decided that it was time to strike out on his own, so he and Durante amicably parted company. Moore was taking a chance by leaving the popular *Durante-Moore Show*, but he did not have to wait long for another break.

Take It or Leave It

Moving to Los Angeles, he replaced Phil Baker as the host of the quiz show, *Take It or Leave It* on NBC in the fall of 1947. Contestants were drawn from the studio audience and, playing one at a time, were asked a series of seven questions. The first question was worth $1 and each succeeding question doubled in value to $2, $4, $8, $16, $32, and finally $64. Naturally, the questions were more difficult as they increased in value. Players had the option of quitting anytime and leaving with their winnings or risking it all to go for the next question.

The popularity of Bert Parks' big money quiz show *Stop the Music,* where contestants could win as much as $20,000, prompted the sponsor of *Take It or Leave It* to raise the top prize from $64 to $6,400.

Garry Moore (Look *magazine September 22, 1964):*
"I told him that if he did raise the ante, I would quit. For a top prize of $64, no contestant got hurt if he lost. For $6,400, the loss could be devastating: a college education for his kid,

a last payment on a mortgage, and all because he didn't know the name of the first Chief Justice of the United States or the capital of Bolivia. Also, it would have changed my position from master-of-the-revels to a croupier. And nobody loves a croupier."

In fact, several years later when *Take It or Leave It* was revised as *The $64,000 Question* for television in 1955, Moore was asked to host the program.

> *GM:*
>
> "I turned it down on the basis that $64,000 was too much money for anybody to play games with and, almost surely, at that price, some backstage hanky-panky would creep in."

Moore was right about the "hanky-panky" business as *The $64,000 Question* left the air after three years amid charges that the show was fixed.

Going Back East

Offered the chance to host his own series for CBS radio in New York City, Moore moved back east and opened *The Garry Moore Show* on September 12, 1949. It was here that he perfected the format that made him a television star. He became a relaxed low-key entertainer who told jokes, conducted interviews with the studio audience, and featured singing guest stars who worked with him in comedy skits.

In June 1950, *The Garry Moore Show* moved to television airing five nights a week. Moore

Garry Moore, Betsy Palmer, Henry Morgan, Bess Myerson, and Bill Cullen promote a time change for *I've Got a Secret* in 1961 (Fred Wostbrock).

opened each show with a monologue, which he wrote himself, then followed with a comedy skit featuring his regular cast. A series of musical numbers filled the rest of the show. The show later became a daily afternoon entry. A new feature was the appearance of naturalist Ivan Sanderson, who brought unusual animals to the show on Fridays.

Moore was the spark plug that held the show together. Although he was a low-key host, he often brought life to the party with outrageous stunts such as boxing a bear, flying on a trapeze, and bouncing on the trampoline. On one occasion, series regular Denise Lor demonstrated jujitsu by flipping Moore on the floor.

At times the program devoted itself to charitable causes. On one occasion, Moore urged each of his viewers to send a nickel to a Michigan housewife and her husband. By the end of that week, the couple had received around $7,000 in nickels.

Don't Tell Anyone, But I've Got a Secret

On June 19, 1952, Moore began hosting *I've Got a Secret* on CBS. *I've Got a Secret* featured a panel of four celebrities who questioned a contestant with a secret. At the beginning of each round, Moore introduced the contestant who whispered the secret in Moore's ear while it flashed on the television screen for the audience to see. The panelists were given thirty seconds each to question the contestant and guess their secret. The contestant received $20 for each panelist they stumped and $80 if they stumped the entire panel. Three rounds were played on each program with the third round featuring a celebrity guest with a secret for the panel to identify. Some celebrities who stopped by *I've Got a Secret* were Boris Karloff, Ronald Reagan, Paul Newman, Desi Arnaz, Lucille Ball, and Johnny Carson.

There was a considerable turnover in the panel during the show's first season, but by the second year, the panel consisted of game show host Bill Cullen, comedian Henry Morgan, and actresses Jayne Meadows (wife of comedian Steve Allen) and Faye Emerson. Meadows and Emerson were replaced by Betsy Palmer and Bess Myerson in the late 1950s.

The Secret of Success

The simple format of *I've Got a Secret's* helped the show frequently rank among the top 20 programs. The humorous questioning sessions in each round from the witty panel members combined with Moore's relaxed hosting kept *I've Got a Secret* on the air for nearly 15 years. Moore may very well be the only television star in history to have a daily 9–5 work schedule. According to an April 1953 *TV Guide* story, Moore caught the commuter train from his home in Rye, New York at 8:18 a.m. and was at his office by 9 a.m.

He wrote material for *The Garry Moore Show* until 11:30 a.m. when he took a taxi to the Mansfield Theater on W. 39th Street to rehearse for the program. At 1:00 p.m., the cast and crew grabbed lunch and from 1:30–2:00 p.m., *The Garry Moore Show* aired live. After the show, Moore went back to his office and met with his writers and sponsors. He hopped on the 4:15 p.m. commuter train and went home to have dinner with his wife and two sons, Mason and Garry Jr. On Thursday nights when *I've Got a Secret* aired, Moore stayed in town for dinner.

TV Is Too Commercial

In 1958 Moore stepped down from his daytime series. One reason that he quit the show was, as he put it, "the gradual over commercialization of daytime TV." Most television viewers would agree with Moore's belief that there were too many commercials for one program. When *The Garry Moore Show* started in 1950, there were only four commercial spots per episode. As the costs of television production increased, the number of sponsors increased, until the mid 1950s when there were 39 different sponsors for his program, all of whom sponsored the show on a different day of the week.

During the 1950s and 1960s, it was common for the stars of the programs to perform the commercial spots. For Moore, this meant memorizing and knowing all about 39 different products. He once remarked to *Harper's Magazine* in June 1958 that he couldn't remember "which is crispy and which is crunchy."

Things only got worse as rising production costs increased the number of commercials per week to a whopping 60 by 1958. This was accomplished by CBS allowing sponsors to advertise three different products every 15 minutes on the show. If this all sounds confusing, it was.

> *Garry Moore (***Look** *magazine September 22, 1964):*
> "How can one guy possibly know thoroughly about 60 different products? How can he rehearse 60 commercials a week and still have time to worry about his real product: the entertainment content of the show? The tail was wagging the dog into insensibility, so I called it a daytime."

Moore was a man who strongly believed that if someone endorsed a sponsor's product, they should know all about it.

> *GM:*
> "You're being asked to recommend it to your friends: the viewers. If the product doesn't live up to the sponsor's claims, you have two choices: you demand that the sponsor reduce his claims to fit the facts, or, failing that, you don't accept the product as an advertiser."

A Bigger Show

After performing for the 2,040th time, *The Garry Moore Show* faded on June 27, 1958. Moore returned to CBS that fall with a primetime variety series. The nighttime show used much of the same format as his daytime program, but with a much larger budget. Moore could now afford to hire more writers and big-name guest stars. The new *Garry Moore Show* featured Allen Funt's popular *Candid Camera* series as a regular segment in which a hidden camera focused on unsuspecting people in public places with comical results.

Moore made so much money for CBS that the network signed him to a 15 year contract in 1959. Away from television, Moore generously gave his time to several organizations. He served as national chairman of the National Society for Crippled Children and Adults and on the board of governors for the National Hospital for Speech Disorders. He also served as chairman of the board of the Royal Crown Beverage Company (RC). Moore spent his free time playing golf, sailing his yacht, raising tropical fish, and collecting old and rare jazz records. He also enjoyed walking and was frequently seen walking around New York City where his fans always warmly greeted him.

Burnout

By 1964 Moore had tired of television. He faced the same commercial problems on his primetime shows that had plagued his daytime series. He decided to try public affairs broadcasting by anchoring a series of reports for CBS Radio. He soon found that the network only wanted him to read the news and not participate in the actual writing and research.

When ratings for *The Garry Moore Show* dropped during the 1963-1964 season, CBS axed the series. For Moore, it was a relief rather than a tragedy. The loss of privacy became another factor in Moore's desire to get out of television. He was simply burned out. He had grown discouraged with the direction television was taking in the 1960s and decided to step out of the limelight.

A World Tour

Moore remained with *I've Got a Secret* until September 14, 1964, when he turned the show over to comedian Steve Allen. Although he no longer hosted the show, Moore retained joint ownership of *I've Got a Secret* with CBS. Moore took his wife on a nine month cruise around the world visiting Egypt, Africa, India, Thailand, Japan, Australia, and Tahiti.

During his absence, Moore deliberately kept himself ignorant of everything going on in the television business. Returning from his worldly journey in May 1965, Moore talked to CBS about releasing him from the contract he had with the network. The contract guaranteed him $100,000 a year even if he did not work, but Moore wanted to be free to do other projects for NBC or ABC.

Taking to the Streets

When CBS refused to release him from the deal and did not offer any work, Moore spent another year in retirement. Still wanting to host a show dealing with public affairs, Moore produced and hosted an ABC special, *Garry Moore's People Poll*, in February 1966. Moore took to the streets in San Francisco, Washington D.C., Chicago, St. Louis, and New Orleans interviewing average people and getting their opinions on public issues.

CBS rejected the idea, but since Moore's contract allowed for guest appearances on other networks, ABC agreed to air the special. However, *Garry Moore's People Poll* was a major flop and Moore decided to give up on public affairs broadcasting.

Since CBS wanted Moore to act, he decided to pitch the idea for a new comedy-variety series to the network. The new *Garry Moore Show* featured zany skits and blackouts (short comedy bits strung together in a lightning-fast format). Moore's new series returned to CBS in September 1966. Running against NBC's *Bonanza*, the top-rated program on television, *The Garry Moore Show* vanished in mid-season.

A Legal but Not a Moral Right

Since Moore owned a piece of *I've Got a Secret*, which was still running on CBS with Steve Allen as host, someone asked him if he planned to return to that show. According to a November 1966 *New York Times* story, Moore pointed out that he had a legal, but not a moral right, and would never push out Steve Allen. CBS was still paying him, but not offering any work, so Moore retired for the second time from television.

He spent most of the next two years sailing a boat he owned in Northeast Harbor, Maine. He also did some benefit luncheons and stumped for presidential candidate Joseph McCarthy in 1968. Moore also anchored *Voice of America* radio interviews called *New York, New York*. These interviews were on the light-hearted side and a break from the usual hard news.

By 1969 Moore was at a crossroads in his life. At 54 years of age, he was not interested in returning to a regular series, yet was not happy in retirement. Then one day, Mark Goodson called and asked Moore if he would consider hosting a revival of the game show *To Tell the Truth*. Since taping the show would not take up much of Moore's time and allow him plenty of opportunities to do other work, the idea sounded good. With CBS's permission, Moore gladly took the job.

A New Beginning

To Tell the Truth was syndicated daily beginning in September 1969. The game featured four celebrity panelists who questioned three contestants all claiming to be the same person. The job of the panel was to guess which one was the real person. This new version of *To Tell the Truth* paved the way for a massive game show revival in the 1970s.

When game shows became popular again in the 1970s with bigger prizes and loud, flashy sets, Moore insisted that *To Tell the Truth* not follow the trend and become a big money game show with large prizes. He was obviously not happy with the way producers staged game shows in that era.

Illness and Recovery

Moore's lifetime smoking habit finally caught up with him in late 1976. During an examination, doctors found a malignant tumor near his larynx. The tumor could be removed since doctors caught it early enough. On December 21, 1976, the show taped its last cycle of episodes before going on its regular two week Christmas hiatus. Moore entered the hospital where the cancer was successfully removed, but the operation left his voice slightly weaker. While Moore recovered from the surgery, *To Tell the Truth* resumed production in January 1977 with Bill Cullen hosting for two weeks.

Meanwhile, Moore was beginning to feel that he would not be able to return to the show. Because of his weakened voice, taping the routine five shows in one day would be a serious strain. Moore decided to hang it up permanently and turned the hosting over to NBC sportscaster Joe Garagiola. There was no mention of Moore's retirement on *To Tell the Truth* since he did not know at the time that the December 21, 1976, taping would be his last.

During the spring of 1977, there was some confusion among the viewers as to who was actually hosting *To Tell the Truth*. Since the show was syndicated to individual stations, some markets were still playing episodes with Moore as host, while others aired episodes with Garagiola hosting. Rumors circulated that Moore was dying and volumes of viewer mail poured into the Goodson-Todman offices demanding an explanation.

Who Really Is the Host of the Show?

In reality, Moore had made a full recovery and was enjoying a life of retirement. *To Tell the Truth* producer Bruno Zirato called Moore and asked him to make a special appearance on the show and officially announce his retirement. On June 26, 1977, the episode was taped in New York with Moore formally handing the reigns of the show over to Joe Garagiola. The episode aired in September 1977 as the opening show of *To Tell the Truth's* ninth season.

What You See Is What You Get

Moore happily retired for the last time from television and spent his remaining years with his second wife, Mary Elizabeth DeChant, whom he married in 1975. Moore enjoyed sailing, snorkeling, and playing in a jazz band at his new home in South Carolina. He spent the summers sailing his 40-foot ketch at a second home in Northeast Harbor, Maine.

Moore developed emphysema around 1986 and wrestled with the disease for the next seven years. His health slowly declined and eventually made it difficult for Moore to travel back and forth between his two homes in Maine and South Carolina. Moore finally lost the battle to emphysema on November 28, 1993, at the age of 78. He was survived by his second wife Mary "Betsy" Moore and two sons, Garry and John, from his first marriage.

In a business where performers frequently come and go, Garry Moore thrived as an entertainer for nearly five decades. Through it all, he was never afraid to stand up for his beliefs, even if it meant losing a job or a sponsor. Yet with all his successes, he retained the common touch.

Ira Skutch (I've Got a Secret *director, February 2006 telephone interview):*
"He was a truly wonderful human being. He was exactly what you saw. His public persona as a performer was exactly what he was in person."

JACK NARZ

Birth Name: John L. Narz, Jr.

Born: November 13, 1922, in Louisville, Kentucky

Marriages and Family: Mary Lou Roemheld (1947–1961) (Divorced) 3 sons, 1 daughter; Dolores Vaiksnor (1968–Present)

Military Service: United States Army Air Force (1942–1946)

Radio Career: Announcer (KXO-AM, El Centro, CA) 1947; Announcer (KWIK-FM, Burbank, CA) 1947–1948; Announcer (KIEV-AM, Glendale, CA) 1948–1949; Announcer (KLAC-AM, Los Angeles, CA) 1949–1951

TV Career: ANNOUNCER—Staff Announcer (KLAC-TV, Los Angeles, CA) 1949–1951; *The Colgate Comedy Hour* (NBC Primetime) September 10, 1950–December 25, 1955; *Space Patrol* (ABC Daytime) September 11, 1950–February 26, 1955; *Place the Face* (NBC Primetime) July 2, 1953–August 20, 1953, (CBS Primetime) August 27, 1953–August 26, 1954, (NBC Primetime) September 18, 1954–December 25, 1954; *Life with Elizabeth* (Syndicated) September 1953–September 1955; *The Bob Crosby Show* (CBS Daytime) September 14, 1953–August 30, 1957; *The Spike Jones Show* (NBC Primetime) January 2, 1954–May 8, 1954; *Kollege of Musical Knowledge* (NBC Primetime) July 4, 1954–September 12, 1954; *The George Gobel Show* (NBC Primetime) September 17, 1957–December 1957; *The Eddie Fisher Show* (NBC Primetime) September 24, 1957–December 1957; *The Gisele MacKenzie Show* (NBC Primetime) September 28, 1957–December 1957; *The All-New Beat the Clock* (CBS Daytime) September 17, 1979–February 1, 1980; *Card Sharks* (NBC Daytime) 1981 (Substitute for Gene Wood) HOST—*Parley* (Unsold Game Show Pilot) 1957; *Dotto* (CBS Daytime) January 6, 1958–August 15, 1958, (NBC Primetime) July 1, 1958–August 12, 1958; *Top Dollar* (CBS Daytime) November 17, 1958–October 23, 1959; *Kollege of Musical Knowledge* (Unsold Game Show Pilot) 1959; *Video Village* (CBS Daytime) July 1, 1960–September 2, 1960; *The Marriage Game* (KTLA-TV, Los Angeles, CA) September 11, 1960–October 23, 1960; *Seven Keys* (KTLA-TV, Los Angeles CA) September 12, 1960–April 28, 1961, (ABC Daytime) April 3, 1961–March 27, 1964, (KTLA-TV, Los Angeles, CA) April 12, 1964–January 15, 1965; *I'll Bet* (KTLA-TV, Los Angeles, CA) May 28, 1964–August 27, 1964, (NBC Daytime) March 29, 1965–September 24, 1965; *The Movie Game* (Unsold Game Show Pilot) 1966; *The Who, What, or Where Game* (Unsold Game Show Pilot) 1966; *Beat the Clock* (Syndicated) September 15, 1969–September 1972; *Concentration* (Syndicated) September 10, 1973–September 1978; *Now You See It* (CBS Daytime) April 1, 1974–June 13, 1975; *Phrase It* (Unsold Game Show Pilot) 1980

Jack Narz (Jack Narz, courtesy Fred Wostbrock)

Theatrical Movie: *Phone Call From a Stranger* (1952)
Other Career: Flight Instructor: Van Nuys Metropolitan Airport (1946–1947)

On a game show, there are two different people who are seen and heard by the viewers. One is the host and the other is the announcer. These are two very important jobs, and it takes special people to handle the tasks. Hosts get most of the publicity because they are seen on camera, but announcers are usually relegated to being the second banana. While some hosts are lousy announcers, some announcers make terrible hosts. There are only a few people who can handle both chores with equal ease.

Jack Narz worked the audiences as a game show announcer and later hosted a number of game shows in his own right. Possessing a pleasant voice, a great sense of humor, and a calm disposition, Narz could pep up a studio audience as the announcer. Flip the coin, and he presided over the festivities as a host by putting contestants at ease with his warm personality. He invited the viewers to join in the fun.

Born as John L. Narz, Jr., in Louisville, Kentucky on November 13, 1922, he enjoyed fishing, hunting, and working with the Boy Scouts. His two primary interests as a boy were radio and airplanes.

> *Jack Narz (October 2004 telephone interview):*
> "All my book covers and things were covered with my drawings of airplanes. I read all of the dime novels in those days about flying and I used to go out to the local airfield in Louisville. My dad would take me out and I'd sit out there most of the day waiting for an airplane to land or take off. I was crazy about flying."

"I Was Bombed a Few Times"

After high school, Narz worked for a year to earn money for college, but after the United States entered World War II, he enlisted in the Army Air Force in early 1942. Now he had the chance to put his flying skills to work. After training in the Aviation Cadets, he earned his wings in February 1943 and became a pilot.

> *JN:*
> "I never shot anybody down and nobody ever shot me down. I was bombed a few times, but that was in the officer's club, if you know what I mean."

Narz was discharged on November 14, 1946, and he headed for California to work as an instrument flying instructor at the Van Nuys Metropolitan Airport.

> JN:
> "There were restrictions on how many hours you could fly in a month as a flight instructor. At the time, the pay was [about] $5 dollars an hour and you were restricted to five hours a week, so it was a great way to starve. Right after the war, there were thousands of former pilots looking for work. We were a dime a dozen at that point."

Getting into Radio

Narz considered other career options. His other interest had been radio since he had listened to it for countless hours as a child. In January 1947 a friend, who worked in public relations for a movie studio, told Narz that he had a good voice for radio and encouraged him to try his luck in the industry. Narz was introduced to a man who worked as an announcer at the Hollywood Bowl and was starting a school for radio announcers. Narz signed up for one year of instruction, and six months later, he sneaked into an audition held at the school by a radio station manager. From that audition he landed a job as an announcer at KXO-AM in El Centro, California, a small farming community located about seven miles from the Mexican border.

After moving to California, Narz met Mary Lou Roemheld, and they married in 1947. They had three sons and one daughter during their 14 year marriage. Narz dropped out of the announcer's school after getting his first radio job. On his days off, he drove to Los Angeles to audition for other radio stations. After a few months, Narz went to work for KWIK-FM in Burbank and later at KIEV-AM in Glendale. Finally in 1949 he was hired by the much larger station KLAC-AM in Los Angeles. Not long after Narz joined the staff, KLAC opened a television station.

> JN:
> "At that point there was no money in television, so none of the staff announcers there wanted to do it, so I volunteered."

On KLAC-TV, Narz did sports, news, station breaks, and served as the on-camera announcer for special shows and remote broadcasts. One of the remote broadcasts was a fireworks show.

"I Worked Every Channel in Town"

Aiming his sights higher, Narz slowly migrated into national television in 1950 doing commercials on the NBC nighttime variety series *The Colgate Comedy Hour*. He also announced for *Space Patrol*, a daily ABC afternoon children's program. By then, Narz had left KLAC to freelance as an announcer for Los Angeles television stations.

> *JN:*
> "I worked every channel in town. I would just go from one [station] to the other seven days a week. You were paid anywhere from $5 to $12 a show. I racked them up. I was doing pretty well."

Gaining Prominence

On the national scene, Narz announced for *The Bob Crosby Show*, a daily afternoon variety series on CBS and *Life with Elizabeth*, the first regular television show to star actress Betty White. In the summer of 1953, Narz became the announcer for *Place the Face*, a game show where contestants tried to identify people from their past after being introduced to them on the air. The host of *Place the Face* was Bill Cullen, who became Narz's brother-in-law. Narz and his wife Mary Lou introduced Cullen to Mary Lou's sister, Anne Roemheld, and they later married.

Through the 1950s, Narz was a high profile television announcer on *The Kollege of Musical Knowledge*, *The Spike Jones Show*, *The George Gobel Show*, and *The Eddie Fisher Show*. He also took a brief stab at acting with a minor role in the 1952 release *Phone Call from a Stranger*. Narz said that he appeared in four to five movies total, but could not recall the names of the other releases. He found movie work boring and decided to stick with announcing.

Connecting the Dots

In 1958 Narz moved before the cameras as a host of the new CBS daytime game show *Dotto*. He moved his family to New York City on January 1, 1958, where the show originated.

> *JN:*
> "I was watching the Rose Bowl game with friends, and that afternoon I got on the airplane and went to New York. It was 100 degrees in Los Angeles when I left and about 25 or 30 degrees when I got to New York that night. I didn't even own an overcoat. I wore what was known in those days as a car coat. It came down to just above the knees. I had a sports car, a Thunderbird. I was in golf slacks, a golf shirt, and a car coat, and people thought I was out of my mind."

Five days after his arrival in New York, *Dotto* went on the air on January 6, 1958. Based on the children's game "Connect the Dots," two contestants answered questions for the right to connect a series of 50 dots on the board. Players selected questions worth five, eight, or ten dots, and the difficulty of the question increased with point value. Each player had his or her own

Jack Narz steers the action on *Dotto* in 1958 (Jack Narz, courtesy Fred Wostbrock).

Dotto board with the same picture, but could not see their opponent's board. That way if one player had more dots connected on his/her picture, the opponent would not have an unfair advantage. The first player to identify the person, place, or thing on the picture won the game. The amount of money won was determined by the number of unconnected dots on the player's board.

Within three months of its premiere, *Dotto* was the number one-rated daytime show on television. A home game in which viewers sent in postcards for the right to guess a picture drew more than a million responses each week. The show was so popular that a weekly nighttime edition was soon in the works. In an unusual move, the primetime version was picked up by NBC rather than CBS, who aired the daily show. Nighttime *Dotto* went on the air July 1, 1958, and drew respectable ratings.

Rigged

Dotto seemed to be an indestructible show, but a major scandal brewing behind the scenes was waiting to cut the game's life short. The infamous quiz show scandals of the late 1950s, where many games were rigged to ensure a more entertaining program, hit home in the *Dotto* family. According to Joseph Stone's book *Prime Time and Misdemeanors*, a young actor named Edward Hilgemeier was waiting backstage to appear as a contestant on May 20, 1958. While in the dressing room, he found a notebook belonging to Marie Winn, a young lady who was appearing on the program at that very moment. Upon examining the notebook, Hilgemeier found a page containing answers to questions and pictures being used on that day's program. He tore the page from the notebook and walked to the stage area where the broadcast was airing live.

On the show, Winn defeated her opponent Yeffe Kimbal Slatin. As Slatin walked backstage, Hilgemeier confronted her and showed Winn's notebook page he found in the dressing room. Hilgemeier and Slatin took the notebook page to a lawyer, who contacted *Dotto*'s producers about a settlement in exchange for an agreement not to sue. Frank Cooper Associates, the packager of *Dotto*, initially offered $2,000 to Slatin and $500 to Hilgemeier. Hilgemeier balked at the offer, but on June 18, 1958, Frank Cooper Associates doubled its offer to $4,000 for Slatin and $1,000 for Hilgemeier. Again Hilgemeier refused, but Slatin accepted the money and quietly left the situation.

On July 10, Hilgemeier told the story to a *New York Post* reporter named Jack O'Grady. The next day, Hilgemeier met with the *Dotto* producers and they offered him $1,500 to keep quiet about the whole affair. Hilgemeier accepted and signed an agreement for the money. Then, with the help of O'Grady, he drafted an affidavit on the whole matter to be submitted to *The New York Post*. The newspaper refused to publish the story since Hilgemeier had no copies of the agreement he signed with Frank Cooper Associates.

"I Had No Idea"

On August 7, Hilgemeier went to the offices of Dotto's sponsor, Colgate-Palmolive, and showed them the affidavit. This time, Hilgemeier told them he did not want any money, but wanted them to stop the gossip circulating about him through the entertainment industry. Hilgemeier claimed that the bad talk was affecting his ability to get acting work. The following week he met twice with officials of Colgate-Palmolive concerning the matter. Then on Friday, August 15, 1958, the sponsor met with CBS officials and the producers of *Dotto*, who finally admitted that the show was fixed. All agreed that *Dotto* would have to be canceled now that the truth was known.

CBS canceled *Dotto* immediately after its August 15, 1958, broadcast while NBC axed the nighttime version. One of the people who had no clue of the rigging was Narz.

> *JN:*
> "That came as a shock to me. I left the studio one Friday afternoon with the number one show on daytime TV, and that night I got a call from one of the fellows in the advertising agency. I went over to his house and he gave me a couple of martinis and told me, 'Don't go to work on Monday. The show has been canceled.' I went from the top of the heap to no job in a matter of hours. I had no idea."

"Oh They Had Big Plans"

Not only did Narz lose his show, but he lost an opportunity to make a fortune. Before the scandal broke, Narz had recorded an album of folk songs called "Sing the Folk Music With Jack Narz." The album was part of a promotional campaign for Colgate-Palmolive, the sponsor of *Dotto*. Viewers who purchased the sponsor's product at the stores could send in the box tops and a small cash amount to receive a copy of the album.

> *JN:*
> "Oh they (the sponsor) had big plans. We figured we were going to sell thousands and thousands of them. When the scandal happened it dropped dead."

Although the album was released, it never sold well. Narz recalled an incident told to him by a friend.

> *JN:*
> "[He] came back from Japan on vacation and said he went to a nightclub and there was a Japanese guy lip-synching to my album. It was the funniest thing he had ever seen. A little Japanese guy lip-synching to me."

When it was discovered that other quiz shows were fixed, the New York District Attorney's office investigated the matter. Narz testified before a grand jury and was cleared of any wrongdoing. Fortunately, Narz had the support of *Dotto's* sponsor. After the show was canceled, Colgate-Palmolive promised to put Narz back on the air in a new program as quickly as possible.

Since *Dotto* had ended under suspicious circumstances, the sponsor decided to let things cool off before putting Narz back on the air. *Dotto* was replaced by the game show *Top Dollar* on August 18, 1958. Warren Hull hosted the first 13 weeks of the show before turning the game over to Narz in November 1958. The show ran until October 1959 when CBS cleared its daytime schedule of all game shows.

"Now What Do I Do?"

While in California on a Christmas vacation in 1959, Narz hosted a game show pilot called *Kollege of Musical Knowledge*. NBC wanted the show, so Narz' agent told him to sell his house in New York and move back to California. No sooner had Narz returned to California when NBC changed its mind and scuttled plans for the show.

> *JN:*
> "I thought, 'Well now what do I do?'"

However, a call from NBC in New York brought Narz back before the cameras. Bill Cullen, who hosted *The Price Is Right*, was going on a lengthy vacation, and the network asked Narz to substitute for him. Narz headed back to New York leaving his family in California since this was only a temporary gig.

Narz was approached by producer Merrill Heatter to host a new game show called *Video Village*. Narz agreed and the show hit the CBS airwaves on July 1, 1960. *Video Village* played like a home board game because a large game board placed on the floor of the studio was used and the contestants acted as the playing pieces moving around the board. A single die with the numbers one through six was rolled in a chuck-a-luck cage to determine the number of spaces a player could move. *Video Village* originated from New York, so Narz commuted back and forth from his home in California to host the show.

About a month later, producer Carl Jampel asked Narz to host a game show called *Seven Keys* for Los Angeles station KTLA-TV. Narz was unable to take the job since *Video Village* aired live during the weekdays and he was only in California on the weekends. Jampel offered to tape several episodes of the show in advance, allowing Narz to host it during his visits home. Narz took the job. For a few weeks, he flew back and forth between New York and California hosting his two shows until marital problems forced him to give up *Video Village* and return to California in September 1960. Narz tried to save his marriage, but it ended in divorce in 1961.

Keys to Success

Meanwhile, he opened his new show, *Seven Keys*, over KTLA-TV on September 12, 1960. Contestants earned keys to win prizes by moving from the bottom to the top of a game board containing 70 squares. The trick was to make the connection from bottom to top in 15 moves. If the player won a key, they could quit and take their prizes or risk it all and play another game to win a second key. Players could win up to seven keys before retiring from the show. *Seven Keys* drew large enough ratings on KTLA to interest ABC in airing a weekday version. *Seven Keys* moved to ABC in April 1961 and ran for three years. The show then returned to KTLA for one more season.

In addition to *Seven Keys*, Narz hosted a string of short-lived game shows for KTLA during the early 1960s.

> *JN:*
> "Whenever they had an idea for a new show, KTLA was willing to put it on. We just did one after the other. I don't even remember the names of them. One crazy idea after another."

I'll Bet

One of the shows that made it to the network was *I'll Bet* in the spring of 1965. It fared poorly in the ratings and left the air after 26 weeks. On a side note, while Narz hosted *I'll Bet*, his brother Tom Kennedy hosted NBC's *You Don't Say*. One week the brothers traded shows and Kennedy hosted *I'll Bet* while Narz did *You Don't Say*.

> *JN:*
> "Both shows were produced by Ralph Andrews and Bill Yagemann. That was their idea to have us switch and do each other's show. It was fun trading off."

Hiatus

For the next four years, Narz had no regular television program. During 1966 he hosted two game show pilots that failed to become a series: *The Movie Game* and *The Who, What, or Where Game*. Both shows later hit the airwaves in 1969, but with different hosts. Sonny Fox hosted *The Movie Game* in syndication while Art James emceed *The Who, What, or Where Game* for NBC.

Narz also served as a celebrity guest on his brother's game show *You Don't Say* on NBC. Once a year between 1964 and 1966, the brothers switched positions and Narz hosted while Kennedy played the game. While his career was at a standstill, his personal life took a turn for the better when Narz married Dolores Vaiksnor in September 1968.

Clocking in to Work

An offer to host a revival of *Beat the Clock* brought Narz back to television in September 1969. On *Beat the Clock,* contestants played against a large clock completing embarrassing stunts for cash and prizes. The first season of the show taped in New York City, but in 1970, moved to Montreal, Canada, to cut production costs.

> *Ira Skutch (***Beat the Clock*** director, February 2006 telephone interview):*
> "Jack was an absolutely marvelous emcee and a lovely human being. Talk about a lack of performer's ego, he has none. He would do anything you asked him to do. We were doing *Beat the Clock* in Canada and he flew up there from Los Angeles. One January, we got to Montreal and it was very, very cold. They were having a heat wave in California and he [Narz] got on the plane in Los Angeles and the temperature was 100 degrees. Six hours later, he got out of the plane in Montreal and it was 50 degrees below zero. (Laughing) If that isn't a shock to the system, I don't know what else is."

A Game of Concentration

In the fall of 1973, Narz moved on to host *Concentration*, a revival of the popular NBC game show. Based on the children's card game of the same name, *Concentration* pitted two contestants in a memorization contest. The players faced a board containing 30 squares. Each player in turn selected two squares and was shown prizes. Prizes ranged from small items to appliances and cars.

All prizes were hidden in two locations on the board and the players tried to remember where they were located as the game progressed. If a player matched two prizes, the boxes opened to reveal a portion of a rebus puzzle. The first contestant to solve the puzzle won all prizes he/she accumulated in the game. Narz settled in for a five year run on *Concentration*.

Now You See It...Now You Don't

In April 1974 Narz took a second show, *Now You See It*. Based on the popular word search puzzles in newspapers, players were asked general knowledge questions and searched for the answers on a large board of letters. Narz remembered some peculiar things about *Now You See It*.

> *JN:*
> "It went on the air on April Fools' Day; it was on the air for 13 months, 13 days; and the last show was on Friday the 13th."

According to Narz, *Now You See It* drew a large following of fans during its short run.

JN:

"It was doing very well in the ratings and we were getting fabulous mail. We heard from one company down in Florida. The company actually took an entire lunch hour and went into the auditorium to watch the show while they had their lunch."

According to Narz, CBS program executive Fred Silverman disliked the show and pulled it from the daytime schedule on June 13, 1975.

Family Feud

The following year, Narz did some run-throughs for the Goodson-Todman game *Family Feud*. Narz was assured that he would host the show, but a few days later, an unexpected telephone call brought the news that Richard Dawson would host *Family Feud* instead. Dawson was a celebrity panelist on Goodson-Todman's *Match Game '76*, but his contract with that show had expired and he wanted off of the series. The only way to get Dawson to renew his *Match Game* contract was to promise him the hosting job of the next Goodson-Todman game show developed.

"Well, I Think I've Had It"

Narz remained with *Concentration* until it folded in September 1978. By now, he was tired of the business and was less than thrilled at the new shows being produced.

JN:

"I was not too interested and things were changing quickly, and not to the way I liked things to be. I did not approve of a lot of things that were going on, a lot of the shows that were on, and the way people were acting. I had some meetings with some people [in] their torn jeans and their sandals up on their desks. When I walked in, they would say, 'Hi, what's your name and what have you done?' I thought, 'Well, I think I've had it. I think I'll just hang it up and start traveling.' So I did."

Narz was coaxed out of retirement in 1979 to serve as the announcer and associate producer of a new version of *Beat the Clock* for CBS.

JN:

"I didn't want to produce the show. I didn't want anything to do with it."

The other reluctant draftee on this version of *Beat the Clock* was the new host, Monty Hall, who also wanted no part of the venture. When the show delivered low ratings, *The All-New Beat the Clock*, to no one's surprise, was put out to pasture on February 1, 1980, after less than five months in production. After this fiasco, Narz gladly called it a career.

JN:

"I guess the word got out that I was not interested [in hosting any more shows] and therefore [the producers] were not interested and the phone just didn't ring anymore. About the only thing I got calls to do were telethons and benefits, and I thought, 'Well, I've had enough of that too so goodbye everybody.'"

He briefly came back in 1981 to substitute for Gene Wood as announcer on NBC's *Card Sharks*. Narz made one final television appearance with his brother Tom Kennedy on a week of NBC's *Password Plus* in March 1982. Narz appeared as a celebrity player while Kennedy hosted the program.

Switcheroo

As mentioned previously, Narz and Kennedy had been famous for occasionally trading off the hosting chores of their shows during the 1960s. This *Password Plus* appearance featuring both brothers gave them one last chance to pull the old switcheroo on the viewers. While taping an episode, Narz and Kennedy jokingly argued over whether it was easier to be the host or a celebrity guest player on the show.

On the spur of the moment, without consulting with the producer, the brothers traded places, with Kennedy playing the game while Narz hosted the rest of the episode. It was the last time that Narz ever hosted a game show.

> JN:
> "We had no idea it would happen. We were just kidding around. The producer [of *Password Plus*] at that time was a young fellow named Bobby Sherman. Bobby just went along with it and said, 'Let them go. Let them do it.'"

Traveling

Since the early 1980s, Narz has enjoyed retirement by traveling extensively around the globe with his wife Dolores and with friends, although he has curtailed his traveling in recent years. He has taken few trips since the September 11, 2001, terrorist attack on the United States in which four hijacked airplanes crashed into the World Trade Center, the Pentagon, and a field in Pennsylvania.

> JN:
> "I used to go all around the world, but not anymore. It's not any fun anymore on the airlines. They are not what they used to be, and the security [measures] at the airport is a pain. My buddy and I went to Maui to play golf a few months ago and we stood in the line at Maui for almost three hours. Thank goodness I did all my traveling when it was nice and when it was fun."

Although he does not travel much these days, Narz enjoys his retirement. He lives with his wife Dolores in Beverly Hills, California, and stays active by playing golf and participating in charity tournaments.

> *Tom Kennedy (Brother of Jack Narz, October 2004 telephone interview):*
> "Jack is a golf nut. You can quote me on that."

Narz maintains close ties with his family and spends time with his four children and six grandchildren. He and his brother Tom Kennedy and their sister are all very close.

Recognition

In August 2004 Narz joined his brother Tom and game show hosts Bob Barker, Dick Clark, and Betty White at the third annual meeting of the Game Show Congress which convened in Burbank, California. The congress offered a salute to game show hosts Bill Cullen and Ralph Edwards. Narz and his fellow emcees shared their memories of working with the two men over the years. In 2005 Narz and his brother Tom were jointly honored with The Bill Cullen Lifetime Achievement Award for their years of service to the game show industry.

In more than three decades as a broadcaster, Jack Narz had a long and healthy career and he never took himself too seriously as a performer. And he enjoyed it. For Narz, it was a fun and profitable way to make a living.

> JN:
> "All we were trying to do, as far as I was concerned, was provide about 30 minutes of lighthearted entertainment and then go home."

BERT PARKS

Birth Name: Bertram Jacobson
Born: December 30, 1914, in Atlanta, Georgia
Died: February 2, 1992, in La Jolla, California
Marriage and Family: Annette Liebman: (June 8, 1943–February 2, 1992) 2 sons, 1 daughter
Military Career: United States Army (1942–1946)
Radio Career: Announcer (WGST-AM, Atlanta, Georgia) 1931–1933; Staff Announcer (CBS Network, New York) 1933–1939; *Renfrew of the Mounted* (CBS) March 3, 1936–March 5, 1937; *The Eddie Cantor Show* (CBS) March 28, 1938–June 26, 1939; *The Camel Caravan* (NBC) June 27, 1939–September 1940; *The Adventures of Ellery Queen* (CBS) April 1940–September 22, 1940; *Matinee at Meadowbrook* (CBS) January 18, 1941–March 22, 1941; *How'm I Doin'?* (CBS) January 9, 1942–July 3, 1942, (NBC) July 9, 1942–October 1, 1942; *McGarry and His Mouse* (NBC) June 26, 1946–September 25, 1946, (Mutual) January 6, 1947–March 31, 1947; *Break the Bank* (ABC) July 5, 1946–September 23, 1949, (NBC) October 5, 1949–September 21, 1951, (ABC) September 24, 1951–March 27, 1953, (NBC) September 28, 1953–July 15, 1955; *Second Honeymoon* (WAAT-AM, Newark, New Jersey) 1947; *Stop the Music* (ABC) March 21, 1948–August 10, 1952; *Second Honeymoon* (ABC) September 20, 1948–November 11, 1949, (Mutual) November 14, 1949–January 16, 1950
TV Career: HOST—*Party Line* (NBC Primetime) June 8, 1947–August 31, 1947; *Break the Bank* (ABC Primetime) October 22, 1948–September 23, 1949, (NBC Primetime) October 5, 1949–January 9, 1952, (CBS Primetime) January 13, 1952–February 1, 1953, (NBC Primetime) June 23, 1953–September 1, 1953, (ABC Primetime) January 31, 1954–June 20, 1956; *Stop the Music* (ABC Primetime) May 5, 1949–April 24, 1952, (ABC Primetime) September 7, 1954–June 14, 1956; *The Bert Parks Show* (NBC Daytime) November 1, 1950–January 11, 1952, (CBS Daytime) January 14, 1952–June 26, 1952; *Double or Nothing* (CBS Daytime) October 6, 1952–July 2, 1954, (NBC Primetime) June 5, 1953–July 3, 1953; *Balance Your Budget* (CBS Primetime) October 18, 1952–May 2, 1953; *Two in Love* (CBS Primetime) June 19, 1954–September 11, 1954; *The Miss America Pageant* (ABC, NBC, & CBS) September 1955–September 1979; *NBC Bandstand* (NBC Daytime) July 30, 1956–November 23, 1956; *Break the $250,000 Bank* (NBC Primetime) October 9, 1956–January 15, 1957; *Giant Step* (CBS Primetime) November 7, 1956–May 29, 1957; *Hold That Note* (NBC Primetime) January 22, 1957–April 2, 1957; *Bid 'N' Buy* (CBS Primetime) July 1, 1958–September 23, 1958; *County Fair* (NBC Daytime) September 22, 1958–September 25, 1959; *Masquerade Party* (NBC Primetime) October 2, 1958–September 24, 1959, (CBS Primetime) October 26, 1959–Janu-

Bert Parks (Fred Wostbrock)

ary 18, 1960, (NBC Primetime) January 29, 1960–September 23, 1960; *The Big Payoff* (CBS) September 28, 1959–October 23, 1959; *Yours for a Song* (ABC Primetime) November 14, 1961–September 22, 1962, (ABC Daytime) December 4, 1961–March 29, 1963; *Hollywood Squares* (Unsold CBS Game Show Pilot) April 1965; *Circus!* (Syndicated) September 1971–September 1973; *Strike It Rich* (Syndicated) September 1973–September 1974   ACTOR—*Fast Lane Blues* (Unsold ABC Drama Pilot) 1978

Broadway Career: *The Music Man* (June 27, 1960–September 1961); *Mr. President; Damn Yankees*
Theatrical Movies: *That's the Way of the World* (1975); *The Freshman* (1990)

"There she is, Miss America." For a quarter of a century, these words were sung by Bert Parks to the excited and often emotional winners of the Miss America Pageant. Not only did Parks host one of the highest rated annual events on television, he could also be found giving away thousands of dollars in cash and prizes most days and evenings on quiz shows. A man who wore many hats in the business, Parks entertained viewers with charisma, humor, class, and frequently added to the festivities by breaking into a song with his rich voice.

Bert Parks was born as Bertrand Jacobson on December 30, 1914, in Atlanta, Georgia, the second of two boys born to Aaron and Hattie Jacobson. His father and mother had moved from New York to Atlanta before Parks' birth to open a haberdashery shop. From the age of 12 until he graduated six years later, Parks attended Marist College, a boys' military institution founded by a Catholic order called the Marist Fathers.

Singing for His Supper

A gifted singer, Parks first sang publicly at the age of 15 in a movie house in Atlanta, Georgia. It was here that he changed his name from Bertrand Jacobson to Bert Parks to make it easier to fit his name on theater marquees. The following year, he got his first job at radio station WGST in Atlanta at a salary of $7 a week. Over the next two years he worked his way from an errand boy and record guardian to become the station's chief announcer at $15 per week.

After graduating from high school, Parks went to New York City in 1933 and lied about his age and his level of education to get an audition as a CBS staff announcer. Parks won the job and, at 18, became the youngest network announcer in the United States at the time. One of his earliest assignments called for Parks to act on a radio western called *Bobby Benson* in which he played Little Luke Leadbetter, the best friend of the hero. Parks' ability to ad-lib and sing gave him great flexibility and helped cultivate his career.

How'm I Doin'?

His first big break came in 1938 when he was assigned to announce for *The Eddie Cantor Show*, then one of the most popular programs on the radio. Parks also worked as a vocalist and straight man with Cantor in skits on the series. After that show left the air, Parks was hired to announce for *The Camel Caravan* on NBC radio. The early 1940s saw Parks in two dramas: *The Adventures of Ellery Queen* and *Matinee at Meadowbrook*. His first game show experience was in January 1942 as the announcer for a CBS quiz show called *How'm I Doin'?* He remained with this show until he joined the United States Army as a private in the fall of 1942.

Parks was shipped to China where he worked in reconnaissance operations and established underground radio stations behind the Japanese lines. One of his most dangerous assignments had him working for three weeks in enemy territory with a wire recorder. He also announced on a weekly radio series for the Army and later received the Bronze Star. He was discharged in 1946 with the rank of captain.

During the war, Parks married his girlfriend, Annette Liebman, whom he had met on a blind date while she was a student at Columbia University and he was a CBS staff announcer.

They married on June 8, 1943, just before he was shipped overseas. After the war, they had twin sons Jeffrey and Joel and later a daughter Annette.

Laughing All the Way to the Bank

Upon his return to civilian life, Parks was recommended by game show host Bud Collyer for the job as host of *Break the Bank*, a new quiz program developed for ABC radio. On July 5, 1946, Parks hosted the first of more than a dozen game shows in his long career.

On *Break the Bank*, Parks and his co-host Bud Collyer selected contestants from the studio audience and asked them a series of questions ranging from $25 to $500. Along the way, if a player missed two questions, they lost the game and their winnings were added to the bank. Contestants who successfully earned $500 could answer one more question and "break the bank." The bank started with a base value of $1,000 and grew over a period of weeks until someone broke it.

Break the Bank catapulted to the top of the ratings and in 1948, ABC rewarded Parks by making him the host of *Stop the Music*. On this game, a band played a song while three telephone operators contacted listeners at home who had submitted their names on postcards to compete on the show. As soon as a connection was made, Parks yelled "stop the music." The listener then guessed the mystery tune and won prizes if correct.

These ladies try to *Break the Bank* by answering Bert Parks' question (Fred Wostbrock).

Baby Steps

In the meantime, Parks had taken his first baby steps in the new medium of television with a summer game show called *Party Line* in 1947. He followed the next year with a television version of *Break the Bank*, which had a healthy run of eight years on ABC, CBS, and NBC. In 1949 *Stop the Music* successfully moved to television with a five year run on ABC. By the early 1950s, Parks was fronting his own daytime variety series, *The Bert Parks Show* and the game shows *Double or Nothing*, *Balance Your Budget*, and *Two in Love*.

There She Is

In 1955 he became the host of the annual *Miss America Pageant*, which originated from Atlantic City, New Jersey each September. It was here that Parks became a television superstar and established his trademark by serenading the winners with the tune, "There She Is, Miss America." He hosted the pageant for the next quarter of a century.

When describing what it was like to host the pageant in a 1970 *TV Guide* interview, Parks noted that very little of the show was scripted and that he had to ad-lib most of the program. The only scripted parts of the show were lead-ins for commercials and the entertainment segments. With two hours to fill, Parks called the show "Russian roulette."

Despite his popularity with the viewers, Parks was frequently slammed by critics for his high energy performances. As a host, Parks lit up the place with his constant motion, his dancing and singing, and his booming baritone voice. He told *TV Guide*'s Edith Efron in 1962 that some people thought his bubbly personality was phony adding that many thought there was no way anyone could smile that much. Parks insisted that it was not difficult at all. He was genuinely a happy man most of the time and that was simply his personality.

Turning Down $64,000

In 1955 Parks was offered the job as host of *The $64,000 Question*, but he turned it down. Prior to that time, all quiz shows gave away rather modest prizes and Parks felt that $64,000 was too much money. He also figured that the show would not succeed. In what turned out to be a grave mistake for Parks, actor Hal March signed for the series, and the show became the top-rated television program during the 1955-1956 season. Part of the show's appeal was Hal March with his new low-key style of hosting. Before long, Parks' loud and bouncy manner began losing favor with the viewers.

Now that quiz shows gave away larger prizes than before, Parks' low budget games seemed out of place. To keep up with the times, his two shows *Stop the Music* and *Break the Bank* souped up their formats. On *Stop the Music*, the mystery melody jackpot increased to a possible win of $10,000. Nevertheless, ABC canceled the show in June 1956.

That fall *Break the Bank* jumped on the big money bandwagon and was branded *Break the $250,000 Bank*. NBC dropped the show after a mere three months before anyone could win the grand prize. Parks attempted another big money show, *Giant Step*, during the 1956–1957 season. This game gave kids aged 7 to 17 the chance to win a four year all-expenses-paid college education. *Giant Step* left the air in the spring of 1957.

No Place on the Tube

Now no longer in demand as a host, Parks was unemployed for the first time in his career. His only television work during the 1957-1958 season was hosting the *Miss America Pageant*. Parks decided that if he was going to stay in the business, he would have to follow the trend and subdue his hosting style. He returned to television in July of 1958 with CBS's *Bid 'n' Buy*. Here four contestants started the game with $10,000 and bid against each other for clues to guess a mystery object.

Although *Bid 'n' Buy* only lasted two months as a summer series, it did the trick and Parks was soon back in business. In September 1958 he landed two NBC game shows: the daytime *County Fair* where contestants competed in a series of stunts for cash and prizes and the night-time *Masquerade Party*. Here, four celebrities questioned a guest celebrity disguised by heavy makeup and costumes. The object was for the panel to identify the mystery guest.

The Music Man

During his long career, Parks had always wanted to act, but never had the chance. He finally won the part to replace Eddie Albert as the lead in the Broadway show *The Music Man* in June 1960. Parks was a big hit playing a con man reformed by love. The show lasted 462 performances before closing in 1961. Parks called that period the greatest success of his career in a 1962 *TV Guide* interview. He later performed in the Broadway musicals *Mr. President* and *Damn Yankees* during the 1960s.

In the fall of 1961, Parks returned to television hosting ABC's *Yours for a Song*. In a twist from the usual guess-the-name-of-the-song format, contestants won money by filling in the missing lyrics to popular songs. There were six words missing from the first stanza of each song and two songs were played per game. Players collected money for each correct lyric they supplied. *Yours for a Song* allowed Parks to return to his high energy style of hosting, and the show was popular enough to air both in daytime and nighttime during its year and a half run.

Bands and Whistles

After *Yours for a Song* folded in March 1963, Parks dropped from view as a regular performer. Although he still hosted *The Miss America Pageant*, Parks was largely retired, though not entirely of his own choice. He was hurt by the continuing criticism of his hosting style. Parks told *TV Guide* in 1962 that society in general, not just television, had become bland. He thought that people everywhere were too low key and that there should be more bands and whistles playing.

Maintaining his home in Greenwich, Connecticut, Parks and his family also spent part of the year at a home in Hollywood, Florida where he enjoyed swimming, gardening, tennis, and boating. He indulged in his passion for acting with guest appearances on the ABC detective shows *Burke's Law* and *Honey West* in the mid 1960s. In the spring of 1965, Parks hosted the game show pilot *Hollywood Squares* for CBS. The show was not picked up by the network, although it was purchased by NBC in 1966 with Peter Marshall as host. Except for his one night per year on *The Miss America Pageant*, Parks was mostly out of the limelight.

Women's Lib Speaks Out

Although the pageant remained popular with the general public, it began drawing criticism from women's liberation groups in the late 1960s. A group of women's lib protesters crashed the 1968 show as the winner was making her final speech. The police quickly restored order by escorting the group out of the auditorium. Off camera, the criticism by women's lib groups continued as Parks was burned in effigy.

Parks philosophically addressed the issue to *TV Guide* in 1970. He could not understand why people would be turned off by the pageant because it represented something happy. But he also conjectured that the women's libbers may have had some disappointments in their past causing them to be disgruntled.

Let's Have a Circus!

Parks came out of retirement in 1971 to host the syndicated effort *Circus*. Parks and the producers traveled around Europe for the next two years taping the best circus acts they could find and presented them in a half hour format. In the fall of 1973, Parks hosted his last game show,

Strike It Rich. This one brought down-on-their-luck contestants on the show to win money by answering a series of questions. It was canned after one season.

With his game show career finished, Parks made guest appearances on *Ellery Queen* and *The Bionic Woman*. He also had a prominent role in the 1975 theatrical movie *That's the Way of the World*. In 1978 Parks starred in an ABC pilot for a drama series called *Fast Lane Blues*. Here he played an oil company mogul sponsoring a cross-country scavenger hunt. A group of people race their cars through 12 different U.S. cities. The object of the race: collect as many gold stars hidden throughout the cities as possible. The winner was paid $1 million dollars by the oil company. *Fast Lane Blues* never saw the light as a regular series.

Happy Birthday, You're Fired!

On December 30, 1979, just after Parks returned home from a surprise party celebrating his 65th birthday, he received a shocking telephone call. The caller was a news reporter seeking comments from Parks about being fired as host of the *Miss America Pageant*. As it turned out, Parks had been dumped as the pageant's host, but the reports of his dismissal had hit the newspapers before he was even notified. A letter from the pageant's officials informing Parks of his firing was said to have been sent to his home, but Parks claimed he never received it.

Why was Parks fired so abruptly? The producers of the pageant considered Parks too old to continue hosting the show and wanted to project a more youthful image despite the high ratings. In a 1990 *People Weekly* interview, Parks compared his firing with the fact that 69-year-old Ronald Reagan was not too old to be elected President of the United States.

Survival of the Fittest

The barrage of publicity surrounding Parks' dismissal from the pageant worked in his favor. Johnny Carson, host of NBC's *Tonight Show*, organized a letter-writing campaign to get Parks reinstated as the pageant's host. Despite widespread protests, the pageant officials would not rehire Parks.

In April 1980, he received a special award at the National Association of Broadcasters Convention honoring his 48 years in broadcasting. Parks also received a flood of offers for guest appearances on television sitcoms and talk shows. Through the 1980s, Parks turned up in *The Love Boat*, *WKRP In Cincinnati*, *227*, and *Roseanne*. He also landed lucrative contracts as a television commercial spokesman.

Tongue-in-Cheek

Parks remained interested in beauty pageants and found himself hosting the *Mrs. America Pageant*, the *Miss Young International*, the *Mother-Daughter Pageant*, and the *U.S. Man of the Year Pageant*. The offers did not stop there, however. Parks also hosted the *Purina Chow Dog Contest* and the *Miss Glamorous Kitty Pageant* where he serenaded the winning cat with a takeoff of his famous "There She Is" song. The new lyrics were "There she is, the Glamorous Kitty Queen of America."

And if that seemed far-fetched, Parks also hosted the "Coast-to-Coast Shower Sing-Off" and a tugboat contest. To Parks, however, this kind of work was enjoyable. The work was financially rewarding too because combined with his television assignments, Parks made half a million dollars annually.

In 1990 Parks appeared in his second theatrical movie, *The Freshman*, starring Marlon Brando and Matthew Broderick. Parks played himself singing a satirical version of the song "There She Is" to a lizard. This appearance brought Parks back into the national spotlight and paved the way for a return to the *Miss America Pageant*. The pageant's chief executive officer, Leonard Horn, asked Parks to come back as a guest for the 70th anniversary of the show. Parks would not serenade the 1990 winner, however, since that was the responsibility of the current host Gary Collins.

Name Calling

At the pageant on September 8, 1990, Parks was introduced by Collins and received a standing ovation. The evening turned into a bit of an ordeal for Parks. As he was introducing the former winners, two pages of his script stuck together causing Parks to skip an entire page of names. Despite that embarrassing moment, Parks brushed it off telling *USA Today* in 1990 that those were the risks of live television. He took full responsibility for the gaffe and moved on with his life. Parks did not return to the pageant the following year.

At the end of 1991, Parks was diagnosed with lung cancer. At the age of 77 years, he died in his sleep after a short illness at the Scripps Memorial Hospital in La Jolla, California on February 2, 1992. Parks was survived by his wife of nearly 49 years, Annette, their three children and two grandchildren.

Make Lemonade

Parks' life and career seemed to follow the old adage about making lemonade out of lemons. He went from serenading beauty queens to serenading beauty cats. For a spell, he went from loud and bouncy to a more subdued hosting style to stay in show business. After making all of those adjustments, he still virtually disappeared from television after the 1960s except for the *Miss America Pageant*. A track record like that would dishearten many people, but not Bert Parks. He never saw his later work as a comedown from his glory days of the 1950s. He took the jobs that were offered in later life, enjoyed them to the utmost, and in the end, laughed all the way to the bank.

JIM PECK

Birth Name: James Edward Peck

Born: June 5, 1943, in Milwaukee, Wisconsin

Marriages and Family: Camille McGreevy (Divorced) 1 son; Colleen Shannon Dooley (1999–Present)

Military Service: United States Army Reserves (1964–1970)

TV Career: ANNOUNCER—Booth Announcer (WISN-TV, Milwaukee, WI) 1968–1969   HOST— *Confrontation* (WVTV-TV, Milwaukee, WI) 1969–1971; *Jim Peck's Hotline* (WTMJ-TV, Milwaukee, WI) 1971–1973; *Take It from Here* (WRC-TV, Washington D.C.) 1973–1976; *The Big Showdown* (ABC Daytime) December 23, 1974–July 4, 1975; *Caught in the Act* (Unsold ABC Game Show Pilot) 1975; *Money Machine* (Unsold Game Show Pilot) 1976; *Hot Seat* (ABC Daytime) July 12, 1976–October 22, 1976; *Second Chance* (ABC Daytime) March 7, 1977–July 15, 1977; *Seventh Sense* (Unsold Human Interest Pilot) August 1978; *You Don't Say* (Syndicated) September 18, 1978–March 1979; *The Answer Machine* (Unsold NBC Game Show Pilot) 1979; *Three's a Crowd* (Syndicated) September 17, 1979–February 1, 1980; *Everything's Relative* (Unsold Game Show Pilot) 1980; *The TV Game* (Unsold Game Show Pilot) 1982; *The Joker's Wild* (Syndicated) 1983–1986; *Deception* (Unsold Game Show Pilot) 1984; *The Buck Stops Here* (Unsold Game Show Pilot) 1985; *Divorce Court* (Syndicated) September 1986–September 1991; *Suit Yourself* (Unsold ABC Game Show Pilot) May 1990; *I Remember Milwaukee/I Remember* (WMVS-TV, Milwaukee, WI) 1995–Present   ACTOR—*1st and Ten* (HBO) 1986–1993 (Recurring Role)

Other Careers: Admissions Counselor, Marquette University, Milwaukee, WI (1966–1968); Staff Member in Public Relations and Fund Raising, Marquette University (1994–Present)

Jim Peck (Fred Wostbrock)

Hosting a television game show can be difficult at times. A good game show host has to think and act quickly, especially when things go wrong. Almost every host has experienced a moment when something embarrassing takes place on their game show. Often these humiliating moments involve the contestants. When the poor host, the person in charge of steering the action on stage, is the target, he or she must take the embarrassment in stride and keep the show moving. Jim Peck is one host who can well relate to this scenario. He experienced one such humiliating moment where he was the victim, but being the professional that he is, Peck saved the day and proved that he could, and still can, handle the unpredictable.

James Edward Peck was born on June 5, 1943, in Milwaukee, Wisconsin, the second of two boys born to Harry F. and Patricia Peck. By his own account, Peck had his sights on a broadcasting career from the time he was a little boy.

Jim Peck (June 7, 2002 telephone interview):
"I used to sit and listen to radio shows. We had a station here in town (WTMJ) which was the NBC station back then. They used to produce radio shows and they had a big auditorium theater. I used to go down there and watch them do radio shows and think 'boy, someday I'd like to do that.'"

After graduating from Marquette University High School in Milwaukee, Peck enrolled in Marquette University where he acted in some theatrical plays. He graduated with a double major in English and Psychology in 1964, and went on to earn his master's degree in Psychology. While pursuing his advanced degree, Peck served in the United States Army Reserves. Stationed at Fort Jackson in Columbia, South Carolina, Peck eventually attained the rank of Sergeant before his discharge in 1970. While serving in the Army Reserves, he worked in the admissions office at Marquette University. He also acted in the summer stock theatrical productions "The West Side Story" and "Brigadoon."

Confrontation

In 1968 Peck joined the staff of WISN-TV in Milwaukee as a booth announcer. The following year, he moved across town to WVTV hosting the talk show *Confrontation*. This show brought together people who passionately disagreed on certain issues and let them argue it out on the air. He also hosted *Jim Peck's Hotline*, which allowed viewers to call in and voice their opinions on the various subjects discussed with studio guests.

During one week while Peck was interviewing actor Richard Benjamin, the taping for the 30 minute show suddenly stopped. The engineer in charge of operating the videotape recorder had accidentally loaded a 30 second tape to record the program instead of a 30 minute reel. By the time the engineer discovered that the tape had run out, they were about 20 minutes into the program.

JP:
"We had to redo the whole show. Thank God it was an actor [who was being interviewed] and he could pretend to be answering the questions for the first time."

Showdown

By 1973 Peck was ready to try something new, so he turned his attention to game shows. While watching the popular NBC game show *Who, What, or Where*, Peck noticed that the show was produced by Ron Greenberg, so he contacted Greenberg about an audition. Greenberg just happened to be developing a new game show called *Showdown* for ABC, and he needed a host. After auditioning several people, Greenberg decided to try the 30-year-old unknown from Milwaukee. Impressed by what he saw, Greenberg showed Peck's audition tape to ABC and the network ordered a pilot episode for *Showdown*.

The pilot was not picked up immediately for a regular series. In the meantime, Peck took a job hosting *Take It from Here*, a talk show for WRC-TV in Washington D.C. Each show featured three guests who all had something in common such as three authors or three midwives. The subjects ranged from lighthearted to controversial.

JP:
"You would have three people leaning forward and interrupting each other in a nice way. Not like Jerry Springer. It worked most of the time."

Bonafide Host

In 1974 ABC ordered another pilot taped for *Showdown*. The game was renamed *The Big Showdown*. This time, ABC picked it up, and the show debuted on December 23, 1974. Peck continued hosting *Take It from Here* in Washington D.C. and commuted to New York every third week to tape three weeks of shows for *The Big Showdown*.

Three contestants faced a game board with six categories, each worth one to six points. The object was to answer questions and be the first to reach a target number established at the beginning of the round. A payoff amount was selected to determine the cash value of the round. The payoff amounts ranged from $25 to $500. For example the target number for one round might be 23 points and the payoff amount $500.

Peck read a toss up question, and the first player to answer correctly received one point and control of the board. The player chose a category and Peck asked a question. The first player to buzz in with the correct answer added the point value of that question to their score. The idea was to reach the exact target number without going over. The first player to reach the target number (in our example, 23) received the payoff amount (in this case, $500). The winner after three rounds moved to the bonus game.

The bonus round featured a special pair of oversized dice with the sixes replaced by the words "show" and "down." The contestant rolled the dice and if the words "show" and "down" appeared, $10,000 was won. If not, the number rolled became the payoff point. The player was given 30 seconds to roll the dice as many times as possible. Every time the payoff point was rolled, the contestant collected $250. If the contestant rolled "showdown" on the dice during the 30 seconds of play, he or she won $5,000.

The Big Showdown garnered moderate ratings during its run, but there were problems with the game. One of the biggest problems, according to Peck, was the bonus round. The odds of rolling the words "show" and "down" on the very first roll were slim so there were not many $10,000 winners.

JP:
"We went I don't know how long before someone actually hit the big showdown. And that was always very anti-climactic."

The Big Falldown

In the spring of 1975, one of the funniest bloopers in game show history took place during a taping of *The Big Showdown*. Peck stumbled while making his entrance into the studio.

JP:
"Almost invariably a game show host walks onto the stage from the side, comes through a curtain, or is standing there when the cameras go on. But we had a set director who obviously thought we should do something different so he built a spiral staircase."

As Peck descended the steps on each episode, the show's announcer said, "Here's your host, Jim Peck." The director then cut to a close-up of Peck, which is called the star shot.

JP:
"That's where you give a big smile, wave your hand and say 'Hi.' Sixty some shows I had [made the entrance] perfectly, and then I hit the narrow end instead of the wide end of a step. As I went to say 'Hi,' I fell on my credits and bounced down the steps."

Amazingly, Peck played it cool. He was not hurt in the fall so he quickly rose to his feet and told the laughing audience, "Sure, you people would applaud a lynching." When the audience laughed at his joke, Peck decided to proceed with the program rather than re-tape the entrance.

JP:
"I thought, 'Well I'm not going to quit on a laugh.' I thought if Ronnie Greenberg (the producer) wants to stop he can do that, but I'm going to keep going. I just got up and dusted off my posterior."

Greenberg thought that the fall was a wonderful moment since Peck was unhurt and the audience loved it. He decided to leave it in the tape, and the moment aired on national television in April 1975.

Come on! Let's win $10,000 on *The Big Showdown* **(Fred Wostbrock)**

Will he do it? (Fred Wostbrock)

"Oh, so close," says Jim Peck (Fred Wostbrock)

JP:

"I think it has made every blooper show. I still get [a residual check for] about $1.37 from Holland, Thailand, or some place where they decide to run it."

"Even at the Time It Was Very Odd"

When Fred Silverman became the head of ABC's daytime programming in 1975, he began changing the schedule to make room for new shows. One of the victims of his cancellations was *The Big Showdown*.

JP:

"It's interesting to note that the show was canceled with a 28 share (meaning that 28 percent of the audience was tuned to the show), which you would kill to have today. Even at the time it was very odd, but Dick Clark was doing [*The $10,000 Pyramid*] and they didn't want to drop Dick's show even though I think we were getting better numbers. But he was Dick Clark, and they wanted to keep him on the network. It was just one of those things that happen in the business."

The Big Showdown left the air on July 4, 1975, after a run of nearly seven months. Later that year Peck received a call from ABC to host *Caught in the Act*, a celebrity-oriented game show pilot for Bob Stewart Productions. The network had forced Stewart to audition a soap opera actor as the host. During rehearsals it was evident that the actor would not work because he could not ad-lib. The network did not want to simply tell the actor to take a hike, so Peck was called in to watch the pilot tape session, which was done on a Saturday.

JP:

"I sat way in the back and sort of hunched down and watched the guy do the show. I sneaked out and met [the producers] at the deli on 7th Avenue. The next day we called everybody back and I did the pilot."

ABC passed on the show.

Sizzling in the Hot Seat

In the summer of 1976 Peck returned to the national scene with ABC's *Hot Seat*. This game involved two married couples and a lie detector. One mate was placed in the "hot seat" and connected to the lie detector. Peck asked the team three provocative questions worth $100, $200, and $400. The other mate tried to predict how the one hooked to the lie detector would respond. The team won money if the prediction was accurate. The couple with the most money won the game.

Peck recalled an incident on *Hot Seat* where one contestant, as Peck put it "wasn't a very nice person." The man was hooked to the lie detector and had to match his wife on one final question to win the game and a new car. When he failed to match her response, he blew his stack.

JP:

"He just yanked his hands out of the cords he was attached to and he said, 'How did we blow the damn car?' It just fumed the audience."

Since *Hot Seat* taped in Los Angeles, Peck commuted from Washington D.C., where he was still hosting his local talk show *Take It from Here*. By now, Peck was divorced and the long commute to California prevented him from spending enough time with his son, so he moved with his son to Los Angeles. They had just settled in California when ABC canceled *Hot Seat* in October 1976.

A Second Chance

Fred Silverman put Peck under exclusive contract for ABC. One of his first assignments was substituting for David Hartman as co-host on *Good Morning America* in the fall of 1976. In March

1977, Peck landed *Second Chance*, a new ABC game show produced by Bill Carruthers, who later revised the show as *Press Your Luck* in the 1980s.

Three players wrote down their responses to questions and were then shown three possible answers. Contestants earned three spins on the game board if they kept their first answer, but only one spin if they changed their response.

After three questions, the players faced the large game board containing 18 squares of prizes and various dollar amounts. A flashing light bounced rapidly around the squares and contestants in turn hit a plunger to stop the bouncing light. The player won the prize or cash amount in the illuminated square. Also on the board were "devils" which took away a player's winnings. Four "devils" knocked a player out of the game. The player with the highest cash score after two rounds won the game. ABC canceled *Second Chance* after four months in July 1977.

After Hours

Since he was still under contract to ABC, Peck developed a late-night offering, *After Hours: The Jim Peck Special.*

JP:
> "We were doing a sketch where we needed a girl dressed rather seductively. We interviewed a lot of models. The one that I fell for head over heels and thought would be perfect was Loni Anderson (who later starred in the sitcom *WKRP in Cincinnati*). The problem was that she was too sexy for the sketch."

The special also included a repertoire of improvisational players. While putting together some actors and actresses for the group, Peck attended a show at the Comedy Club in Los Angeles where he spotted a young unknown comic named Robin Williams.

JP:
> "No one really knew his name and he came on stage and just lit the place up. I've never seen anybody work like that in my life. We called him in and talked to him, but he had just signed to do a show for NBC and couldn't do this one for ABC. I almost gave him his start."

With ABC Entertainment President Fred Silverman's support, *The Jim Peck Special* began production. However, when Silverman left ABC to become programming chief at NBC in early 1978, the special languished on a shelf and never aired. After his ABC contract expired that year, Peck moved on to other projects.

"It Ended Up on the Cutting Room Floor"

In September 1978, Peck won a small role on the premiere episode of the ABC science fiction series *Battlestar Galactica*. Peck played a reporter broadcasting from a peace conference when all of a sudden the Earth is attacked by a group of aliens called the Cylons. The scene was so brief that it was almost cut from the episode.

JP:
> "It ended up pretty much on the cutting room floor. If you have a magnifying glass and look really closely, you can actually see part of it."

Peck also returned to game shows with a syndicated revival of *You Don't Say*. Two contestants tried to guess the names of famous people or places with clues provided by four celebrities. The first player to reach $500 won the game and played a bonus round where he or she tried to guess as many famous names or places as possible using more clues from the celebrities. This revamped version of *You Don't Say* vanished after six months. In 1979 Peck hosted *The Answer Machine*, another pilot that failed to become a series.

Game show producer Chuck Barris gave him his next break. Barris first met Peck in Washington D.C. in the mid 1970s when he appeared on Peck's talk show *Take It from Here*. Barris rolled out a new game called *Three's a Crowd* and hired Peck to host the show.

An Odd Show

Three's a Crowd's premise sought to answer the question, "Who knows a man better, his wife or his secretary?" The game employed three husbands, their wives, and their secretaries. To start the show, the husbands came on stage while their wives and secretaries were secluded backstage. Peck asked the husbands three questions, usually of the embarrassing nature, about their personal lives. (Example: "Have you ever necked with your secretary?")

After the husbands answered, the secretaries were brought out and asked the same three questions. The secretaries tried to match the answers their bosses had given. Every match earned one point for the team of secretaries. The wives were brought out for the last part of the game and were asked the same questions. Every answer that matched their husbands' answers gave the team of wives one point. The team (secretaries or wives) with the most points at the end of the show split $1,000.

Peck said that the idea for the show had been given to Chuck Barris in the late 1960s by Jess Oppenheimer, who was a writer for the sitcom *I Love Lucy*. Oppenheimer's original idea was to have questions such as "What is your boss'/husband's favorite restaurant?" or "What is his favorite color of socks?" As the game progressed, the questions would get racier to make the show more interesting. However, by the time *Three's a Crowd* reached the air in 1979, Barris wanted nothing but racy material.

> *JP:*
> "It was an odd show. We could never figure out why anyone would come on it."

The racy questions made each episode of *Three's a Crowd* a three-ring circus. The wives and secretaries frequently got so angry at each other that the women often wanted to scratch out each other's eyes. Although *Three's a Crowd* drew sizeable ratings during the fall of 1979, many women around the country protested that the show gave secretaries a negative image. In Detroit, where it was number one at 7:30 p.m., the station carrying the show was picketed by secretarial groups.

As the protests spread around the country, *Three's a Crowd* plummeted in the ratings. Barris finally pulled the plug on the show in February 1980 after he saw his other game shows suffer because of the negative publicity.

> *JP:*
> "It was so controversial and way ahead of its time. If you think about some of the things we did on there, we predated [Jerry] Springer, Maury [Povich], and all the others."

Lean Years

Peck's career stalled after the demise of *Three's a Crowd*. He survived by guest-hosting on talk shows and home shopping specials. Finally, in 1983, Peck was called by Barry & Enright Productions to substitute for Jack Barry as host on *The Joker's Wild* for a couple of weeks. Soon, Barry regularly began calling on Peck to substitute for him during the 1983-1984 season. Peck revealed that Barry planned to eventually retire from hosting the show.

> *JP:*
> "Jack really wanted to phase himself out, and he didn't just want to stop the show. So I came in and did a week here and a week there. Pretty soon it was a couple of weeks here and there. By the time Barry died, I was probably doing about half of the year."

A Near Miss

The reason that Barry wanted to retire from *The Joker's Wild* was because of a serious heart condition he had suffered since the late 1970s.

> *JP:*
> "They were doing two weeks of tapings in one week, five shows on Wednesday and five shows on Thursday. Jack would take one and I would take the other because he just didn't feel up to coming in and doing another five shows that week."

When Barry died of a heart attack in May 1984 just after completing the seventh season of *The Joker's Wild*, it looked as if Peck would become the new host. That was not to be the case, however, since the job went to game show veteran Bill Cullen.

> *JP:*
> "Jack passed away during the hiatus. If the show had been in production, I most likely would have gotten the job because I knew the show, and we could have just kept going without a glitch. The syndicator (Colbert TV Sales) was afraid that I didn't have a big enough name, and he was probably right. So they went with Bill Cullen."

Despite not getting *The Joker's Wild* hosting gig, Peck spoke highly of Cullen, whom he had first met on the game show pilot *Caught in the Act* back in 1975.

> *JP:*
> "He was just a delightful guy."

Peck came back to substitute for Cullen on *The Joker's Wild* one more time during its last season in 1986. Another funny experience in Peck's career came during this two-week stint. While taping an episode, about three fourths of the way into the show, the producer suddenly yelled, "Stop tape." The reason: they had run out of questions! Since Cullen hosted the show at a much slower pace, the writers used fewer questions for each game than they had available when Barry and Peck hosted.

> *JP:*
> "I work fast. Jack and I worked at about the same pace. Bill, I didn't realize, had a whole different demeanor and whole different way of doing it, and he worked slowly."

The taping stopped for nearly an hour while members of the network Standards and Practices met with the producers to approve the new questions added to finish the game. Show announcer Charlie O'Donnell entertained the studio audience during the down time while Peck went back to his dressing room until taping resumed.

"They Weren't Doing Anything That I Did"

After completing his stint on *The Joker's Wild*, Peck moved out of the game show arena. He became the court reporter on the syndicated series *Divorce Court* in the fall of 1986. The show used actors to portray the husbands and wives who came to settle their cases before retired California Superior Court Judge William B. Keene. Peck interviewed the couples after their cases were settled. *Divorce Court* became Peck's longest-running series lasting five seasons.

Divorce Court producers Peter Locke and Donald Kushner also produced the long-running HBO sitcom *1st and Ten* during the 1980s. As a result, Peck guest-starred once or twice a season on the sitcom playing different roles.

> *JP:*
> "I got a chance to do a little bit of acting, which is about all I can do." (Laughing)

Peck made one last stab at game show hosting in 1990 with the ABC pilot *Suit Yourself*. Contestants answered questions to earn cards from a deck of oversized playing cards. The object was to acquire three cards of the same suit. This was Peck's last pilot. After *Divorce Court* left the air in 1991, he spent the next two years hunting for television work. Peck finally decided it was time to get out of show business.

> *JP:*
> "They [the producers] weren't doing anything that I did. All the talk shows turned to freak shows and they stopped doing game shows. I didn't want to do a freak show so that was pretty much the end of it."

Not Ready to Retire

Peck retired in 1993 and headed back to his home state of Wisconsin. He rented a large farm near Spring Green and spent his time walking the hills, reading, and traveling. He soon grew restless from the inactivity and by the end of the year decided that he needed to get back to work.

> *JP:*
> "I thought I would open a vein if I didn't find something to do."

He talked with some friends at his alma mater, Marquette University. Soon he was hired to work in a number of Marquette's departments including Public Relations and fund raising.

> *JP:*
> "I love being in the university setting. It's a great way to stay young, and if you can give something back, then it's wonderful. It's worked out very well for both the university and me."

I Remember Milwaukee

In 1995 Peck's son, Jim Peck Jr., wrote, produced, and directed a special on Frank Lloyd Wright's wing-spread building for WMVS-TV, the public television station in Milwaukee. The senior Peck was hired as host and for one month worked for his son.

> *JP:*
> "He won an Emmy and I didn't, so I was a little upset by that." (Laughing)

Jim Peck Jr. soon went to work as a reporter for Idaho Public Television where he has won several awards. For Jim Peck Sr., the Frank Lloyd Wright special led to a regular series on WMVS-TV called *I Remember Milwaukee*, which Peck calls "an oral history of the city." What began as a limited run series of ten to twelve episodes soon turned into a weekly series on the WMVS schedule. Now more than 200 episodes later, *I Remember Milwaukee* continues to flourish. In recent years, the show's title shortened to *I Remember*.

"And They Said It Wouldn't Last"

After moving back to Wisconsin in 1993, Peck renewed a friendship with an old friend, Colleen Shannon Dooley. He and Dooley had known each other for many years since their families went back three generations. Dooley's grandmother worked with Peck's father.

Their friendship led to a long-term romance, and the two finally wed in 1999.

> *JP:*
> "And they said it wouldn't last." (Laughing)

Although much of Jim Peck's television career has been filled with short-lived programs and a number of disappointments, he expresses no regrets for the route that his career has taken. What started as a broadcasting career on the local level in Milwaukee in the 1960s later led to national television exposure along with a certain amount of stardom and recognition. Now that his career has come full circle back to Milwaukee, Wisconsin, Jim Peck is a happy man.

> *JP:*
> "I'm supposed to be retired and I'm working full time at Marquette [University] and hosting a show on public television every week. I love it! I'll never fully retire again. I need to be more active than that. The trick is to retire to something and not from something. I like being active."

JIM PERRY

Birth Name: James Edward Dooley
Born: November 9, 1933, in Camden, New Jersey
Marriage and Family: June Wiatrak (1959–Present) 1 son, 1 daughter
Military Service: United States Army (1955–1956)
TV Career, Canada: Host—*Fractured Phrases* (CTV) September 1965–September 1966; *Words and Music* (CTV) September 1966–September 1967; *Miss Canada Pageant* (CTV) (Annually) 1966–1989; *Money Makers* (Syndicated) March 3, 1969–May 30, 1969; *Eye Bet* (CTV) September 1972–September 1974; *Headline Hunters* (CTV) September 1972–September 1982; *Definition* (CTV) September 1974–September 1989
TV Career, United States: ANNOUNCER—*That Show Starring Joan Rivers* (Syndicated) September 1968–September 1969 HOST—*Talking Pictures* (Unsold NBC Game Show Pilot) 1963; *It's Your Move* (Syndicated) September 18, 1967–December 15, 1967; *Card Sharks* (NBC Daytime) April 24, 1978–October 23, 1981; *Twisters* (Unsold Game Show Pilot) October 1982; *Sale of the Century* (NBC Daytime) January 3, 1983–March 24, 1989, (Syndicated) January 1985–September 1986; *Lottery Cash Explosion* (Pilot for State Lottery Franchise) July 18, 1993
Radio Career, United States: Staff Announcer/Newscaster (WABC-AM, New York, NY) 1968–1972; *The Jim Perry Show* (WABC-AM, New York, NY) 1970–1972
Other Careers: Singer for Grossingers, New York (1956–1959); Straight Man to Comedian Sid Caesar (1959–1963)
Books: *The Sleeper Awakes: A Journey To Self Awareness* (1991); *There's Got to Be a Pony in There Somewhere* (Unpublished)

Not many television personalities have worked in two different countries on a regular basis in their careers. One game show host trekked back and forth between the United States and Canada hosting television shows for almost 25 years. That man was Jim Perry, who became a household name in two different nations. Ironically, most viewers in Canada had no idea that Perry was American and many U.S. viewers had no clue that Perry also worked in Canada. His unusual career path left some people scratching their heads wondering how he accomplished this milestone.

Jim Perry was born as James Edward Dooley on November 9, 1933, in Camden, New Jersey. He experienced an unhappy childhood growing up during the Depression. His parents divorced when he was young leaving Perry and his two sisters with a feeling of loneliness.

Jim Perry (Fred Wostbrock)

Jim Perry (March 10, 2005 telephone interview):
   "That kind of set a tone of wanting to be liked and wanting to have the world love me. It's the kind of thing that leads one toward becoming an entertainer. I find with a lot of entertainers that they start out with a need in finding, if you will, a surrogate family."

After his parents divorced, Perry was raised by his mother, but he was plagued by his rough childhood in the coming years. What followed was a childhood of constantly moving from one place to another. During his high school years alone, Perry and his mother moved from Chester, Pennsylvania to Biloxi, Mississippi, and finally to Pleasanton, California.

JP:
   "[I] was constantly meeting new people. [I was] always having to meet new people, [to] make an impression, [to] try to be loved. I didn't realize that, in many ways, I was attuning myself to the things that were going to be an aid to me later in life. Meeting new people has never bothered me."

"That Turned Out to Be the Best Thing That Ever Happened"

After graduating from high school, Perry moved back east to live with his father while going to college at the University of Pennsylvania where he studied Psychology.

JP:
   "I thought things were going to be better with my father, but they weren't."

Perry was unable to pay his bills and was forced to withdraw from college after two years. His fortunes finally turned around when he was drafted into the United States Army in 1955. He was stationed in Germany and worked for Armed Forces Radio as an announcer and singer.

JP:
   "That turned out to be the best thing that ever happened. I toured with a couple of soldier shows, and I came to the conclusions that if I can sing, and have a bunch of guys applaud, I can do something with this."

Upon his discharge in 1956, Perry worked as a singer for Grossingers in the Catskill Mountains in New York. There he met June Wiatrak, a catalogue model who was making a name for herself. They married in 1959 and had a daughter named Erin and a son named Sean, both of whom followed in their parents' footsteps with careers in show business.

Sid Caesar

One of the morning shows at Grossingers was an audience participation "Simon Says" game. Perry stood with a microphone outside the breakfast room to talk with the customers and lure them to the "Simon Says" game in the entertainment lounge. His ability to attract the customers caught the attention of Mort Curtis, who told Perry that comedian Sid Caesar was looking for a straight man for his nightclub act. Perry was not convinced that merely talking was a talent.

JP:
   "There are tangible talents where you say, 'I think I can do something with this. It's very difficult to say, 'I think I'd like to talk for a living.' I rather denigrated talking for quite some time. It was so natural to me."

Perry met with Caesar and the two hit it off leading to a four-year stint of Perry working as the comic foil to Caesar.

"Why Don't You Try This?"

In 1963 Caesar left the act when he landed a role in a Broadway show called *Little Me*. Looking for something new, Perry tried his luck in game show hosting. He did a run-through for a game produced by musician Harry Salter, which never made it to the pilot stage. One of the people at the run-though was game show producer Howard Felsher, who later worked for Goodson-Todman Productions. Perry said that Felsher was instrumental to him in learning the ropes of game show hosting.

> *JP:*
> "Howard [would say] 'Now you did this well, but why don't you try this.' It was like having a school teacher all the way along the line. It was wonderful for me and I really learned the business with Howard Felsher."

> *Howard Felsher (TV producer, June 2006 telephone interview):*
> "He became a good [host]. He's a good man and an honorable man. There are not too many hosts as good as Jim was potentially."

Perry was working under his birth name, Jim Dooley, when he auditioned for an NBC pilot, *Talking Pictures*. The network confused him with another Jim Dooley, who was a commercial spokesman for Northeast Airlines. Taking his wife's advice, Perry adopted his mother's maiden name and began performing under the stage name Jim Perry. NBC passed up the *Talking Pictures* pilot in favor of a new game show called *Jeopardy!*

Hello Canada

Meanwhile, Perry went to Canada to host a folk music special, which led to his next break. In 1965 Art Baer and Ben Johlson created the game show *Fractured Phrases*. Perry was asked to host the pilot episode, which was taped in Canada.

> *Jim Perry:*
> "They (Baer and Johlson) asked the Canadians if they could bring me up just to do the pilot because they wanted something to show down in the U.S."

The Canadian television executives remembered Perry from the folk music special he had recently hosted and gladly approved of him. *Fractured Phrases* was sold to NBC, but Art James landed the hosting gig. Baer and Johlson sold another version of the game to CTV (The Canadian Television Network) and Perry had his first regular television job. Rather than move to Canada, Perry commuted from his home in New York to tape the show in Montreal.

On *Fractured Phrases*, contestants were shown jumbled phrases and then phonetically sounded out the words to figure out the fractured phrase. The American version lasted only 13 weeks, but *Fractured Phrases* fared much better in Canada running for two years.

A Complicated Game

In 1966 CTV assigned Perry the game show *Words and Music*. This complicated game called for players to identify a person, place, or thing through a series of musical clues. An organist played a medley of three songs, all of which shared one particular word in their titles (for example: Blue Moon, Blue Skies, and Blue Moon of Kentucky. The common word is "blue").

Once this word was guessed, it was placed on a crossword puzzle consisting of several words. Another medley of songs was performed and game play moved in the same fashion. All of the words in the crossword puzzle served as clues to a mystery word. The first player to guess the mystery word was the winner. Viewers were baffled by the complex rules and *Words and Music* failed after one season.

> *JP:*
> "It was very literate. You had to know some music and then you had to solve a crossword puzzle. It was a very static show and I don't think it would ever have any success here [in the United States]."

In the fall of 1966, Perry began hosting the annual *Miss Canada Pageant*. He used his singing skills to serenade the contestants much in the same manner Bert Parks did with the *Miss America Pageant*. Perry hosted the pageant for 24 consecutive years.

It's Your Move

In 1967 Perry started his first American game show, *It's Your Move*. Two teams of two players bid on how much time they needed to act out words for their teammates. Contestants who bid the least amount of time earned the right to play. After 13 weeks on the air, a television strike stopped production of the show in December 1967. By his own admission, *It's Your Move* was one of Perry's favorite games.

> **JP:**
> "It was a shame because I thought it was the best charade show ever. It never really got its due."

A Brief Radio Interlude

After spending a few months out of work, Perry won a job as a staff announcer at WABC-TV in New York with the help of Dirk Fredericks, who had served as Perry's announcer on *It's Your Move*. Perry was initially limited to doing station identifications. He soon moved to the station's radio division delivering a five minute newscast every 30 minutes during the overnight hours. As he settled into his new radio environment, Perry feared that his light and easy-going voice would not fit in with the station's rock music format.

> **JP:**
> "I made it work because I could sight read very well. I did the news very quick, very fast, and it suited rock radio."

Bingo!

In the spring of 1969, Perry attempted another game show, *Money Makers*. Future game show producer Jay Wolpert also worked on this show. Similar to the popular game Bingo, *Money Makers* required contestants to answer questions worth from one to nine points. After successfully answering a question, the contestants placed that point value anywhere they chose on a large bingo-type board consisting of four rows of four columns.

When a player successfully put four markers in a row up and down, across, or diagonally, the contestant won the sum total of those point values in cash by answering another question. The row of four numbers served as the last four digits to a home viewer's telephone number that Perry called giving the person a chance to win cash. *Money Makers* died after 13 short weeks.

Goodbye Radio, Hello Television...Again

Back at WABC, Perry was given an early Sunday morning disc jockey show that aired from 3 to 5 a.m. beginning in 1970. He continued to deliver the news during the week nights and would pinch hit for other announcers at the station when needed. After four years in radio, Perry was itching to get back into television. The problem was that by the early 1970s, New York was rapidly dying as a television production center because everything was moving to Los Angeles. With no television prospects in New York, Perry considered other options.

"We Left as Dooley and Arrived as Perry"

In 1972 during his annual excursion to Toronto to host the *Miss Canada Pageant*, Perry was approached by the head of station CFTO-TV about hosting a regular series.

> **JP:**
> "I said, 'If you find a show for me, we'll move here.' I was as good as my word and he was as good as his word."

Perry was offered the daytime game show *Eye Bet*, which was seen nationally over the CTV network. Perry quit his job at WABC and moved the family to Canada where they remained for the next six years. At the time of his move, Perry's legal name was still Jim Dooley. Since he was becoming well known in Canada as Jim Perry, he decided to legally adopt his professional name.

JP:
"We literally left the U.S. as Dooley and arrived in Canada as Perry, and it's been Perry ever since."

When CTV realized that Perry was serious about moving to Canada, the network also offered him a weekly primetime show. *Headline Hunters* was a game that required its contestants to keep abreast of current affairs in the news. *Headline Hunters*, became a top ten hit and lasted for a decade. Perry also found time to host the annual *Santa Claus Parade* for CTV.

The Definition of Success

In 1974 he began his longest running series, the game show *Definition*. Similar in format to *Wheel of Fortune*, the show aired at 6:00 p.m. every weeknight. Two celebrity/contestant teams solved puzzles by calling out letters a la *Wheel of Fortune* except that the players did not spin a wheel. Contestants solved puns and correct guesses allowed them to call out letters. An example pun had a four-letter answer. The pun was, "What happens when the smog lifts in California?" The answer: "U.C.L.A."

Definition became a ratings hit in Canada attracting an average of 750,000 viewers each night. *Definition* not only featured Canadian celebrities, but it also attracted a number of American television and movie stars.

JP:
"We had a lot of celebrities who would not do game shows in [the United States]. For a trip to Toronto on a weekend and to get paid, a lot of people went up and did it."

Although most Americans do not recall ever seeing *Definition*, many have heard the program's theme song. The opening music used in the popular movie *Austin Powers* was the same music from *Definition*. The catchy tune was written by musician Quincy Jones.

JP:
"My son asked Mike Myers (the star of Austin Powers), 'Was that [theme] from my father's show? Myers said that it was. He said he wanted to throw in a little homage to the Canadians that the Canadians would get and the Americans wouldn't."

Compared to American game shows where thousands of dollars in cash and new cars were given away daily, *Definition* only gave away modest prizes such as color television sets, washers and dryers, and encyclopedias. The show did not give away a car until 1982 when a contestant won a mid-size Chevrolet during the show's annual tournament of champions. Perry felt that a show like *Definition* would never be a hit in the United States.

JP:
"The Canadians have a very English background and the English are very big on word play. So too are the Canadians. The Canadian audience will watch a more literate game."

Play Your Cards Right

Perry breezed though the 1970s with multiple successes in Canada, but wanted to crack the larger U.S. television market. Since he was doing well in Canada and because the CTV network had been so good to him, Perry continued hosting his game shows in that country. Perry went to Los Angeles and hired an agent to help him find a job. He was told to see Jonathan Goodson at Goodson-Todman Productions. At the time, the company was developing a new NBC game show called *Card Sharks*.

Perry had an advantage because there were two people on the Goodson-Todman staff who

Jim Perry starts a new game with two *Card Sharks* players (Fred Wostbrock).

already knew him: Howard Felsher and Jay Wolpert. With Felsher and Wolpert pulling for him, Perry was signed to host *Card Sharks* in short order. He purchased a home in Los Angeles and brought his family back to the U.S. *Card Sharks* debuted over NBC on April 24, 1978.

On *Card Sharks*, two contestants were each given five oversized cards from two standard decks of 52 playing cards. The first card was revealed and the object of the game was for players to guess whether each succeeding card was higher or lower in value than the one preceding it. Before playing their cards, contestants first had to guess how many from a group of 100 people gave a specific answer to a survey question.

One player predicted how many people gave the answer while their opponent guessed if the actual number was higher or lower. The player coming closest won the right to play their cards. The first contestant to work his/her way across the board of five cards won $100 and the first player to win two games advanced to the "Money Cards."

In the bonus game, the winner was dealt a total of seven cards on a three-level board. The player started with $200 and a base card was revealed. The contestant wagered all or part of his/her money as to whether the next card was higher or lower. A player could win a total of $28,800 if they could successfully double their bet with each play of the cards. Calling a card incorrectly cost the player the amount of their bet.

Card Sharks hit the ground running and became a solid hit. Perry was now a bona fide television star in both the United States and Canada.

JP:

"When I started *Card Sharks*, as far as most of the American public was concerned, they didn't know me. The U.S. networks, most of them did not know me. I used to laughingly say to people, 'I was the most experienced unknown in American television.' They think, 'How did somebody get that good who has never done a game show?' Well, I had done about 5,000 [shows] up to that point."

"I Bent a Few of Them"

One of the trademarks of *Card Sharks* was the oversized playing cards used in the game. When revealing cards during the show, Perry would quickly turn them over with a sharp twist of his hand for dramatic effect.

JP:
"I banged the cards so much that they were constantly having to replace them. I'm sure that [the producers] wished I had handled them a little more gingerly when I put them up [on the board]. I bent a few of them and they were very expensive to replace. Anything that got nicked, [out] it went, but I thought it was important to the show so I banged the hell out of those cards."

Shuffling the cards to ensure fair game play was no picnic for the show's staff.

JP:
"They were very heavy and shuffling those cards was an ordeal. They would shuffle them in front of the network censors. Right before they went on, the contestants would cut the cards. The contestants were not called on to shuffle them, which would have been a really difficult thing to do. By having the contestants do the last act of cutting the cards, there was no way that anybody could do any kind of shenanigans. The ultimate fall of the cards was because of the way the contestants cut them."

The Fall of the Cards

While hosting *Card Sharks* in the United States, Perry was busy flying to Canada to tape episodes for *Headline Hunters* and *Definition*. He also continued hosting the annual *Miss Canada Pageant*. In June of 1980, NBC reshuffled its daytime lineup and moved *Card Sharks* to 12 noon. The move ultimately hurt the show since many NBC affiliates dropped the game to air local news.

To help boost the ratings, the producers opened the third season of *Card Sharks* with a three-week tournament in which eight game show hosts played for charity. The hosts who participated were Jack Clark, Bill Cullen, Tom Kennedy, Jim Lange, Allen Ludden, Wink Martindale, Gene Rayburn, and Alex Trebek. Nothing helped as *Card Sharks* slowly eroded in the ratings and left the air on October 23, 1981.

Shortly after *Card Sharks* ceased production, Perry was approached by the producer of NBC's *Wheel of Fortune* about taking over as host from Chuck Woolery, who was leaving the series. However, NBC nixed the idea because Perry had just gone off the air and felt it was too soon to bring him back. In 1982 *Headline Hunters* stopped production in Canada leaving only *Definition* as Perry's livelihood.

A Twist

In the fall of 1982, producer Bob Stewart called Perry to host an NBC game show pilot called *Twisters*. The game was a combination of shuffleboard and answering riddles. Stewart was having a problem finding an emcee and was hurrying to beat a deadline to get the pilot episode recorded. Knowing that Perry had a knack for learning the rules of a game quickly, Stewart called him in, and in one single day, Perry learned the game and taped the pilot. While *Twisters* did not sell, it helped Perry land his next American game show.

The Sale of the Century

Australian television producer Reg Grundy had just sold a version of the game show *Sale of the Century* to NBC. *Sale of the Century* had aired on that network in the early 1970s, but had only been a moderate hit. Grundy purchased the rights to the show and made it a hit in Australia. After seeing how successful the show was in that country, NBC entertainment president

Brandon Tartikoff bought back the American rights from Grundy. Perry was well known to Reg Grundy since Grundy produced an Australian version of Perry's show *Definition*. Reg Grundy wanted Perry to host *Sale of the Century*, but Tartikoff was not convinced that Perry was right for the show.

Card Sharks had been a very high energy show and Tartikoff was having trouble envisioning Perry hosting a lower energy series like *Sale of the Century*. However, when Tartikoff saw Perry hosting the *Twisters* pilot and realized that he could run a completely different type of game from *Card Sharks*, Tartikoff changed his mind. He gave the thumbs up for Perry to take the reins and *Sale of the Century* opened its NBC run on January 3, 1983.

Sale of the Century had a very simple format: three contestants answered a series of rapid-fire questions for the right to purchase merchandise. The players started the game with $20. Correct answers added $5 to the contestants' scores while wrong answers cost them $5. The game was periodically interrupted with "Instant Bargains." The player in the lead was offered the chance to buy a prize at a greatly reduced price. For example, a $400 television set could be purchased for $11. If the player bought the prize, the purchase price was subtracted from their score. Perry frequently sweetened the deal by offering additional cash to the contestant.

Another game played during the show was "The Fame Game." Perry read a series of clues pertaining to a famous person. The first player to buzz in with the correct answer chose one of nine numbers on a board. Behind each number were prizes and also money cards, which were added to the contestant's score if selected. The game ended with a 60-second speed round of questions and the contestant with the most money went on to shop in the "sale of the century."

On the stage were large and extravagant prizes such as cars, boats, and trips that the player could purchase using his/her winnings from the main game. The shopping segment was later replaced by contestants selecting numbers from a 20 square board until matching two identical prizes. In the last year of the show's run, budget cuts by NBC resulted in another bonus round where the winner solved four puzzles in 20 seconds for a cash jackpot.

The End of the Ride

Sale of the Century was popular enough to spawn a syndicated nighttime edition from January 1985 to September 1986 with Perry hosting both versions. Through the 1980s, Perry continued to hopscotch between the U.S. and Canada, but his career was about to undergo a drastic change. In March 1989, NBC canceled *Sale of the Century* after six years on the air. Simultaneously, *Definition*, which had been running for 15 years in Canada, was given the axe by CTV. In September 1989, Perry hosted his last *Miss Canada Pageant*. After 24 straight years on radio and television, Perry was suddenly out of a job.

"The Sleeper Awakes"

The year 1989 marked a turning point for Perry. With a lot of time on his hands, he was forced for the first time in his life to deal with emotional problems that had plagued him throughout his career. As mentioned earlier in the chapter, Perry's childhood was filled with loneliness and neglect. Despite a successful career and a long and happy marriage, Perry still felt hollow on the inside. No amount of money and success could fill the void that he felt within himself. Perry had been running nonstop for so long that he had never taken the time to find out what his life was all about.

JP:
"It was kind of interesting that the shows went off the air at the time they did. Suddenly I was looking at, 'What am I, who am I, and what's going on with my life?'"

After deeply exploring and confronting the darker areas of his life, Perry was moved to write a self-help book called *The Sleeper Awakes: A Journey To Self-Awareness*, which was published by

Summit Books in 1991. In the book, he talked in-depth about the emotional roller coaster he rode while putting his life back in order.

Gradually, Perry emerged as a different man. He finally made peace with his past and was able to put the successes and failures of his life into perspective. Having been out of the television business for a few years, Perry discovered that he had no desire to go back.

> *JP:*
> "I bumped into some people and they asked me, 'How can you be retired? How do you feel about it?'" I feel great. I feel very complete. I was fortunate in how things worked out for me when I was done [in television] and moved on to other things and wrote books. I look back, and the idea of walking out on a stage, and everybody starting to applaud, seems like the silliest thing in the world to me."

This is the picture of Jim Perry seen on the cover of his first book, *The Sleeper Awakes* (Tracy Frankel, courtesy Jim Perry).

"There's Got to Be a Pony in There Somewhere"

After his last game shows left the air in 1989, Perry worked on two more television assignments. In the early 1990s, he co-hosted an infomercial with his daughter Erin. He later hosted the pilot for a state lottery franchise produced by Jonathan Goodson that was sold in several states, but Perry did not host any of the regular shows. In the late 1990s, he wrote a sequel to *The Sleeper Awakes* called *There's Got to Be a Pony in There Somewhere*. He has yet to find a publisher for the second book as of 2006.

He explained how that book title applies to his own life:

> *JP:*
> "There's something good that happens in everything. There's a joke about a group of psychologists taking two young boys and they put one young boy in a room full of all these wonderful toys. The little boy sits there. [The psychologists] say, 'Why won't you play with these toys?' [The boy] says, 'Well, if I play with this one, you'll take it away from me. If I play with this one, it'll break and I'll be unhappy.' It goes on and on. They put the other boy into a room that is empty except for a pile of horse manure and a shovel. He happily starts digging away at the pile of horse manure. The psychologists say, 'Why are you so happy?' And he says, 'Because there's got to be a pony in there somewhere.'"

To Perry, that says it all. He feels that every part of his life had something good to offer.

> *JP:*
> "I regret none of it. It was all wonderful. I learned from all of it and I had great experiences. I look back and there was a pony in all of it."

These days, Perry and his wife June reside in Cocoa, Florida, where they moved in 2001 to be near his two sisters. Their daughter Erin currently is a rock singer living in Germany and son Sean works in Los Angeles as a talent agent and has developed a number of reality-based shows. In 2004 Perry and his wife purchased a summer home in Bakersville, North Carolina, as a mountain getaway from the hot summers in Florida.

> *JP:*
> "June is a potter, and a very good one. Bakersville, North Carolina, is noted for crafts people and pottery. We're building a new pottery studio for her up there and looking forward to another chapter of our lives."

REGIS PHILBIN

Birth Name: Regis Francis Xavier Philbin

Born: August 25, 1931, in New York, New York

Marriages and Family: Kay Faylan (1955–1968) (Divorced) 1 daughter, 1 son; Joy Senese (1970–Present) 2 daughters

Military Career: United States Navy (1953–1955)

Radio Career: Newscaster (KSON-AM, San Diego, CA) 1957–1959

TV Career: HOST—News Anchor (KFMB-TV, San Diego, CA) 1959–1960; News Anchor (KOGO-TV, San Diego, CA) 1960–1964; *The Regis Philbin Show* (KOGO-TV, San Diego, CA) October 1961–October 1964; *That Regis Philbin Show* (Syndicated) October 1964–February 1965, (KTTV-TV, Los Angeles, CA) 1965–1967; *The Joey Bishop Show* (ABC Late Night) April 17, 1967–December 26, 1969; *National Celebrity Test* (Unsold ABC Game Show Pilot) May 1968; *Philbin's People* (KHJ-TV, Los Angeles, CA) August 23, 1969–May 1970; *Tempo/Philbin & Co.* (KHJ-TV, Los Angeles, CA) August 10, 1970–January 25, 1974; *Target* (KHJ-TV, Los Angeles, CA) June 12, 1971–June 1972; *A.M. Chicago* (WLS-TV, Chicago, IL) June 1974–October 1974; *A.M. Los Angeles* (KABC-TV, Los Angeles, CA) January 6, 1975–November 27, 1981; *The Neighbors* (ABC Daytime) December 29, 1975–April 9, 1976; *Almost Anything Goes* (ABC Primetime) January 24, 1976–May 9, 1976; *The Regis Philbin Show* (NBC Daytime) November 30, 1981–April 9, 1982; *Regis Philbin's Health Styles* (Lifetime Network) 1982–1988; *The Morning Show* (WABC-TV, New York City) April 4, 1983–September 9, 1988; *Live, with Regis and Kathie Lee* (Syndicated) September 12, 1988–

Regis Philbin (Fred Wostbrock)

September 2000; *Live, with Regis and Kelly* (Syndicated) September 2000–Present; *Who Wants to Be a Millionaire?* (ABC Primetime) August 16, 1999–August 29, 1999, (ABC Primetime) November 7, 1999–November 21, 1999, (ABC Primetime) January 8, 2000–June 27, 2002; *Super Millionaire* (ABC Primetime) February 22, 2004–February 27, 2004, (ABC Primetime) May 16, 2004–May 23, 2004; *America's Got Talent* (NBC Primetime) June 21, 2006–August 17, 2006

Theatrical Movies: *Everything You Always Wanted to Know About Sex* (1972); *The Bad News Bears Go to Japan* (1978); *Sextette* (1978); *The Man Who Loved Women* (1983); *Funny About Love* (1990); *Night and the City* (1992); *Open Season* (1995); *Dudley Do-Right* (1999); *Little Nicky* (2000); *People I Know* (2002); *Pinocchio* (2002); *Cheaper by the Dozen* (2003); *The Breakup Artist* (2004); *Miss Congeniality 2: Armed and Fabulous* (2005)

Made-for-TV Movies: *Mad Bull* (1977); *SST: Death Flight* (1977); *Mirror, Mirror* (1979); *Lily for President* (1982); *California Girls* (1985); *Perry Mason: The Case of the Telltale Talk Show Host* (1993)

Other Careers: Page, NBC Television Network, New York City (1955); Stagehand/News Writer, KCOP-TV, Los Angeles, CA (1955–1957)

Books: *Cooking with Regis and Kathie Lee* (1993); *Entertaining with Regis and Kathie Lee* (1994); *I'm Only One Man* (1995); *Who Wants to Be Me?* (2000)

Regis Philbin tends to be noted more as a talk show host than as a quizmaster. His resume is loaded with talk shows, but includes only three rounds as a game show host. That first game show came after 15 years in the talk arena and was a complete disaster. As a talk show host, Philbin's four cracks at national stardom never achieved real success. Unlike many performers, he achieved success later in life. Not until Philbin was 57 years old did he finally make it. He later added the icing to the cake becoming one of the most celebrated game show hosts of all time a mere two years before his 70th birthday. Hey, it's never too late to achieve and enjoy success.

Regis Francis Xavier Philbin was born on August 25, 1931, in Manhattan, New York City. His first name came from Regis High School in Manhattan, his father's alma mater. Philbin grew up in the Bronx section of New York City and began weightlifting as a teenager, a ritual he continues to the present day. In college at the University of Notre Dame in Indiana, Philbin participated in intramural boxing and took up resistance training. He graduated in 1953 with a degree in Sociology.

His first stop after college was a two year stint in the United States Navy where he was stationed at Coronado, California. According to his 1995 autobiography, *I'm Only One Man*, Philbin drove to Los Angeles on the day of his discharge in an old Hudson convertible seeking a job with KCOP-TV. The station had no immediate openings for him, but asked for his address and phone number. Meanwhile Philbin headed back to New York to rejoin his family. An uncle who worked for CBS radio helped Philbin get a job as a page for NBC. He worked as an usher for *The Tonight Show* with host Steve Allen.

New York or California

Then, as luck would have it, KCOP-TV called him about a job as a stagehand and stage manager. Philbin weighed his options as he pointed out in *I'm Only One Man*. He had just started working for NBC in New York and loved his job, but New York was quickly declining as a major broadcasting center. All of the work and talent was headed for Los Angeles. He accepted KCOP's offer and moved to California.

Along with setting up props for shows and driving a film delivery truck, Philbin cued on-air talent during the live shows and held cue cards. What he really wanted was to get on the air, so he began writing funny critiques of the KCOP-TV shows and posted them anonymously on the bulletin board. The station manager was not amused when he found out Philbin was the guilty party. He dressed Philbin down, but then decided that he liked his writing style. Before long, Philbin added the duties of news and sports writing along with his stage hand work.

Now for the News

The long 12-hour shifts at KCOP-TV eventually wore Philbin down and he moved to San Diego in 1957 as a newscaster for KSON radio. In those days, San Diego was such a quiet town that news stories were hard to find. For Philbin, it meant having fun taking dull stories such as a piggy bank robbery and punching them up with more action without distorting the facts. His prowess earned him a spot on San Diego's KFMB-TV in 1959 doing those same feature stories.

By 1960 KOGO-TV just across town offered Philbin a job anchoring the evening news and hosting a Saturday night talk show. For the next four years, Philbin interviewed guests and talked about everything and anything (within reason that is). He was happy as a lark.

The Big Time (For a Little While)

In the fall of 1964, when Steve Allen left his syndicated talk show to take over as host of CBS's *I've Got a Secret*, Westinghouse Broadcasting tapped Philbin to take over the 90 minute nationally syndicated series. He was so excited about his shot at the big time before he realized how different things would be.

His new show would be taped and far more structured than his live San Diego talk show. He also had no real creative control over the series. Philbin pointed out in *I'm Only One Man* that because of the tape delay, he could not talk about current events during his off-the-cuff chats. Adding insult to injury: the writers were giving him jokes to tell, something Philbin was clearly uncomfortable doing.

Branded with the title *That Regis Philbin Show*, the premiere in October 1964 featured a well-known astrologer who surprised Philbin on the air with his prediction that the show would flop. Sure enough after 20 weeks Philbin was dropped by Westinghouse and replaced by Merv Griffin. Philbin then took his show to Los Angeles station KTTV for the next two years.

Second Banana

In the spring of 1967, Philbin was back on late night national television again. Facing fierce competition from NBC's *Tonight Show* with Johnny Carson, ABC launched a talk show with comedian Joey Bishop as host. Philbin came aboard as Bishop's sidekick. The premiere night of *The Joey Bishop Show* on April 17, 1967, was one Philbin never forgot. Actress Debbie Reynolds chased him across the stage and threw him on the floor. For the next two and a half years, Philbin worked his secondary role, but generally was unhappy. Despite those unpleasant years, Philbin recounted in *I'm Only One Man* that Bishop taught him a lot about the business.

When Philbin learned that ABC considered replacing him, he walked off in the middle of the July 8, 1968, show. Philbin confided in his book that the walk-out was somewhat planned by him and Bishop to get the attention of ABC executives. But Philbin was unsure whether or not

Regis Philbin and Joey Bishop were ABC's answer to Johnny Carson's *Tonight Show* in the late 1960s (Fred Wostbrock).

he would return to the show because he really feared that ABC wanted him out. The outpouring of viewer mail in his favor prompted him to come back the following week.

A Funky Period

Philbin was in a funk during the mid to late 1960s. While his career was less than thrilling, his shaky 13 year marriage to Kay Faylan ended in 1968. To this day, Philbin has remained close to his son and daughter from that marriage. He also lost his house overlooking Universal City courtesy of California's infamous mudslides in February 1968. When two weeks of heavy rains washed out his back yard, the city of Los Angeles declared the house unsafe and forced him to move.

Philbin first tried his luck as a game show host with the 1968 pilot *The National Celebrity Test*. Produced by Chuck Barris for ABC, the network passed on the game. After *The Joey Bishop Show* left the air in 1969, Philbin largely disappeared from the national scene, but remained very active as a talk show host in Los Angeles. Signing with KHJ-TV, he hosted *Philbin's People*, *Tempo* (which was renamed *Philbin & Co.* in July 1973), and *Target*. Here he continued in the format he loved most: live television with ad-libbed conversations. Although he had no network series, Philbin appeared in occasional guest roles on *Big Valley*, *The Danny Thomas Hour*, *Love, American Style*, and *That Girl*.

What a Joy!

The beginning of the 1970s signaled the end of Philbin's late 1960s funk. His time on *The Joey Bishop Show* yielded one truly great reward: the meeting of his second wife Joy Senese. She worked as Joey Bishop's executive secretary and Philbin asked her out. Their wedding was March 1, 1970, at the chapel in Forest Lawn Cemetery in Los Angeles. As strange as that sounds, Philbin mentioned in *I'm Only One Man* that the beauty of Forest Lawn's chapel was the reason the couple selected it. Regis and Joy later had two daughters.

Not Again!

In January 1974 Philbin's KHJ show was canceled leaving him unemployed. There were no openings on any Los Angeles stations, so Philbin set out across the country auditioning for new gigs. He finally got a break in June 1974 as temporary morning host for *A.M. Chicago*, a mixture of news and talk. He spent the summer hoping to be made permanent host but was bypassed in favor of someone else that fall.

By the end of the year, Philbin was at the end of his rope when he was offered a job doing movie reviews for KABC-TV in Los Angeles. KABC subsequently launched *A.M. Los Angeles* in January 1975 and paired Philbin as co-host with Sarah Purcell. Using his simple format of informal chatting with Purcell about their personal lives and interviewing guests, the show burned up the morning ratings in southern California.

Howdy Neighbor

In December 1975 Philbin received a third chance at national stardom, this time as a game show host. ABC unveiled *The Neighbors*, a game where five women, all of whom lived in the same neighborhood in real life, competed. Two of the women played as contestants while the other three composed a panel. Philbin read a statement to one of the two contestants. The player's job was to guess if that bit of information pertained to her or to one of her three neighbors sitting on the panel. Contestants scored $25 for each correct guess.

In round two, Philbin read gossipy tidbits about the two players and they guessed which of the three neighbors made those statements. Matching the statements to the correct neighbors was worth $100 apiece. In the final round, Philbin read one more piece of gossip and the players guessed which one of the women was the subject of that statement. The player with the most money won the game.

The Neighbors never set the woods on fire and ABC stopped the game on April 9, 1976, after 15 weeks. Philbin actually worked triple duty (he continued hosting *A.M. Los Angeles*) that spring because ABC hired him as one of the four hosts of *Almost Anything Goes*. This primetime entry pitted three teams of contestants from around the country in a series of athletic events ranging from egg balancing to obstacle courses. After ABC canceled *Almost Anything Goes* in May 1976, Philbin left the game show world (as a host) for almost 25 years.

The Art of Complaining

For the next five years, *A.M. Los Angeles* continued as a ratings juggernaut and Philbin's star continued to shine. The opening banter of each show where Philbin and Sarah Purcell (later replaced by Cyndy Garvey) chatted about their private lives and personal opinions was the secret to the show's success. Viewers loved to watch Philbin complain about everyday life because it was funny and he knew how to poke fun at himself. He made it an art.

By 1981 those high numbers caught the attention of NBC president Grant Tinker, who contacted Philbin about hosting a daytime talkfest. Since Philbin's KABC contract was about to end, he jumped at his fourth chance at national fame. *The Regis Philbin Show* debuted as a taped 30 minute affair on November 30, 1981, but once again he could not capture a large audience with the shorter format. NBC axed the show in April 1982 and Philbin was again out of work. He could not go back to *A.M. Los Angeles* because KABC management was angry at him for leaving the show to go national. For all practical purposes, Philbin's career in California seemed dead.

Going Home

After losing his NBC show, Philbin learned that the newly formed Lifetime Network was in need of new programming. With his wife Joy, they developed *Regis Philbin's Health Styles*, a show about fitness, and cooking. Despite a meager production budget and the fact that the Lifetime Network was not carried on many cable systems around the country at the time, the show lasted six years. Philbin was not altogether happy with this assignment. He missed his morning gabfests on television, but there were no opportunities knocking at his door.

Finally in January 1983 Philbin received a call about hosting a new morning show on WABC-TV in his hometown: New York City. He signed a one year deal to host *The Morning Show* with his former *A.M. Los Angeles* co-host Cyndy Garvey. By the end of that first year, the ratings on WABC-TV were on the rise and Philbin signed a new four year contract. Kathie Lee Gifford succeeded Garvey as co-host in 1985 as the ratings continued to climb.

Live! With Regis and Kathie Lee

In 1988 Philbin turned 57 years old, but he had good reason to celebrate. After five years as a local show, *The Morning Show* was going national. That fall, the newly renamed *Live! With Regis and Kathie Lee* moved into syndication and handily won its time slot in most markets. For Philbin, fifth time was the charm and he finally hit the big time to stay.

Each morning, Philbin and Gifford opened the show at 9:00 a.m. with informal chatter. Philbin used his trademark complaining about everyday life and how it seemed that the world was out to get him. Gifford effectively counterpunched his needling. Some of Philbin's funniest gripes included his inability to figure out cell phones, fax machines, computers, or just about anything mechanical.

His wife, Joy, was often the subject for family gripes. She received her chance to poke back at Philbin during the occasions she substituted for Gifford as co-host. The audiences laughed and ate it up. There were also daily guests who stopped by to promote their latest movies, books, to help with cooking segments, or to participate in a comical routine with Philbin often the butt of the joke.

There were also some serious moments. In 1993 when Philbin suffered chest pains and underwent an angioplasty to clear a blocked artery, he shared his experience on *Live!* To his surprise, a number of viewers wrote letters telling him that he helped them recognize the symptoms of heart disease and saved their lives.

Over the next decade, Philbin enjoyed success with the show, but by the late 1990s, he seemed restless again. He was not tired of his daily chores on *Live!* but since he was done with work at 10:00 a.m. each morning, he had nothing to do for the rest of the day. Philbin told *TV Guide* in 1999 that Joy was tired of having him around the house for most of the day after work. Since he had no real hobbies, she told him that he needed to find something to do with his afternoons. That answer came in short order.

Let's Play for a Million

In the spring of 1999, ABC announced something unheard of in years: they were adding a game show to their primetime schedule that summer. The new game show offered a top prize of $1 million to anyone who could answer 15 multiple choice questions in a row without missing any along the way.

When Philbin heard about *Who Wants to Be a Millionaire?* he immediately told ABC that he was interested in hosting it. ABC executives were cool to the idea, but Philbin persisted until they gave him the chance. His game show, *The Neighbors*, had been a flop in the 1970s and Philbin's talk show personality seemed out of place on a game show. Nevertheless, he proved to be exactly what the show needed. Philbin provided light banter with his contestants by toning down the loud complaining that carried his daytime series. He fooled all of the critics and proved to be a capable host.

Who Wants to Be a Millionaire? had been a popular game show in the United Kingdom before ABC gave it a try in America. Executive Producer Michael Davies originally wanted to revive the mega-hit 1950s quiz show, *The $64,000 Question* for ABC, but decided to develop *Millionaire* instead. Both shows were similar in format: contestants, playing one at a time, answered a series of progressively harder questions doubling in value for a large payoff. Unlike *The $64,000 Question*, contestants on *Millionaire* sat with the host at the center of the stage rather than stand inside an isolation booth.

The game began with 10 contestants participating in the "Fastest Finger" round. Philbin posed a question requiring four answers to be placed in sequence. The player who correctly placed all four items in sequence in the shortest time advanced to the "hot seat." The simple game presented 15 general knowledge questions worth from $100 to $1,000,000. The player selected one of four possible answers for each question and won the corresponding dollar amount. The contestant could quit and keep his/her winnings or risk it all on the next question.

Is That Your Final Answer?

There was no time limit to answer and Philbin told *TV Guide* in 1999 that one contestant took 14 minutes to answer. Eight of those minutes were deleted from the tape for broadcast. Aiding the contestants during the game were three "lifelines" that could be used anytime. One was called "50-50" where two of the incorrect answers were eliminated from the possible four. Another gave the player the option of "Asking the Audience." The audience voted which of the remaining answers they thought was correct. The third lifeline was "Phone a Friend." The player could telephone a friend at home and ask for assistance.

Who Wants to Be a Millionaire? began with a 13-night run in August 1999 and became the hit of the summer. ABC scheduled another 15 night run during the ratings sweeps period in November 1999 where the ratings soared. The show also crowned its first millionaire on November 21, 1999, when John Carpenter went all the way to the top. A regular berth on ABC's prime-time schedule was a sure bet and beginning on January 8, 2000, *Who Wants to Be a Millionaire?* aired three nights every week. By the end of the 1999-2000 season, the game show was a top ten attraction.

Philbin often joked that he saved ABC because of the show. In *Who Wants to Be Me?* Philbin said that it began during an interview on *Larry King Live* one evening. King asked him why he was hosting the game. Philbin joked that he was there to save ABC, but the punch line hit the media and caught the fancy of the viewers.

Who Wants to Watch?

By the fall of 2000, *Who Wants to Be a Millionaire?* could be seen four nights per week by an average of 13.6 million viewers. It started a wave of new big money game shows that had not been seen since the 1950s and that trend continues today. A number of special *Millionaire* episodes where celebrities played for charity began in the spring of 2000. Within months, one or two of the four weekly shows were devoted to celebrity players. Whether or not ABC burned the show out by running it four nights per week or because there were too many celebrity episodes or a combination of the two is up for debate. In either case, by the fall of 2001, the future of *Who Wants to Be a Millionaire?* was bleak.

Ratings dropped to 7.8 million viewers and ABC reduced the show to twice per week. By the spring of 2002, the once powerful game was down to only Thursday nights. Executive producer Michael Davies announced a new daily half hour syndicated edition of *Who Wants to Be a Millionaire?* available to local stations for the fall of 2002. Philbin was offered the job to host the new show, but declined since he was already seen each weekday morning on *Live!* Meredith Viera, one of the hosts of ABC's *The View*, became host of the daytime version.

On June 27, 2002, Philbin hosted a special 90 minute sendoff of *Who Wants to Be a Millionaire?* on ABC. The daytime version premiered in September 2002 with healthy ratings, definite proof that the show had staying power.

Let's Raise the Stakes

Although the primetime version was gone, ABC kept *Who Wants to Be a Millionaire?* on the back burner as a possible midseason replacement show or as a series of specials. Not until February 2004 did the show return to primetime. Philbin came back to host a special week of new shows called *Who Wants to Be a Super Millionaire?* with a possible jackpot of $10 million. ABC aired two rounds of specials from February 22–27, 2004, and May 16–23, 2004.

Got Talent?

More recently in the summer of 2006, Philbin found himself hosting *America's Got Talent*, NBC's answer to *American Idol*. After a successful summer run, NBC announced plans to bring the show back during 2007. Overall, Philbin has, and is having, an extraordinary run. His morning series *Live!* continues drawing the viewers as Philbin trades barbs with co-host Kelly Ripa, who replaced Kathie Lee Gifford in 2001.

Away from the cameras, Philbin lives with his wife Joy in a New York City apartment and a country home in Connecticut. He enjoys playing tennis, but describes himself a poor loser since he has demolished several rackets over the years. He enjoys cooking, though he remarked in *Who Wants to Be Me?* that he has difficulty operating a grill. Regis Philbin may be limited in mechanical abilities or Tennis matches, but there is no doubt that he has "got talent."

Gene Rayburn

Birth Name: Eugene Rubessa
Born: December 22, 1917, in Christopher, Illinois
Died: November 29, 1999, in Gloucester, Massachusetts
Marriage and Family: Helen Tickner: (1940–1996) (Deceased) 1 daughter
Military Career: United States Army Air Force (1942–1945)
Radio Career: *The Rayburn and Finch Show* (WNEW-AM, New York) 1946–1953; *Monitor* (NBC) 1961–1973
TV Career: ANNOUNCER—*Tonight* (NBC Late Night) September 27, 1954–January 25, 1957; *The Steve Allen Show* (NBC Primetime) June 24, 1956–June 7, 1959   HOST—*Where Are You From?* (Unsold NBC Game Show Pilot) October 1953; *Bright Ideas* (WNBT-TV, New York City) November 16, 1953–February 26, 1954; *The Sky's the Limit* (WNBC-TV, New York City) November 1, 1954–December 27, 1955; *Make the Connection* (NBC Primetime) August 4, 1955–September 29, 1955; *Choose Up Sides* (NBC Saturday Mornings) January 7, 1956–March 31, 1956; *Tic Tac Dough* (NBC Daytime) September 13, 1956–February 8, 1957; *Dough Re Mi* (NBC Daytime) February 24, 1958–December 30, 1960; *Head of the Class* (Unsold NBC Game Show Pilot) 1960; *Miss Universe Pageant* (Annually) 1961–1965; *Play Your Hunch* (NBC Daytime) October 15, 1962–November 16, 1962; *The Match Game* (NBC Daytime) December 31, 1962–September 26, 1969; *Amateur's Guide to Love* (CBS Daytime) March 27, 1972–June 23, 1972; *Celebrity Match Mates* (Unsold Game Show Pilot) 1972; *Match Game '73–'79* (CBS Daytime) July 2, 1973–April 20, 1979; *Match Game P.M.* (Syndicated) September 8, 1975–September 1981; *Match Game* (Syndicated) September 1979–September 1982; *It Happened Right Here* (WCVB-TV, Boston, MA) March 16, 1982–September 1982; Party Line (*Unsold NBC Game Show Pilot) 1983;* Match Game–Hollywood Squares Hour (NBC Daytime) October 31, 1983–July 27, 1984; Break the Bank (Syndicated) September 16, 1985–December 20, 1985; The Movie Masters (AMC) August 2, 1989–January 19, 1990

Broadway Career: *Bye Bye Birdie* (1961–1962); *Come Blow Your Horn* (1962); *Aqua Carnival* (1962)
Stage Career: *Will Success Spoil Rock Hunter?* (1957); *The Love of Four Colonels* (1957); *Who Was That Lady I Saw You With?* (1959); *Under the Yum-Yum Tree* (1962); *The Impossible Years* (1966); *A Christmas Carol* (1981); *La Cage aux Folles* (1991); *Sugar Babies*
Other Career: NBC Studio Page, Rockefeller Center, New York (1936–1939)

Gene Rayburn had a personal credo that he followed in his professional and personal life: never stop the tape.

Gene Rayburn (Gene Rayburn, courtesy Fred Wostbrock)

One of the things game shows are famous for is the unplanned moment when the unexpected happens. Contestants may say totally outrageous things, props on the show's set may fail to work, the director may keep the camera rolling when the program is going to the commercial forcing the host to keep talking, or the poor host may accidentally say something inappropriate and embarrass the contestant. All of these things happened to Rayburn. Through it all, the video-tape captured every spontaneous and unscripted moment. Spontaneity was only one of the many secrets in Rayburn's bag of tricks.

Born as Eugene Rubessa to Croatian parents in Christopher, Illinois on December 22, 1917, Rayburn dreamed of being an opera singer as a youth. After attending Knox College in Galesburg, Illinois for one year, Rayburn dropped out and moved to New York City to study opera. When he could not afford to take voice lessons, he went all around town hunting for theatrical work. Just when he ran out of money, a friend helped him get a job on NBC's page-and-guide staff.

Rubessa Becomes Rayburn

That was 1936 when Rayburn began working for NBC as a studio page and tour guide. Upon discovering that the network operated a school for announcers, he studied broadcasting. He adopted a new surname figuring that his birth name, Eugene Rubessa, would be difficult for people to remember. Opening a New York City telephone book, he blindly pointed to a name. The name he happened to finger was Rayburn.

In 1939 he landed his first radio job in Newburgh, New York. He later worked at radio stations in Baltimore and Philadelphia before going back to New York as an announcer for WNEW-AM. On New Year's Day 1940, Rayburn married Helen Tickner, whom he had met while working as an NBC page. They had one daughter, Lynn, who was born in 1942 shortly before Rayburn joined the U.S. Army Air Force and trained to be a bombardier during the Second World War.

After his discharge in 1945, Rayburn returned to WNEW radio doing a morning show with Jack Lescoulie. In 1946 Lescoulie was replaced by Dee Finch and the show was renamed *The Rayburn and Finch Show*. For the next seven years, Rayburn and Finch had one of the most popular radio shows in the New York City area. Rayburn used this opportunity to polish his skills as a comedian.

A Bright Idea

In 1953 Rayburn and Finch received an offer to take their show to television on the local NBC affiliate WNBT-TV. Finch declined the offer, but Rayburn decided to try his luck as a single. Rayburn's first television show was a daily 15 minute series of advice on better living called *Bright Ideas*, which went on the air in November 1953.

When the show flopped after a few months, WNBT tried to fire Rayburn. Since he had an exclusive contract, Rayburn's job was spared. The station assigned Rayburn to host a new children's game show called *The Sky's the Limit*. The show featured contestants playing in a series of question and answer rounds and completing comical stunts for prizes.

"Sudden Death"

Rayburn moved to national television in September 1954 as the announcer/sidekick on NBC's *Tonight Show* with Steve Allen as the first host. As the announcer, Rayburn participated in comedy skits playing such characters as a drowning man doing a Life Savers commercial and a mad surgeon carving up a skeleton. In addition to the comedy roles, Rayburn delivered a short news summary each night.

As part of his job, Rayburn warmed up the studio audience before *The Tonight Show* went on the air live. One of his favorite warm-up gags was the "Sudden Death" routine, which he described in a 1956 *TV Guide* interview. Rayburn began by asking the audience if anyone could not see the stage. Whenever someone raised their hand, he would pull a gun out of his pocket and fire a round of blanks at the person. The routine never failed to bring down the house.

Choose Up Sides

Away from *The Tonight Show* and *The Sky's the Limit*, Rayburn served as a panelist on *The Name's the Same* during the 1954-1955 season. In the summer of 1955 he briefly hosted *Make the Connection*, a game where four panelists tried to determine the connection, or the circumstances, that brought two or more contestants together. Rayburn returned to television in January 1956 with a Saturday morning children's game show called *Choose Up Sides* where two teams composed of four kids competed in a series of stunts to see who could accomplish the feat in the shortest amount of time.

In the summer of 1956, Rayburn joined Steve Allen as his announcer when Allen launched his own primetime variety hour for NBC. Allen and Rayburn remained with *The Tonight Show*, but cut back their appearances to Wednesday through Friday since Allen's variety show aired on Sunday nights. The Monday and Tuesday programs of *The Tonight Show* were hosted by comedian Ernie Kovacs. Rayburn also acted in some dramas on *Robert Montgomery Presents* and did commercials for *Playwrights '56*, an NBC anthology series, and the Sunday afternoon documentary show *Wide Wide World*. He also did some summer stock theater work.

Allen and Rayburn remained with *The Tonight Show* until January 1957 when they left to concentrate on Allen's variety series. Meanwhile, Rayburn filled in for Jack Barry as the Friday host of NBC's *Tic Tac Dough* until breaking his leg in a skiing accident in February 1957. Barry hosted the show Monday through Thursday, but since he was also hosting *Twenty-One* on Thursday evenings, he was given a breather on Friday. Working on *Tic Tac Dough* helped Rayburn get his foot in the door with Barry-Enright Productions.

"He Managed to Coax It Along"

In 1958, Barry and Enright tapped Rayburn to host *Dough Re Mi*. This musical game called for three contestants to identify songs played by the orchestra. Each player started the game with $200 and the orchestra played the first three notes of a tune. The players bid portions of their bankrolls for the right to hear the fourth note. Players continued bidding until a bell sounded or until nobody wanted to bid any higher. The player bidding the most listened to the fourth note. If he/she correctly identified the song, they collected $100. If incorrect, the player could challenge one of the other two contestants to name the song. If the challenged player answered incorrectly, the challenger collected $50. Three songs were played in each round worth $100, $300, and $500.

> **Robert Noah (Dough Re Mi** *executive producer, June 2006 telephone interview):*
> "Gene was good on it, but the show itself was not the greatest. He managed to coax it along."

Rayburn injected as much humor into the show as he could by singing songs, tap dancing, and doing an opening monologue each day.

On Radio and Broadway

In 1961 Rayburn became one of the rotating hosts of the NBC radio series *Monitor*, which was a combination of news, music, skits, and chatter. He remained with this series for the next 12 years. Rayburn also hosted the annual *Miss Universe Pageant* from 1961 to 1965 when he turned the show over to Bob Barker.

In a change of pace, Rayburn hit the Broadway stage in 1961 replacing Dick Van Dyke as the star of *Bye Bye Birdie*. He later toured in the musical comedy *Come Blow Your Horn* and the short-lived *Aqua Carnival* in 1962. Throughout his career, Rayburn enjoyed acting, but those opportunities were very few.

> *Howard Felsher (TV producer, June 2006 telephone interview):*
> "I remember liking [Gene] a great deal. He was a very funny man and he was kind of lost because he didn't become the big star that he wanted to be. He was kind of disappointed. If you yourself wanted to write the great American novel and you couldn't do it, wouldn't you be disappointed? He wanted to be a star like Marlon Brando. Not like a he-man, but he wanted to walk down the street and everybody recognize him."

I Have a Hunch

Returning to game shows in October 1962, Rayburn took over hosting *Play Your Hunch*, a Goodson-Todman effort that had been on the air four years. The original host was Merv Griffin and the show involved four contestants divided into two teams solving a group of problems or answering questions. The players were given three possible answers which were labeled "X," "Y," and "Z."

When Rayburn took over from Griffin as host of *Play Your Hunch*, the ratings declined according to producer Ira Skutch in his 1989 book *I Remember Television*. *Play Your Hunch* lost five points of its rating and the network insisted on another emcee. Rayburn was replaced by Robert Q. Lewis.

Making a Match

Despite being fired from the show, the timing was fortuitous for Rayburn. Goodson-Todman Productions introduced a new show called *The Match Game*. Ira Skutch pulled for Rayburn, persuaded Mark Goodson to give him a chance as host, and *Match Game* premiered on December 31, 1962.

On *The Match Game*, two teams composed of a celebrity and two contestants were asked questions such as "Name a brand of cereal." The team members secretly wrote down their answers on cards. If two players matched answers the team scored 25 points and if all three players matched, the answer was worth 50 points. One hundred points won the game and the team played the bonus round called "Audience Match." Here the team guessed how members of the studio audience responded to questions. There was also a home game where Rayburn telephoned a viewer and asked a question. The viewer tried to match his/her answer with a selected member from the studio audience.

The Match Game picked up steam during its first season and was one of NBC's most popular daytime shows. It dominated the 4:00 p.m. slot for the next seven years. In a move the network later regretted, *The Match Game* was canceled in September 1969 even though it was still beating its competition. Rayburn stayed in the limelight with guest appearances as a panelist on *What's My Line?* and *To Tell the Truth* during the early 1970s. He also worked the weekends hosting *Monitor* for NBC radio.

Professional and Personal Setbacks

In 1970 Rayburn and his wife moved to the Osterville section of Barnstable, Massachusetts near Cape Cod. Unfortunately this period brought some tough times for Rayburn. A car accident near his home in November 1970 put Rayburn in the hospital with cuts and bruises.

In March 1972 he returned to television with the CBS comedy game show *Amateur's Guide to Love*. Guest celebrities went to various locations in southern California involving average citizens in humorous situations that were recorded by a hidden camera. The unsuspecting victim was placed in a situation requiring him/her to make a decision on love and marriage. A celebrity panel in the studio watched the taped segments and voted on how the subject should best handle the situation.

Robert Noah (AGTL producer):
"It was an impossible assignment. The show was just too hard to do in those days on a day-time budget. [We did] two [recorded] spots a day, 10 spots a week, on a very small game show budget. It couldn't be done right."

For Rayburn, the show was too constricting for his freewheeling personality.

RN:
"He was in a strait jacket because so much of the game was on tape."

Not surprising, *Amateur's Guide to Love* left the air after 13 weeks. Shortly after the series ceased production, a three-alarm fire destroyed Rayburn's three story Osterville home on June 6, 1972.

RN:
"He had just finished building it. It broke his heart."

Rebuilding Home and Career

Rayburn and his family built a new home and remained near Cape Cod. During the 1972-1973 season, he appeared as a semi-regular panelist on the syndicated revival of *I've Got a Secret* hosted by Steve Allen. Rayburn also hosted *Celebrity Match Mates*, a failed game show pilot that later aired under the title *Tattletales* with Bert Convy as host.

Rayburn finally got a break when Goodson-Todman reactivated *The Match Game* and brought him back to host the festivities. The show was overhauled to include two contestants and six celebrities and was renamed *Match Game '73* to distinguish it from the original version. *Match Game '73* bowed over CBS on July 2, 1973. In the beginning, the questions were much like the ones in the 1960s version with the humor coming from mismatched answers and the celebrities clowning around.

Rayburn thought that the show needed more comedy, so he began injecting his spontaneous humor much to the chagrin of Mark Goodson. Some of it included touches of slapstick comedy.

Burt Dubrow (TV producer, May 2006 telephone interview):
"Gene told me that, originally, Mark Goodson did not want him to be walking around [on the set], and he wanted him to stay put. I don't know if that show would have worked if Gene had stayed put. I think it took Gene awhile to convince Goodson of what he wanted."

Rayburn's ideas slowly took hold. Several weeks into the run, the questions changed to include double-entendre humor such as, "Herman's ____ looks like a prune," or "Captain Hook lost his ____ on the poop deck."

"It Was Like a Party"

Within months, *Match Game '73* was the number one-rated daytime show. Rayburn and his celebrity panelists, including regulars Richard Dawson, Brett Somers, and Charles Nelson Reilly, became the toast of the town. The comedy resulting from the great chemistry between Rayburn and the celebrities was the glue that held the show together.

Ira Skutch (Match Game producer, February 2006 telephone interview):
"That was a wonderful family affair. We all got along well together. I would say almost 95 percent of the stars who did it really enjoyed it and looked forward to coming back. That was the whole essence of that show. It was like a party."

Unplanned Moments

For the viewers, it was the unplanned moments that made the show funny and popular. One embarrassing incident that did not air with the original episode in 1974 has consistently made the rounds of blooper specials. Rayburn introduced a lady contestant at the start of the game and meant to compliment her beautiful dimples when she smiled. Instead, Rayburn accidentally said, "Doesn't she have pretty nipples?"

A winning team: Charles Nelson Reilly, Brett Somers, Gene Rayburn, and Richard Dawson on the set of *Match Game '73* **(Gene Rayburn, courtesy Fred Wostbrock).**

In another show, Rayburn tossed to a commercial break, but show director Marc Breslow decided to keep the camera on Rayburn forcing him to continue ad-libbing. Finally he jumped off the stage, climbed over the audience in their seats, and put his hand over the lens on the camera at the back of the studio. On still another episode, Rayburn made his entrance by knocking down the sliding doors on the set rather than waiting for the doors to open for him.

> *Burt Dubrow:*
> "I don't think there was anybody on television that could control six celebrities, two civilians, and that game and keep it going to that degree. The moment that camera went on, he turned on [the energy]. He was not the same guy on camera as he was off. Off camera he was quieter. I would call him a bit of an intellect. He knew just a little bit about everything and he was fairly serious. On camera, he was just up and high as a kite."

A Popular Match

One of the highlights of the show was the annual New Year's Eve episode where elaborate ceremonies were held to formally change the show's name to reflect a new year. After 1973, the show was titled *Match Game '74, '75,* and so forth.

In 1975 the producers launched *Match Game P.M.,* for nighttime syndication. The questions were considerably racier than the daytime series, which only enhanced the show's popularity. Rayburn flew back and forth between his Cape Cod home and Los Angeles to tape the series. He

A cameraman cues Gene Rayburn on *Match Game '73* (Gene Rayburn, courtesy Fred Wostbrock).

flew to California every other Friday to tape six episodes of the show on Saturday and another six on Sunday. Then he flew home on Mondays. After awhile, the commute began to wear on Rayburn so he and his wife Helen maintained an apartment in Los Angeles where they lived a few months out of the year.

CBS Fumbles the Match

In late 1977, CBS moved *Match Game '77* to the mornings and the ratings began falling. Much of the show's audience consisted of teenagers who routinely watched the game each afternoon upon coming home from school. After three months, CBS switched the show back to the afternoons, but the damage was done. By then it was pre-empted by stations for local programming in many markets. The daytime version faded on April 20, 1979.

The show's evening version continued pulling strong ratings and audience response prompted Goodson-Todman to re-launch the daytime version in syndication. Both versions of the show continued until 1981 when *Match Game P.M.* departed leaving only the daytime series.

The End of the Match

By the ninth season, *Match Game* was showing its age. Rayburn had grown increasingly weary of the Los Angeles commute. *Match Game* was finally canceled in 1982 after nine years on the air. Rayburn, in the meantime, began searching for work closer to home.

In the spring of 1982, he co-hosted a short-lived Boston human interest series called *It Happened Right Here* for station WCVB-TV. Each show featured unusual people performing incredible feats such as a man lying on a bed of nails as assistants piled 1,100 pounds of concrete on his chest. Rayburn also became co-owner and operator of a roller skating rink in Hyannis, Massachusetts. Having a lifelong interest in skating, he and his wife found a roller skating rink in the San Fernando Valley during the 1970s and began skating there regularly during their California visits.

A Misbegotten Show

In October 1983 Rayburn returned to television joining Jon Bauman as co-host of NBC's *The Match Game–Hollywood Squares Hour*. Two contestants played *The Match Game* for the first half hour using the same format as the 1970s version. The winner of this segment faced the previous day's champion in the *Hollywood Squares* portion of the show. When the *Hollywood Squares* segment began, three more stars were added to the set to form the tic tac toe board. The winner of the *Hollywood Squares* round played the Super Match for a chance to win up to $30,000. Rayburn hosted the *Match Game* portions of the show while co-host Jon Bauman played as one of the six panelists. During the *Hollywood Squares* segment, Rayburn and Bauman traded places with Rayburn playing as a celebrity square.

The Match Game–Hollywood Squares Hour finished dead last in the ratings for its time slot. It was canceled after 39 weeks on July 27, 1984.

> *Ira Skutch:*
> "That whole thing was misbegotten. They (Mark Goodson Productions) tried to marry two things that didn't marry terribly well. One of the reasons I left Goodson-Todman was because of that [show]. When they were putting it together, I felt very strongly that Gene should emcee the entire show. It was a mistake to have two emcees. It made it look like two different shows. I don't think the show would have succeeded anyway, but I think that hurt it more than anything."

Short-Lived Comebacks

Rayburn tried again in the fall of 1985 with *Break the Bank*, a complex game of answering questions, guessing puzzles, and performing stunts. As he had done on many occasions, Rayburn turned on the spontaneous humor. This time, however, it failed to turn the trick. Rayburn was dismissed from the show in December 1985 and replaced him with Joe Farago, but *Break the Bank* was gone by 1986.

After *Break the Bank*, the telephone stopped ringing for Rayburn as producers turned to younger people for hosting jobs. He retired to his home in Massachusetts where he enjoyed playing tennis and tending to his vegetable garden. He came out of retirement in 1989 to host one more show, *The Movie Masters*, for the American Movie Classics cable channel. Three celebrity panelists, playing for members of the home audience, answered movie trivia questions. Correct answers allowed the celebrity to view a portion of a scene from a famous movie. The first celebrity to identify the movie from the scene won prizes for his/her home player. *The Movie Masters* was broadcast on an infrequent basis during the 1989-1990 season.

Restless Retirement

Around this time, ABC announced a revival of *The Match Game* for its daytime schedule. Rayburn might well have returned as host if not for an unfortunate incident. In a July 1990 *Los Angeles Times* interview, Rayburn said that just prior to ABC's announcement of *The Match Game* revival, the show *Entertainment Tonight* aired a birthday greeting for Rayburn and gave his real age (68 at the time). When producers and network executives learned that Rayburn was older than he looked, they went out of their way to avoid hiring him. In his place, the producers hired

Ross Shafer, the former host of FOX's *The Late Show*. The new version of *Match Game* only lasted the 1990-1991 season.

With no job offers, Rayburn was restless in retirement. Immersing himself in a variety of hobbies, he enjoyed growing his own vegetables, herbs, and flowers in a variety of gardens. He also kept physically fit by riding a bicycle, playing tennis, croquet, and cruising the roads near his home on his Honda motorcycle. His other talents included gourmet cooking, needlepoint, and woodworking.

He returned to acting in 1991 with *La Cage aux Folles* performing at the Bucks County Playhouse in New Hope, Pennsylvania. Rayburn had performed in a number of summer stock plays through the years whenever his schedule permitted. He continued to pop up periodically in game show reunion specials on talk shows during the 1990s. In 1994 he found a whole new generation of fans when Game Show Network began airing reruns of the 1970s version of *Match Game*. Just as it did for CBS two decades earlier, *Match Game* soon became the number-one rated series on GSN!

Lifetime Achievement

After the death of Rayburn's wife, Helen, in October 1996, his health steadily declined. He moved to Los Angeles in 1998 to be near his game show colleagues, but heart trouble soon forced him to move back east. In 1999 he moved in with his daughter at Gloucester, Massachusetts where she took care of him in his final months of life. On October 26, 1999, after years of neglect by the industry, Rayburn was finally honored with a Lifetime Achievement Award at the National Academy of Television Arts and Sciences.

Just over a month later, Gene Rayburn succumbed to congestive heart failure on November 29, 1999, at the age of 81. His well-rounded career in radio, television, and the stage caused Rayburn to have the same complaint of many hosts: that the public tended to brand him as just another game show host with no other talents.

> *Burt Dubrow:*
> "I don't think he died knowing how good he was. He was a broadcaster, and you don't have many of those left anymore. He just knew how to do it. He was just loads and loads of fun."

Pat Sajak

Birth Name: Patrick Sajak
Born: October 26, 1946, in Chicago, Illinois
Marriages and Family: Sherrill [last name unknown] (1977–1985) (Divorced) 1 stepson; Leslie Brown: (December 31, 1989–Present) 1 son, 1 daughter
Military Service: United States Army (1967–1970)
Radio Career: Newscaster (WEDC-AM, Chicago, Illinois) 1966–1967; Disc Jockey (WNBS-FM, Murray, Kentucky) 1971–1972; *The Pat Sajak Baseball Hour* (MLB Radio) 2002–Present
TV Career: HOST—Staff Announcer/Weatherman (WSM-TV, Nashville, Tennessee) 1972–1977; Weatherman (KNBC-TV, Los Angeles, CA) 1977–1982; *The Sunday Show* (KNBC-TV, Los Angeles, CA) July 22, 1979–January 10, 1982; *Puzzlers* (Unsold Game Show Pilot) 1979; *Press Your Luck* (Unsold Game Show Pilot) 1980; *Wheel of Fortune* (NBC Daytime) December 28, 1981–January 9, 1989, (Syndicated) September 12, 1983–Present; *The College Bowl* (NBC Primetime Special) May 23, 1984; *The Pat Sajak Show* (CBS Late Night) January 9, 1989–April 13, 1990; *Pat Sajak Weekend* (Fox News Channel) March 2, 2003–October 26, 2003; *Pat Sajak's American League Ballpark Tour* (Travel Channel) 2004; *Pat Sajak's National League Ballpark Tour* (Travel Channel) 2004; Producer: Black Jack Bowling (Taiwan & Slovenia); Run For the Money (Taiwan & Slovenia)
Theatrical Movie: *Airplane II: The Sequel* (1982)
Business Interests: Owner, WNAV-AM, Annapolis, Maryland (1998–Present); President, P.A.T. Productions, Los Angeles, Ca. (1998–Present); Co-owner, BoJak Records (2000–Present)
Other Careers: Desk Clerk, Madison Hotel, Washington, D.C. (1970–1971); Desk Clerk, Howard Johnson's Hotel, Nashville, TN (1972)

Pat Sajak (Fred Wostbrock)

Pat Sajak once noted that if he pitched the idea for *Wheel of Fortune* to a network today, executives would laugh at him. Take the premise of spinning a giant wheel and guessing letters to puzzles. Who would have thought that a show based on a simple game like Hangman could run for three decades? For more than a quarter of a century, Sajak has presided over the most popular syndicated series in America. Since 1984, *Wheel of Fortune* has set the record for the most consecutive seasons as the number one-rated syndicated show.

Pat Sajak was born in Chicago, Illinois on October 26, 1946. His father worked as a trucking foreman who loaded and unloaded cargo. Sajak decided that he was not interested in the trucking business after accompanying his father to work one day. He took an interest in show business after watching *The Tonight Show* with host Jack Paar. Using a wooden spoon as a make-believe microphone, Sajak practiced talking as if he were on the radio. In high school, however, he was shy and private, but still displayed his sense of humor. Upon graduation, Sajak attended Columbia College in Chicago.

In 1966 he took a job with WEDC-AM, a small 250 watt radio station located in a Cadillac showroom in Chicago. At WEDC, Sajak did a five minute newscast every hour between midnight and 6:00 a.m. The overnight programming was hosted by a Spanish disc jockey who spoke no English. Sajak, who spoke no Spanish, read the news in English.

"Good Morning Vietnam!"

In 1967 Sajak dropped out of Columbia College and enlisted in the United States Army. Hoping to be assigned to Armed Forces Radio, instead he worked as a finance clerk in Long Binh, which was 35 miles from Saigon in South Vietnam. After repeated attempts to get a transfer to radio duty, he wrote his former WEDC employer, Roman Pucinski, who just happened to be a member of the U.S. Congress. With Pucinski's help, Sajak was transferred to the Armed Forces Vietnam Network in Saigon where he worked as a radio disc jockey.

One of his assignments was the *Good Morning Vietnam* radio show where he played rock and roll music and began each show by shouting, "Good Morning, Vietnam!" This phrase became the title for a 1987 theatrical movie starring Robin Williams in which he played a U.S. soldier working in Vietnam radio.

As a military disc jockey, Sajak had to work under certain restrictions, but being the clown, he always found a way to get around some of the rules. A 1988 *Broadcasting* article told how Sajak frequently made sarcastic remarks that his fellow soldiers understood but the officers usually had no clue. One such example involved Sajak's program director, who ordered him to play Christmas tunes starting in October. Figuring that playing Christmas music so early would make the soldiers homesick, Sajak bent the rules by introducing rock tunes as Christmas songs.

In 1969 Sajak was transferred to a military base in Texas, but convinced a captain to move him to the Pentagon where he ran a slide projector used by Generals for war briefings. After his discharge in 1970, Sajak worked as a desk clerk at the Madison Hotel in Washington D.C. for about six months. Yearning to get back into radio, a friend told Sajak about a job opening at WNBS-AM, a 250 watt station located in Murray, Kentucky. At WNBS, Sajak worked as a disc jockey in the 7 p.m. to midnight shift.

Nashville Shenanigans

By 1972 Sajak was floundering. With no job prospects, Sajak headed for Nashville, Tennessee hoping to break into radio or television there. Instead he wound up working as a desk clerk for the Howard Johnson Hotel. After making the rounds of radio and television stations seeking employment, Sajak finally landed a job as a staff announcer at WSM-TV (now WSMV-TV).

Sajak started out announcing station breaks and eventually began substituting on a local talk show. He also filled in for the sports anchor and weatherman when needed. When the regular weekend weatherman resigned, Sajak took the position. His sense of humor shined at WSM-TV. He pulled hilarious stunts to jazz up otherwise mundane broadcasting duties.

One of Sajak's assignments was to read the job listings provided by the state labor department each morning. He related in a 1988 *Broadcasting* interview how on one occasion, he sank lower in his chair behind the desk after reading each listing until only the top of his head was showing. Sometimes he read the listings backwards.

Another of his favorite pranks was to put a good job listing in his pocket and not give out the telephone number. One evening, Sajak appeared on the station's late night movie by having someone superimpose his image in a small corner of the screen. Sajak then talked back to the characters in the movie. The occasional reprimands from his bosses never stopped Sajak from having fun.

Keeping Up the Shenanigans in L.A.

In 1977 executives from KNBC-TV in Los Angeles caught Sajak's on-air shenanigans and offered him a job as a weatherman. Sajak jumped at the chance and moved with his new bride Sherrill and his seven-year-old stepson to the west coast. Working in the second largest television market in the country did not change Sajak one bit.

His weather reports were filled with crazy antics such as forecasting Canadian cold fronts in Los Angeles. In 1988 Merv Griffin related the story to *The New York Times Magazine* of how he watched Sajak one night doing the weather with a bandage covering his right eye. When he came back from the commercial break, the bandage was over his left eye. Sajak continued with the weather forecast as if nothing had happened. He also hosted *The Sunday Show*, a weekly 90 minute magazine series on KNBC spotlighting the offbeat happenings in Los Angeles such as frying eggs on the sidewalk.

Too Low Key

Wanting to expand his horizons, Sajak began auditioning to host game shows. The first was a failed pilot for Goodson-Todman called *Puzzlers*. He followed in 1980 with the pilot *Press Your Luck*, which was based on the Simon electronic memory games sold in stores. *Press Your Luck* reached the air in 1983 with a whole different format and different host.

Sajak was criticized by producers for being too low key and not projecting enough energy and the result was that nobody would hire him. Producers wanted Sajak to yell and get excited when contestants won, but that was not his style. Sajak told the *New York Times Magazine* that after he had been in the business for a few years, producers started telling new hosts to tone down their style much in the way Sajak worked.

NBC Takes a Spin

In 1981 producer Merv Griffin was looking for someone to take over from Chuck Woolery as the host of NBC's *Wheel of Fortune*. At the time, the show was in last place in its time slot and on the brink of cancellation. Griffin had been watching Sajak's antics on KNBC-TV and thought he would be a natural host for *Wheel of Fortune*.

Griffin went to NBC to sell the network on Sajak as a game show host. NBC executives refused, fearing that Sajak did not have a big enough name for a network show. Griffin then used a more subtle approach. He threatened to stop taping of the show immediately unless NBC accepted Sajak. Since the network did not want to lose *Wheel of Fortune*, the executives relented, and on December 28, 1981, Sajak became the new host.

On *Wheel of Fortune*, three contestants spun a giant wheel for the right to guess letters and solve a puzzle. Guessing letters in the puzzle earned contestants money based on the spin of the wheel. Players who solved the puzzles earned the right to shop from a large gallery of prizes. *Wheel of Fortune* had started on NBC in January 1975 and had only been a moderate success.

A new bonus round was added to the game on Sajak's first episode. The winning contestant tried to solve one more puzzle for additional prizes. The player selected five consonants and one vowel and any of those letters appearing in the puzzle were revealed. The player then tried

An early publicity photo of Pat Sajak on *Wheel of Fortune* (Fred Wostbrock).

to guess the puzzle in 10 seconds or less. Susan Stafford, who had served as the co-hostess and letter turner on the show during Chuck Woolery's tenure, remained until October 1982 when she was replaced by Vanna White.

White was one of 200 women who auditioned for the role as letter turner. Some years before as a college student, she had written to audition as a contestant on *Wheel of Fortune* but was never selected. At her audition with Sajak, White was a little shaky, but she credited Sajak with helping her get through the ordeal.

Syndication: The Saving Grace

In 1983 Merv Griffin Productions President Murray Schwartz got the idea of syndicating *Wheel of Fortune* for nighttime viewing with much larger prizes than the daytime version. Since NBC owned the rights to syndicate the series, Schwartz made a deal with the network to extend its daytime contract in exchange for the syndication rights. King World bought the rights to distribute the series for $100,000.

Some of the changes for the nighttime series included raising the top dollar value on the wheel from $2,000, the current amount, to $5,000. The prize gallery was upgraded to include sable coats and luxury cars. The syndicated *Wheel of Fortune* launched on September 12, 1983, with only nine stations in the country carrying the show. Not a very good beginning.

The early ratings success in the first few weeks caused other stations to take notice. Within a few months, there were approximately 150 stations carrying the show and by April 1984, *Wheel of Fortune* had displaced *Family Feud* as the number one rated syndicated series in America. The success of the evening version boosted the ratings for the daytime counterpart on NBC. Part of the show's success was the simplicity of the game.

Other ingredients in the formula for *Wheel of Fortune's* success were Pat Sajak and Vanna White, who were now two of the most familiar faces on television. The high ratings of *Wheel of Fortune* allowed Sajak and White to branch out in the entertainment field. On May 23, 1984, Sajak hosted a one hour special on NBC celebrating the 30th anniversary of the long-running quiz show *College Bowl*. The college teams on the special competed for $20,000 in scholarship money. During the mid 1980s, Sajak co-hosted the *Macy's Thanksgiving Day Parades* and the *Tournament of Roses Parades* for NBC.

In the fall of 1987, *Wheel of Fortune's* producers tweaked the format of the syndicated version by dropping the shopping segment and letting the contestants keep the cash they won in each round. This change picked up the pace of the game considerably and allowed for more rounds of playing, thus allowing players to rack up more money. The bonus round allowed for winnings up to $25,000. The shopping segment remained on the daytime version because of a lower prize budget. *Wheel of Fortune* was the number one rated syndicated series through the late 1980s and paved the way for Sajak to try a new kind of television show.

Late Night Talk

In the spring of 1988, CBS announced that Sajak had signed to host a late night talk show for the network. For years, CBS had tried to compete against *The Tonight Show*, but was never successful. The network viewed Sajak as someone who could provide some competition. As a testament of the network's confidence, CBS gave him a two year contract guaranteeing him $60,000 a week and spent $4 million to build a new 280-seat studio for his show.

Sajak viewed running against Johnny Carson with a realistic attitude according to a 1990 *Newsweek* interview. He honestly did not think that he would beat Carson in the ratings, but noted that *The Pat Sajak Show* actually cost CBS a lot less than its previous programming of old sitcoms and police action shows that aired at 11:30 p.m.

With his new CBS deal in place, the question remained of what would happen to *Wheel of Fortune*? Contractually Sajak was forced to leave the daytime series since it was on NBC, a competing network. Since the popular nighttime edition was syndicated to individual stations, he could stay with that version.

CBS delayed the premiere of *The Pat Sajak Show* until early 1989 when Sajak's NBC contract expired. He hosted his last daytime episode of *Wheel of Fortune* on January 9, 1989, the same day that his new talk show premiered. Former football place kicker Rolf Benirschke became the new host of the NBC version and remained until it was canceled in June 1989.

Meanwhile, *The Pat Sajak Show* got off to a strong start during its opening weeks. Sajak kept the show non-controversial, opting instead to emphasize humor and interesting conversation. His guests were an assorted mix: actors Chevy Chase, John Forsythe, and Charlie Sheen, politician Barry Goldwater, and his *Wheel of Fortune* co-host Vanna White. Joining Sajak each night were bandleader Tom Scott and sidekick Dan Miller, who worked with Sajak at WSM-TV in Nashville.

The Pat Sajak Show's ratings began sliding after its first few weeks. Not only did the show fail to out-draw Johnny Carson in the ratings, but another talk show hosted by Arsenio Hall on FOX was luring away the younger viewers. Sajak's show was cut to 60 minutes in October 1989 and he began using guest hosts on the Friday episodes. A new set was introduced in early 1990 and Sajak dropped his opening monologue, but nothing seemed to work. CBS pulled the plug on *The Pat Sajak Show* on April 13, 1990.

A New Family

With his talk show gone, Sajak continued on *Wheel of Fortune*, which was still the top rated syndicated show. The show began taping episodes in major cities around the country. Sajak also started a new family life. His first marriage having ended in divorce in 1985, Sajak married Leslie Brown on December 31, 1989. The couple had a son and a daughter. A longtime fan of baseball, Sajak indulged his interest in the great American pastime when he filled in for Rex Barney as the stadium announcer for the Baltimore Orioles at Oriole Park in Maryland during the summer of 1992.

Since his wife was originally from Maryland, Sajak and his family bought a home in Severna Park, but he commuted to Los Angeles to tape *Wheel of Fortune* every few weeks. He began looking at opportunities to get involved in his new hometown. After turning down an offer to buy two Maryland radio stations, Sajak finally purchased station WNAV-AM in Annapolis in 1998.

It's Your Business

Sajak expanded his business interests further by launching P.A.T. Productions with his business partner Bob Burton to produce game and children's television shows. Before long, P.A.T. Productions had the game shows *Black Jack Bowling* and *Run for the Money* on the air in Taiwan and Slovenia. He also ventured into the music business forming Sajak Music Publishing and later BoJak Records to produce recordings for country artist Jude Johnstone in Nashville.

The *Wheel of Fortune* host continued stretching his legs into the new millennium. Sajak returned to the talk show desk as an occasional substitute on *Larry King Live*. In September 2001, Sajak starred as Felix Unger with his former Army buddy Joe Moore in a stage version of the Neil Simon comedy *The Odd Couple* at the Hawaii Theater in Honolulu. To Sajak, this was no first time experience as an actor. He had played a lawyer in a 1993 drama written by Moore and also staged in Hawaii.

Who's on First, What's on Second...

Taking his interviewing skills and coupling that with a big interest in baseball, Sajak launched a new radio talk show called *The Pat Sajak Baseball Hour* in 2002. The show is heard weekly on the Major League Baseball radio network. He also produced two specials for the Travel Channel: *Pat Sajak's American League Ballpark Tour* and *Pat Sajak's National League Ballpark Tour*. For these two specials, Sajak spotlighted famous stadiums around the country used by the baseball leagues. After 13 years of resisting several offers to do a regularly scheduled talk show, Sajak signed with Fox News Channel to host a one hour Sunday evening program. *Pat Sajak Weekend* debuted in March 2003 and featured Sajak interviewing a variety of guests. However, the show faded from view after just seven months.

In the spring of 2005, Sajak took his love of baseball a step further by becoming part owner of The Golden Baseball League, a new minor league incorporating seven teams in California and Arizona. Sajak threw out the first ceremonial baseball pitch to start the new league at its first game in Surprise, Arizona on May 26, 2005. He then served as the first baseman coach for the first inning.

Not Quite Sure

Of all the accomplishments in Sajak's lifetime, nothing has topped his phenomenal run as host of *Wheel of Fortune*. He dismisses any thoughts that he is the reason for the longevity of *Wheel of Fortune* adding that the game itself is the shining star. During a visit to New Orleans in 2005, Sajak told the *Times-Picayune* that after 24 years of hosting *Wheel of Fortune*, he figured that most viewers would be tired of him. Since they still watched him, he joked that it said something about him, but whatever it was, he was not quite sure.

PETER TOMARKEN

Birth Name: Peter David Tomarken

Born: December 7, 1942, in Olean, New York

Died: March 13, 2006, in Santa Monica, California

Marriages and Family: Dana Jones (1963–1991) (Divorced) 1 son, 2 daughters; Kathleen Eastman (1993–2006) (Deceased)

TV Career: ACTOR—*The Secret Empire* (NBC Primetime) February 27, 1979–May 1, 1979 HOST—*Rodeo Drive* (Unsold Game Show Pilot) October 1980; *Duel In the Daytime* (Unsold NBC Game Show Pilot) August 1981; *Hit Man* (NBC Daytime) January 3, 1983–April 1, 1983; *Press Your Luck* (CBS Daytime) September 19, 1983–September 26, 1986; *The Hollywood Reporter* (Unsold Entertainment News Show Pilot) December 1985; *The Extra Censory World of Char* (Unsold ABC Human Interest Pilot) May 23, 1987; *Bargain Hunters* (ABC Daytime) July 6, 1987–September 4, 1987; *Wipeout* (Syndicated) September 12, 1988–September 8, 1989; *TKO* (Unsold Game Show Pilot) November 1989; *Monopoly* (Unsold Game Show Pilot) 1989; *Live Wire* (Unsold NBC Game Show Pilot) January 1990; *2 Heads Are Better Than One* (Unsold Game Show Pilot) October 1990; *Prime Games* (Game Show Network) December 1994–December 1996; *Decades* (Game Show Network) February 1995–December 1996; *Paranoia* (Fox Family Channel) April 14, 2000–May 7, 2000; *Whammy: The All-New Press Your Luck* (GSN Pilot) 2002 PRODUCER/DIRECTOR—*America's Funniest People* (ABC) 1991–1992; *Real Stories of the Highway Patrol* (Syndicated) 1992–1994

Non-Broadcast Shows (Host): Luxor Live (Las Vegas, NV) 1990–2000; *The $25,000 Game Show* (Pigeon Forge, TN) 1997–1998

Theatrical Movies: *Heaven Can Wait* (1978); *Haunted* (1998); *Divorce: The Musical* (2002); *19 at 11* (2004)

Made-For-TV Movies: *Secrets* (ABC) February 20, 1977; *The Awakening of Candra* (CBS) December 16, 1983; *Running Mates* (HBO) October 4, 1992

Other Careers: Clothing Editor, *Daily News Record & Women's Wear Daily* (1964–1965); Writer, *House and Home Magazine* (1965–1966); Public Relations Work, Larwin Company, Los Angeles, CA (1966–1968); Vice President of Public Relations, Great Southwest, Los Angeles, CA (1968–1972); President, OTB Advertising, Los Angeles, CA (1972–1975); Television Commercial Director (1975–1979); Partner, John Aaroe & Associates Real Estate Brokerage, Los Angeles, CA (1998–2000); Owner & Operator, T&S Construction/T&S Financial/T&S Realtors, Los Angeles, CA (2000–2006)

Peter Tomarken (Peter Tomarken, courtesy Fred Wostbrock)

One of the biggest reasons Americans watch game shows is to see an average Joe get on television and win lots of money. In the 1980s, greed was the way to go and making big money was a way of life. What better way to make some fast money than to appear on a game show! Get on a show, answer some questions, and win the dough. It looks simple enough, but looks can be deceiving. However, there was one contestant who figured out a way to legally beat the system, humiliate a major television network, and walk away with over $100,000 in cash in just a little over an hour. The host who presided over that major television event was Peter Tomarken, who had no idea that he was taking part in a historical event that would be remembered in game show circles for years to come.

Peter David Tomarken was born in Olean, New York on December 7, 1942. Tomarken and his two brothers Edward and James moved with their parents to Los Angeles in 1950 where the family operated a jewelry store. When he was about 12 years old, Tomarken got his first job as, of all things, a watch winder in his parents' store.

Peter Tomarken (March 2005 telephone interview):
"On Saturdays I would go down and wind the watches, clean the diamonds and clean the cases."

Sadly, his father committed suicide when Tomarken was a teenager leaving his mother to care for the three boys.

Writing

Yearning to become a writer, Tomarken enrolled at the University of California in Los Angeles. During his college years, he married his girlfriend, Dana Jones, in 1963. By the time he graduated with a degree in English the next year, Tomarken and his new bride were off to New York City where he landed a job as a clothing editor for the newspapers *Women's Wear Daily* and *The Daily News Record*. The next year, he switched to McGraw-Hill Publishers as a writer for their magazine *House and Home*. Since it was only published monthly, Tomarken did not enjoy the work, so in 1966 he and his wife moved back to Los Angeles.

Tomarken then segued into public relations work for the Larwin Company, a building contractor. He then moved up to become Vice President of Public Relations and Advertising for a larger company called Great Southwest. Finding advertising work especially rewarding, he opened his own advertising agency where one of his clients was Texas International Airlines.

"I Was a Comic in the Sense of a Wise Guy"

By the mid 1970s, Tomarken had worked a number of different jobs, but he also had another talent that was rapidly becoming evident.

PT:
"As a kid, I was always a comic in the sense of a wise guy. [I was] the child who was the performer in the family. There was a kind of duality. I wound up starting off as a journalist in my career and it just gravitated to the entertainment business in a kind of strange, circuitous fashion."

Tomarken broke into show business as a television commercial producer and director. Finally, someone suggested that he move before the cameras and start selling the products. As he became a familiar face on TV ads, Tomarken parlayed this success into a series of occasional guest starring roles on CBS's *Medical Center*, NBC's *Rockford Files*, and the ABC series *240 Robert*.

In 1977 he landed a supporting role in the ABC made-for-television movie *Secrets*. The next year, he appeared in his first theatrical release, *Heaven Can Wait* starring Warren Beatty. February 1979 brought his first regular television series, *Cliffhangers*, a one hour drama on NBC that was comprised of three 20 minute serials called *Stop Susan Williams*, *The Curse of Dracula*, and *The Secret Empire*. Each week, an episode of the three serials aired with cliffhanger endings designed to lure the viewers back for the next installment.

"It Wasn't Acting, It Was Posturing"

Tomarken appeared in *The Secret Empire*, which was the story of how a U.S. Marshal in 1880s Wyoming discovered the entrance to a secret underground city while pursuing outlaws. The people of this underground world came from another planet and the city was ruled by an evil dictator. Tomarken's character was a citizen who led a group of people with the intent of freeing themselves from the dictator's iron hand. *The Secret Empire* was unique in the fact that the episodes were filmed in both black and white and color. The scenes taking place in the old west were in black and white while the underground world segments were in living color.

The entire *Cliffhangers* series failed to draw a substantial audience and was canceled after three months. In true cliff hanger fashion, *The Secret Empire* ended before a final episode could be filmed leaving the viewers wondering what happened.

> *PT:*
> "I didn't like [*Secret Empire*] because to me, it wasn't really acting, it was posturing."

Four Days, Six Figures

He continued producing and acting in commercials to make ends meet until one day in 1980 when his agent asked how he felt about hosting game shows. Tomarken was not thrilled.

> *PT:*
> "Why would I want to be a game show host?"

When he was told that he could work four days a month and make a six figure salary, Tomarken quickly changed his mind, so his agent began sending him on game show auditions.

His first game show was *Rodeo Drive*, a syndicated pilot produced by Jay Wolpert. The show featured a set resembling the famous Beverly Hills, California shopping street of the same name. Contestants answered questions for the right to shop in "stores" on the drive to win merchandise. Although *Rodeo Drive* was not picked up as a series, it reached the air a decade later on the Lifetime Network with Louise Duart as host.

In the summer of 1981, Tomarken tried again with the NBC game show pilot *Duel in the Daytime*, which was also created by Jay Wolpert. This unusual game was set in the medieval period and featured a variety of different games based on the medieval theme. However, *Duel in the Daytime* was one hour in length, too complicated, and too costly to make it to NBC's schedule.

Hit Man

Third time was the charm for Tomarken when his next game show pilot, *Hit Man*, another Jay Wolpert production, was picked up by NBC for its daytime schedule beginning January 3, 1983. On *Hit Man*, three contestants watched a film clip accompanied by narration from Tomarken. The players then were asked questions based on the film. The first player to correctly answer five questions received $300. The second player to correctly answer five questions collected $200 while the third contestant was eliminated.

In round two, the two contestants played against the previous day's champion. The players watched another film clip and then received a number of "hit men." The champion received seven "hit men" while the player with $300 was given four and the third place contestant received three. Contestants answered another series of rapid-fire questions. Correct answers enabled a player to knock out their opponents' "hit men." The first player to knock out all of his/her opponents' "hit men" won the game and played a bonus round for a possible $10,000.

Hit Man's 11:30 a.m. time slot put the show at a major disadvantage because it ran against CBS's *The Price Is Right*, the top-rated game show on television. *Hit Man* was knocked out on April Fool's Day 1983. Tomarken noted that *Hit Man's* producer and creator, Jay Wolpert, never really got his due in the business.

> *PT:*
> "The issue of independent producers who don't have a lot of clout is they just don't get the opportunities that the others do. They don't get the opportunity to let their shows build audiences and they wind up getting canceled. If the show isn't a hit in 15 minutes, it's kind of disconcerting."

Hit Man had a short life, but the show went out with a laugh. At the end of the last episode where announcer Rod Roddy usually gave the address and telephone number for potential contestants to try out for the game, Roddy instead said, "If you would like to be a contestant on *Hit Man*, forget it. And now back to you Peter."

PT:

"That was prepared because there was a kind of bitterness that we were canceled. I think we were basically trying to screw the network."

It's Time to Press Your Luck

Shortly after *Hit Man*'s demise, Tomarken was offered the hosting position for CBS's *Press Your Luck*. Little did Tomarken know what he was getting into when he took this job. *Press Your Luck* was a big money game that pitted three contestants against a large board containing 18 squares filled with prizes and various amounts of money. The players answered a series of four questions to win spins on the big board. After the question round, the contestants faced the mammoth board. A light surrounding each of the squares bounced rapidly around the board and the player in control hit a plunger to stop the light. Whatever was in the square on which the light stopped was awarded to the player. Prizes ranged from $100 to $5,000 in cash to trips, cars, sailboats, TV sets, and other assorted goodies.

Also scattered throughout the board were little animated cartoon figures called Whammies that, if hit, took the player's winnings. An animated Whammy crossed the screen in front of the contestant with a short zany cartoon sequence where it took the player's money. In most cases, the Whammy was injured in some Wile E. Coyote–like fashion by crashing into trees, getting pounded with a hammer, or swallowed by a shark adding humor to the segment. After each spin, players had the option of passing any of their remaining spins to the other contestants to protect their winnings, or could continue "pressing their luck" to win more money. Hitting four Whammies put a player out of the game. The contestant with the most money after two rounds won the game.

The Whammy Wins Big

Sandwiched between two established game shows, *The $25,000 Pyramid* and *The Price Is Right* on CBS, *Press Your Luck* shot to the top of the ratings in its time slot. It averaged a 20 share during the 1983-1984 season (meaning that 20 percent of the audience watched the show, which was a good number for daytime television). Each episode of *Press Your Luck* was packed with high energy excitement, suspense, and loads of laughs.

The animated Whammies that taunted the contestants as they stole their winnings were popular with the viewers. Some Whammy animations were parodies of famous people. Rock musicians Michael Jackson, Boy George, Tina Turner, and the Beatles were among the people parodied on the show. One popular sequence featured a Whammy break dancing to music, a popular fad of the 1980s. Supplying the high-pitched voices of the Whammies was none other than the show's creator Bill Carruthers. Tomarken's free-spirited personality was a perfect fit for this show.

PT:

"I would do stuff to alleviate my boredom. I'd run around the table or I'd stand on something. People liked me on *Press Your Luck* because I was a wise guy. In other words, I wasn't nasty, but I was able to say to a guy who missed a question, 'Don't worry about it. You just blew a question and 14 million people saw you make a fool of yourself,' and everybody would laugh. It was me being a little edgy."

By far the most memorable aspect of *Press Your Luck* was its flashy and colorful game board with the light that bounced randomly around the squares of prizes. Or was the light moving around the board randomly? As it turned out, the bouncing light moved in a sequence of only

Peter Tomarken and *Press Your Luck* gave viewers a frenetic and suspenseful half hour each day (Peter Tomarken, courtesy Fred Wostbrock.).

six different patterns. When *Press Your Luck* was developed, CBS felt that there was no need to spend an extra $10,000 on additional light patterns since the computers operating the board would have to be upgraded. CBS executives wagered that because the light moved so rapidly around the board, nobody would have time to figure out that it was not moving randomly. They were wrong.

The Show Gets Whammied

During the show's first season, one of the viewers was Michael Larson, an unemployed ice cream truck driver from Lebanon, Ohio. Larson enjoyed watching the show every day and soon he started videotaping it. He began watching the light as it bounced from square to square on the game board and suspected that there was a pattern to the way it moved. For weeks, Larson intensely studied videotapes of the show, frequently watching them in slow motion and pausing the tapes to watch the light movements on the board. He finally figured out the show's secret that there were only six light patterns. After memorizing the patterns, Larson knew exactly when to hit the plunger and stop the light on the squares containing the largest money prizes. He knew how to avoid the Whammy.

Larson immediately flew to Los Angeles and tried out for the show. Bill Carruthers, the show's executive producer and director, was impressed with Larson. Bob Edwards, the contestant coordinator, had a bad feeling about Larson that he could not quite put a finger on, but Carruthers overruled him and booked Larson as a contestant. On Saturday, May 19, 1984, Larson reported to CBS Television City in Los Angeles where the show taped. He was scheduled to appear on the fifth show to be taped that day.

During the game, Larson played only moderately well in the first round. He hit a Whammy on his very first spin and was in third place when the game moved to round two. When his turn to play the big board came, Larson pulled out all the stops and began hitting the big money square at the top of the board which contained anywhere from $3,000 to $5,000 in cash plus an extra spin. Since Larson repeatedly hit the square giving him an extra spin, he was able to keep going. Before long, he had racked up over $50,000, more than any contestant on the show had ever collected. He was still on a roll. And to top it off, he had avoided the Whammy.

"I'll Be Working for Him Instead of CBS"

Did Tomarken suspect that Larson had figured out the board's patterns during the game?

PT:

"I knew he was doing something. What it was, I didn't know because I wasn't privy to that kind of information in terms of the number of patterns [on the board]. I was privy to it after the fact. I just figured that pretty soon, I'll be working for him instead of CBS. When the camera was off of me, I would be looking around like, 'Are you kidding me, what is going on here?'"

Meanwhile in the control booth, it was total pandemonium as the show's staff watched in amazement. By the end of the game, Larson had won $110,237 in cash and prizes. After the taping, CBS tried to deny Larson his money charging that he had cheated. When Larson finally told them how he had figured out the board's six light patterns, CBS's lawyers decided that Larson had done nothing illegal and gave him the money.

The game aired over CBS as a two-part episode on Friday June 8 and Monday June 11, 1984. Larson set a record for winning the most money in a single day on a game show. Sadly, life for Larson was all downhill after his *Press Your Luck* appearance. He invested his winnings in a real estate development deal that went sour and later was robbed of the rest of his money. He died of cancer in 1999 at the age of 49. After Larson's appearance, the *Press Your Luck* game board was reprogrammed to include over 20 new light patterns making it virtually impossible for anyone to memorize them.

PT:

"An amazing story, an amazing guy, and a tragic guy. He had done nothing illegal. He had really done his homework and succeeded. The tragedy is that he went on later and used that same kind of zeal and drive to pretty much bring himself to ruination. He was a man who was clearly gifted and had an insight, but he just self-destructed. I've always viewed him as a rather tragic guy, but I think the network viewed him as a villain."

The Luck Runs Out

Press Your Luck sailed through its first two years on the air drawing high ratings for CBS. However, by late 1985, the network was in a financial crunch. At that time, the contract for *The Price Is Right*, which aired immediately after *Press Your Luck*, was up for renewal. Tomarken explained that CBS could not afford to pay Mark Goodson Productions, the owners of *The Price Is Right*, the kind of money they wanted to continue the show on that network. Goodson came up with an alternative.

> *PT:*
> "Basically Goodson said that they wanted our time slot (10:30 a.m.) since we were such a juggernaut."

The result was that *Press Your Luck* was moved from 10:30 a.m. to 4:00 p.m., although in some markets the show aired at noon. The show's 10:30 time slot was taken over by the Mark Goodson game show *Card Sharks*, which was hosted by Bob Eubanks. The time change hurt *Press Your Luck* since many CBS stations pre-empted the show in favor of local programming. By the summer of 1986, *Press Your Luck* had fallen to 25th place out of 26 daytime shows and played its last game on September 26, 1986.

"My Personality Is What I Am"

In the fall of 1986, Tomarken auditioned for a new NBC game show called *Wordplay*.

> *PT:*
> "What was interesting is that I auditioned for *Wordplay* and was asked to behave like Pat Sajak in the sense that I was asked to minimize my style. I agreed to it and it was a mistake. The show tested well, but I tested poorly. I was not hired to do it."

In the summer of 1987, Tomarken popped up on ABC's *Bargain Hunters*. Contestants on this show played a series of games in which they were shown prizes and the idea was to determine which ones were the bargains. Between rounds of game play, home viewers were given the opportunity to buy merchandise at reduced prices. *Bargain Hunters* died a quick death after less than two months on the air.

> *PT:*
> "What's ironic is when I did *Bargain Hunters*, as I recall, the show tested poorly and I tested through the roof. It was interesting [to learn] that my personality is what I am and I'm not suited for some shows."

A Wipeout

Tomarken found his next assignment interesting. The fall of 1987 brought the game show pilot *Wipeout*. The audience response to the pilot was terrible, so Tomarken went to Paramount Television, the show's packager, and made some suggestions on how to improve the game.

> *PT:*
> "Somehow, I talked them into letting me produce the show and to go on the road pitching it to the affiliates in various cities on how we were going to do it. It was the most incredible experience I can recall in the business in that I was on the road as a salesman."

Wipeout cleared enough stations to launch as a syndicated series on September 12, 1988. In the game, Tomarken asked three players questions, all of which had multiple answers. The answers were displayed on a game board and the object was for players to pick the correct answers. Choosing an incorrect answer was a "wipeout," which cost the player control of the board. Tomarken doubled as the show's host and supervising producer, a task he felt was a mistake.

> *PT:*
> "I needed someone strong to pull me back or direct me because my personality is too strong. You lose your objective eye when you try to do too many things. I think I shortchanged myself."

Plagued by budget restrictions, *Wipeout* flopped after just one season.

"I Thought the Days of Slavery Were Over"

The late 1980s and early 1990s were professionally tough for Tomarken. He hosted two more failed game show pilots in the fall of 1989. The first was *TKO* (Technical Knockout) for Mark Goodson Productions. The second was a Merv Griffin Productions pilot called *Monopoly* that was based on the Parker Brothers board game. The game play was similar to the box version in that contestants rolled giant dice and moved around the large *Monopoly* board buying properties and building houses and hotels.

Tomarken was appalled when he discovered that a female midget had been hired to play Mr. Pennybags, the little man with a moustache and tall hat featured in the board game. The midget's role was simply to run around the board on the show's set.

> PT:
> "I was told, 'You can't talk to this person because it's an entity and she has a woman's voice.' I remember saying, 'You mean there's a human being in front of me constantly and I can't talk to it and I treat it as if it's an inanimate object? I thought the days of slavery were over.' It was so tasteless."

Many station managers who viewed the pilot episode took offense at the midget being used as part of the game. Only about 20 stations signed to carry the series so that scuttled plans for the syndicated version. Griffin reworked the concept, dropped the idea of using a midget as part of the game, and sold *Monopoly* to ABC for a 12 week primetime run during the summer of 1990. However Tomarken was out as the host since he and Griffin had clashed over the use of the midget in the series. Instead, Griffin chose Michael Reilly, one of the contestants from the pilot, to host the show.

More Frustration

Tomarken hosted another NBC game show pilot in January 1990 called *Live Wire.*

> PT:
> "It was to be done live every morning and the questions were based on the news of the night before [from the newspapers] whether it be the society pages, the front page, or the sports section. It was topical and dated so that people had to be really aware of what happened the day or night before."

The idea of doing the show live each day presented numerous problems and NBC passed on the series.

Tomarken tried one more time in the fall of 1990 with the pilot *2 Heads Are Better Than One*, which was packaged by his former boss Bill Carruthers. By now, game shows were slowly vanishing from the tube and talk shows began taking their place. Tomarken decided that his time in the game show spotlight was over.

> PT:
> "My prime was during that time when game shows were out of favor and that was too bad. I started trying to write more and produce more because game shows were out of favor. I had to make a living."

Producing

In January 1991, Tomarken joined the staff of the ABC comedy series *America's Funniest People* as a segment producer. The show featured people from around the country performing comedy acts, and Tomarken's job was to travel to different locations and record people for use on the series. He left *America's Funniest People* after one season to become a producer and director for the new syndicated drama *Real Stories of the Highway Patrol.* Using material taken from actual police files in different segments of America, the stories were recreated using actors. Again, Tomarken traveled the country producing and directing episodes of the series.

Tomarken also hosted a non-televised talk show called *Luxor Live* for 10 years. He taped the show in Los Angeles for viewing at the Luxor Hotel in Las Vegas as part of their entertainment package for the guests.

PT:

"They did it with this technique that made it look like I was live at the hotel sitting and doing this talk show. Clearly it was on tape, but when you saw the show, it appeared as though I was live. People would come to see me in Los Angeles and say, 'How did you get here? I just saw you in Vegas.'"

Tremendous Challenges

Times were still tough for Tomarken. The ups and downs of his career and frequently being out of work disintegrated his marriage of almost 30 years leading to a divorce in 1991. After four years out of the game show business, he got his foot back in the door when he joined the staff of the new cable channel Game Show Network in late 1994.

Game Show Network featured a massive library of classic game shows from such producers as Goodson-Todman, Barry-Enright, Merv Griffin, and Chuck Barris. Interspersed with reruns of the classic game shows were interactive segments allowing home viewers to play along and win prizes. This was where Tomarken came into the picture. He hosted two interactive shows called *Prime Games* and *Decades*, which were seen at various times throughout the evening.

PT:

"It was a tremendous challenge because first, nobody was watching us to begin with. Second of all, I was in a room that measured probably 12' × 12'. There were two remote controlled cameras and I was alone in the room. There was no audience. I would do the most outrageous stuff to entertain myself because I figured if I could entertain myself, maybe I could entertain someone else. It was a kick. It was different, new and innovative."

Tomarken spent two years with Game Show Network, but by 1996, new management had taken over and the network began altering its programming. Less emphasis was placed on the classic shows and the network began producing new game shows, many of which failed during the late 1990s. Tomarken was unhappy with the direction that Game Show Network had taken, and with the cancellation of his two interactive shows, left the network.

Tomarken bided his time hosting occasional infomercials. In 1997 Bob Eubanks hired him as one of the rotating hosts of a live non-televised game show staged at Pigeon Forge, Tennessee called *The $25,000 Game Show*. Tourists visiting Dollywood, Gatlinburg, and Pigeon Forge were given the opportunity to be called on stage to play a variety of games for cash and prizes. Tomarken alternated with Eubanks and Jamie Farr as host of the show during the 1997-1998 season.

Paranoia

In the spring of 2000, Tomarken returned to television as host of the big money game show *Paranoia* for the Fox Family Channel. *Paranoia* came along when game shows were back in vogue after the resounding success of ABC's *Who Wants to Be a Millionaire?* Unlike the other game shows, *Paranoia* aired live and featured a studio contestant competing against three people in other cities linked by a satellite. The studio player started with $10,000 and answered questions to keep the money. The contestant also challenged the satellite players to answer the questions. If the satellite players answered correctly, they took a portion of the studio player's money. There were also segments of the show allowing people to call a telephone number or participate by internet. *Paranoia* faded from view after less than a month on the air.

In September 2001, Game Show Network began airing reruns of *Press Your Luck*. The high ratings prompted the network to launch a new version of the game called *Whammy: The All-New*

Press Your Luck as a daily series. Tomarken auditioned for the job, but was beaten out by game show newcomer Todd Newton. At his audition, he was told to change his on-screen persona from the wise guy type of host he had been on the original *Press Your Luck*.

> PT:
> "It was terribly hurtful and I think I was doomed before I did it. I remember being told, 'No, no. Be nice. Be sure everybody likes you.' I took that advice with the pilot. I made the same mistake."

Tomarken also figured that the heads of Game Show Network wanted to make the new version of *Press Your Luck* more youth-oriented by going with a younger host.

"There's Much More Stability to It"

By now, Tomarken had decided to entirely pursue another line of work outside of the entertainment business. He had been dabbling in real estate since the late 1990s and had obtained his realtor's license. In 1998 he joined the staff of John Aaroe and Associates in Los Angeles as a realtor. Then in 2000, he started his own mortgage brokerage, real estate firm, and contracting company called T&S Construction, T&S Financial, and T&S Realtors. The company helped people finance for buying houses and home repair.

> PT:
> "I enjoy it. There's much more stability to it. It's challenging. I've kind of started a new life and I've been happier. I'm pleased to be out of [the entertainment] business. I don't want to sound bitter because there were some wonderful years in it and I had some great fun. But the huge ups and downs were just debilitating. They cost me one marriage and cost me my sanity too often. I think if I had to do it over again, I would try to do it differently."

Tomarken lived in Los Angeles with his second wife, Kathleen Eastman, whom he married in 1993. From his first marriage, Tomarken had a son named Jason, who is currently an actor in New York, and twin daughters Alexis and Candace.

Although he was primarily out of the entertainment industry by the late 1990s, Tomarken returned for special occasions. He appeared in three theatrical movies between 1998 and 2004: *Haunted*, *Divorce: the Musical*, and *19 at 11*. The latter movie was a graduate student film produced at the University of Southern California that made the rounds of film festivals across the nation.

Fifteen Minutes of Fame

In March 2003, Tomarken hosted a two hour Game Show Network documentary called *Big Bucks: The Press Your Luck Scandal*, which told the inside story of how Michael Larson won $110,237 by memorizing the light patterns on the game board. To commemorate the event, Game Show Network invited Tomarken to guest host a special episode of *Whammy: The All New Press Your Luck* featuring Larson's brother, James, in a rematch against the two contestants defeated in the 1984 game.

When not working, Tomarken enjoyed piloting his own airplane.

> PT:
> "I fly a lot, and that keeps me focused and takes me away from the humdrum of the business anxieties. You don't have time to be anxious about anything other than what you are doing. My wife loves it. We take flights and go to different places whether it's lunch in Santa Barbara, or Monterey, or Las Vegas."

In August 2005, Tomarken volunteered his services for Angel Flight West, a nonprofit organization that provided free air transportation for medical patients. Using his 1973 Beechcraft A36 airplane, Tomarken flew people needing medical assistance to hospitals.

On March 13, 2006, just minutes after taking off for San Diego to pick up a cancer patient for the UCLA Medical Center, Tomarken's plane experienced engine trouble. He tried to turn back for the Santa Monica Airport, but the small craft crashed into the Pacific Ocean about 200 yards off the Santa Monica Pier. Tomarken and his 41-year-old wife Kathleen died in the crash. Tomarken was 63 years old and was survived by his ex-wife Dana and their three children.

In a career full of ups and downs, *Press Your Luck* remained Tomarken's crowning achievement in the world of game shows. Reruns of the show aired on the USA cable network from 1987 to 1995 and currently can be seen on GSN: The Network for Games. Although he later found success and happiness in the world of real estate, Tomarken held fond memories of his three years on *Press Your Luck*.

PT:

"*Press Your Luck* was a perfect fit for me. There really wasn't anything before or after that fit me as well as that show. I really look at it as my 15 minutes of fame. I don't think I've ever heard of a game show set being as much fun and as happy as ours was. Nobody had an attitude and it was just a lot of fun."

ALEX TREBEK

Birth Name: George Alexander Trebek

Born: July 22, 1940, in Sudbury, Ontario, Canada

Marriages and Family: Elaine Callei (1974–1981) (Divorced) 1 step-daughter; Jean Currivan (April 30, 1990–Present) 1 son, 1 daughter

Radio Career: Staff Announcer (CBO-AM, Ottawa, Canada) 1961–1963

TV Career, Canada: ANNOUNCER—Curling Sports Coverage (CBC) 1966–1970; Championship Tennis (CBC) September 7, 1968–December 28, 1968; Fabulous World of Skiing (CBC) November 22, 1969–February 14, 1970   HOST—Music Hop (CBC) October 3, 1963–June 25, 1964; Vacation Time (CBC) June 29, 1964–September 25, 1964; Reach for the Top (CBC) 1966–1973; Trans-World Top Team (CBC) October 3, 1968–April 4, 1970; Strategy (Syndicated) April 1, 1969–October 7, 1969; Pick and Choose (CBC) July 4, 1971–September 12, 1971; Outside/Inside (CBC) November 26, 1972–May 13, 1973; TGIF (CBC) January 5, 1973–May 11, 1973; Stars on Ice (CTV) 1974–1977

TV Career, United States: HOST—*Wizard of Odds* (NBC Daytime) July 17, 1973–June 28, 1974; *High Rollers* (NBC Daytime) July 1, 1974–June 11, 1976, (Syndicated) September 8, 1975–September 19, 1976; *Double Dare* (CBS Daytime) December 13, 1976–April 29, 1977; *The $128,000 Question* (Syndicated) September 1977–September 1978; *The New High Rollers* (NBC Daytime) April 24, 1978–June 20, 1980; *Pitfall* (Syndicated) September 14, 1981–September 1982; *Battlestars* (NBC Daytime) October 26, 1981–April 23, 1982; *Starcade* (Unsold NBC Game Show Pilot) 1982; *The New Battlestars* (NBC Daytime) April 4, 1983–July 1, 1983; *Malcolm* (Unsold NBC Game Show Pilot) 1983; *Jeopardy!* (Syndicated) September 17, 1984–Present; *M'ama Non M'ama* (Unsold ABC Game Show Pilot) December 1984; *Lucky Numbers* (Unsold Game Show Pilot) May 1985; *Second Guess* (Unsold NBC Game Show Pilot) July 1986; *Value Television* (Syndicated) January 19, 1987–April 18, 1987; *Classic Concentration* (NBC Daytime) May 4, 1987–September 20, 1991, (NBC Daytime) October 28, 1991–December 31, 1993; *Super Jeopardy!* (ABC Primetime) June 16, 1990–September 8, 1990; *To Tell the Truth* (NBC Daytime) February 4, 1991–May 31, 1991   PRODUCER—*Jeopardy!* (1984–1987)

Theatrical Movies: *Dying Young* (1991); *White Men Can't Jump* (1992); *Short Cuts* (1993);

Alex Trebek (Fred Wostbrock)

Spy Hard (1996); *Jane Austen's Mafia!* (1998); *Random Hearts* (1999); *The Male Swagger* (1999); *Charlie's Angels* (2000); *Finding Forrester* (2000)
Book: *The Jeopardy! Book* (1990)

Okay, think quickly and answer this question: what is the name of the fruit also known as an alligator pear? How about this one: the name of an angle exceeding 90 degrees but less than 180. While you are pondering these questions, you suddenly notice that a pipe has ruptured in the house and water is everywhere. You also remember that the roof leaks because it is raining.

Who will you call to help you fix these problems and answer these questions? Never fear because Alex Trebek is here to set everything straight. Not only can he answer the questions, but he can also repair the leaky roof, the ruptured pipe, and even whip up an elegant dinner in your kitchen. Have you figured out the answers to those questions? Okay, the answers are "avocado" and "obtuse." Now, while Trebek repairs your plumbing and roof, have some of the meal he fixed in the kitchen and read his fascinating story.

George Alexander Trebek was born in Sudbury, Ontario in Canada on July 22, 1940. He was one of two children born to George Edward and Lucille Lagace Trebek. As a shy and introverted youth, Trebek usually sat off to the side watching other children play. He described himself as "shy" and "bright" but also a "loner."

> *Alex Trebek (April 2006 telephone interview):*
> "I never really made plans as to what my future would be in terms of jobs as an adult."

He once considered becoming a priest, but quickly changed his mind.

> *AT:*
> "I discovered girls."

Late in his teenage years, Trebek spent one summer in Cincinnati working as a garbage man.

> *AT:*
> "My mother was working in Cincinnati for a family and I came down to spend a summer with her. I got a job working in this large apartment project."

Reaching for the Top

Returning to Canada, Trebek considered majoring in medicine or law, but settled on philosophy at the University of Ottawa. During his senior year in February 1961, Trebek needed money for his college expenses. He took a job as a radio announcer for CBO-AM, an affiliate of the Canadian Broadcasting Corporation (CBC). He soon found himself doing news, weather, and sports on radio and television. He became a full time broadcaster after graduating from college.

In 1963 he became the host of *Music Hop*, a popular CBC television series.

> *AT:*
> "It was a live variety music show. We had singers appear as guests, and we had our own band and backup singers, [but unlike *American Bandstand*] there was no dancing."

Through the 1960s, Trebek was also a popular sports announcer broadcasting curling, tennis matches, and Canada's Triple Crown of Horse Racing. Wanting to try something new, Trebek turned to game shows and really found his calling. In 1966 he began a seven year run hosting *Reach for the Top*, a tough quiz show pitting two teams of high school students. It became so popular, that Trebek co-hosted a spin-off series, *Trans-World Top Team*, for two seasons beginning in 1968.

> *AT:*
> "That was an international competition. We competed against an American group of students and a British group. In fact we traveled to England and Hawaii. It was a fun thing. It was a new experience for me traveling abroad to do shows."

For 26 weeks in 1969, Trebek hosted the game show *Strategy*. The show's set revolved around a large dartboard on the studio floor. The teams of contestants started at the outside and answered questions for the right to move toward the center of the board. When a team correctly answered a question, they could choose to advance themselves toward the center or use their turn to block an opponent's progress. The first team to cross to the center of the dart board won the game.

Cracking the U.S. Market

By 1973 Trebek was a very familiar face in Canadian television. Meanwhile in the United States, his friend, actor Alan Thicke (also from Canada), became one of the writers for *Wizard of Odds*, a new NBC game show. Thicke urged Trebek to come to New York and audition as the show's host. He won the job and *Wizard of Odds* debuted July 17, 1973.

Trebek moved to California where the show taped, but fearing that the game might not last, he hesitated to buy or rent a home. For the first two weeks that *Wizard of Odds* aired, Trebek camped out on the floor at Thicke's residence. Trebek then rented an apartment and, when NBC renewed the series for six months, he felt comfortable enough to buy a house and remain in the United States.

Wizard of Odds involved six contestants who answered questions based on the law of averages posed by the "Wizard" (Trebek). Two rounds were played with three contestants competing in each segment. In the bonus round, a wheel containing the names of all six players was spun and the chosen contestant played one more question to win a car. While *Wizard of Odds* was only moderately successful, it introduced Trebek to American audiences. His next game show became his trademark of the 1970s.

Rolling the Dice

Wizard of Odds left the air on June 28, 1974. The following Monday on July 1, Trebek was back on NBC in the same time slot (11:00 a.m. Eastern Time) with *High Rollers*. Two contestants answered toss-up questions for the right to roll a pair of oversized dice on a long rectangular table. Actress Ruta Lee served as the official dice roller for the contestants. Before the players was a board with the numbers 1–9. The player winning the question had the option of rolling the dice or passing to their opponent.

The object was to roll the dice and eliminate numbers from a board. For example, if a contestant rolled a seven, he/she could knock off either the number seven or a combination of numbers adding up to seven. Players lost the game by rolling a number already eliminated. Henceforth, there was a lot of suspense as players often passed the dice to each other to prevent rolling a bad number.

Each of the nine numbers contained a prize that was given to the player who rolled that number. Contestants kept their prizes by winning the round. The game ended when someone either knocked off the last number on the board or rolled a bad number. The first player to win two games advanced to the Big Numbers bonus round. The winner rolled the dice and tried to eliminate all nine numbers on the board receiving $100 for each successful roll. Knocking off all nine numbers won the player $10,000. *High Rollers* ran until June 1976.

> *Robert Noah (**High Rollers** producer: June 2006 telephone interview):*
> "Alex did [that show] so well. He is an extremely bright man and he just plain doesn't make mistakes. If he did, you didn't see them."

> *Alex Trebek:*
> "I thought the premise of the show was good. You needed a little bit of intelligence to answer the questions and gain control of the dice. Then you needed to have your wits about you to know whether to pass or take the roll yourself. You had to understand odds and averages to make the right decision. If the only good roll up there was a two, you weren't likely to keep the roll yourself even if the prize was tremendous. It would just be a sucker move."

Alex Trebek holds the lucky dice on *High Rollers* in 1974 (Fred Wostbrock).

Two Tough Quizzes

In December 1976, Trebek popped up on CBS's *Double Dare*. Two players stationed in isolation booths guessed the names of people, places, and things. While one contestant played, the sound was eliminated in the opponent's booth. Trebek provided clues and a player correctly guessing the word could "dare" his/her opponent to guess it. If the opponent failed, the first player could "double dare" the opponent to guess the word for double stakes. The opponent collected the money if he/she was successful on a dare.

AT:

"On a scale of difficulty, *Double Dare* would probably compare to *Jeopardy!* But it didn't endear itself to the public."

When *Double Dare* left the air in the spring of 1977, Trebek took over as host of *The $128,000 Question*, a revival of *The $64,000 Question*. Contestants answered a series of progressively harder questions starting at $64 and doubling in value to $64,000. One wrong answer along the way lost the player all of his/her winnings. All of the $64,000 winners returned at the end of the season in a championship match with the big winner collecting another $64,000.

AT:

"I wore some of the most awful tuxedos [on that show] ever created. They wanted to jazz it up."

Another Roll of the Dice

In the spring of 1978, Trebek returned to NBC with *The New High Rollers*. The format was basically the same as the original with a few changes. The board of nine numbers was now divided into three columns with three numbers. Each column contained a prize rather than all nine numbers concealing prizes.

A player who knocked off the numbers in a column added that prize to their collection. For each time a column was not cleared, another gift was added up to a maximum of five prizes per column. This often led to payoffs of $30,000 worth of merchandise. The other major change was that Trebek had no co-host and contestants now rolled their own dice. *The New High Rollers* lasted two years before falling victim to NBC's massive game show wipeouts in June of 1980.

Out of Work

After seven straight years on American television, Trebek was suddenly unemployed. In August 1980, he filled in for one week hosting *Wheel of Fortune* when host Chuck Woolery took ill. The following month, Trebek competed in a special tournament on *Card Sharks* where eight game show hosts played for charity. After three weeks of competition, Trebek won the tournament.

Aside from these guest appearances, he could not find any steady work. Not only did he have financial problems, but his seven year marriage to Elaine Callei was unraveling leading to divorce in 1981.

"They Bounced My Check"

In what appeared to be a break, Trebek landed two jobs in the fall of 1981. The first was *Pitfall*, a syndicated game produced in Vancouver, Canada. Trebek posed questions to the studio audience and the two contestants selected the answers they felt the majority of the audience chose from four possibilities.

In the bonus game, the winner crossed an eight section bridge in 100 seconds by answering questions. Two of the eight sections were designated "pitfalls." The player could use two pitpasses earned in the main game to avoid the "pitfalls." If the player failed to use the pitpass at the proper time, they lost time on the clock and had to answer another question to get back on the bridge.

AT:

"*Pitfall* was not a pleasant experience. They bounced my payment check. It came at a bad time because my father had died and my marriage had dissolved. I was in bad, bad straits and could have used the money."

Pitfall ceased production when its packager, Catalena Productions, went bankrupt in 1982. Trebek still has the bounced check for $49,000 framed and hanging on a wall in his home.

AT:

"Interestingly, in a career that spans 45 years, the only time I've been done that way was by fellow Canadians. Fellow Canadians shafted me."

Those Are the Battlestars

Trebek's second show in 1981 was NBC's *Battlestars*, a show that he called, "the son of *Hollywood Squares*." The game used two contestants and six celebrities, who sat in triangles instead of squares. The players chose stars and the celebrities listened to a question. When the celebrity gave his/her answer, the contestant had to determine if the celebrity was correct or not. If the player guessed correctly, they captured one third of the triangle (each triangle contained three lights). The first player to capture three complete triangles won the game. *Battlestars* died after 26 weeks.

AT:

"That was a lot of fun, and I enjoyed that show because there was a lot of humor."

Trying Again

In 1982 Trebek hosted the pilot for *Starcade*, a video arcade game show produced for NBC. The network passed on the idea, but *Starcade* later turned up on Ted Turner's WTBS Superstation and in syndication with two different hosts. In the spring of 1983, Trebek tried again with *The New Battlestars*, a revival of the 1981 series. With only a few changes in the game's format, the new version was canceled after three months. He then hosted *Malcolm*, another NBC game show pilot that never made it to the air.

By now, Trebek was at the lowest point of his professional and personal life. He lived alone in a sparsely furnished studio apartment in Hollywood. With a lot of time on his hands, he used his self-taught carpentry skills to build a 10 room house in the Hollywood Hills.

Robert Noah:

"Alex is unbelievable in terms of his physical capabilities. The only thing he did not do [on that house] was the plumbing and the electrical work mostly because it had to be done to building code. He did the rest of it himself. I think he had occasional helpers, but let me tell you, he got his hands dirty."

Finally in late 1983, Trebek received a call from Robert Murphy, the vice president of Merv Griffin Productions, asking him to host the pilot for an updated version of *Jeopardy!*

AT:

"The producers were familiar with my work because they remembered that I had stepped in quickly to replace Chuck Woolery on *Wheel of Fortune* [back in 1980]. I didn't have to audition [for *Jeopardy*]."

The Remaking of a Hit

The *Jeopardy!* pilot was taped in the fall of 1983 utilizing a game board with pull cards similar to the one from the original 1964 series. After reviewing the pilot, executives at Merv Griffin Productions were not pleased. They felt the show looked too dated with the old pull card system and decided that drastic changes were necessary.

Starting from scratch, the game board was redesigned into a group of video monitors displaying the categories and answers. In the first round, the answers ranged from $100-$500 and in the "Double Jeopardy!" round, the amounts doubled to $200-$1,000. After taping a second pilot with the new set, King World Productions sold the show in syndication and *Jeopardy!* returned in September 1984.

AT:

"They weren't going to pay me very much money. So I asked them, 'Can I produce it also?' and they said, 'Okay.' So for the first three years, I produced, and that way I was able to earn as much money as I had earned hosting my previous shows."

Jeopardy! Is in Jeopardy

AT:

"We had to find our audience. Some people thought we were too difficult for the mainstream television audience."

Consequently, in many markets, the show was relegated to late night time slots. Therefore, many viewers did not even know the show existed. In New York City, the game aired at 2:00 a.m. By the middle of the 1984-1985 season, *Jeopardy!* lost a crucial market when the Los Angeles station carrying the show canceled it.

King World Productions came to the rescue, however. By now, King World distributed *Wheel of Fortune*, television's top-rated syndicated show. With the hottest syndicated series in America, King World used its clout to sell *Jeopardy!* to different stations who promised to put the show in better time slots.

In many markets, *Jeopardy!* was paired with *Wheel of Fortune* in the early evening hours. When *Jeopardy!* returned for its second season in the fall of 1985, it climbed in the ratings until it was the second most watched syndicated series in the country. The show's theme music became one of the most recognized songs in America. Many schools began playing mock versions of *Jeopardy!* as part of their classroom instruction.

Super Classic

With his career finally back on track, Trebek sought additional work. He hosted three more game show pilots during the mid 1980s that never came to fruition. In May 1987 he became host of NBC's *Classic Concentration*. Two contestants, in turn, called out pairs of numbers on a 25 square game board. Each square concealed a prize and the object was to match two identical prizes. When players made a match, the two boxes opened revealing a portion of a rebus puzzle.

The first player to solve the puzzle won their accumulated prizes. In the bonus round, the winner competed for a new car. A board with 15 squares concealed seven matching cars. The player was given 35 seconds to match all seven cars by calling out two numbers at a time. The last car matched was awarded to the contestant.

With two successful shows running five days a week, Trebek moved to ABC primetime in the summer of 1990. The network picked up *Jeopardy!* for a special 13 week tournament in which 36 previous winners were invited back to compete. One of the contestants was a champion on the show in the 1960s, while the remaining 35 players were selected from the first six years of the current version. The souped up show was called *Super Jeopardy!* and the grand prize was $250,000.

Getting Back a Personal Life

Trebek's schedule of taping two daily game shows and spending five months of the year on the road for *Jeopardy!* promotional appearances and contestant searches left him with little time for a personal life. He remained single after his 1981 divorce, but Trebek's concerned friends insisted that he try dating again. They fixed him up with several well-known women including Stephanie Powers, Rona Barrett, Susan Sullivan, and Beverly Sassoon. None of these ladies were quite right for him, however.

Life as he knew it changed in 1988 when Trebek met 25-year-old Jean Currivan at a dinner party. There was no initial attraction and the two went their separate ways. But several months later at another dinner party, the two met again and this time Trebek asked her out and she accepted. After seriously dating for a year, the two wed on April 30, 1990.

A New Show, an Unexpected Event

Meanwhile, back in his professional life, Trebek became one of the few television personalities to have three daily game shows at the same time. In February 1991, Trebek took over from

Lynn Swann to host the last three months of NBC's *To Tell the Truth*, a revival of the popular 1950s show. Interestingly enough, Trebek was seen back to back on NBC each weekday morning. *To Tell the Truth* aired at 11:00 a.m. while *Classic Concentration* followed at 11:30 a.m. In most cities, Trebek could be seen on *Jeopardy!* in the early evening hours giving him a total of 90 minutes television time each day.

One day, just after taking over as host of *To Tell the Truth*, Trebek was suddenly called away from the studio. On February 3, 1991, in the middle of taping five *To Tell the Truth* episodes, Trebek received a call that Jean was in labor with their first child. Trebek rushed to the hospital to be with Jean while Mark Goodson, the show's packager, stepped in and hosted the remaining two shows taped that day. Jean gave birth to their son Matthew, and two years later, the Trebeks had a daughter, Emily.

Double the Fun

After 1991, Trebek's heavy schedule lightened with the cancellations of *To Tell the Truth* and *Classic Concentration*, although reruns of the latter show remained on NBC's daytime schedule through December 1993. *Jeopardy!* was a different story, and the show rolled through the 1990s as the second highest-rated syndicated series in America. In 2001 with game shows now giving away multimillion dollar prizes, *Jeopardy's* producers doubled all the dollar amounts on the game board. In round one, the dollar amounts ranged from $200-$1,000 while the Double Jeopardy! round increased the values to $400-$2,000.

Further changes came during the 2003-2004 season when the producers waived the five day winnings limit imposed on contestants. The new rule allowed for contestants to remain on the show until defeated. While several players remained on the show for more than five days, no one was prepared for what happened next.

The Ken and Alex Show

On June 2, 2004, Ken Jennings, a software engineer from Salt Lake City, Utah, defeated the show's current champion. Jennings won his first five games, but before long, viewers realized that this was no ordinary contestant. For 15 weeks, Jennings triumphed over his opponents and raked in the green. His run on the show captured the attention of the news media and viewers were glued to their televisions each night wondering if Jennings would retain his crown. In the ratings race, *Jeopardy!* finally surpassed *Wheel of Fortune* as the top-rated syndicated series.

> *AT:*
> "It got [to the point that the show] became 'The Ken and Alex Show.' (Laughing) Then it was 'Ken: Also Featuring Alex Trebek.' I'm glad he let me stay on as host of the program."

After 74 straight wins, Jennings was finally defeated at the end of his 75th game on November 30, 2004. All told, Jennings won $2,520,700, the highest regular winning total ever for any *Jeopardy!* contestant. Jennings later competed in a 2005 Tournament of Champions but was defeated.

> *AT:*
> "He was great for our show and the show was great for him. He was the perfect contestant. He was bright, he knew his material, understood how to play the game, knew when to wager big, when to hold back, and was lucky. It's possible that we will see his kind again as a contestant on a game show, but I am not holding my breath. It was a great time for us, and I had a tear in my eye when he lost."

Horsing Around

Trebek and his family divide their time between homes in Studio City, California and a second place in Central California. Trebek also owned Creston Farms, a 700 acre horse breeding and training ground. He bought the property in 1996 and unexpectedly found himself with a new business.

AT:

    "It just happened by accident. I bought the property and the person who was leasing it at the time was running a horse operation. He decided to move after six months and left me with a 700 acre vacant property that was a great spot for thoroughbred horses."

Although he managed and took care of the horses, Trebek never took up horseback riding.

AT:

    "I've got a bad back and I don't care to put myself on a horse, bounce myself along, and compress all those discs."

Owning and managing three different properties demanded so much of Trebek's time that he finally sold Creston Farms in August 2005.

Alex of All Trades

Trebek's hobby is primarily working around the house. Through the years, he became handy as an electrician, plumber, and carpenter. In the early 1990s, he helped renovate the Studio City, California home he purchased shortly after his marriage.

AT:

    "I enjoy doing it and it keeps me pretty busy in a house this size. It's difficult to get a repairman who can get there when the crisis is at its peak so you learn to do stuff yourself."

Trebek also enjoys gourmet cooking and was noted for arranging the spices in his cabinets in alphabetical order. Another of his many interests is languages, although he is fluent only in English and French.

AT:

    "I know a smattering of languages, but not enough to converse, but certainly enough to make myself understood if I'm in one of those countries. The problem is that I speak with a very good accent. That causes problems because when you speak with the correct accent, the people think you are fluent in the language and they just shoot back a paragraph of words. You're standing there looking kind of sheepish and stupid because you didn't understand half of what they said. You're a lot better if you give a highly American accented interpretation."

It Comes with the Territory

After nearly 25 years of living and working in the United States, Trebek finally became an American citizen in 1996. He was welcomed as a new citizen in true American fashion when, two weeks later, he received a summons for jury duty.

AT:

    "Amazing coincidence. I was randomly chosen."

Besides hosting *Jeopardy!* Trebek also hosts the annual National Geographic Bee sponsored by the National Geographic Society. He is also a member of the Society's Education Foundation. In his long and successful career, Alex Trebek has remained so busy that he never stops to worry about how long things will last. His outlook has always been to just get out there, do the work, and enjoy the ride.

AT:

    "I've never thought about things like that for any of the shows I've hosted. I just get out and if I enjoy doing them, I do them. I don't think, 'Gosh, this could end next week. It could be canceled after 13 weeks. It could be canceled at the end of the season.' I don't give it any thought. I've usually been surprised when shows were canceled. Hey, that's part of the business. It comes with the territory."

CHUCK WOOLERY

Birth Name: Charles Herbert Woolery

Born: March 16, 1941, in Ashland, Kentucky

Marriages and Family: Margaret Hayes (1963–1970) (Divorced) 2 Sons, 1 Daughter; Jo Ann Pflug (1973–1980) (Divorced) 1 Daughter; Teri Nelson (1985–2004) (Divorced) 2 Sons; Kim Barnes (2006-Present)

Military Career: United States Navy (1960–1962)

TV Career: ACTOR—*The New Zoo Revue* (Syndicated) September 1973-September 1974   HOST—*Your Hit Parade* (CBS Primetime) August 2, 1974-August 30, 1974; *Wheel of Fortune* (NBC Daytime) January 6, 1975-December 25, 1981; *Hittin' Home* (Unsold Talk Show Pilot) 1981; *Love Connection* (Syndicated) September 19, 1983-September 1994; *America's Music Tracks* (TBS) October 2, 1983-February 5, 1984; *Scrabble* (NBC Daytime) July 2, 1984-March 23, 1990; *The Big Spin* (California State Lottery) October 28, 1985-November 18, 1985; *The Chuck Woolery Show* (Syndicated) September 16, 1991-January 24, 1992; *Scrabble* (NBC Daytime) January 18, 1993-June 11, 1993; *Home and Family* (FAM) April 1, 1996-January 10, 1997; *The Dating Game* (Syndicated) September 8, 1997-September 1999; *Greed* (FOX Primetime) November 4, 1999-July 14, 2000; *Lingo* (GSN) August 5, 2002-Present; *Chuck Woolery: Naturally Stoned* (GSN) June 15, 2003-July 27, 2003

Theatrical Movies: *Sonic Boom* (1974); *The Treasure of the Jamaican Reef (a.k.a. Evil in the Deep)* (1976); *Six Pack* (1982); *Cold Feet* (1989)

Made-for-TV Movie: *Guide for the Married Man* (ABC) October 13, 1978

Other Careers: Sales Representative, The Pillsbury Corporation (1960s); Country/Rock Music Singer (1967–1974)

Chuck Woolery once noted that his life was a series of recoveries. Indeed, when one looks at the life of this man, there seems to be a pattern of extremely happy times followed by crushing lows. But in the end, things always worked out for Woolery. Each time he was knocked down by a low point, Woolery recovered himself and kept on going like the Energizer Bunny. Through eight game

Chuck Woolery (Chuck Woolery, courtesy Fred Wostbrock)

shows, two talk shows, two musical variety programs, one children's series, one reality show, five movies, several music recordings, four marriages, six children, two stepchildren, and two close brushes with death, Woolery's life story is anything but dull.

Early Life

Born as Charles Herbert Woolery in Ashland, Kentucky, on March 16, 1941, his father, Dan, owned a fountain supplies company while his mother, Katherine, was a homemaker. Woolery enjoyed a happy childhood with his sister and parents. One of the family's favorite pastimes was singing. As a seventh grader in Ashland Junior High School, Woolery sang for a special first-day assembly to the students.

After high school, Woolery attended the University of Kentucky in 1960, but dropped out shortly afterward to enlist in the U.S. Navy. After his discharge, Woolery returned to school at Morehead State University in Kentucky as an economics major. While in college, he married Margaret Hayes and the couple had a son, Chad, and a daughter, Katherine. They also adopted another son named Cary. Woolery held a number of jobs during his college years including a stint as a salesman for the Pillsbury Corporation.

Making Music

By 1967 Woolery had set his sights on a musical career, so he left college and moved his family to Nashville, Tennessee. He scored a top 40 country rock tune called "Naturally Stoned" with his music group Avant-Garde in October 1968. Although he recorded a number of records over the next six years, "Naturally Stoned" turned out to be a one-hit wonder for Woolery.

By the early 1970s, his music career had stalled and his marriage had ended. While recovering from these blows, Woolery received a telephone call from comedian Jonathan Winters, one of his childhood idols. Winters called to compliment Woolery on one of his songs leading to a friendship that paid dividends.

A role in the theatrical comedy movie *Sonic Boom* brought Woolery to Los Angeles in 1972. Jonathan Winters helped book Woolery as a guest on NBC's *Tonight Show*, a move that pointed to a new career. In 1973 he starred in the syndicated children's series *The New Zoo Revue* playing an old man called Mr. Dingle.

In a guest spot on *The Merv Griffin Show*, Woolery performed a song. After his number, Griffin interviewed Woolery for about 15 minutes and was impressed by his talents. Woolery was not, however, keen on Griffin's next offer: a job as a game show host.

Spinning Wheels

Griffin had just developed a new game show called *Shopper's Bazaar*, which was soon renamed *Wheel of Fortune*. Woolery reluctantly auditioned and beat out actor Edd Byrnes as host. Little did Woolery know that he was making history when *Wheel of Fortune* premiered over NBC on January 6, 1975. The game featured three contestants who solved puzzles by guessing letters one a time. The players in turn spun a giant wheel containing various dollar amounts. When the wheel landed on a dollar amount, the player called out only consonant letters. Each time the letter appeared in the puzzle, the contestant won the corresponding amount of money. Guessing a letter that appeared several times in the puzzle could lead to large payoffs. Players could also call out vowels, but the price was $250 deducted from their score. The letters in the puzzle were revealed manually by co-host Susan Stafford, who served as the official "letter turner."

Players continued spinning and guessing letters, but two pitfalls on the wheel added a twist to the game. If the wheel landed on "Bankrupt," players lost their accumulated winnings for the round. There were also "Lose a Turn" spaces that lost the player control of the game. The first player to correctly solve the puzzle won the round and used their accumulated money to shop for prizes.

On the stage was a large assortment of merchandise including fur coats, trips, and furniture all marked with their purchase prices. The contestant selected prizes until they ran out of money. There were four or five rounds played per show depending on time. The player with the biggest cash value in prizes won the game.

Woolery's laid-back style quickly won over the viewers. His initial reluctance to be a game show host vanished after he settled into his role on *Wheel of Fortune*. He truly enjoyed talking with the contestants and cheering them on to victory.

Everything Is Wrong, But It Works

Being a newcomer in the hosting business, Woolery frequently stumbled on his own words and made mistakes, but that was part of his appeal. Fellow host Peter Marshall noted in his book *Backstage with the Original Hollywood Square* that an NBC executive asked him to attend a taping of *Wheel of Fortune* to see if he could give Woolery some pointers on hosting. Marshall noted that Woolery was doing several things wrong, but he did it in such a way that it enhanced his performance. Bob Eubanks echoed Marshall's sentiments in his autobiography *It's In the Book Bob*. He called Woolery "a terrific guy and a good friend," and that he could make mistakes, laugh at himself, and people loved it.

In December 1975 *Wheel of Fortune* expanded to one hour and featured two complete games per show. The winner played a bonus round for additional prizes. It was soon obvious that one hour of the show was too much and in January 1976, *Wheel of Fortune* reverted to its half hour format. *Wheel of Fortune* drew average ratings during the late 1970s, but was never a huge success. In early 1980 Merv Griffin attempted to syndicate a weekly nighttime version of the show but failed.

In June 1980 NBC canceled the game shows *Hollywood Squares*, *High Rollers*, and *Chain Reaction* to make room for a new 90 minute talk show hosted by comedian David Letterman that aired from 10:00 to 11:30 a.m. NBC planned to cancel *Wheel of Fortune* that August in favor of *Today at Midday*, a half hour news magazine that would air in *Wheel's* then-current time slot at 11:30 a.m. However, when *The David Letterman Show* tanked in the ratings that summer, NBC scrapped plans for *Today at Midday* and *Wheel of Fortune* was spared from the axe.

Hitting Rock Bottom

Just when life seemed to be going well for Woolery, he was hit with another crushing blow. A second marriage to actress Jo Ann Phlug, with whom he had a daughter, Melissa, ended in divorce in 1980. Then, in a move he came to regret, Woolery stepped down as host of *Wheel of Fortune* after a salary dispute with Merv Griffin. Woolery hosted his last episode of *Wheel of Fortune* on Christmas Day 1981. He was replaced by Los Angeles TV weatherman Pat Sajak.

The breakup of his marriage and losing his spot on *Wheel of Fortune* put Woolery in a deep depression. In a 1999 interview with Julie Moran on *Entertainment Tonight*, Woolery talked about his suicide attempt by taking a lethal mixture of prescription drugs and alcohol. Fortunately Woolery's friends found him and rushed him to the hospital where he promptly received treatment. Emerging from this experience a changed man, Woolery pulled a 180 degree turn and began putting the pieces of his personal and professional life back together.

Making a Love Connection

Getting back on track in 1982, Woolery appeared in the theatrical movie *Six Pack* starring Kenny Rogers. By the fall of 1983, he was hosting two television shows: the short-lived *America's Music Tracks* for the TBS cable channel and *Love Connection*, a game show. *Love Connection* took the format of the *Dating Game* where a bachelor or bachelorette chose a date from three possibilities one step further. Rather than the dates appearing on stage, the contenders were seen through videotaped interviews. The on-stage contestant viewed tapes of three possible dates and the studio audience secretly voted for one of them. The contestant then chose one and the couple were sent on a date with the show picking up the tab.

After their date, the couple told the audience about the experience. The voting results of the studio audience were revealed. If the majority of the audience voted for the same date as the studio contestant, the couple had the option of going on a second date with the show paying all expenses.

Love Connection quickly became a hit as viewers never knew what to expect each day. Couples who failed to hit it off exchanged comical insults although sometimes the hostility was too evident. On the other hand, if a date went exceptionally well, the couple revealed juicy details, much to the delight of the audience.

Woolery presided over *Love Connection* with his trademark relaxed style, but he also kept the show from turning into a free-for-all. He calmly reined in contestants who went out of control. As a result, *Love Connection* went on to a phenomenal 11-year run. Woolery soon developed his catchphrase, "We'll be back in two and two," when going to a commercial. "Two and two" meant that the show would be back in two minutes and two seconds, the average length of commercial time during the show. After *Love Connection* folded, Woolery continued to use the popular slogan in his other game shows.

Scrabble

In the summer of 1984, Woolery scored another homerun hosting NBC's *Scrabble*. Ironically, the show aired immediately after *Wheel of Fortune*. Based on the board game, *Scrabble* featured two contestants who guessed a series of words.

The game board revealed a number of blank spaces for a word and Woolery provided a clue. The player in control selected two numbered tiles and two letters were revealed that may or may not be in the word. The contestant chose a letter and if it was part of the word, it was placed in its proper space on the board. The player could guess the word or play the second letter. As long as the player selected letters contained in the word, he or she kept control of the game. Selecting a "stopper," or a letter not part of the word, gave the opponent control of the game.

The winner faced the previous day's champion in the "Scrabble Sprint" round. One player guessed a series of three words with Woolery again providing clues while a clock counted upward. Using the time established by the first player, the second contestant tried to beat that time by guessing three different words. The player using the least amount of time collected $1,500. Contestants who won the sprint round five times received $20,000.

Big Spin

With two daily game shows, Woolery squeezed in a third assignment in October 1985. The California state lottery launched *Big Spin*, a weekly series seen over a network of 11 ABC affiliates in the state. Contestants won payoffs determined by the spin of a giant lottery wheel.

Problems quickly plagued the series when one of the contestants turned out to be an illegal alien. A scheduling conflict coupled with low ratings led to Woolery departing the show after four weeks. After *Big Spin's* format was revamped, Geoff Edwards became the new host.

Family Life

Woolery enjoyed his greatest career success during the mid to late 1980s. His personal life changed for the better in 1985 when he married Teri Nelson, the granddaughter of sitcom stars Ozzie and Harriet Nelson. Joining the household were Teri's two daughters from a previous marriage, Courtney and Jennifer. Chuck and Teri later had two sons, Michael and Sean.

In January 1986, Woolery was struck by tragedy when his 19-year-old son, Chad, was killed

Chuck Woolery pays the happy winner her money on *Scrabble* (Chuck Woolery, courtesy Fred Wostbrock).

in a motorcycle accident in Brentwood, California. In what had to be an extremely gut-wrenching experience, Woolery remembered in a 1997 *People Magazine* interview that he had to tape 10 episodes of *Scrabble* the day he selected Chad's funeral casket. Woolery's strong Christian faith helped pull him and his family through the ordeal.

Running Out of Scrabble Tiles

In September 1987, *Scrabble* shifted to 12:30 p.m., a move that hurt the series. The combination of low station clearances in that slot and CBS's *The Young and the Restless* put a significant dent in *Scrabble's* ratings. Another time change to 10:00 a.m. in 1989 also failed and *Scrabble* faded from view on March 23, 1990. Woolery stayed afloat with *Love Connection*, which was now in its seventh season.

More Games and Talk

After 15 years of trying, Woolery finally got his own syndicated talk show in the fall of 1991. *The Chuck Woolery Show* rebuffed the current trend of tabloid talk television. Woolery preferred an old-fashioned talk show with celebrities dropping by to talk about non-controversial issues. After a strong start, *The Chuck Woolery Show* vanished after just four months.

In January 1993, NBC reactivated *Scrabble* for a five month run with Woolery returning as host.

*Robert Noah (*Scrabble *executive producer, June 2006 telephone interview):*
    "It was only [meant to be] temporary. We knew that going in. NBC wanted to air soap operas. By that time, the network was only running games from 10 a.m. to 12 p.m."

Love Connection left the air the following year, but Woolery's career was far from over. After a brief respite, he joined Christina Ferrare as co-host of *Home and Family* in April 1996. The two-hour series aired live each afternoon. *Home and Family* was a mixed bag of celebrity interviews, cooking segments, and unusual spots such as pig racing along with useful household tips such as how to make your own soap.

A Brand New Ferrari

Not long into his run on *Home and Family*, Woolery experienced repeated shortness of breath. Doctors discovered that Woolery was on the brink of having a major heart attack, so on September 23, 1996, Woolery underwent a successful quadruple bypass operation.

After six weeks of recuperation, Woolery returned to work on *Home and Family*. He quit his 37-year smoking habit and began walking five miles a day. In December 1996 he told *TV Guide's* Ty Holland that he felt "like a brand new Ferrari."

Woolery resigned as co-host of *Home and Family* at the end of his contract in January 1997 to pursue other plans. He developed two game shows, *Treasure Hunt* and *It's a Date,* and planned to bring back *Love Connection.* None of these projects came to pass. Instead, an unexpected offer to host a syndicated revival of *The Dating Game* brought Woolery back to the small screen for the next two years.

The Tower of Greed

In November 1999 Woolery joined the big money bandwagon when the FOX network developed the game show *Greed* after the success of ABC's *Who Wants to Be a Millionaire? Greed* offered the ultimate jackpot of $2 million to its winners. The game featured five players with one acting as the team captain. The object was for the team members to answer a series of eight multiple choice questions and climb the "Tower of Greed."

The first question was worth $25,000 and progressed to $2 million. Woolery asked one of the teammates a multiple choice question. The contestant selected an answer, but the team captain had the option of accepting the answer or changing it. Correct answers added the money to the team's pot with everyone receiving a share of the winnings. Woolery asked questions to the other three players with the team captain deciding whether to accept or change the answers given. One wrong answer ended the game and everyone lost their money.

Greed premiered with an unprecedented two hour episode on November 4, 1999. The show drew large audiences during its early weeks. When it appeared that *Greed* would be renewed for a second season, FOX abruptly canceled the show on July 14, 2000.

It's Not Just Letters, It's Lingo

Woolery and his family sold their California home and moved to Park City, Utah to be near the mountains where they enjoyed skiing. After a two-year absence, Woolery returned to the air in the summer of 2002 on Game Show Network's *Lingo.* Two teams of two players each were given a "lingo" board with 25 numbers.

The team in control was shown the first letter of a five letter word and received five chances to guess the word. Players not only had to guess the word, but had to spell it correctly. Teams then selected two numbered balls from a reservoir on their podium. The object was to cover five numbers on their board in a row across, up and down, or diagonally. In the bonus round, players guessed more five letter words and tried to complete a line of five numbers for a possible $5,000 jackpot.

Within a short period of its debut, *Lingo* was the top rated original program on Game Show Network's schedule. To reduce production costs, the first 20 episodes of *Lingo* were taped in the Netherlands on the set of that country's version of the show. When these episodes pulled high ratings, Game Show Network taped new episodes and built a set for the series in Los Angeles.

Reality Stinks

Capitalizing on *Lingo's* success and Woolery's popularity, Game Show Network developed a reality series based on Woolery's everyday life called *Chuck Woolery: Naturally Stoned*. The title came from Woolery's 1968 one hit wonder song "Naturally Stoned." The six episode series was culled from more than 400 hours of videotape obtained by a camera crew that followed Woolery around at home and at work.

Taping the reality series put tremendous pressure on Woolery's already troubled marriage. Chuck and Teri separated in June 2003 and divorced a year later. In July 2006, Woolery married Michigan native Kim Barnes in Las Vegas.

Motolure

Away from the cameras, Woolery enjoys skiing and fishing. He parlayed his love of fishing into a profitable venture when he helped promote a new fishing lure called the Motolure in 2002. Because scientific tests proved that fish were more likely to attack objects in motion, creator Frank Pearce designed the lure to look exactly like a fish that vibrated using a tiny non-electrical motor powered by the pull of a string. Woolery promoted the Motolure on QVC television and helped sell 100,000 of the products in a few short hours.

I'm Too Saccharine

Woolery currently lives in Los Angeles and continues hosting *Lingo* and occasional infomercials. He also does voice-overs for promotions on the Game Show Network. The life of Chuck Woolery has been anything but dull. Once when talking about his game show *Love Connection* to *People Magazine* in 1991, Woolery said that he would never be interesting enough to be a contestant on his own show feeling that he was "too saccharine." He paused a beat and then added, "I really am."

Bibliography

Adams, Val. "About Garry Moore: The Perennial Playboy." *The New York Times*, 7 Mar. 1954: II. 11.

_____. "Bingo on TV Jams Telephone Lines." *The New York Times*, 19 Feb. 1958: 55.

_____. "Daly Quits ABC in Policy Battle." *The New York Times*, 17 Nov. 1960: 75.

_____. "Garry Moore Seeks Release from CBS Contract." *The New York Times*, 29 Nov. 1966: 87.

_____. "TV Bingo in the Home." *The New York Times*, 18 Feb. 1958: 54.

Alexander, Ron. "College Quiz Show, Favorite of the 60s, Tests Wits Again." *The New York Times*, 17 Nov. 1979: 48.

"All About Balloons and Waffle Batter." *TV Guide*, 5 June 1953: 13.

"Allen Ludden Stricken with Massive Stroke." *The Los Angeles Times*, 8 Oct. 1980: 22.

"Allen Ludden, TV Host." *The New York Times*, 10 Jun. 1981: B6.

Allis, Tim, and John Griffiths. "A Man for All Species: Chuck Woolery Will Talk to Just About Anyone." *People Magazine*, 28 Oct. 1991: 113–114.

Andersen, Christopher. "Dick Clark." *People Weekly*, 27 Jan. 1986: 69–72.

"As We See It." *TV Guide*, 16 Feb. 1980: A-4.

Badger, K. Reka. "A Magnificent Vision: Irma Eubanks' Peppertree Ranch Art Show Lives On...." *The Santa Ynez Valley Magazine*, Spring 2004: 3.

"Banko! It Pays to Watch!" *Broadcasting and Cable*, 6 Jan. 1986: 157.

Barks, Ed. "'Feud' Host Has High Hopes." *The Dallas Morning News*, 4 Jul. 1988: 5C.

Barol, Bill. "Taking a Spin at Late-Night." *Newsweek*, 16 Jan. 1989: 63.

"Barry, Jack." *Who's Who in America*. 42nd ed. 1983.

"Barry & Enright to Take Bigger Plunge in Production for Television, Cable." *Broadcasting*, 28 Feb. 1983: 97–98.

Bauer, Nancy. "Rayburn and Exuberance—That's a Match." *The Boston Globe*, 22 Sep. 1982: 5.

Bayliss, John. "TV Game Shows." *The Saturday Evening Post*, Dec. 1975: 24.

Beck, Ken. "Pat Sajak Makes His 'Fortune' Behind the Wheel." *The Tennessean*, 5 Sep. 1999.

Bernstein, Sharon. "Failure of Hospital Closet Bar Cited in TV Host's Suicide." *The Los Angeles Times*, 6 Jun. 1996: B1.

_____. "Friends, Family Remember TV Host for Laughter, Love." *The Los Angeles Times*, 8 Jun. 1996: A1, A22–A23.

"Bert Convy, 57, an Actor and Host of Television Game Shows, Dies." *The New York Times*, 16 Jul. 1991: Sec 2, P-2.

"Bert Parks: A Winning Loser." *Broadcasting*, 5 May 1980: 105.

Beverly, Steve. "Game Show Convention Center." 14 Apr. 2003 <http://www.tvgameshows.net>.

_____. "TVgameshows.net: Your Weekly Game Show Magazine." 14 Mar. 2006 <http://www.tvgameshows.net>.

"The Big Commute." *TV Guide*, 20 Nov. 1954: 13–15.

Bloom, Anna. "Park City Resident Settles Out of Court." *Park Record*, 1 Oct. 2005.

Blumenthal, Norm. *The TV Game Shows*. New York: Pyramid, 1975.

Boivin, Paola. "Remembering The 'Miracle on Ice' 10 Years Later." *The Los Angeles Daily News*, 22 Feb. 1990: S7.

Bolstad, Helen. "Winner's Circle." *TV Radio Mirror*, May 1960: 38–39.

Bowman, Harry. "Peter Marshall Isn't Square About His Role in 'La Cage.'" *The Dallas Morning News*, 17 May 1985: 24A.

Brady, James. "In Step With: Pat Sajak." *Parade Magazine*, 25 Sep. 1988: 23.

"Breakfast with Garry." *Newsweek*, 17 May 1948: 64.

Brooks, Tim, and Earle Marsh. *The Complete Directory to Primetime Network TV Shows 1946–Present*. 4th ed. New York: Ballantine, 1992.

Brown, James. "Edwards, Martindale Move to TV." *The Los Angeles Times*, 12 Nov. 1979: IV. 18.

_____. "Wink Martindale Returns to KMPC." *The Los Angeles Times*, 7 Aug. 1983: 84.

Brunt, Stephen. "Definition Turns 10 with Pride." *The Globe and the Mail*, 3 Mar. 1984: P8.

Buckley, Tom. "Game Shows—TV's Glittering Gold Mine." *The New York Times Magazine*, 18 Nov. 1979: 176.

"Bud Collyer Dies; Host of Shows." *The New York Times*, 9 Sep. 1969: B2.

Burgi, Michael. "Sajak Buys Letters W, N, A, V for $2 Million." *Mediaweek,* 13 Apr. 1998: 28.

"Busiest Man on the Air." *Look,* 8 July 1958: 28–30.

"Buss Stop." *TV Guide,* 13 Aug. 1988: 19.

"Busy Bud Collyer." *TV Guide,* 26 June 1953: 16–17.

Campbell, Cynthia V. "Peter Marshall Spreads Rumors." *The Baton Rouge Sunday Advocate,* 11 Mar. 1990: 7-Mag.

Carroll, Jerry. "KABL Swings to Local Programming." *The San Francisco Chronicle,* 28 Jan. 1997: E1.

Castro, Peter, et. al. "The Mourning After: Wealth and Fame Are No Protection from the Death of a Child." *People Magazine,* 31 Mar. 1997.

"Cheeky King Richard." *Newsweek,* 25 Jun. 1979: 92–93.

Christopher, Rita. "Bert Parks: Mr. Survival." *Maclean's,* 12 Sep. 1983: 12.

Clark, Dick. Personal letter to David Baber. 2 May 1995.

Collins, Bill. "TV/Radio Talk: Atlantic City Show Hits Jackpot." *The Philadelphia Inquirer,* 20 Aug. 1981: E15.

"Combs' Comedy Club Closed." *The Cincinnati Post,* 19 Jan. 1995: 2.

"Combs Psyched." *The Cincinnati Post,* 29 Mar. 1994: 12A.

"Conflicting Voices." *Newsweek,* 17 Jun. 1968: 103.

"Court Remands F.C.C. Decision Denying License to Quiz Figures." *The New York Times,* 9 Apr. 1965: 67.

Cullen, Ann. Telephone interview with David Baber. 6 Mar. 2006.

"Daly Quits as Host of Channel 13 Series." *The New York Times,* 4 Jan. 1969: 55.

"Dan Enright: Back on Top of His TV Game." *Broadcasting,* 19 Dec. 1988: 87.

Darrell, Margery. "Hal March...He Got a $64,000 Break." *Look,* 18 Sept. 1956: 58–59.

Davidson, Bill. "The Wheel of Fortune Stops (Surprisingly) at No. 1." *TV Guide,* 28 Jul. 1984: 59–64.

"Dennis James and the Talent Are Making Good." *TV Guide,* 14 Aug. 1953: 4–5.

"Dennis James Speaks at Roanoke Conference." *The Roanoke Times and World News* 21 Oct. 1994: Extra 10.

Dennison, Georgeanne. "Lange, Others Laid Off by KFRC Radio." *The San Francisco Chronicle,* 13 Aug. 1993: C13.

"Do the Youngsters Have the Answers?" *TV Guide,* 4 Sep. 1953: 15–16.

Doan, Richard K. "End of the Line." *TV Guide,* 17 Jun. 1967: 30–35.

Drake, Ross. "With a Gleam in His Eye and a Bounce in His Step...." *TV Guide,* 6 Apr. 1974: 41–44.

Dubrow, Burt. Telephone interview with David Baber. 26 May 2006.

Dunning, John. *The Encyclopedia of Old-Time Radio.* New York: Oxford University Press, 1998.

_____. *Tune in Yesterday: The Ultimate Encyclopedia of Old-Time Radio 1925—1976.* Englewood Cliffs, N.J.: Prentice-Hall, 1976.

Dutka, Elaine. "Memories of a Game Mind." *The Los Angeles Times,* 22 Dec. 2002: E3.

Edwards, Geoff. Telephone interviews with David Baber, 15 Mar. 2004, 17 Mar. 2004, and 3 May 2004.

Efron, Edith. "Life Is a Spiral Staircase." *TV Guide,* 26 May 1962: 22–25.

_____. "The Original Personality Kid." *TV Guide,* 21 Jul. 1962: 11–13.

Eubanks, Bob. Telephone interview with David Baber. 8 Sep. 2004.

Eubanks, Bob, and Matthew Scott Hansen. *It's in the Book, Bob!* Dallas: Benbella, 2004.

Fabe, Maxene. *TV Game Shows.* New York: Doubleday, 1979.

Fates, Gil. *What's My Line? The Inside History of TV's Most Famous Panel Show.* Englewood Cliffs, N.J.: Prentice-Hall, 1978.

Feder, Robert. "Fan Dials His Dream with Old-Time Radio." *The Chicago Sun-Times,* 17 Jan. 1990: 33.

Felsher, Howard. Telephone interviews with David Baber. 6 and 7 Jun. 2006.

"Fired Game Show Host Sues Burt Reynolds and Bert Convy." *The San Francisco Chronicle,* 21 Jul. 1989: E11.

Fleming, Art. *Art Fleming's TV Game Show Fact Book.* Salt Lake City: Osmond, 1979.

"Fluent Broadcaster: John Charles Daly." *The New York Times,* 17 Nov. 1960: 75.

Folkart, Burt A. "Jack Barry, TV Game Show Host, Dies After Jogging." *The Los Angeles Times,* 3 May 1984: II. 1 and 3.

Fong-Torres, Ben. "DJ's Doing Disappearing Act at 'Magic 61.'" *The San Francisco Chronicle,* 12 Jan. 1992: 34.

_____. "Jim Lange Leaves TV Behind." *The San Francisco Chronicle,* 23 Aug. 1991: E3.

_____. "Radio Waves." *The San Francisco Chronicle,* 7 Aug. 2005.

"For the People." *Broadcasting,* 20 Jan. 1986: 9.

"Forward, March!" *TV Guide,* 5 Mar. 1956: 13–15.

Gallus, Maya. "Portrait of a (Game) Showman." *The Globe and the Mail,* 16 Apr. 1983: F2.

"Game Over." *People Weekly,* 17 Jun. 1996: 52.

"Game Show Without TV." *The Houston Chronicle,* 19 Nov. 1993: 2.

"Garry Moore: Commuting Comedian." *TV Guide,* 17 Apr. 1953: 5–7.

"Garry Moore, 78, the Cheery Host of Long-Running TV Series, Dies." *The New York Times,* 29 Nov. 1993: D8.

Gehman, Richard. "He's Now Making News." *TV Guide,* 15 Apr. 1961: 17–19.

Gehr, Richard. "Love That Bob." *Village Voice,* 4 May 1993: 44.

Gibbons, Diana. "The Other Half." *The New York Times,* 18 Nov. 1945: II. 5.

Goldberg, Lee. *Unsold Television Pilots 1955 Through 1988.* Jefferson, N.C.: McFarland, 1990.

"The Good-Luck Kick." *Time,* 16 Aug. 1954: 65.

Goodman, Mark, and F.X. Feeney. "Top of His Game." *People Weekly,* 14 Nov. 1994: 67–68.

Graham, Jefferson. *Come On Down!!! The TV Game Show Book.* New York: Abbeville, 1988.

_____. "Woolery Keeps the Banter Light." *USA Today,* 10 Oct. 1991: 3D.

Grant, Tim. "The Answer: Retired Game Show Host." *St. Petersburg Times,* 7 Mar. 1993: City 1.

Greenberg, Nikki Finke, and Eric Gelman. "Clark Around the Clock." *Newsweek,* 18 Aug. 1986: 26–29.

Greenberg, Peter S. "The Day the Game Show Got Whammied." *TV Guide,* 26 Nov. 1994: 26–29.

Grossman, Gary H. *Saturday Morning TV.* New York: Dell, 1981.

"Guilty Only of Success." *TV Guide,* 10 Sep. 1960: 8–11.

Hackett, George, and Julia Reed. "Garry Moore Has No Secrets." *Newsweek,* 1 Aug. 1983: 9.

"Hal March, Actor, TV Quizmaster, 49." *The New York Times,* 20 Jan. 1970: 40.

Hall, John C. *Majoring in the Minors: A Glimpse of Baseball in a Small Town.* Stillwater, Oklahoma: Oklahoma Bylines, 1996.

Hall, Monty. Telephone interviews with David Baber. 6 Mar. 2000 and 16 Feb. 2004.

Hall, Monty, and Bill Libby. *Emcee Monty Hall.* New York: Grosset & Dunlap, 1973.

Hawn, Jack. "TV's Money Man: For Cullen, It's Still a Game." *The Los Angeles Times,* 19 Dec. 1980: VI. P-27.

Hawthorn, Tom. "Didn't You Used to Be...? Art Fleming Still in the Biz." *The Globe and the Mail,* 4 Dec. 1987: A2.

"He Covers All Bases: Gene Rayburn *Is* Steve Allen's One-Man Team." *TV Guide* 10 November 1956: 18–19.

"He Ranks Right Along with Zworykin, Sarnoff, DuMont and Doody." *TV Guide,* 9 Nov. 1963: 24–26.

Hickley, Neil. "Garry Moore Takes to the Streets to Get Back into Television." *TV Guide,* 29 Jan. 1966: 24–26.

_____. "There She Is ...Or Through the Years with Bert Parks." *TV Guide,* 5 Sep. 1970: 11–13.

Higgins, Robert. "Garry Moore Returns—To What?" *TV Guide,* 3 Dec. 1966: 6–10.

Hodges, Ann. "Networks Borrow from Povich's 'Current Affair.'" *Houston Chronicle,* 31 Jul. 1989: 2 Star, p-6.

Holland, Ty. "Life Connection: A Brush with Mortality Gives Chuck Woolery a New Outlook." *TV Guide,* 14 Dec. 1996: 7–8.

Horning, Jay. "Rayburn Grew Up with Television Series: Newsmakers Revisited." *St. Petersburg Times,* 14 Feb. 1993: 13A.

Howe, Elena Nelson. "Whatever Works Bob Eubanks: A Talent at Having Fun with the Newly Wed." *The Los Angeles Times,* 12 Jul. 1999: E1.

Hudis, Mark. "No Wheels on Pat's Radio Deal." *Mediaweek,* 29 Apr. 1996: 46.

Hyatt, Wesley. *Short-Lived Television Series 1948–1978: 30 Years of More Than 1,000 Flops.* Jefferson, N.C.: McFarland, 2003.

Inman, David. *The TV Encyclopedia: The Most Comprehensive Guide to Everybody Who's Anybody in Television.* New York: Perigee, 1991.

"The Internet Movie Database." 30 Sep. 2006 <http://www.imdb.com>.

"It's an Easy Life." *TV Guide,* 16 Oct. 1953: 10–11.

"It's Show Time Again." *St. Petersburg Times,* 31 Aug. 1994: City 1.

"Jack Barry and Patti Preble." *The New York Times,* 15 Feb. 1960: 23.

"Jack Barry's New Deal." *TV Guide,* 3 Aug. 1957: 18–19.

"Jack of All Ages." *TV Guide,* 24 Dec. 1955: 13–15.

"Jack's Work Is All Play." *TV Guide,* 29 Mar. 1958: 6.

Jacobs, Tom. "The Celebrity Tic Tac Toe Board Made Him Famous, But He Was First and Foremost an Actor." *The Daily News of Los Angeles,* 15 Jan. 1987.

James, Art. "I Used to Be Live, But Now I'm on Tape." *TV Guide,* 11 Jun. 1977: 31–33.

_____. Telephone interviews with David Baber. 3 Mar. 1999 and 16 Feb. 2004.

_____. "Will Blunders Never Cease?" *TV Guide,* 26 Jan. 1980: 33.

James, Dennis. "Those Housebroken Wrestlers." *TV Guide,* 27 Nov. 1954: 18–19.

"Jim Lange: Magic in the Air." *Bay Area Radio Digest,* Mar.-Apr. 1992.

"John Daly; Hosted TV's What's My Line?" *The Los Angeles Times,* 26 Feb. 1991: A28.

"John Daly, Panel Moderator, Also Is a News Expert." *TV Guide,* 23 Jul. 1960: 9–11.

"John Daly Weds Virginia Warren in a Methodist Church on Coast." *The New York Times,* 23 Dec. 1960: 22.

"John's Other Life." *Newsweek,* 28 Nov. 1960: 59.

Johnson, Chip. "New Family Feud TV Host Injured in Crash." *The Los Angeles Times,* 13 Jul. 1994: B4.

Johnson, Peter. "Bungles Are the Risk of a Live Pageant, Parks Says." *USA Today,* 11 Sep. 1990: 3D.

Johnston, Gaby. Telephone interview with David Baber. 8 Jun. 2006.

"Journey into Night." *Newsweek,* 26 May 1958: 70.

"Junior Grows Up." *Newsweek,* 7 Apr. 1947: 54.

Kallan, Carla. "Game Show Hosts Recall Their Most Embarrassing Moments." *TV Guide,* 27 Jun. 1987: 30–32.

Kava, Brad. "Jim Lange Has a Date in San Jose." *San Jose Mercury News,* 12 Aug. 1994: 20.

_____. "On-Air Employment Offers Few Guarantees." *San Jose Mercury News,* 1 Oct. 1993: 22.

Keating, John. "College (Bowl) Graduate Goes into the Word Game." *TV Guide*, 25 Aug. 1962: 22–24.

Kennedy, Tom. Telephone interview with David Baber. 4 Oct. 2004.

King, Larry. Televised interview with Bob Barker. *Larry King Live*, 26 Dec. 2002.

King, Susan. "Play 'em Again. Monty Hall and Co. Recall the Good Ol' Games." *The Los Angeles Times*, 8 Jul. 1990: TV Times, 2.

Kisseloff, Jeff. *The Box: An Oral History of Television 1920–1961*. New York: Penguin, 1995.

Kline, Richard. Telephone interview with David Baber. 3 May 2006.

Koenigsberg, Alice. "Bert Convy Wants More Time with His Family." *Daytime TV Magazine*, May 1976.

Lange, Jim. Telephone interview with David Baber. 11 Sep. 2006.

Levine, David. "Who Wants to Be a Mid-Two-Figures-Aire? *American Heritage*, Jul/Aug. 2001: 63–68.

Lidz, Franz. "What Is Jeopardy?" *Sports Illustrated*, 1 May 1989: 94–105.

Lieberman, Jane. "Edwards Scratches a 7-Year Itch: Back on Radio." *The Los Angeles Times*, 11 Dec. 1987: VI. 30.

"Life Begins at 43." *Newsweek* 15 May 1961: 73–74.

MacMinn, Aleene. "TV & Video." *The Los Angeles Times*, 17 Oct. 1989: F2.

"The Man with the Velvet Whip." *TV Guide*, 20 Nov. 1953: 15–17.

March, Hal. "The $64,000 Question and I." *Saturday Evening Post*, 30 Nov. 1957: 21, 89–94.

Marill, Alvin H. *Movies Made for Television: The Telefeature and the Mini-series 1964–1986*. New York: Zoetrope, 1987.

Marion, Jane. "Family Feuds? He's an Expert." *TV Guide*, 5 Aug. 1989: 11.

Marshall, Peter. Telephone interviews with David Baber. 19 May 2005 and 2 Jun. 2005.

Marshall, Peter, and Adrienne Armstrong. *Backstage with the Original Hollywood Squares*. Nashville: Rutledge Hill, 2002.

Martindale, Wink. Telephone interview with David Baber. 16 Feb. 2004.

_____. *Winking at Life*. California: Century Hill, 2000.

"Match Maker." *People Magazine*, 20 Dec. 1999: 140.

McClellan, Stephen. "ABC Takes Chance on Prime Time Game Show Block." *Broadcasting*, 21 May 1990: 33.

McDougal, Dennis. "Jockeying for Position in New Year." *The Los Angeles Times*, 27 Dec. 1983: VI. 1.

McKinnon, George. "Marquee! Gene Rayburn Likes the Stage Game Too." *The Boston Globe*, 22 Nov. 1981:

McNeil, Alex. *Total Television: A Comprehensive Guide to Programming from 1948 to the Present*. 3rd ed. New York: Penguin, 1991.

Meisler, Andy. "It's Paradise Found (if you don't look too hard)." *TV Guide*, 13 Aug. 1983: 37.

Meyers, Robert. "They Pay Him $1,000 an Hour to Listen to Jokes." *TV Guide*, 6 May 1972: 19–21.

Miller, Holly G. "Dick Clark's Role After Rock." *The Saturday Evening Post*, Jul/Aug. 1995: 34–35, 88.

Miller, Mark Crispin. "Mark Crispin Miller on Television: Family Feud." *New Republic*, 18 & 25 Jul. 1983: 24–27.

Missanelli, M.G. "Sajak Takes Job with New Spin." *Philadelphia Inquirer*, 7 Jul. 1992: Sec. D P-5.

Mitchell, Emily, and Ken Baker. "Those Left Behind." *People Weekly*, 7 Oct. 1996: 105–106.

"Moore for Housewives." *Time*, 2 Feb. 1953: 47.

Moore, Garry. "Comedian's Evolution: Mr. Moore Tries His Hand at Autobiography." *The New York Times*, 12 Sep. 1948: II. 9.

_____. "Fame Is a Funny Thing." *Look*, 22 Sep. 1964: 77–88.

Moran, Julie. Televised interview with Chuck Woolery. *Entertainment Tonight*, 17 Nov. 1999.

Morrow, Terry. "Ubiquitous Eubanks Is Back in the Game." *The Knoxville News-Sentinel*, 31 Jul. 1998: T17.

Murphy, Mary. "TV's Game Show Hosts: The Prizes...The Applause...The Pain." *TV Guide*, 21 Jan. 1984: 35–42.

Narz, Jack. Telephone interview with David Baber. 4 Oct. 2004.

Nash, Jay Robert, et al., eds. *The Motion Picture Guide Index M-Z*. Chicago: Cinebooks, 1987.

Nelson, George, Jefferson Graham, Peggy Orenstein, and Laurie Werner. "NBC Makes a Match." *Esquire*, Jan. 1984: 88.

"Networks Running Neck and Neck and Shoulder in Daytime." *Broadcasting*, 14 Jul. 1986: 31–33.

The New York Times, 13 Nov. 1970: 74.

The New York Times, 8 Jun. 1972: 51.

The New York Times. *The New York Times Directory of the Theater*. New York: Arno, 1973.

Njeri, Itabari. "Revisiting TV's Stone Age." *The Miami Herald*, 13 Nov. 1982.

Noah, Robert. Telephone interview with David Baber. 29 Jun. 2006.

Norbom, Mary Ann. *Richard Dawson and Family Feud*. New York: Signet, 1981.

Novak, Ralph. Review of *The Running Man*. *People Weekly*, 30 Nov. 1987: 18.

O'Brien, Tim. "Opryland's Silver Anniversary Touts '$25,000 Game Show.'" *Amusement Business*, 4 Mar. 1996: 7.

O'Connor, John J. "TV: Tribute to 'My Line'" *The New York Times*, 28 May 1975: 83.

Oliver, Myrna. "Bill Cullen: Fixture as Game Show Host." *The Los Angeles Times*, 8 July 1990: A29.

_____. "Dennis James; Pioneering TV Host, Commercial Spokesman." *The Los Angeles Times*, 5 Jun. 1997: B18.

Ottinger, Matt. "The Bill Cullen Homepage." 27

Sep. 2006 <http://userdata.acd.net/ottinger/Cul len/>.

_____. "The Game Show Home Game Home Page." 27 Sep. 2006 <userdata.acd.net/ottinger/games.htm>.

Paeth, Gary. "Ray Combs' Crash Injuries Cloud Future." *The Cincinnati Post*, 13 Jul. 1994: 5B.

Parke, Richard H. "Bookish Day Camp Seeking Children." *The New York Times*, 6 Mar. 1960: 56.

"Pat Sajak: On a Roll." *Broadcasting*, 14 Mar. 1988: 48–51.

"Pat Sajak to Star in 'The Odd Couple.'" *AP Online*, 21 Jul. 2001.

Peck, Jim. Telephone interviews with David Baber. 7 Jun. 2002 and 12 Aug. 2002.

"People in the News." *The Associated Press*, 14 Apr. 1990.

Perry, Jim. *The Sleeper Awakes: A Journey to Self-Awareness*. Los Angeles: Summit, 1991.

_____. Telephone interview with David Baber. 10 Mar. 2005.

"Phi Beta Kappa Key to Success." *TV Guide*. 23 Oct. 1954: A-2.

Philbin, Regis. *Who Wants to Be Me?* Massachusetts: Wheeler, 2000.

Philbin, Regis, and Bill Zehme. *I'm Only One Man!* New York: Hyperion, 1995.

"Pied Piper of Teen-Age Set." *TV Guide*, 24 May 1958: 8–11.

Pike, Lori E. "'Wink and Bill,' KABC-AM's Afternoon 'Ken and Bob.'" *The Los Angeles Times*, 2 Jan. 1989: VI. 8.

Plummer, Bill. "Who Says 'It's Not Easy'? Marriage Has Been a Breeze for Bert and Anne Convy." *People Weekly*, 31 Oct. 1983: 115–117.

Prial, Frank J. "Jack Barry, 66, Dies." *The New York Times*, 4 May 1984: II. 6.

Prouty, Howard H., ed. *Variety Television Reviews Vol. 4 1951–1953*. New York: Garland, 1989.

_____. *Variety Television Reviews Vol. 1963–1965*. New York: Garland, 1989.

_____. *Variety Television Reviews Vol. 9 1966–1969*. New York: Garland, 1989.

_____. *Variety Television Reviews Vol. 10 1970–1973*. New York: Garland, 1989.

_____. *Variety Television Reviews Vol. 12 1978–1982*. New York: Garland, 1989.

Puig, Claudia. "Edwards Says Goodbye KFI After Dispute." *The Los Angeles Times*, 6 Mar. 1989: VI. 1.

_____. "KFI Suspends Edwards in Dispute with Leykis." *The Los Angeles Times*, 28 Feb. 1989: VI. 1.

"The Quiz Biz." *Forbes*, 1 Apr. 1975: 48.

"Radio." *The Los Angeles Times*, 24 Mar. 1987: VI. 2.

"Ray Combs Cincinnati Comedy Connection to Locate in Belvedere's Carew Tower." *Business Wire*, 12 Jul. 1991.

Rayfield, Fred. "Traveling Quizmaster." *The New York Times*, 27 Jun. 1954: II. 3.

"The Real Deal." *People Weekly*, 9 Dec. 1996: 154.

"The Region." *The Los Angeles Times*, 28 Nov. 1985: I. 2.

"Regis Forever!" *TV Guide*, 2 Mar. 2002: 35–36.

Reid, Richard. Telephone interview with David Baber. 22 Jun. 2006.

Roberts, David. "'La Cage aux Folles' to Play at National." *Washington Post*, 5 Sep. 1984.

Rosen, Marjorie. "And the Winner of the Miss America Pageant for 1990 Is...Bert Parks, Back from His Crowning Indignity." *People Weekly*, 10 Sep. 1990: 120.

Ross, Chuck. "CBS Wants New Host When It Gets 'Wheel of Fortune.'" *The San Francisco Chronicle*, 17 Jun. 1989: C7.

Russel, Dick. "The Return of a TV Outcast." *TV Guide*, 1 Dec. 1979: 21–24.

Ruth, Daniel. "No Couches? No Problem, Says Pat Sajak." *Chicago Sun-Times*, 22 Feb. 1990.

Ryfle, Steve. "Ex-Host of Family Feud Had Attempted Suicide, Death: Ray Combs, Upset Over Marital and Career Problems, Was Found Hanged in Closet of His Hospital Room Sunday." *The Los Angeles Times*, 4 Jun. 1996: B4.

Sanchez, Jorge. "Art Fleming Remembered As Celebrity, Neighbor." *St. Petersburg Times*, 1 May 1995: 11.

Schleler, Curt. "LBS Making a Fuss About New Feud." *Advertising Age*, 22 Feb. 1988: S8.

Schwartz, David, Steve Ryan, and Fred Westbrock. *The Encyclopedia of TV Game Shows*. 2nd ed. New York: Facts on File, 1995.

Schwartz, Marla Schram. "Viewers' Views." *The Los Angeles Times*, 29 July 1990: 4.

Schwed, Mark. "Prime Chuck." *TV Guide*, 14 Jun. 2003: 25–27.

Scovell, Nell. "Johnny Come Lately." *Rolling Stone*, 23 Feb. 1989: 23.

See, Carolyn. "He's One of the Nicest Guys in the Business." *TV Guide*, 30 Dec. 1978: 18–22.

Shah, Diane. "The Good Fortune of Pat Sajak." *The New York Times Magazine* 11 Dec. 1988: 42, 80–96.

Shales, Tom. "Fast 'Feud'—with Relish." *The Washington Post*, 29 Nov. 1978: B1, B11.

_____. "Pat Sajak, CBS' Johnny on the Spot." *The Washington Post*, 10 Jan. 1989: B1, B4.

_____. "The Pyramid at Any Price." *The Washington Post*, 26 Jan. 1981: C1, C8.

Shanley, J. P. "Back in Business: Jack Barry, Who Once Quit Commerce, Becomes a Business Tycoon." *The New York Times*, 17 Feb. 1957: II. 13.

Shepard, Richard F. "Man of Many Words." *The New York Times*, 20 July 1958: II. 9.

Siano, Joseph. "'Love Connection' Meets 'The Osbournes.'" *The New York Times*, 15 Jun. 2003: XIII. 4.

Skutch, Ira. *I Remember Television: A Memoir*. Metuchen, N.J.: Scarecrow, 1989.

_____. Telephone interview with David Baber. 10 Feb. 2006.

"Smell of Success." *Time,* 30 May 1960: 74.

Soloman, Michael. "Hosts We Love the Most." *TV Guide,* 27 Jan. 2001: 42.

Smith, Cecil. "Allen Ludden Knew the Password to TV Success." *The Los Angeles Times,* 14 June 1981: 2.

Spindler, Joan. "Where Are They Now? Answer: Ex-Quizzers Go On, in and Out of TV." *The New York Times,* 15 Nov. 1959: II. 13.

Stanley, John. "Comic Makes It—Ends, Begins Family Feud; Ray Combs Reconciles with Wife, Begins Hosting TV Game Show." *The San Francisco Chronicle,* 18 Sep. 1988: 45.

Stewart, Bob. Telephone interviews with David Baber. 19 Apr. 2005 and 25 Jan. 2006.

Stone, Joseph, and Tim Yohn. *Prime Time and Misdemeanors: Investigating the 1950s T.V. Quiz Scandal—A D.A.'s Account.* New Brunswick, N.J.: Rutgers University Press, 1992.

"Stricken TV Host Ludden Reported Making Progress." *The Los Angeles Times,* 8 Nov. 1980: 27.

"Superman in the Flesh." *Time,* 14 Sep. 1942: 70.

Tamaki, Julie. "Ex–Miss America Host Bert Parks Dies." *The Los Angeles Times,* 3 Feb. 1992: A3 and A24.

Taylor, Chuck. "Wink Martindale: Back in the Game." *Billboard* 14 Dec. 1996: 70–72.

"Television: What's His Line?" *Time,* 28 Nov. 1960: 62–64.

Terrace, Vincent. *Fifty Years of Television: A Guide to Series and Pilots 1937–1988.* New York: Cornwell, 1991.

"Tests Run on Game Show Host." *The Los Angeles Times,* 27 Apr. 1990: I. 9.

Thomas, Jack. "TV and Radio: Jack Thomas, Why Did It Happen Here?" *The Boston Globe,* 12 Mar. 1982.

Thomas, Robert McG., Jr. "Art Fleming, 70, Television Host Who Gave Polish to 'Jeopardy!'" *The New York Times,* 27 Apr. 1995: D25.

_____. "Dennis James, 79, TV Game Show Host and Announcer, Dies." *The New York Times,* 6 Jun. 1997: B10.

Tinker, Grant, and Bud Rukeyser. *Tinker in Television: from General Sarnoff to General Electric.* New York: Simon & Schuster, 1994.

"Together Again." *The Los Angeles Times,* 14 Jan. 1993: F2.

Tomarken, Peter. Telephone interview with David Baber. 17 Mar. 2005.

Tomasson, Robert E. "John Daly, Newsman, Dies at 77; Host of TV's What's My Line?" *The New York Times,* 26 Feb. 1991: D2.

Townsend, Dorothy. "Allen Ludden, 63, Winner of Emmy, Dies of Cancer." *The Los Angeles Times,* 10 June 1981: 20.

Trebek, Alex. Telephone interview with David Baber. 3 Apr. 2006.

Trebek, Alex, and Peter Barsocchini. *The Jeopardy! Book.* New York: HarperCollins, 1990.

Trinkaus, Janet. "Jim Lange: Content as Host." *The Times Union,* 1 Jan. 1989: T8.

"TV & Video." *The Los Angeles Times,* 20 Jul. 1989: VI. 2.

"TV Host Ludden Is Recovering." *The Globe and the Mail,* 9 Jan. 1981: P15.

"TV Host's Condition Upgraded." *The Los Angeles Times,* 14 Jul. 1994: B6.

"2 in Quiz Scandal Must Sell Station." *The New York Times,* 10 Mar. 1966: 67.

Walker, Dave. "Sitting Pat—In a Business Usually Fueled by Ambition and Restlessness, Game-Show Icons Pat Sajak and Vanna White Remain Content to Light the Letters and Spin the 'Wheel of Fortune.'" *The Times-Picayune,* 23 Aug. 2005.

Walley, Wayne. "Ray Combs, SeaGull Launching Talk Strip." *Electronic Media,* 19 Dec. 1994.

Wellons, Nancy Imperiale. "Fox Is Hoping 'Paranoia' Sweeps Game Show Fans." *The Orlando Sentinel,* 14 Apr. 2000: E2.

"What Did They Do with Them?" *TV Guide,* 5 July 1958: 17–19.

"Where Are They Now?" *Newsweek,* 7 Nov. 1966: 20.

"Who's Who Among Concert Tour Jerks." *The Knoxville News-Sentinel,* 23 Oct. 1998: WE2.

Wilkes, Paul. "The Applause Still Rings in His Ears." *TV Guide,* 12 Apr. 1969: 14–19.

"Wink Martindale Chasing Riches." *Advertising Age* 16 Jan. 1986: 16 and 19.

"Word May Be 'Fraud' for Man Seen on TV." *The New York Times,* 15 Jan. 1988: 14.

Wostbrock, Fred. Interview with Bob Barker. Archive of American Academy of Television Arts and Sciences. 7 Jul. 2000.

"Young Old Trooper." *Harper's Magazine,* Jun. 1958: 80–81.

Zehme, Bill. "Question Authority." *TV Guide,* 6 Nov. 1999: 16–21.

Zoglin, Richard. "Game Shows Get Gamier." *Time,* 28 Sep. 1992: 70–71.

Zorn, Eric. "Family Skeleton Rattles Network." *Chicago Tribune,* 27 May 1993: Chicagoland Section, P-1.

Index